LUFTWAFFE CAMOUFLAGE AND MARKINGS

1933-1945 Volume Two

LUFTWAFFE
CAMOUFLAGE
AND MARKINGS
1933-1945 Volume Two

Code Systems & Markings
Night Fighters
Ground-Attack
Reconnaissance
Bombers
Maritime
Transports & Trainers

K.A.Merrick

with Jürgen Kiroff

J. Richard Smith
and Tom Willis

C L A S S I C

An imprint of
Ian Allan Publishing

The Author

Ken Merrick has been researching and writing about British and German aviation subjects for the last 40 years, producing books ranging from the history of individual aircraft types, through to a highly detailed history of Allied clandestine air operations in World War Two. He became particularly interested in the subject of German camouflage systems some 30 years ago and has since written a number of highly acclaimed books on the subject in the intervening years including *Luftwaffe Camouflage and Markings 1935-1945 Volume One* (1973), *German Aircraft Markings 1939-1945* (published by Ian Allan in 1977), *The Official Monogram Painting Guide for German Aircraft 1935-1945* (with Thomas H. Hitchcock, 1980) and *German Aircraft Interiors 1935-1945 Volume One* (1998).

This work is a compilation of all those years of research, melded with intriguing new information culled from a mass of official RLM and German paint industry documentation. The result is a complete and radical reappraisal of all that has appeared on this contentious subject during the intervening years.
He lives in Australia.

Paint Technology Advisor

Jürgen H. Kiroff was born in Nürnberg in 1956, where he later studied precision instrument engineering. One of his main interests is aviation history and readers of some modelling magazines may be familiar with his aircraft drawings. In 1988 he joined the family business, Farben-Kiroff-Technik in Fürth/Bavaria, a manufacturer of paints, whose primary work involves solving surface chemistry problems for the paint industry (chemical preparation problems, varnishes and paints with the desired properties as well as chemical removal of various paints and the sealing of surfaces). In these areas he assumed responsibility and with his brother Peter has run the company (now in the second generation) since 1991 with the 50th anniversary of Farben-Kiroff-Technik taking place in 2005. Jürgen recognized the importance of historical chemical formulae and used the company's contacts to collect many of them and also studied their technical applications. The knowledge and vast experience of his father Werner, who died in June 2003, always helped when the archives proved incomplete.

The result of collating this research and technology means that today, Farben-Kiroff-Technik is able to replicate and produce almost all the RLM LDv.521 colours. More and more German aviation museums are making use of this knowledge to reproduce RLM colours (the German Technical Museum Berlin, the Luftwaffe Museum Gatow, the Luftfahrtmuseum Laatzen etc.) as well as other European aircraft restoration ventures. Today, many historical aircraft have been restored and displayed with the use of Kiroff aviation paint.

First published 2005

ISBN 1 903223 39 3

Produced by Chevron Publishing Limited

Project Editors: Eddie J. Creek and Robert Forsyth/Chevron Publishing

Jacket Design by Colin Woodman Design

Published by Classic Publications an imprint of Ian Allan Publishing Ltd. Hersham, Surrey, KT12 4RG

Printed in England by Ian Allan Printing Ltd, Hersham, Surrey KT12 4RG

Visit Ian Allan Publishing at www.ianallanpublishing.com

Contents

Introduction

With the publication of Luftwaffe Camouflage and Markings 1933-1945 Volume Two, the reader is presented with as complete an analysis of the colours, markings and usage of German aviation paints as possible, drawn from all the known surviving technical and historical data of the period under review. It is hoped that this compilation will provide a reliable source document, not just for daily use by researchers, aircraft restorers and enthusiasts, but also as a basis against which to test future original documentary evidence as, inevitably, it arises. No one would be foolish enough to claim that all that is possible to know about this vast and complex subject is contained within these two volumes.

Inevitably, no sooner had Volume One been published than some additional information pertinent to its contents turned up, along with detection of some minor errors. In this regard, my thanks go to John Vasco for correcting some photographic captions involving Bf 110s, a subject area in which he has great expertise, and to Jim Crow for the others.

There were also some questions to be addressed about a few of the colours on the colour card 'Tafel 3' nicht in den RLM – Karten veröffentlichte Farbtöne', included with Volume One. The technical difficulties encountered with the production of completely accurate colour chips forced changes to the contents of this colour card after the book itself had been printed. These various pieces of information are given in the Addendum on page 448. Readers will also find a fuller explanation in this volume for some of the RAL colours included on the third colour card. Included with this volume are two more of Herr Kiroff's superb reproductions of colour cards containing original colours, including the remaining wartime camouflage shades. Once more his technical expertise has provided the reader, researcher and restorer with a unique resource. Included with this volume are two more of Herr Kiroff's superb reproductions of colour cards containing original colours, including the remaining wartime camouflage shades. Once more his technical expertise has provided the reader, researcher and restorer with a unique resource.

Included with this volume are two more of Herr Kiroff's superb reproductions of colour cards containing original colours, including the remaining wartime camouflage shades. Once more his technical expertise has provided the reader, researcher and restorer with a unique resource. Readers will find some colour description names for the late war colours which may seem unusual. However, as Herr Kiroff has pointed out, in the last published consolidated paint industry document, "LS Farbtonkarte für Tarnfarben (Gebäude- und Bodentarnung)" 24 July 1944, only colour descriptions, not RLM numbers, were used for the corresponding ground camouflage colours for airfields and buildings, - schwarz, dunkelbraun, dunkelgrün, olivgrün, ziegelrot, erdgelb, grau and weiß. Olivgrün is known to have been RAL 6003; and in other official documents the ground/equipment camouflage colour listed as RAL 6003 was the same colour as RLM 62; and thus also RLM 82 (see page 106 Volume One). The written description of 'dunkelbraun' in this last industry document corresponded to RLM 81's successive descriptive terms of 'olivbraun' and then 'braunviolett' in RLM approved aircraft industry documents, and echoed the 1936 original RLM 61 colour description), while 'dunkelgrün' corresponded to RLM 83. This serves to illustrate further the confusion over written colour descriptions, as described on page 113 of Volume One. To illustrate further the eclectic nature of written colour descriptions on Tafel 5 Herr Kiroff has appended these alternative colour descriptions (used in the paint industry's consolidated reference document that served a broader user-base than just the Luftwaffe), for the RLM colours 81, 82 and 83. The reader is thus provided with the full spectrum of written (albeit confusing at times) colour terms. He has also emphasised the very important (but often not understood) fact that the RAL system recycled some reference numbers as the war progressed. Thus, at a later date, the same number could identify a replacement different shade of the same colour, or even a completely new colour. Thus one has to be careful of the time sequence when extrapolating from RAL numbers to specific shades/colours. Post war, the same process has continued and some colours on the current RAL colour card swatch no longer have any relationship to a specific original colour or shade of the pre-war and wartime period. This applies to the full range, not solely those associated with the aircraft industry.

To the production team of Eddie Creek and Robert Forsyth at Chevron Publishing, and to Jürgen Kiroff for his technical skills, I add my enduring thanks.

To my own personal production manager, my wife Rae, I add my lasting thanks for her continuous support.

K. A. Merrick
June 2005

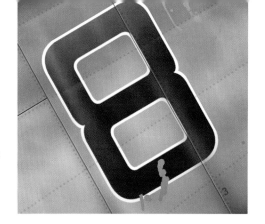

Five-Character Military Code System

by J. Richard Smith

On 1 April 1934, six Luftkreiskommando (Regional Air Commands) were established in Germany, ostensibly to co-ordinate civilian air traffic movements over the country. In fact, these were territorial areas of command for the then still secret air force. The six Regional Air Commands, their headquarters cities and their commanders were:

Luftkreiskommando I	Königsberg	Gen.Lt. Wachenfeld
Luftkreiskommando II	Berlin	Gen.Lt. Kaupisch
Luftkreiskommando III	Dresden	Gen.Maj. Schweickhardt
Luftkreiskommando IV	Münster	Gen.Lt. Halm
Luftkreiskommando V	München	Gen.Lt. Eberth
Luftkreiskommando VI	Kiel	Konteradmiral Zander

When the Luftwaffe was publicly revealed in March 1935 its aircraft initially retained their existing civil registration, plus the dual fin and rudder markings of the horizontal tricolours on the starboard side and the National Socialist blood banner emblem on the port side, which had been introduced on 6 July 1933.

JG 132, the first fighter unit, was formed from the DVL Reklame-Staffel Mitteldeutschland (Publicity Squadron Central Germany) Döberitz on 14 March 1935. Given the name 'Richthofen', initially its aircraft retained their civil registrations and dual tail markings. The second of the new fighter units, JG 134 'Horst Wessel', was presented to the Führer, on the occasion of his birthday in April 1935, by SA senior personnel in an elaborate ceremony that was recorded in the June 1935 edition of *Der Deutsche Sportflieger*. The eight civil-registration marked He 51s visible in the photographs wore no traditional colouring on the engine cowlings.

On 15 September, tail markings were revised, the starboard-side tricolour being replaced by the National Socialist blood banner marking. The five-character military code marking was either introduced at the same time as this change, or soon after, judging by a photograph of four Ju 52s which are now thought to be from KG 753, which appeared in the November 1935 issue of *Der Deutsche Sportflieger;* the photograph would have had to have been taken in October or earlier. Application of the new code system to single-seat fighter aircraft is less well defined than for bombers, but some clues exists which help date the process to the same time range as that involved for the Kampfgeschwadern. Some photographs of He 51s of JG 132 and JG 134 wearing the new five-character code show them retaining the starboard side tricolours marking which indicates that they adopted the new codes very soon after promulgation of the 15 September instruction. However, such instructions carried a grace period, usually of approximately two months, for compliance, indicating that the

ABOVE: A Ju 52/3m g3e of Kampfgeschwader z.b.V1. This photograph is of historical significance because it proves that the five-character code system was in use in 1935, a copy of this photograph appearing in the November 1935 issue of 'Der Deutsche Sportflieger'. The aircraft coded 27+E11, 27+E13 and 27+D13 were from I. Gruppe, and 27+B23 from II.Gruppe.

Jagdgeschwader took up the new code system markings at the same time as the Kampfgeschwader.

One interesting example of a precursor to the new code system appears in several photographs taken at Döberitz when JG 132's He 51s still retained their civil registrations and dual tail markings. A single machine from the Stab appears wearing the code 'A1' in black, on both sides forward of a Balkenkreuz marking. It also carried two narrow black bands around the rear section of the fuselage (see Chapter 11). The nature and origins of this proto-code marking are not explained in any surviving RLM documentation and appear to have been unique to both this unit and the time period. It is recorded here only in light of revisions to the fighter code system in July 1936.

ABOVE: Photographed after the change to their tail markings, the aircraft of the two leading Ketten of He 51s wear the five-character codes destined to be used by single-seat fighter aircraft for only a brief period. The leading three, 21+G13, 21+F21 and 21+E21 were from II./JG 132 and wear the distinctive red nose colouring of that unit. The lead aircraft of the port trio, 21+C21, was also from the same unit, while the other two, 23+X12 and 23+E (or F)12, were from 2./St. G 162. Note the distinctively larger size Balkenkreuz markings and code letters on the latter two machines. The starboard trio comprises three new replacement He 51 B-1 aircraft, supplies of which began to reach JG 132 during the early months of 1936. The three retain their white production numbers, 45, 53 and 55, which were used for temporary identification for delivery flights during this period.

In most fighter, bomber, and transport units, a Luftwaffe Gruppe was identified by a Roman numeral and initially comprised a Staff Flight (Stab) and three Staffeln each of nine aircraft. Each Staffel was identified by an Arabic number. Three, or possibly four Staffeln could be combined together to form a Gruppe, which also contained a Stab flight. For example, the composition of Jagdgeschwader 132 at its zenith was as follows:

Geschwader Stab/JG 132	**(Geschwader staff flight)**
I.Gruppe Stab/JG 132	(first Gruppe staff flight)
1.Staffel/JG 132	(first Staffel)
2.Staffel/JG 132	(second Staffel)
3.Staffel/JG 132	(third Staffel)
II.Gruppe Stab/JG 132	(second Gruppe staff flight)
4.Staffel/JG 132	(fourth Staffel)
5.Staffel/JG 132	(fifth Staffel)
6.Staffel/JG 132	(sixth Staffel)
III.Gruppe Stab/JG 132	(third Gruppe staff flight)
7.Staffel/JG 132	(seventh Staffel)
8.Staffel/JG 132	(eighth Staffel)
9.Staffel/JG 132	(ninth Staffel)
IV.Gruppe Stab/JG 132	(fourth Gruppe staff flight)
10.Staffel/JG 132	(tenth Staffel)
11.Staffel/JG 132	(eleventh Staffel)
12.Staffel/JG 132	(twelfth Staffel)

Therefore, III./JG 132 would indicate the third Gruppe of JG 132, while 3./JG 132 would indicate the third Staffel of the same Geschwader. As time progressed the original system was modified – Staffel strength being increased to 12, then 16 aircraft. With some Geschwadern having four Gruppen, a Jagdgeschwader of the 1944 period could control well over 200 aircraft.

The designation 'Jagdgeschwader 132' indicated that it was the first (1), Jagd (3), Geschwader formed within Regional Air Command II (2). Other examples included KG 254 – the second (2), Kampf (5), Geschwader formed within Regional Air Command IV (4) and JG 141 – the first (1), Zerstörer (4) Geschwader formed within Regional Air Command I (1).

The codes designating the various types of units were as follows:

0   Naval reconnaisance units (See Aufklärungsflieger)
1   Army co-operation reconnaissance units (Heeres Aufklärungsflieger)
2   Long-range reconnaissance units (Fernaufklärungsflieger)
3   Normal fighter units (Jagdflieger)
4   Heavy fighter units (Zerstörerflieger)
5   Bomber units (Kampfflieger)
6   Dive Bombers (Sturzkampfflieger)
7   Transport (Transportflieger)
8   Carrier-borne units (Trägerflieger) [i]
9   Shipboard floatplane units (Bordflieger) [ii]

The unit code markings comprised a five-character sequence comprising two numbers, a letter and two further numbers. This sequence was painted on both sides of the fuselage, and repeated above

and below the wings. When applied to the wings, the first two figures were painted on the port side of the top wing, the second two on the starboard side, all inboard of the Balkenkreuz. The individual letter was sometimes painted on the top of the fuselage, on the centre of the wing, or omitted altogether. An example was the Ju 87 A-1 dive bomber, W.Nr. 0163, operated by II./St.G 165 based at Schweinfurt coded 52+A26. The latter contained the following information:

5   The fifth Geschwader formed within...
2   Luftkreiskommando 2 (in this case Stukageschwader 165)
A   The individual aircraft identification letter
2   II. Gruppe
6   6. Staffel

Some units recorded the Gruppe and Staffel differently. For example, instead of indicating the 6. Staffel they would record this as the 3. Staffel in the II.Gruppe. The distinction in choice of recording a particular Staffel as either part of an entire Geschwader establishment, or, as part of an individual Gruppe, appears to have been excercised by the individual Geschwader, rather than something set down by the RLM. In the above example the code then would have read as 25+A23. The Geschwader Stab or headquarters flight would appear to have had the Gruppe and Staffel numbers replaced by the letters 'OK'.

ABOVE: A line-up of Do 23 Gs of 3./KG 253, finished overall in RLM 02, probably photographed at the I. Gruppe home airfield at Gotha. The individual elements of the code group were applied in the same positions as for the upper surfaces, and the first element, '33' can be seen under the starboard wing tip.

In the case of an autonomous Gruppe (into which most reconnaissance units were formed) the code was broken down somewhat differently; for example, the He 46 E-1 operated by 3.(H)/15 based at Göppingen, coded 50+E23, whose code is broken down as follows:

50 An autonomous Gruppe within Luftkreiskommando 5
E   The individual aircraft identification letter
2   The second autonomous Gruppe formed within Luftkreiskommando 5 (in this case Aufklärungsgruppe 15).
3   3. Staffel

A list of pre-war Luftwaffe units follows, together with the code (where known) for each one:

---

i   Only only such unit was ever formed, Träger Geschwader 186 which was equipped with the Ju 87 and Bf 109.
ii Only only such unit was ever formed, Bordflieger Gruppe 196 which was equipped with the He 114 and Ar 196.

Luftwaffe High Command

Although it has not been proven from documentary evidence, it is thought that codes beginning with the numeral 0 were used by aircraft attached directly to the Luftwaffe High Command (Oberkommando der Luftwaffe).

ABOVE: This photograph records an unusual code. Only two photographic examples are known showing a code group beginning with '0'; such usage is thought to indicate use of aircraft attached directly to the Luftwaffe High Command (Oberkommando der Luftwaffe). Judging by the aircraft types in the background, and the various styles of fin and rudder markings, plus a civil registration, this photograph of an He 51 marked 03+F(or E)20, was possibly was taken either in late 1935 or 1936.

02+105	He 59 C	Berlin Grünau Olympic Regatta Course, May 1937
03+F(E?)20	He 51	late 1935/1936

Luftkreiskommando I

10+A1?   Aufklärungsgruppe (F) 121 (later 3.(F) Aufklärungsgruppe 11)

Reconnaissance units underwent several changes in designation between 1935 and 1938, e.g., designated as 1.(F)/121 in March 1935, it was redesignated (F)/22 sometime early in 1937, before returning to its earlier designation of (F)/122 under the general redesignation of reconnaissance units in November 1938.

10+A2?   Aufklärungsgruppe (H) 121 (later 1. and 2.(H) Aufklärungsgruppe 11)

Luftkreiskommando II

20+A?   Aufklärungs Lehrgruppe

A unique four-character code system was in use for this unit in spite of the standing five-character codes system employed by all other units at this time.

20+A1?	Aufklärungsgruppe 122 (later Aufklärungsgruppe 22)
20+A2?	Aufklärungsgruppe 112 (later Aufklärungsgruppe 12)
20+A3?	Aufklärungsgruppe 212 (later Aufklärungsgruppe 52)
20+A4?	Aufklärungsgruppe 212
21+A1?	I./Jagdgeschwader 132 'Richthofen'
21+A2?	II./Jagdgeschwader 132 'Richthofen'
21+A3?	III./Jagdgeschwader 132 'Richthofen'
21+A4?	IV./Jagdgeschwader 132 'Richthofen'
23+A1?	I./Stukageschwader 162 'Immelmann'
23+A2?	II./Stukageschwader 162 'Immelmann'
25+A1?	I./Kampfgeschwader 152 'Hindenburg'
25+A2?	II.(Kampf) Lehrgeschwader
	Formed from II./KG 152.
25+A3?	III.(Kampf) Lehrgeschwader
	Formed from III./KG 152.
27+A1?	I./Kampfgeschwader z.b.V 1
	Formed from IV./KG 152.
27+A2?	II./Kampfgeschwader z.b.V 1

Luftkreiskommando III

30+A1?	Aufklärungsgruppe 123 (later Aufklärungsgruppe 23)
30+A2?	Aufklärungsgruppe 113 (later Aufklärungsgruppe 13)
32+A1?	I./Kampfgeschwader 153
32+A2?	II./Kampfgeschwader 153
32+A3?	III./Kampfgeschwader 153.
33+A0K	Geschwader Stab/Kampfgeschwader 253 'General Wever' ?
33+A1?	I./Kampfgeschwader 253 'General Wever'
33+A2?	II./Kampfgeschwader 253 'General Wever'
33+A3?	III./Kampfgeschwader 253 'General Wever'
35+A1?	I./Stukageschwader 163
35+A2?	II./Stukageschwader 163
35+A3?	III./Stukageschwader 163

Luftkreiskommando IV

40+A1?	Aufklärungsgruppe 124 (later Aufklärungsgruppe 24)
40+A2?	Aufklärungsgruppe 14
40+A3?	Aufklärungsgruppe 114 (later Aufklärungsgruppe 14)
41+A1?	I./Kampfgeschwader 154 'Boelcke'
41+A2?	II./Kampfgeschwader 154 'Boelcke'
41+A3?	III./Kampfgeschwader 154 'Boelcke'
42+A1?	I./Kampfgeschwader 254
42+A2?	II./Kampfgeschwader 254
42+A3?	III./Kampfgeschwader 254

Luftkreiskommando V

50+A1?	Aufklärungsgruppe 125 (Aufklärungsgruppe 25)
50+A2?	Aufklärungsgruppe 115 (Aufklärungsgruppe 15)
51+A1?	I./Jagdgeschwader 135
52+A1?	I./Stukageschwader 165
52+A2?	II./Stukageschwader 165
52+A3?	III./Stukageschwader 165
53+A1?	I./Kampfgeschwader 155
53+A2?	II./Kampfgeschwader 155
53+A3?	III./Kampfgeschwader 155
54+A1?	I./Kampfgeschwader 255 'Alpen'
54+A2?	II./Kampfgeschwader 255 'Alpen'
54+A3?	III./Kampfgeschwader 255 'Alpen'
55+A1?	I./Kampfgeschwader 355
55+A2?	II./Kampfgeschwader 355
55+A3?	III./Kampfgeschwader 355
56+A1?	Unknown

Luftkreiskommando VI

60+A1?	Küstenfliegergruppe 106
60+A2?	Küstenfliegergruppe 206
60+A3?	Küstenfliegergruppe 306
60+A4?	Küstenfliegergruppe 406
60+A5?	Küstenfliegergruppe 506
60+A6?	Küstenfliegergruppe 606
60+A7?	Küstenfliegergruppe 706
60+A8?	Küstenfliegergruppe 806

Luftkreiskommando VII

On 12 October 1937, Luftkreiskommando VII, with headquarters in Hamburg, was formed from areas formally covered by Luftkreiskommando II, IV & V.

ABOVE: A Kette of He 111 E bombers of 6./KG 157 Boelcke in 61/62/63/65 camouflage and marked in the standard code style of the period. The lead aircraft is 71+H26, the second 71+K26 and the third 71+G26.

70+A1?	Aufklärungsgruppe 127 (later Aufklärungsgruppe 27).
71+A1?	I./Kampfgeschwader 157 'Boelcke'
71+A2?	II./Kampfgeschwader 157 'Boelcke'
71+A3?	III./Kampfgeschwader 157 'Boelcke'
71+A1?	I./Stukageschwader 167
72+A1?	I./Kampfgeschwader 257
72+A2?	II./Kampfgeschwader 257
72+A3?	III./Kampfgeschwader 257

Luftkreiskommando VIII

After German forces marched into Austria on 12 March 1938, most of the country was placed under the control of an eighth Luftkreiskommando with its headquarters in Vienna, although the Tyrol (Western Austria) was incorporated into Luftkreiskommando V.

80+A1?	Aufklärungsgruppe 128
80+A2?	Aufklärungsgruppe 18

While this system is generally accepted as the norm, it is possible that an earlier variant was used for a short time in 1935. Two unit codes have been discovered which may have been used during this period. At this time five Kampfgeschwader were in service; I. and II./KG 252, I./KG 254, KG 652 and KG 753. The theory is that the *second* number in the marking sequence referred directly to the *first* number in the unit designation.

Code	Aircraft	Notes
27+E11	Ju 52/3mg3e	Possibly 1./KG 753, October 1935
27+D13	Ju 52/3mg3e	Possibly 3./KG 753, October 1935
27+E13	Ju 52/3mg3e	Possibly 3./KG 753, October 1935
27+D23	Ju 52/3mg3e	Possibly 3. Staffel II./KG 753, October 1935
56+E12	He 111 B-1	Possibly 2./KG 652

Shortly after this time KG 652 formed the basis of KG 153 and KG 753 were expanded and re-designated KG 253.

A special instructional unit was formed in 1935, under the designation Lehrgeschwader 1, to develop tactics. As such it used a five-character code system, but with a distinct variation that indicated its special status, the usual two-numeral prefix being replaced with 'L1'. A second such unit, Lehrgeschwader 2, was formed late in 1938 and employed the same code style. 10.(See)/LG 2 was formed on 1 November 1938 at Travemünde for maritime development work, equipped with He 114 A and Do 18 D aircraft, and at least one Ju 87 B, (on 15 September 1939 it became 3./KG 30). As such it was allocated a further distinctive code, '6L+', followed by three letters rather than the usual form of one letter and two numerals, in this instance 'OS' being used for the last two symbols of the code group. The individual identification letter of each of the few aircraft on strength was marked immediately after the Balkenkreuz.

L1+A1?	I./Lehrgeschwader 1
L1+A2?	II./Lehrgeschwader 1
L1+A3?	III./Lehrgeschwader 1
L2+A1?	I./Lehrgeschwader 2
L2+A2?	II./Lehrgeschwader 2
L2+A3?	III./Lehrgeschwader 2
6L+?OS	10.(See)/LG 2

Trainer markings

At the same time as the five-character code system was introduced for front line aircraft, a similar system was adopted by the training units. The system comprised the letter 'S' (indicating Schule – school), a number (indicating the Luftkreiskommando), a letter (indicating the identity of the Staffel within the school) and a two or three-digit number which identified the individual aircraft within the school. This marking system was retained by Luftwaffe training units until 24 October 1939, when it was replaced by the four-letter Stammkennzeichen markings described in Chapter 17. The 'S' codes are given below, but the significance of the 'S13' and 'S17' remain a mystery, because there were only eight Luftkreiskommando established.

Luftkreiskommando II	S2+???
Luftkreiskommando V	S5+???
Luftkreiskommando VI	S6+???
Luftkreiskommando VII	S7+???
Unknown	S13+???
Unknown	S17+???

RIGHT: A Ju 52/3m of C Staffel brought to its metaphorical knees by a landing accident. While the complete details of the code are difficult to see, the first element 'S5' can be seen forward of the Balkenkreuz on the fuselage, while the remaining portion, 'C16', is clearly visible on the starboard wing tip of W.Nr. 572. The 'S5' coding identified a training unit from within Luftkreiskommando V. This form of code marking remained in use by the Luftwaffe until (at least on paper) repealed on 24 October 1939. (Morten Jessen)

LEFT: This He 46 was operated by the Flugzeugführer Schule at Dresden-Grossenhain. Its marking of 'S7' identified it as belonging to a training school within Luftkreiskommando VII; the letter 'A' was its Staffel identity, while the number 18 was that of the individual aircraft within the school. (G. Long via R. Lutz)

BELOW: Thee Do 23 bombers of the Heereskriegsschule at Kitzingen, carry training school codes of S17+D66, S13+C17 and with a third, S13+C25, just visible to far left. As explained in the text, the significance of the S13 and S17 code allocation is not known. The aircraft in the centre has standard 70/71/65 finish while the other two retain their pre-war 02-overall finish. (Rudolf Langhans via Mark Clayton)

Four-Character Military Code System
by J. Richard Smith

Following the successful occupation of the Czechoslovakian Sudetenland in October 1938, Hitler created the 'Greater German Reich'. This resulted in a reshuffle of the Luftwaffe's command structure, the eight Luftkreiskommando being replaced by three Luftwaffengruppenkommando (Air Force Group Commands). These covered north-east Germany, with headquarters in Berlin; north-west Germany, with headquarters in Braunschweig; and southern Germany, with headquarters in München. A fourth command, Luftwaffenkommando Ostmark, was established to cover Austria and the Sudetenland, with headquarters in Vienna.

In February 1939 the three Luftwaffengruppenkommando were redesignated Luftflotten (Air Fleets). During the German occupation of the remainder of Czechoslovakia in March 1939, Luftwaffenkommando Ostmark became Luftflotte 4, controlling Austria and Czechoslovakia with headquarters in Wien.

On 1 May 1939, all operational Luftwaffe Geschwader were redesignated, units under Luftflotte 1 being numbered from '1' onwards, those within Luftflotte 2 from 26 onwards, those within Luftflotte 3 from 51 onwards and those within Luftflotte 4 from 76 onwards. In addition to the four Luftflotten, the Luftwafe Lehrdivision operated as a separate entity. At this time the following reconnaissance, bomber and ground-attack groups were operational:

Luftflotte 1 (Berlin)

Aufkl.Gr.10	Hs 126, Do 17	Neuhausen
Aufkl.Gr.11	Hs 126, He 46, Do 17	Grossenhain
Aufkl.Gr.21	Hs 126, He 45	Stargard
Aufkl.Gr 41	Hs 126, He 46	Reichenberg
Aufkl.Gr.120	Do 17	Neuhausen
Aufkl.Gr.121	Do 17	Prenzlau
I./KG 152	He 111	Neubrandenburg (later II./KG 1)
I./KG 1	He 111	Kolberg (ex IV./KG 153)
I./KG 2	Do 17	Liegnitz (ex I./KG 252)
II./KG 2	Do 17	Liegnitz (ex II./KG 252)
II./KG 3	Do 17	Heiligenbeil (ex II./KG 153)
III./KG 3	Do 17	Heiligenbeil (ex III./KG 153)
I./KG 4	He 111	Gotha (ex I./KG 253)
II./KG 4	He 111	Erfurt (ex II./KG 253)
III./KG 4	He 111	Nordhausen (ex III./KG 253)
I./St.G 1	Ju 87	Insterburg (ex I./St.G 160)
I./St.G 2	Ju 87	Cottbus (ex I./St.G 163)
II./St.G 2	Ju 87	Stolp-Reitz (ex I./St.G 162)
III./St.G 2	Ju 87	Langensalza (ex II./St.G 163)
II.(S)/LG 2	Hs 123	Damm

Luftflotte 2 (Braunschweig)

Aufkl.Gr.12	Hs 126, He 45, He 46	Münster
Aufkl.Gr.122	Do 17	Goslar
I./KG 26	He 111	Lübeck (ex I./KG 257)
II./KG 26	He 111	Luneburg (ex II./KG 257)
I./KG 27	He 111	Langenhagen (ex I./KG 157)
II./KG 27	He 111	Wunstorf (ex II./KG 157)
III./KG 27	He 111	Delmenhorst (ex III./KG 157)
II./KG 28	He 111	Gütersloh (ex II./KG 254)

Luftflotte 3 (München)

Aufkl.Gr.13	Hs 126, He 45, He 46	Göppingen
Aufkl.Gr.22	Hs 126, Do 17	Rothwesten
Aufkl.Gr.23	Hs 126, He 45, He 46	Ober-Olm
Aufkl.Gr.123	Do 17	Würzburg
I./KG 51	He 111	Landsberg (ex I./KG 255)
III./KG 51	He 111	Memmingen (ex III./KG 255)
I./KG 53	He 111	Neukirchen (ex I./KG 355)
II./KG 53	He 111	Schwäbisch Hall (ex II./KG 355)
III./KG 53	He 111	Giebelstadt (ex III./KG 355)
I./KG 54	He 111	Fritzlar (ex I./KG 254)
I./KG 55	He 111	Langendiebach (ex I./KG 155)
II./KG 55	He 111	Giessen (ex II./KG 155)
I./St.G 51	Ju 87	Wertheim (ex III./St.G 165)

Luftflotte 4 (Wien)

Aufkl.Gr.14	Hs 126, He 46, Do 17	Bad Vöslau
Aufkl.Gr.31	Hs 126, He 46, Do 17	Brieg
Aufkl.Gr. 124	Do 17	Wiener-Neustadt
I./KG 76	Do 17	Wiener-Neustadt (ex I./KG 158)
III./KG 76	Do 17	Wels (ex III./KG 158)
I./KG 77	Do 17	Prague (ex I./KG 153)
II./KG 77	Do 17	Brünn (ex II./KG 158)
III./KG 77	Do 17	Königgratz (ex II./KG 255)
I./St.G 76	Ju 87	Graz (ex I./St.G 168)
I./St.G 77	Ju 87	Brieg (ex I./St.G 165)
II./St.G 77	Ju 87	Breslau (ex II./St.G 165)

Luftwaffe Lehrdivision

II.(K)/LG 1	He 111	Schwerin
III.(K)/LG 1	He 111	Greifswald
IV.(St)/LG 1	Ju 87, Do 17	Barth
7. & 8.(F)/LG 2	Do 17	Jüterbog
9.(H)/LG 2	Hs 126, He 46	Jüterbog
10.(K)LG 2	He 111	Werder

On 24 October 1939, all operational Luftwaffe units with the exception of the Jagdverbände, (single-engine fighter units) and later the Schlachtverbände (ground-attack units) adopted a new four-character code system. The first two characters (always made up of a letter and figure), painted to the left of the fuselage Balkenkreuz marking identified the Geschwader (or autonomous Gruppe) to which the aircraft belonged. The third character, positioned immediately to the right of the fuselage Balkenkreuz was the aircraft's individual identification letter, and the last letter identified the Staffel or Stabsschwarm (headquarters flight). It was intended that the aircraft's individual code letter would be applied above and below each wing, inboard of the respective Balkenkreuz, but sometimes the entire code was painted on both wing surfaces. The official German painting guide, Der Flugzeugmahler of 1944 detailed how this code should be applied:

'Aircraft are to be marked in block characters irrespective of whether letters or numerals are used. An even thickness of the characters used is of special importance. Characters are defined by their height, width, thickness and the space between each character. Spacing of the characters has to be even otherwise they will appear distorted. The letters C, E, F, J and L will be narrower, since they would otherwise appear too wide. M and W appear much wider.

Centreline of characters is parallel to the Balkenkreuz centreline. It runs parallel to the horizontal plane in flight, not to the fuselage centreline. On and under the wings, the centreline is at rightangles to the direction of flight.'

The 1944 edition of Der Flugzeugmahler reiterated also the amended application standard that had been in force since 1939, for how codes were to be placed on the wing surfaces:

'Codes, such as numbers and letters, are not to be applied to the upper surfaces of military and operational aircraft. The third letter is, however, to be applied to the under surfaces of operational aircraft, centred between wingtip and Balkenkreuz. On military (i.e. non-operational) aircraft, all four codes are to be placed underwing.'

All Luftwaffe units to employ the four-character code system had three Staffeln in each Gruppe. The exception was the transport units, which

LEFT: Unit 'hack' aircraft – those used for moving personnel or key staff usually were marked with the full code of the parent unit. Here a Bü 131 of 3./Aufkl.Gr.21 displays its code, P2+OL, on its pre-war 02-overall finish. In the background is an Fw 44 marked NM+AX (or Y), an He 111 with black under surfaces, and a Bf 109. (D. Wadman)

ABOVE AND RIGHT: A Ju 52/3m, H8+ZM, used by 4.(F)/33 for transport duties. It was common practice for such aircraft to use the individual letter 'Z'. These two photographs afford a good record of how the codes were marked on both sides of the same aircraft. In the background is one of the unit's Bf 110s, H8+EM, also wearing winter temporary white finish. The Bf 110 has its yellow 04 tactical band marking placed between the end of the wing root and the beginning of the unit code. The Ju 52 however wears its yellow band marking squarely behind the Balkenkreuz. (D. Vincent)

had four Staffeln in each Gruppe and therefore utilized a slightly modified system. The Staffel letters used by both variations are shown below:

Operational units		Transport Units	
A	Geschwader Stab	A	Geschwader Stab
B	I. Gruppe Stab	B	I. Gruppe Stab
H	1. Staffel	H	1. Staffel
K	2. Staffel	K	2. Staffel
L	3. Staffel	L	3. Staffel
		M	4. Staffel
C	II. Gruppe Stab		
M	4. Staffel	C	II. Gruppe Stab
N	5. Staffel	N	5. Staffel
P	6. Staffel	P	6. Staffel
		R	7. Staffel
D	III. Gruppe Stab	S	8. Staffel
R	7. Staffel		
S	8. Staffel	D	III. Gruppe Stab
T	9. Staffel	T	9. Staffel
		U	10. Staffel
		V	11. Staffel
F	IV. Gruppe Stab	W	12. Staffel
U	10. Staffel		
V	11. Staffel	F	IV. Gruppe Stab
W	12. Staffel	X	13. Staffel
		Y	14. Staffel
		Z	15. Staffel
		Q	16. Staffel

As the war progressed, one or two Geschwader had a V.Gruppe added to provide a 13., 14. and 15.Staffel. In most cases these units carried the same Staffel letters as those allocated to the transport units, but there were exceptions. Notable among these was V./KG 2 which utilized the following system:

J	V. Gruppe Stab
E	14. Staffel
F	15. Staffel
G	16. Staffel

As far as is known, the letters 'I' and 'O' were never used for Staffel identification, but all other letters were used at some time.

The Geschwader and Staffel characters were normally painted black with the individual aircraft letter usually painted in its Stab or Staffel colour. These colours were:

Geschwader Stab	Blue (RLM 24)
	I., II., III., IV. and V.
Gruppe Stab	Green (RLM 25)
1.Staffel within a Gruppe	White (RLM 21)
2.Staffel within a Gruppe	Red (RLM 23)
3.Staffel within a Gruppe	Yellow (RLM 27)
4.Staffel within a Gruppe [i]	Blue (RLM 24)

In practice, the red or yellow individual codes were often outlined in black or painted plain black. The Staffel colours originated from the unit identification system used by the old German Imperial Army with white for the first sub-unit, red for the second, yellow for the third, blue for the fourth, green for the fifth and brown for the sixth. This Stab or Staffel colour was often repeated on the aircraft's spinner.

This system continued virtually unchanged until the end of the war, the one major innovation being the painting of the first two characters approximately one-fifth the size of the remaining letters from July 1943, or possibly earlier, ostensibly for security reasons as it then became difficult to distinguish unit identity other than from close quarters. The value of such intelligence is clear from an instruction contained in the 1941 edition, Part V, of Middle East Training Memorandum No. 1, issued to British ground forces. It stated:

'38. Aircraft.

Enemy aircraft. It is sometimes possible to distinguish the recognition letters of low flying enemy aircraft. These markings are most useful to the R.A.F. for identification purposes and, if seen should be noted and reported back to H.Q.'s. without delay.

    Points to be noted are:-

(a) *Ju 87, Me 110 and multi-engine types have four large letters on either side of the fuselage. Two in front and two after the cross.*

(b) *Me 110s have coloured noses and the number before the cross on the side of the fuselage, and sometimes a dash after it.*

(c) *Italian aircraft tend to stay higher, but their markings are equally important.'*

While the state of intelligence on Bf 110 markings was still sketchy, the ability to recognize unit markings, even in flight at low-level, is evident.

Again the Geschwader code and Staffel letters were painted black with the individual letter in the colour given earlier. An exception was the Versuchsverband Ob.d.L., which had its 'T 9' code painted in white.

Luftwaffe Codes

A1	Kampfgeschwader 53 'Legion Condor'.
A2	I./ZG 52, II./ZG 2 and various transport units in Finland. Also used later by Flugbereitschaft Komm.Gen.d.dt Luftwaffe Finnland and Transportstaffel Fliegerführer Nord.
A3	Kampfgeschwader 200.
A5	Stukageschwader 1 and Schlachtgeschwader 1.
A6	Aufklärungsgruppe 120.
A7	Luftverkehrsgruppe Bronkow.
A8	Kampfschulegeschwader 2.

ABOVE: Test units were also allocated codes and while they usually followed the same broad principles as that applying to front line units, they often incorporated some variations that made them distinctive. This photograph, taken in 1945, of Me 262 A-1a, W.Nr. 170070 operated by the Erprobungsstelle Rechlin, shows a combination of a four-character style code (E7+02) plus a fighter unit-style code (White 12). (Franek Grabowski)

---

i   Transport units only.

A9   Possibly allocated to the Fliegerbrigadestab 4 from 27 May 1944. (e.g., A9+FK, Bf 110, D3620, Gardelegen).

B2   Code B2+AA observed on an He 111 decoy dummy, but probably never carried by a Luftwaffe unit.

B3   Kampfgeschwader 54 'Totenkopf'.

B4   Nachtjagdstaffel Finnland/Norwegen.

B5   Fernaufklärungsgruppe 3.

B7   Wetterkundungstaffel Luftflotte 1.

B8   Sanitätsflugbereitschaft 2.

C1   Erprobungskommando 16. Because of its experimental nature, the unit had two numbers painted to the right of the Balkenkreuz.

C2   Aufklärungsgruppe 41.

C3   Transport Staffel II. Fliegerkorps.

C4   Unit unidentified (e.g., C4+BZ, Do 17 Z-1).

C6   Kampfgruppe z b V 600 and Transportstaffel Fliegerführer 4. Transportstaffel Fl.Füh.4 used the Staffel letter 'H'.

C8   Kampfgeschwader zbV 323 and Transportgeschwader 5 I./KGzbV 323 used the individual letters 'B', 'E', 'F' & 'G'.

C9   Nachtjagdgeschwader 5.

D1   Seeaufklärungsgruppe 126. Also used by Luftdienstkommando 65.

D3   Störkampfstaffel Luftflotte 6 and Nachtschlachtgruppe 2.

D4   Unit unidentified (e.g., D4+CU Ju 88 A-6 Aug 1941, D4+EW Ju 88 A-5 Aug 1941).

D5   Nachtjagdgeschwader 3.

D7   Wetterkundungstaffeln 1 and 6, Luftflotte 5 and Ob.d.L. Staffel letter 'H' was carried by Wekusta 1, Staffel letter 'K' by Wekusta Ob.d.L. 'N' by Wekusta Luftflotte 5 and Staffel letter 'P' by Wekusta 6.

D9   I./Kampfgeschwader 7 and I./Nachtjagdgeschwader 7.

E2   Erprobungsstelle Rechlin E2 (airframes). The 'E' codes used by Rechlin were not true operational unit markings. The two characters painted to the right of the Balkenkreuz often consisted of two numbers or a letter and number.

E3   Erprobungsstelle Rechlin E3 (engines).

E4   Erprobungsstelle Rechlin E4 (Radio Equipment).

E7   Bombs, fuses and ballistics.

E8   I./Fernkampfgeschwader 50 and Nachtschlachtgruppe 9.

F1   Kampfgeschwader 76 'Florian Geyer' and I./Stukageschwader 76. The training Gruppe for KG 76, IV.(Erg)/KG 76 became III./EKG 1 in January 1945, retaining codes of that unit. I./St.G 76 carried last letter codes of the second Gruppe because I. and III./KG 76 existed at its formation, whereas II./KG 76 did not. Code had passed to III./St.G 77 after July 1940.

F2   Ergänzungs (Fern) Gruppe.

F3   Kampfgruppe z b V 23. Also carried by the Verbindungs Staffel Süd Ost.

F4   Seenotstaffel 80.

F5   Flugbereitschaft/Luftflotte 2.

F6   Aufklärungsgruppe 122.

F7   Schleppgruppe 1 and parts of LLG 1 and 2.

F8   Kampfgeschwader 40 and Transportstaffel Condor.

F9   Nachtschlachtgruppe 5.

G1   Kampfgeschwader 55 'Greif'.

G2   Aufklärungsgruppe 124 (possibly also 4.Aufkl.Gr.Ob.d.L)

G3   Possibly Ergänzungsgeschwader 2, (e.g., G3+HL Fw 190 A-6, 3./EJG 2?).

G4   Unit unidentified (e.g., G4+FH Ju 88 A, North Africa).

G5   Transportstaffel V Fliegerkorps and Luftwaffen Kommando Ost.

G6   Transportgeschwader 4 (and others – see below), Code carried by KGrzbV 2 between August and September 1939, then passed to KGrzbV 101 (individual letters 'B', 'H', 'K', 'L' & 'M') KGrzbV 102 (individual letters 'C', 'N', 'P', 'R' and 'S'), KGrzbV 104 (individual letters ('D', 'T', 'U', 'V' and 'W'), KGrzbV

105 (individual letters 'F', 'X', 'Y', 'Z' and 'Q') and Lufttransportstaffel (See) 1 (individual letter 'J').

G9   Nachtjagdgeschwader 1. Also used by I./ZG 1 and III./NJG 4 for a short period and later by Erprobungskommando 410.

H1   Aufklärungsgruppe 12.

H3   Unit unidentified (e.g., H3+BF, Fi 156 C, Russia)

H4   Luftlandesgeschwader 1. Also by various other units including the Fliegerhorstkommandeure, and some transport units.

H5   Possibly Nachtschlachtgruppe 10 (e.g., H5+MK Ju 87 D, Wels, Austria, summer 1945).

H7   Aufklärungsstaffel (F) Ostsee. Also attributed to Stukageschwader 3 but probably confused with the code 'S7', (H7+YH, Fw 189 A, Aufkl.Sta.(F) Ostsee)

H8   Aufklärungsgruppe 33.

H9   H9+?H allocated to Luft Transport Staffel (See) 7, equipped with the French Latecoere 631 and SNCASE 200 aircraft.

J2   Nahaufklärungsgruppe 3. Unit carried fighter-type markings but prefixed with the code 'J 2' painted one fifth the size of the number or numbers.

J3   Nahaufklärungsgruppe 9.

J4   Lufttransportstaffel 290 and Transportstaffel 5.

J6   KGrzbV 500. Also reported to have been used by a detachment of Ju 52/3m floatplanes, and a Ju 87 decoy dummy coded 'J6+AA'.

J8   Nahaufklärungsgruppe 2.

J9   I.(Stuka)/186, III./Stukageschwader 1 and Seenotstaffel 7. After I.(Stuka)/186 was redesignated III./St.G 1 in July 1940, unit retained last letter codes 'B', 'H', 'K' and 'L'. It is possible that the 'J 9' code passed to I./St.G 5, but this has yet to be confirmed.

K1   Unit unidentified. According to one source, this code was allocated to KGrzbV 400, while another source states Stabsschwarm of Luftflotte 6 (e.g., K1+AA Fi 156, K1+EA Bf 110 E, K1+HH Fi 156, Flugbereitschaft L/Kdo 6, von Greim, 5 March 1945, K1+AK Ju 52/3m, W.Nr. 2826, 2./KGrzbV 400, 12 May 1942).

K2   Possibly used by a Transports Staffel equipped with the Ju 52/3m and Do 215.

K3   Seenotstaffel 6.

K4   Wekusta 7.

K5   Einsatzkampfgruppe Ju 88/Gen der Fl.Ausbildung Mediterreanean.

K6   Küstenfliegergruppe 406. War diary of the OKM (Navy High Command) gives the code 'K6+?M' as being used by 4./Kü.Fl.Gr 906.

K7   Aufklärungsgruppe Nacht.

K8   Unit unidentified (e.g., K8+MV Ju 88 S-3, W.Nr. 330934, code found on aircraft's battery cover, 29 Jan 1945).

K9   Aufklärungsgruppe Ob.d.L.

L1   Lehrgeschwader 1. After V.(Z)/LG 1 formed from I.(Z)/LG 1 in October 1939 it retained that unit's Staffel letters. I./NJG 3 also used same codes for a short time after it formed from V.(Z)/LG 1 in October 1940, eventually receiving its own code 'D 5'. The 'L 1' code also carried by the Ju 87s of I./St.G 5 and I./SG 5 following this unit's formation from IV.(Stuka)/LG 1 in February 1942.

L2   Lehrgeschwader 2. When LG 2 was formed late in 1938, its aircraft used a hybrid code system. The code 'L2' was allocated, but the contemporary Staffel identification system in five-character code system in use was retained. 3./Aufkl.Gr.Ob.d.L also used the code 'L1+?S', having been formed from 8./LG 2.

L3   Uncertain, possibly KG 200 (e.g., L3+AE Fi 156, I./KG 200, Ofw. Lange, May 1945).

L5	KGrzbV 5. Some sources state Staffel letters 'B', 'H', 'K', 'L' & 'M' as being used by KGrzbV 5 and 'L5+?R' by 7./Erg.Tr.Geschwader.
L8	Nahaufklärungsgruppe 4.
M2	Küstenfliegergruppe/Kampfgruppe 106.
M3	Fliegerschule der Luftwaffe 2.
M4	One source cites 7. and 8./Aufkl.Gr 32 (e.g., M4+AH Fw 189 A Eastern Front, M4+CM Hs 126 B-1, Nov 1941, M4+BS Hs 126 B-1, Jul 1941, M4+ZS Bü 131, Jul 1941).
M6	Seenotstaffel 3.
M7	Kampfgruppe 806.
M8	I. and II./Zerstörergeschwader 76. Initially carried only by I. and II.Gruppen, but possibly later by the whole Geschwader.
M9	4./Störkampfstaffel Luftflotte 4.
N1	Grossraumtransportstaffel. Only used from 30 January 1945, flying Ju 352s and Fw 200s.
N3	I./Kampfgeschwader zbV 172. Possibly also carried by Stab/KG 3.
N5	Nahaufklärungsgruppe Blomberg.
N6	Possibly Verband Maj Babekuhl equipped with Ju 52/3ms.
N8	Unit unidentified (e.g., N8+IN He 177 A-, W.Nr. 5557 II./KG 40, probably a misprint for 'F8', Dec 1943).
N9	Verbindungstaffel Norwegen. Possibly also used by Verbindungstaffel 4.
P1	I./Kampfgeschwader 60.
P2	Aufklärungsgruppe 21.
P4	Führungskette X Fliegerkorps and Transport Flieger Staffel Nord (Ost).
P5	Sonderstaffel 'Trans Ozean'.
P6	Transportfliegergruppe 110 (Italien).
P7	Seenotstaffel 5 and 51.
P9	Quoted by one source as being an alternative to 'R4' for I./NJG 2.
Q1	Possibly Stab/NAG 1 (e.g., Q1+UB Bf 110 G-3, W.Nr. 4852, Stab/NAG 1, Apostolowo, 24 October 1942, Q1+JC Ju 88 A-14).
Q5	Wekusta 27.
Q8	Seenotdienst Luftflotte 6.
Q9	I./Schlachtgeschwader 5.
R4	Nachtjagdgeschwader 2.
S1	One source states 'S1' used by I./St.G 3 and another by St.G 1.
S2	Stukageschwader 77 and Schlachtgeschwader 77.
S3	Transportgruppe 30 and Stab/SG 10.
S4	Küstenfliegergruppe 506.
S7	Stukageschwader 3 and Schlachtgeschwader 3.
S9	Erprobungsgruppe 210 and Schnellkampfgeschwader 210. Also used by III./ZG 1, which formed from II./SKG 210.
T1	Aufklärungsgruppe 10 'Tannenberg'.
T3	Bordfliegergruppe 196 (also used 6W).
T4	Verbindungstaffel II. Fliegerkorps.
T5	Aufklärungsgruppe Ob.d.L and Aufklärungsgruppe 100. Last letter 'U' used by Wekusta Ob.d.L.
T6	Stukageschwader 2 and Schlachtgeschwader 2 'Immelmann'.
T9	Versuchsverband Ob.d.L/O.K.L.
U2	Nahaufklärungsgruppe 5.
U5	Kampfgeschwader 2 'Holzhammer'. The fifth Gruppe of KG 2, equipped with the Me 410, used last letters 'J', 'E', 'F' and 'G' for Stab flight, respectively 14., 15. and 16.Staffeln.
U8	I./Zerstörergeschwader 26 'Horst Wessel'.
U9	Nachtschlachtgruppe 3.
V1	Transportstaffel VIII. Fliegerkorps.
V2	Ju 52/Fi 156 transport unit of IV. Fliegerkorps (last letter 'H' only).
V3	Kampfschulegeschwader 3.
V4	Kampfgeschwader 1 'Hindenburg'. Early in the war, II./KG 1 used last letter codes of IV./KG 1, because it was formed originally from IV./KG 152.

V5	Luftdienstkommando Finnland.
V7	Aufklärungsgruppe 32. Unit used a unique code system, the second number indicating the Staffel directly, and second letter was the individual aircraft identity.
V8	Nachtschlachtgruppe 1.
W1	Messerschmitt Me 321.
W2	Messerschmitt Me 321.
W3	Messerschmitt Me 321.
W4	Messerschmitt Me 321.
W4	Seenotstaffel 1.
W5	Messerschmitt Me 321.
W5	Stab/Fliegerführer Lofoten.
W6	Messerschmitt Me 321.
W7	Nachtjagdgeschwader 100.
W8	Messerschmitt Me 321.
W9	Messerschmitt Me 323. One source quotes code 'W 9' carried by KGrzbV 40 (I. Gruppe letters), KGrzbV 50 (II. Gruppe letters) and KGrzbV 60 (III. Gruppe letters).
X	Lufttransportstaffel (See) 222 and Seeaufklärungsgruppe 129.
X8	Kampfgruppe zbV 900. In addition to use by KGrzbV 900, aircraft with the Staffel letter 'H' reported to have been operated by Flugber. RLM Staaken, and aircraft with the Staffel letter 'L' by Verbindungsstaffel 58.
X9	Nahaufklärungsgruppe 11.
Y9	Nahaufklärungsgruppe 12.
Z4	Transport Staffel Flieger Führer 3.
Z6	Kampfgeschwader 66.
1A	Wekusta 5.
1B	Wekusta Luftflotte 5 and 13.(Z)/Jagdgeschwader 5 'Eismeer'.
1C	Uncertain. Often confused with '1 Z' for KGrzbV 1.
1D	Unit unidentified (e.g., 1D+GU He 111, Oct 1941).
1E	Ergänzungsgruppe(S) 1.
1G	Kampfgeschwader 27 'Boelcke'.
1H	Kampfgeschwader 26 'Löwen'.
1K	Nachtschlachtgruppe 4.
1L	Nachtjagdgruppe 10.
1M	Seenotstaffel 70.
1R	Various Kurierstaffeln in Finland.
1T	Kampfgruppe 126 and Kampfgeschwader 28.
1Z	Kampfgeschwader zbV 1 and Transportgeschwader 1.
2A	Uncertain. Possibly used by 4./NJG 2, only known example 2A+BL Bf 110 D.W.Nr. 3812, 4./NJG 2, England, 15 October, 1940.
2B	Nachtjagdschwarm Luftflotte 1.
2C	Unit unidentified, given as II./ZG 1 by some sources.
2E	Stabsstaffel/KG 54 'Totenkopf'.
2F	II./KG 28, II./KG 54 'Totenkopf' and Stabsstaffel/St.G 3.
2H	Versuchsstaffel Me 210.
2J	Zerstörergeschwader 1 'Wespen' (third unit).
2K	Nachtschlachtgruppe 7. (see also 4X)
2N	Zerstörergeschwader 76 (later Zerstörergeschwader 1).
2P	X.Fliegerdivision.
2Q	Nahaufklärungsgruppe 15.
2S	Zerstörergeschwader 2 (second unit).
2U	Possibly used by Zerstörergeschwader 1.
2Z	Nachtjagdgeschwader 6.
3C	Nachtjagdgeschwader 4.
3D	Unit unidentified. (e.g., 3D+XD He 114 A-2, Travemünde, 1941).
3E	Kampfgeschwader 6.
3G	Unit unidentified. (e.g., 3G+F? Fi 156 C-2).
3J	Uncertain. Possibly used by 12./NJG 3. Only known example 3J+YW Bf 110 G-4, 12./NJG 3, Stavanger, 1945.

3K	Minensuchsgruppe der Luftwaffe.
3M	I./Zerstörergeschwader 2.
3U	II. and III./Zerstörergeschwader 26 'Horst Wessel'.
3W	Nachtschlachtgruppe 11.
3X	Uncertain. One source quotes '3 X' as being used by I./KG 152 until 18 September 1939 and then passing to II./KG 1. The code was possibly also used by 11./Nahaufklärungsgruppe 11. (e.g., 3X+OL Fw 189 A-3, W.Nr. 01731, 1./NAG 11, Grove, 8 May 1945).
3Y	Unit unidentified (e.g., 3Y+HT Do 24, I./KG 200, Hptm. Braun, Finland, October 1944).
3Z	Kampfgeschwader 77.
4A	IV./Zerstörergeschwader 26 'Horst Wessel'.
4D	Kampfgeschwader 25 and Kampfgeschwader 30 'Adler'.
4E	Aufklärungsgruppe 13.
4F	KGrzbV 400.
4M	Ergänzungszerstörergruppe. Formed at Deblin-Irena on 18 April 1942 with Bf 110s, became the Ergänzungschlachtgruppe in February/March 1943 with Bf 109 and Bf 110, renamed I./SG 152 with Fw 190, Hs 129 and possibly Me 410.
4N	Aufklärungsgruppe 22.
4O	Aufklärungsstaffel XI. Fliegerkorps.
4Q	Verbindungsstaffel 7 Flieger Division.
4R	Nachtjagdgeschwader 2.
4T	Wekusta 51.
4U	Aufklärungsgruppe 123.
4V	KGrzbV 9, 106 and I./Kampfgeschwader 172. KGrzbV 9 used Staffel letters 'B', 'H', 'K', 'L' & 'M', KGrzbV 106 used letters 'C', 'N', 'P', 'R' and 'S' and I./KGzbV 172 used letters 'D', 'T', 'U', 'V' & 'W'. These units became, respectively, I./TG 3, III./TG 2 and IV./TG 3.
4X	Nachtschlachtgruppe 7 (see also '2 K').
5B	Nachtschlachtgruppe 10.
5D	Aufklärungsgruppe 31.
5F	Aufklärungsgruppe 14.
5G	Unit unidentified (e.g., 5G+DA He 111, Finland, June 1944).
5H	Nahaufklärungsgruppe 16.
5J	Kampfgeschwader 4 'General Wever'. When I./KG 4 became I./KG 100 in October 1943, code '5 J' retained by the new unit.
5K	Kampfgeschwader 3 'Blitz'.
5M	Wekusta 26.
5T	Kampfgeschwader 101. Prior to 1 February 1943 the unit was known as Kampfschulegeschwader 1.
5U	Unit unidentified (e.g., 5U+CL Ju 188, 1944).
5W	Seenotstaffel 10 and 50.
5Z	Wekusta 76.
6A	Nachtschlachtgruppe 12. The individual letter 'W' was used by the Verbindungstaffel of Luftflotte 1.
6F	Luftbeobachterstaffel 4.
6G	III./Stukageschwader 51 and II./Stukageshwader 1.
6 H	Fl.Erg.Gruppe (See).
6I	Küstenfliegergruppe 706 and Seeaufklärungsgruppe 130.
6J	Nachtschlachtgruppe 8.
6K	Aufklärungsgruppe 41.
6L	3./KG 30.
6M	Aufklärungsgruppe 11 and Nahaufklärunsgruppe 8. Probably used also by Küstenfliegerstaffel Krim.
6N	Kampfgruppe/Kampfgeschwader 100.
6Q	Schlachtgeschwader 151.
6R	Seeaufklärungsgruppe 127.
6 T	Probably confused with the code '6 I' for Küstenfliegergruppe 706.
6U	Zerstörergeschwader 1 (second unit).
6W	Seeaufklärungsgruppe 128. Staffel letters 'H' and 'K' were used by 1. and 2./SAG 128 and Staffel letter 'N' by 5./BFGr 196.
6X	NSGr Ostland.

6Z	Gruppe Herzog.
7A	Aufklärungsgruppe 121.
7C	Possibly SAGr 125, but more likely typographical error for '7 R'.
7J	Nachtjagdgeschwader 102.
7K	Jagdgeschwader 101.
7R	Seeaufklärungsgruppe 125.
7T	Kampfgruppe 606 and I./Kampfgeschwader 77.
7U	Kampfgruppe zbV 108 and Transportgruppe 20.
7V	Kampfgruppe zbV 700 and IV./Transportgeschwader 4. Used the Staffel letters 'A', 'B', 'C', 'D' and 'E' and later passed to IV./TG 4.
8A	Lufttransportstaffel (See) 1 and 2.
8C	Possibly used by the Störkampfstaffeln of Luftflotte 6 (e.g., 8C+BH Fw 58 1./Störkampfstaffel, Luftflotte 6).
8H	Aufklärungsgruppe 33.
8I	3.(H)/Aufklärungsgruppe 12?. Later NAGr 16 (e.g., 8I+DL Fw 189 A-2.
8L	Küstenfliegergruppe 906 and Seeaufklärungsruppe 131.
8Q	Transportgruppe 10.
8T	KGrzbV 800 and II./Transportgeschwader 2.
8 U	Possibly used by Stab/Transport Fliegerführer 2, with Staffel letter 'C'.
8V	Nachtjagdgeschwader 20.
9A	Unit unidentified, (e.g., 9A+SX Ju 52/3m, Finland).
9G	Fl.Aufklärungsstaffel Perleberg.
9H	Nahaufklärungsgruppe Kroatien.
9K	Kampfgeschwader 51 'Edelweiss'.
9L	Unit unidentified (e.g., 9L+HB Me 323 D-6).
9P	Kampfgruppe zbV 9, 40, 50 and 60. Staffel letters 'B', 'H', 'K', 'L' & 'M' were used by KGrzbV 9 up to January 1941 then passing to KGrzbV 40, Staffel letters 'C', 'N', 'P', 'R' and 'S' by KGrzbV 50 and 'D', 'T', 'U', 'V' and 'W' by KGrzbV 60. Between November 1942 and March 1943 the code was also used by KGrzbV Frankfurt and Wittstock.
9Q	Fliegerverbindungsgeschwader 2.
9V	Fernaufklärungsgruppe 5.
9W	Nachtjagdgeschwader 101.

Revised Glider Markings

The first use of military transport gliders occurred on 10 May 1940, when 42 DFS 230s landed 400 troops near the Belgian fort of Eben Emael and three bridges over the Albert Canal. The gliders that took part in that operation appear to have been unmarked but, sometime later, military gliders adopted a special code system. This comprised two letters to the left of the fuselage Balkenkreuz, the first of which was always 'L' for Lastensegler or troop-carrying glider. To the right of the Balkenkreuz was a single number followed by a hyphen and another, one, two or three-digit number. It is thought that the first numeral may have indicated that the glider was operated by Luftlandesgeschwader 1, while the other numbers were purely a numerical identification. The one variation to this form of marking was where the first number was replaced by the letter 'S', which indicated Schule (School).

Sometime in 1943, (possibly around the time of the revision to second line glider markings as noted below) the unique prefix marking was replaced by the normal Geschwader/Gruppe-style of code, e.g., gliders operated by the Schleppgruppen used the code 'F7' and those by Luftlandesgeschwader 1 used 'H4'. The existing suffix numerical sequence described above appears to have been retained. Again, training units adopted the letter 'S' plus the numerical sequence.

On 25 June 1943, gliders used by the NSFK and Luftwaffe A/B Schulen had their 'D' and 'WL' prefixed registrations replaced by Stammkennzeichen registrations as described in Chapter 17. The letters were painted in black, separated by a hyphen for NSKF machines and by a Balkenkreuz for Luftwaffe machines.

Fighter and Ground-Attack Unit Markings

by J. Richard Smith

Fighter Markings

As recorded in Chapter 8, all operational Luftwaffe units adopted a new five-character code system in September/October 1935. As far as is known, only two fighter units used these markings, JG 132 and JG 134, before a new system was introduced on 2 July 1936. This system, outlined in directive LA II/Fl. In. 3, was introduced to overcome the problems of rapid air-to-air identification associated with fighter operations. The clutter of the five-part codes gave no clear indication of which aircraft was which under such conditions and a simplified system became necessary. This was resolved by introducing for each Staffel a white number from 1 to 12, edged in black, painted in four positions: on each side of the fuselage, on top of the upper wing centre section and on the bottom of the fuselage between the wing roots. The size of the number was identical in all positions.

A series of symbols, used in conjunction with these Staffel numbers, identified the Staffel within the Gruppe, and the Gruppe within the Geschwader. In addition, a distinctive set of symbols was used to identify aircraft of the various Stab (Staff) flights. Official orders called for the introduction of these markings by September 1936.

These can be summarized as follows:

Gruppe	I.	II.	III.	Staffel Symbol	
Staffel	1.	4.	7.	none	
Staffel	2.	5.	8.	white band	Eng 300 mm Fus 200 mm
Staffel	3.	6.	9.	white disc	Eng 300 mm Fus 200 mm
Gruppe Symbol		▬ 1100 mm	〜 1098 mm		

By the spring of 1937, the following Luftwaffe fighter units were operational:

I./JG 131	Ar 68 F	Jesau
I./JG 132	He 51 B	Berlin-Döberitz
II./JG 132	He 51 B & Bf 109 B	Jüterbog-Damm
I./JG 134	Ar 68 E	Dortmund
II./JG 134	Ar 68 E	Werl
I./JG 135	He 51 B	Bad Aibling
I./JG 136	He 51 C	Kiel-Holtenau
I./JG 232	Ar 68	Bernburg
I./JG 234	Ar 68	Köln-Butzweilerhof
II./JG 234	Ar 68	Düsseldorf

To identify the individual Jagdgeschwader, their aircraft had different colours applied to their cowlings and fuselage upper decking. These were as follows:

JG 131	black
JG 132	red
JG 134	brown
JG 135	blue
JG 136	none
JG 232	green
JG 234	orange

As mentioned in Volume One, Chapter 7, 'traditional colours' historically tied to famous individuals or units of previous wars, were not bestowed on JG 132 and JG 134 at time of their official formation, the colours being introduced later in 1935. Photographic evidence however does show the combination of horizontal tricolour marking, in conjunction with the five-character military code and traditional colouring, on the He 51s of JG 132. Repeal of the tricolour marking occurred from 15 September 1935. Allowing for the usual two months grace period for changing to the blood banner marking on both sides of fin and rudder, autumn 1935 appears to be the period of completion of these marking changes. Addition of the cowling colouring may have occurred at the same time that the new codes were marked on the aircraft.

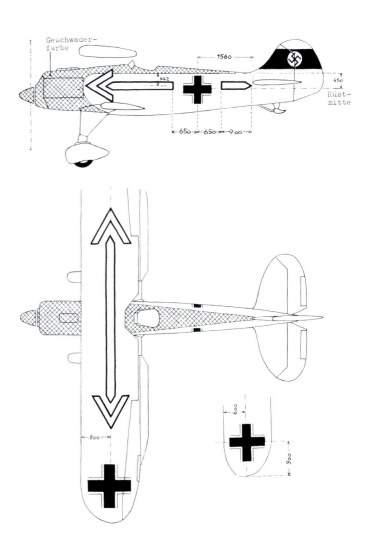

Markings for Geschwaderführer of the Stabskette. Note the dimensions set for the bottom line of the Geschwader colour relative to the aircraft horizontal centre line (Rüstemitte). Dimensions for positioning of the Balkenkreuze on the upper surface of the top wing and bottom surface of the lower wing were also given.

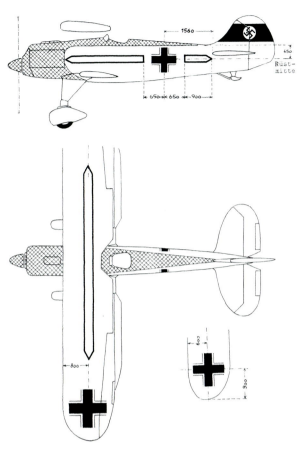

Markings for Geschwaderstab Kettenführer of second Kette.

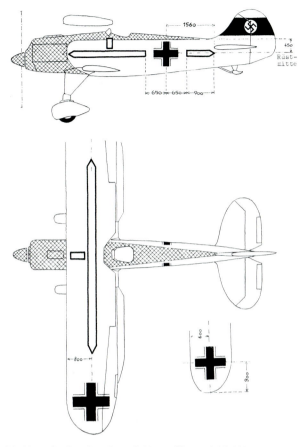

Markings for Geschwaderstab Kettenführer of third Kette.

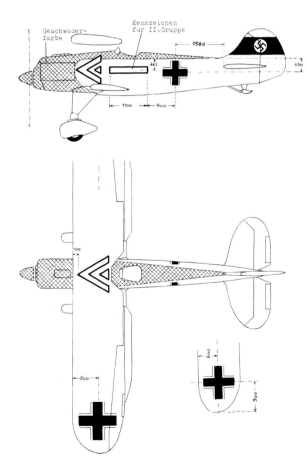

Markings for II./Gruppenstab Kettenführer of first Kette.

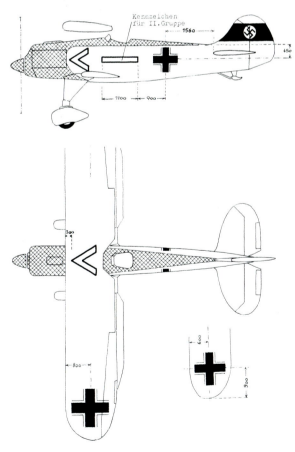

Markings for II./Gruppenstab Kettenführer of second Kette.

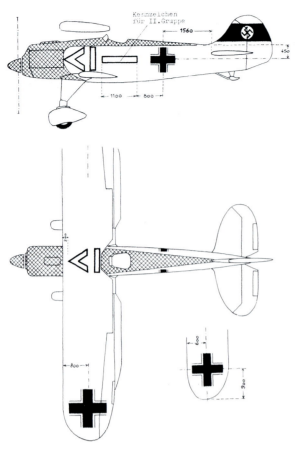

Markings for II./Gruppenstab Kettenführer of third Kette.

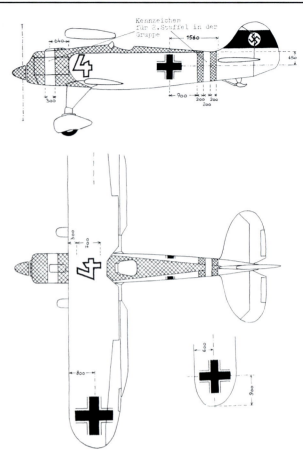

Markings for a 2. Staffel, I. Gruppe aircraft.

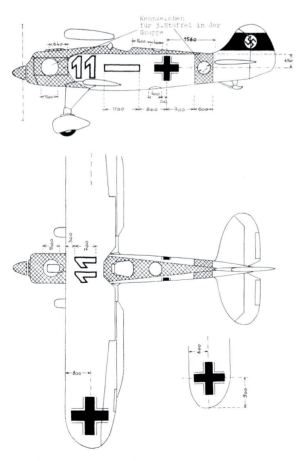

Markings for a 6. Staffel, II. Gruppe aircraft.

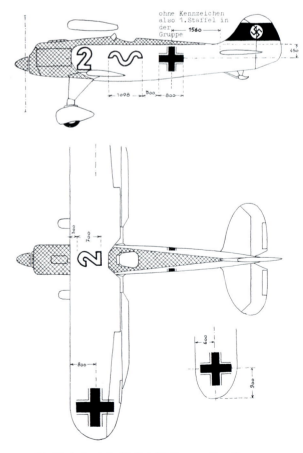

Markings for a 7. Staffel, III. Gruppe aircraft.

ABOVE: A line-up of He 51s of JG 132 wearing a combination of tricolour marking across the fin and rudder plus five-character military code and 'traditional' red cowling colouring, points to a date of around September-October 1935. Marking of the cowl colouring appears to have been done at about the same time that the new codes replaced the civil registration markings. The combination of fine weather and the presence of the tricolour marking reinforce the date as theearlier part of the two months grace period of between 15 September and 15 November 1935.

Of the listed units listed above, only JG 132 and JG 134 had been formed prior to the date of introduction of the revised markings for fighter aircraft. JG 232 did not form until the same month as the revised markings were introduced, with two of the remaining three units forming the following year. Thus the allocation in the listing above was a gradually developed process. Colours used were from the standard L.Dv. 521/1 colour chart – 22 black, 23 red, 26 brown, 24 blue, 25 green and 04 orange. The latter colour was better described as chrome yellow as no true orange colour existed on the chart amongst the paint types specified for external application to an airframe. The decision not to allocate a colour to JG 136, which formed in March 1938, may provide an end date to this practice. Certainly by then the appearance of the Bf 109, and the introduction of fighter camouflage in 1937, must have signalled the decline of this system.

Later in 1937, a seventh Luftkreiskommando was added to the Luftwaffe by dividing into two the area previously covered by

ABOVE: Once unit colours had been introduced and applied, the new air-to-air rapid recognition markings became even more visually effective. This Ar 68 F wears the markings assigned for 3. Staffel aircraft; but the identity of the Jagdgeschwader was not revealed.

ABOVE: Not all fighter units had traditional colours bestowed on them; I./JG 334 was established on 1 April 1937, by which time the new all-metal fighter design, the Bf 109 B, was entering service and such peripheral accoutrements were already becoming redundant. This Ar 68 E of I./JG 334, 'White 6', wears the reduced markings applicable to 1. Staffel, signified by just a number, forward of the Balkenkreuz marking. (G. Long via R. Lutz)

Luftkreiskommando IV. The new command had its headquarters in Hamburg. The reorganization led to I./JG 232 becoming I./JG 137, with a second Gruppe being established in July 1938. At the same time I. and II./JG 334 were formed at Frankfurt-Rebstock and Mannheim-Sandhofen respectively, I./JG 138 at Vienna, and I./JG 131 was redesignated I./JG 130.

Earlier in the year the first of the new Messerschmitt Bf 109 B-1 monoplane fighters had been delivered to II./JG 132. There is little doubt that when this fighter entered service it was the finest in the world. It possessed a maximum speed of 465 km/h, was highly manoeuvrable and introduced an enclosed cockpit and retractable undercarriage. The arrival of the new fighter prompted the Luftwaffe Generalstab to issue a directive, which stipulated a new system of markings to fighters, on 14 December 1937.

Markings of aircraft of the leichten Jagdverbände [i]

7. Marking of the aircraft of the leichten Jagdverbände

All previous instructions regarding marking of aircraft of the leichten Jagdverbände are cancelled. The following markings are introduced with immediate effect.

I. Application of markings
National markings (Balkenkreuz and Hakenkreuz) as before.

The markings will be applied only [ii] on both sides of the fuselage. In order to present a uniform image, the location and dimensions as shown on attached diagram are to be strictly observed.

II. Organization and schematic of unit markings
a) Staffel aircraft (including reserve aircraft) are to carry Arabic numerals from 1 to 12, i.e.
The 1., 4. and 7. Staffel in white colour without border.
The 2., 5. And 8. Staffel in red colour with white border.
The 3., 5. And 9. Staffel in clay yellow with black border.

---

i   Leichten Jagdverbände = in this context 'Single-seat fighter units'.

ii   This was to distinguish from Kampfgeschwader aircraft whose code group was often marked also on wing lower surfaces.

b) Marking of the Gruppen and the Gruppenstabe.

The I. Gruppe of the Geschwader carry no Gruppe marking.

The II. Gruppe a horizontal bar behind the Balkenkreuz in the respective Staffel colour and border. The III. Gruppe a vertical bar behind the Balkenkreuz also in the Staffel colour and border.

The Gruppen aircraft carry a chevron with a triangular section in black with white border in place of the numeral. The Gruppen marking (I. no marking, II. horizontal bar behind Balkenkreuz, III. vertical bar behind Balkenkreuz) likewise black with white edge.

Both Ketten members of the Gruppenstabe are to be marked similarly to the Gruppenführer's aircraft, however carrying only the chevron without the triangular panel.

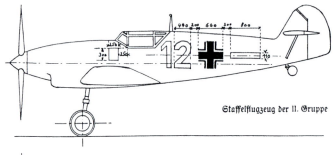

Staffelflugzeug der II. Gruppe

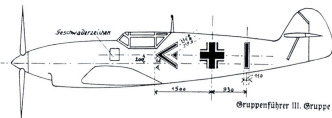

Gruppenführer III. Gruppe

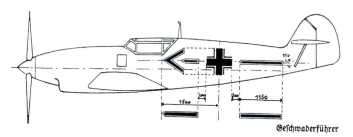

Geschwaderführer

Kennzeichnung BF 109

Maße für Zahlen:

Höhe = 650 mm   Breite = 440 mm   Stärke = 110 mm

Bei Zahlen und Zeichen mit Umrandung tritt ein Rand von 20 mm hinzu. Jedoch darf sich dadurch das Außenmaß nicht ändern. — Bei zweistelligen Zahlen ist der Abstand von Zahl zu Zahl 80 mm. Die Breite der 1 ist 260 mm.

c) Markings of the Geschwader and the three aircraft of the Geschwader.

For the marking of the Geschwader identity a maximum space of 250 x 300 mm (see sketch) is reserved. In this panel the individual Geschwader emblem is to be applied. The Geschwaderkommodore and independent Gruppenkommandeure are to submit proposals for such

ABOVE: The changing state of fighter markings during the mid-1930s sometimes appeared bewildering. Seen here is an Ar 68 E-1 of III./JG 134, photographed in March 1936, wearing a simple numerical identity of a red '8' marked aft of the Balkenkreuz marking on each side of the aircraft. However this simple style was, in fact, only a temporary measure prevalent during the time when Germany was about to reoccupy the Rhineland area in defiance of the terms of the Treaty of Versailles. This involved as much bluff as anything else with subterfuges to inflate the apparent strength of the German forces of the time. Note that JG 134 aircraft were still not marked with their 'traditional' colour of brown at that time.

signs before 1. 2. 38. Emblems are only to be applied after authorization from the R. d. L. and Ob. d. L. The dimensions of 250 x 30 mm are to be strictly adhered to.

The Geschwader leader's aircraft is to have an arrow in front of the Balkenkreuz with the remainder behind. Colour black with white edge.

Both Ketten members carry only the pointed marking before the Balkenkreuz, without the arrowhead marking. Colour black with white edge.

The instruction for group markings applies only to Bf 109 fighter aircraft. The marking of He 51 and Ar 68 aircraft is not necessary as these types will be retired on delivery of the Bf 109. A separate instruction for marking of heavy fighters will be published at a later date.

Genst. d. L., 14.12. 37,
Fl. In. 3 Nr. 730/37 II.

This marking system was later utilized by all single-engine day fighters, and remained virtually unchanged, until the end of the war. Only two changes to the system were introduced during the war. In the first, the Gruppe symbols were changed as is detailed in the accompanying tabular summary. In the second, the red numbers used by the second Staffel within a Gruppe were replaced by black late in 1939, and by the time the Battle of Britain was at its height in the summer of 1940, it was rare for the older colour to be seen. Exceptions were the aircraft of the Jagdgeschwader numbered JG 300 and upwards which, possibly because they operated solely in the defence of the German homeland, re-introduced red numbers in 1943. Retention of black for second Staffel markings is confirmed by an order issued by the Ob.d.L on 21 October 1943, which referred back to a previous instruction issued in 1938.

LEFT: This Bf 109 E, W.Nr. 878 of Stab/JG 53, wears the single chevron Gruppen Adjutant marking forward of the Balkenkreuz, with the horizontal bar marking of II. Gruppe aft. It has been suggested in some writings that addition of a number with the marking (something not included in the RLM instruction) was related to the Adjutant's status within the Gruppe. In this instance it seems to apply to the inset small red (the Gruppe colour) number '2', outlined in white seen here, as this was the mount of the Stab's number two officer.

ABOVE: The contention about the relevance of the addition of a numeral to Stab markings mentioned in the previous caption is challenged by this photograph of an Fw 190 wearing a Gruppen Adjutant's single chevron plus the number '4'. While, with two exceptions, Jagdgeschwadern were not expanded to include a IV. Gruppe until August 1944, there is no sign of a IV. Gruppe marking across the yellow and red RVT bands.
(J. Crow)

RIGHT: This photograph of the Bf 109 E of the Gruppen Adjutant of I./JG 52 (the I. Gruppe Wappen was marked aft of the Balkenkreuz on this aircraft) illustrates the point further with the presence of a normal size numeral aft of the marking.
(S. Wunder via F. Grabowski)

Aircraft Markings

The instruction about markings of aircraft in B.L.B. 1938 S.4 Nr. 7 Abschnitt II is to be carried out as follows:

II. Application of markings

Markings of Staffel Aircraft

a) Staffel aircraft (including reserve aircraft) are to carry Arabic numerals from 1 to 16, i.e.
   The 1. Staffel in the Gruppe white colour.
   The 2. Staffel in the Gruppe black colour.
   The 3. Staffel in the Gruppe clay yellow.
   The 4. Staffel in the Gruppe blue with white border.

b) Marking of the Gruppen and the Gruppenstabe.
   The I. Gruppe; no Gruppe marking.
   The II. Gruppe; a horizontal bar behind the Balkenkreuz in the respective Staffel colour.
   The III. Gruppe; a vertical bar behind the Balkenkreuz in the Staffel colour.
   The IV. Gruppe; a wavy line in the Staffel colour and border.

The aircraft of the Gruppenkommandeur carries a chevron with a triangular section in black with white border in place of the numeral. The Gruppen marking (I. no marking, II. horizontal bar behind Balkenkreuz, III. vertical bar behind Balkenkreuz, IV. wavy line) likewise black with white edge. The remaining aircraft of the Gruppenstabe are to be marked similarly to the Gruppenkommandeur, however carrying only the chevron without the triangular panel.

c) Markings of the Geschwaderkommodore.

The remainder as set down in L.V.Bl. 1943 S. 425 Nr. 788
Der R.d.L. u. Ob. d. L. 21. 10. 1943
Az. 65.a.10. 12. Nr. 16143/43 geh. (Genst. Gen. Qu. 2.Abt.II A)

L.V.
Bl. S. 1103

LEFT: The mount of the Geschwader IA of JG 2, photographed during the winter of 1939/40. The addition of a '1' however was not part of the RLM standard for this Stab marking. The camouflage was the revised style introduced in November/December 1939, with raised demarcation line and 71/02 upper surfaces. The aircraft also was marked with oversize wing Balkenkreuze, a common fault at that time.

RIGHT: The triple chevron marking was an oddity that developed from the manner in which the Gruppen-kommodore marking was applied. The 'triple' chevron marking was a stylised form using the pale edging seen on some markings as an outline over the natural background colouring of the aircraft – a stencilled application in effect. (F. Smith)

BELOW: A Bf 109 E-3 of III./JG 51, bearing the Stab markings of a Gruppe Technical Officer and the III. Gruppe badge, being refuelled at a temporary airstrip sometime in May 1940. In this instance the III. Gruppe marking was the vertical bar type. Camouflage was 71/02/65.

ABOVE: The size of markings could vary quite considerably as this photograph of a late model Fw 190, W.Nr. 440401, of an unidentified II. Gruppe illustrates. It wears tactical markings conforming to the last RLM instruction with a yellow band around the engine cowling and yellow rudder. The solid colouring of the engine cowling matches the tonal value of the 70-colouring of the propeller blades, indicating that it was probably 82, the additional dark streaks around the 76-coloured lower section of the cowling ring possibly being in 81 or 83. The upper surface colouring of the wing tip matches that of the cowling and the rear section of the cockpit hood, in what was otherwise a very minimalist form of camouflage. The under surface of the wing has a slight reflection to it, indicating that it was bare metal without the benefit of the usual extra colouring along the leading section and wing tip; the undercarriage fairing however was painted 76, a sub-contract supplied item. (J. Crow)

LEFT: The normal size and placement of individual aircraft identification numbers is shown in this photograph of a Bf 109 E of I./JG 26. The aircraft also carries the JG 26 Wappen forward of the cockpit, plus the 2. Staffel 'devil's head' badge beneath the cockpit. Camouflage is 71/02/65.

ABOVE: Not all fighter units with numerals marked in the correct location used the most common size of marking for individual aircraft numbers, as can be seen on this Fw 190 A-8 marked with a very small number '9'. While uncommon early in the war, other units are also known to have used this size of marking on Bf 109 Es. By late 1944, small size numerals became more common as part of the drive to improve camouflage effectiveness.

During and after the Battle of Britain, at least two units, III./JG 27 and III./JG 54 carried their identification numbers on the noses of their Bf 109s, the former above the engine exhaust, the latter aft of the supercharger intake. The reason for this is unclear, but may have had something to do with the formation of the former from I./JG 1 and the latter from I./JG 21.

When a fourth Staffel was added to JG 2 and JG 26 in October 1943, in accordance with the new directive, they were identified by use of a blue number. Until August 1944, these were the only two Jagdgeschwadern to have four Staffeln, but after that date most were reorganized in a similar manner. Despite the new directive, the colour used by the fourth Staffel in those Gruppen varied between blue, red and green and the reader is advised to consult the examples given below for details. In addition, some other units used different colours for Staffel identification, such as brown, grey and green, which were recorded by at least one unit and, again, the reader is referred to the examples that follow.

ABOVE: These Bf 109s serving on the Eastern Front provide an interesting insight into the use of small numerals for fighters. 'White 6' in the foreground has a numeral of identical height to that seen on the Fw 190 in the previous photograph (ABOVE LEFT). The third aircraft, 'Yellow 5' also has the same size marking, yet the aircraft in between has a yellow '1' marked in the more usual standard size. (It does however also show signs of having had some previous markings painted out). Careful measurement of the similar numerals shows that in both of the former instances the numeral was 5/10s the size of the Balkenkreuz. JG 52 and JG 3 also have been noted using this size marking; the consistency of size and random spread of samples pointing to the existence of an official standard. (H. Obert)

In addition, some aircraft from the Jabo (fighter-bomber) Staffeln of JG 2 and JG 26 had a white bomb symbol painted aft of the fuselage Balkenkreuz.

Aircraft from the Geschwader and Gruppe staff flights also carried a series of special symbols, as noted earlier, designed to identify the position of a particular pilot. Although these symbols were supposed to show the role of the pilot within the Stab-Kommand structure, experience has shown that this was rarely the case. The only reasonably consistent symbol that reflected the Stab position of the pilot was the double chevron used by the Gruppenkommandeur. Examples of these symbols are shown on page 252.

Gruppe Identification

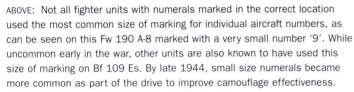

Marking		Gruppe and notes
(No marking)		I.Gruppe
—		II.Gruppe
∿		III.Gruppe
▌		III.Gruppe (used as an alternative to that above from 1939 to around 1941)
● O		IV.Gruppe Plain or white circle, or thick outline circle.
✚		IV.Gruppe (from 1940 until October 21, 1943)
∼		IV.Gruppe (from October 21, 1943)

ABOVE: I. Gruppe aircraft carried no identifying marking aft of the Balkenkreuz, while II. Gruppe carried a horizontal bar, usually marked in the appropriate Staffel colour of white, yellow or red, or simply black outlined in one of those three colours. This late model Fw 190, W.Nr. 681330 of an unidentified unit, shows clear evidence of it having been transferred from III. Gruppe (where it had been marked with a '7' and a vertical bar) to 6. Staffel; its II. Gruppe status is shown by the horizontal bar marking. The aircraft was marked with the last standard of tactical markings, comprising a yellow band around the nose section and yellow rudder. (J.Crow)

LEFT: Identification of III. Gruppe aircraft took two forms, both of which appeared at the same time – either as a vertical bar or as a horizontal 'sine wave' form. The Bf 109 F-4 trop in the background has the latter form of marking, in this instance its white colouring, plus the 'White 4' marking identify it as a 4. Staffel, III. Gruppe aircraft (possibly of JG 77). Note particularly the style of the '4' marking and compare it with the style of the 'White 3' marking on the Gruppen-Adjutant's Bf 109 G-2 trop, W.Nr. 10681. Both aircraft were camouflaged in standard 78/79 tropical finish, with a full array of North Africa tactical markings in white. (J. Crow)

RIGHT: Oversize markings appear to have been a feature of III./JG 52 as this photograph of 'Yellow 1' illustrates. The heavy mottling indicates that this practice was still in force well into the air fighting over Britain. The III. Gruppe emblem of a black running wolf on a yellow oval background was marked on the engine cowling.

LEFT: The original form of IV. Gruppe marking was either a small plain cross, or a circle. This Fw 190 A-4, W.Nr. 555, of JG 1 wears a combination of markings that identify it as the mount of the IV. Gruppe Adjutant. Camouflage is 74/75/76. (E. Mombeek)

251

ABOVE: Bf 109 Es of 2./JG 77 seen during the opening of the war against Poland. 'Red 13', and other aircraft from this Staffel were marked with a red disc, thinly outlined in white. This anomaly resulted from the renumbering of units and transfers that had taken place prior to the war when 1./JG 331 had formed from 10./JG 132 in November 1938; the latter used the IV. Gruppe white spot marking. I./JG 331 was redesignated I./JG 77 in May 1939 and the white spot was retained in the very modified form shown here. As there was no symbol for I. Gruppe, the 'artistic' representation seen here was probably retained only as a memento of the unit's origins.

Geschwader Markings

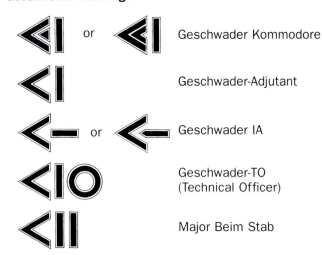

The symbol was normally positioned forward of the fuselage Balkenkreuz but III./JG 27, in particular, painted it on the nose section of its fighters, just behind the spinner. As has been indicated earlier, the same unit also applied its identification numerals in this position.

On 1 November 1938, seven of the 18 fighter groups had been reorganized as heavy fighter units with the eventual intention of re-equipping them with the new and much-vaunted Bf 110 twin-engine

ABOVE: In 1944, when all Jagdeschwadern were expanded to include a IV. Gruppe, the system of Gruppe identification markings were again revised. A new form, very similar at first glance to the old 'sine wave' form of III. Gruppe marking, was introduced, as shown on this 11. Staffel Fw 190, 'Red 31'. (J. Crow)

destroyer. These groups were known initially as Schweregruppen (heavy groups), but on 1 January 1939, the term Zerstörergruppe (destroyer group) was introduced. The seven destroyer groups were:

Luftwaffengruppenkommando 1 (Berlin)

I./JG 141	Bf 109 D	Jüterbog-Damm	(ex II./JG 132)
II./JG 141	Bf 109 C	Fürstenwalde	(ex III./JG 132)

Luftwaffengruppenkommando 2 (Braunschweig)

I./JG 142	Bf 109 B, C & D	Dortmund	(ex I./JG 134)
II./JG 142	Bf 109 D	Werl	(ex II./JG 134)
III./JG 142	Bf 109 B, C & D	Lippstadt	(ex IV./JG 134)

Luftwaffengruppenkommando 3 (München)

I./JG 143	Bf 109 B	Illesheim	(ex III./JG 334)

Luftwaffenkommando Ostmark (Wien)

I./JG 144	Bf 109 B	Gablingen	(ex III./JG 234)

Until their re-equipment with the Bf 110, the Zerstörergeschwader retained the system of coloured numbers and symbols described above, but when the Messerschmitt twin-engine fighter was delivered, the new four-character code was introduced as described in Chapter 9.

As recorded in Chapter 9, creation of the four Luftflotten produced a final major redesignation of all Luftwaffe units on 1 May 1939; operational Geschwader under Luftflotte 1 were numbered from 1 onwards; Luftflotte 2 from 26 onwards; Luftflotte 3 from 51 onwards; and Luftflotte 4 from 76 onwards. The major operational Luftwaffe fighter units at this time were:

Luftflotte 1 (Berlin)

I./JG 1	Bf 109	Jesau	(ex I./JG 130)
I./JG 2	Bf 109	Berlin-Döberitz	(ex I./JG 131)
I./JG 3	Bf 109	Zerbst	(ex II./JG 231)
I./ZG 1	Bf 110	Jüterbog-Damm	(ex I./JG 141)
II./ZG 1	Bf 109	Fürstenwalde	(ex II./JG 141)
I./ZG 2	Bf 109	Bernburg	(ex I./JG 231)

Luftflotte 2 (Braunschweig)

I./JG 26	Bf 109	Köln	(ex I./JG 132)
II./JG 26	Bf 109	Düsseldorf	(ex II./JG 132)
I./ZG 26	Bf 109	Dortmund	(ex I./JG 142)
II./ZG 26	Bf 109	Werl	(ex II./JG 142)
III./ZG 26	Bf 109	Lippstadt	(ex III./JG 142)

Luftflotte 3 (München)

I./JG 51	Bf 109	Aibling	(ex I./JG 233)
I./JG 52	Bf 109	Böblingen	(ex I./JG 433)
I./JG 53	Bf 109	Wiesbaden	(ex I./JG 133)
II./JG 53	Bf 109	Mannheim	(ex II./JG 133)
I./ZG 52	Bf 109	Illesheim	(ex I./JG 143)

Luftflotte 4 (Wien)

I./JG 76	Bf 109	Wien-Aspern	(ex I./JG 134)
I./JG 77	Bf 109	Breslau	(ex I./JG 331)
II./JG 77	Bf 109	Pilsen	(ex II./JG 333)
I./ZG 76	Bf 110	Olmütz	(ex I./JG 144)

Luftwaffe Lehrdivision

I.(Z)/LG 1	Bf 110	Barth
I.(J)/LG 2	Bf 109	Garz

Apart from these operational fighter units, a number of advanced Jagdfliegerschulen (fighter training schools) were formed, these later becoming, by way of 17 Ausbildungsgruppen (training groups), Jagdgeschwader 101 to 108 and JG 110. The aircraft from these units carried coloured numbers, but these often comprised three rather than two numerals. The training and replacement units (Ergänzungsgruppen) carried similar markings.

Marking Examples

Jagdgeschwader 1 'Oesau'

When a fourth Staffel was added to each of JG 1's three Gruppen in August 1944, this unit adopted the following identification colours:

4./JG 1	red numbers
8./JG 1	blue numbers
12./JG 1	blue numbers

The III.Gruppe of JG 1 is also recorded as carrying grey-coloured numbers.

Code	Aircraft	W.Nr.	Notes
black 5	Bf 109 E-4	4892	2./JG 1, 21 January 1942
white 9	Bf 109 F-4	7423	10./JG 1, 4 July 1942
yellow 6	Fw 190 A-4	0575	12./JG 1, Villiers, Ofw. Schippers, 1 September 1942
black <1	Bf 109 G-6	15394	Stab III./JG 1, 25 June 1943
white 11	Fw 190 A-4	0621	4./JG 1, Uffz. Schieweck, 3 November 1943
black 12	Fw 190 A-8	170643	6./JG 1, Argentan, Ofw. Brodbeck, 20 June 1944
grey 23	Bf 109 G-14	784969	Stab/JG 1, Anklam, Uffz. Weichert, 25 November 1943
blue 5	Bf 109 G-10	490663	12./JG 1, Hettersheim, Lt. Hathay, 25 December 1944
red 4	Fw 190 A-9	205226	4./JG 1, Twente, Lt. Kindhäuser, 14 January 14 1945
white 5	He 162 A-2	310018	1./JG 1, Leck, Hptm. Künnecke, 4 May 1945

Jagdgeschwader 2 'Richthofen'

The 10.(Jabo)Staffel of JG 2 carried blue numbers. When a fourth Staffel was added to each of JG 2's three Gruppen in October 1943, this unit adopted the following identification colours:

4./JG 2	blue numbers
8./JG 2	blue numbers
12./JG 2	blue numbers

Code	Aircraft	W.Nr.	Notes
white 1	Bf 109 E-4	2765	4./JG 2, Walderslade, Ofw. Harbauer, 30 August 1940
white 12	Fw 190 A-2	0226	4./JG 2, Dieppe, Gef. Eimers, 19 August 1942
white 2	Bf 109 G-4	16151	7./JG 2, 15 May 1943
blue 16	Bf 109 G-6	19483	12./JG 2, 29 June 1943
yellow 4	Fw 190 A-5	410019	3./JG 2, combat on 15 July 1943
<-+-	Fw 190 A-8	170960	11./JG 2, Avranches, Fhr. Sommer, 3 August 1944
yellow 8	Fw 190 D-9	210132	11./JG 2, St. Trond, Uffz. Schwerwadt, 1 January 1945
black 2	Fw 190 D-9	400222	10./JG 2, St. Trond, Fw. Peschek, 1 January 1945

Jagdgeschwader 3 'Udet'

When a fourth Staffel was added to each of JG 3's four Gruppen in August 1944, this unit adopted the following identification colours:

4./JG 3	green numbers
8./JG 3	red or blue numbers
12./JG 3	blue numbers
16./JG 3	red numbers

Code	Aircraft	W.Nr.	Notes
white 6	Bf 109 E-4	1985	1./JG 3, Kent, Lt. Schnabel, 5 September, 1940
yellow 12	Bf 109 F-4/tp	10110	3./JG 3, 8 May 1942
black 1	Bf 109 F-4	10231	8./JG 3, 15 August 1942
white <12	Bf 109 G-4	19642	1./JG 3, 22 June 1943
red 58	Bf 109 G-6	164999	8./JG 3, Conches, 29 January 1944
red 20	Fw 190 A-8	680848	16./JG 3, Uffz. Wald, 11 August 1944
<<+	Fw 190 A-8	681382	Stab IV./JG 3, Hptm. Möritz, September 1944
green 9	Bf 109 G-14	780706	4./JG 3, Sangerhausen, 2 November 1944
black 4	Fw 190 A-8	682236	14./JG 3, Uffz. Buchholz, 2 December 1944
blue 6	Bf 109 G-10	130315	8./JG 3, Gülow, Uffz. Klotz, 5 March 1945

Jagdgeschwader 4

When a fourth Staffel was added to each of JG 4's four Gruppen in August 1944, this unit adopted the following identification colours:

4./JG 4	blue numbers
8./JG 4	blue numbers
12./JG 4	blue numbers
16./JG 4	blue numbers

Code	Aircraft	W.Nr.	Notes
white 5	Bf 109 G-6	162680	1./JG 4, Lavariano, Uffz. Kier, 9 June 1944
blue 14	Fw 190 A-8	681286	8./JG 4, Alteno, Ofgef. Herget, 6 September 1944
green 5	Bf 109 G-14	460377	3./JG 4, Mörfelden, Oblt. Stark, 21 September 1944
yellow 1	Bf 109 G-14	462922	11./JG 4, Arnhem, Fhr. Reinfelt, 24 September 1944
blue 2	Bf 109 K-4	330323	12./JG 4, Querfurt, Fhr. Schneck, 21 November 1944

Code	Aircraft	W.Nr.	Notes
blue 18	Bf 109 G-10	490707	16./JG 4, Hähnlein, Uffz. Walter, 2 December, 1944
white 18	Fw 190 A-8	682676	5./JG 4, Ofw. Schaar, 1 January 1945
yellow 13	Fw 190 A-9	205056	7./JG 4, Uffz. Niggl, 4 February 1945
black 11	Fw 190 A-9	980570	6./JG 4, Sagan-Sprottau, 12 February 1945
black 1	Bf 109 G-14	465323	10./JG 4, Sellow, Uffz. Kilias, 17 February 1945

Jagdgeschwader 5 'Eismeer'

13.(Z)Staffel of JG 5 carried the four character code '1B' (see Chapter 9). When a fourth Staffel was added to each of JG 5's four Gruppen in August 1944, this unit adopted the following identification colours:

4./JG 5	unknown
8./JG 5	blue numbers
12./JG 5	blue numbers
16./JG 5	unknown

Code	Aircraft	W.Nr.	Notes
yellow 2	Bf 109 F-4	7207	9./JG 5, 2 April, 1942
black 2	Fw 190 A-3	2228	2./JG 5, Uffz. Friedemann, Sola, 28 January 1943
yellow 12	Fw 190 A-2	0459	12./JG 5, Uffz. Jarbee, 11 March 1943
black 4	Fw 190 A-3	0323	14.(Jabo)/JG 5, Murmansk, 5 April 1943
black 15	Bf 109 F-4		11./JG 5, Lt. Meyer, May 1943, black disc aft of cross
white 7	Bf 109 G-6	165839	1./JG 5, Lt. Mors, 6 August 1944
yellow 9	Bf 109 G-6/U2	412284	3./JG 5, Oblt.. Müller, Caen, 17 July 1944
<<+	Bf 109 G-6	413620	Stab II./JG 5, Obstlt. Kettner, 25 August 1944
blue 23	Bf 109 G-14/AS	460310	8./JG 5, Uffz. Steiner, Sudetenland, 16 October 1944
white 4	Fw 190 A-8	732167	9./JG 5, Fw. Amm, Bardufoss, 19 November 1944
blue 1	Fw 190 F-8	350177	12./JG 5, Uffz. Schäfer, Herdla, 9 February 1945

Jagdgeschwader 6 'Horst Wessel'

When the three Gruppen of JG 6 were established in August 1944, the fourth Staffel adopted the following identification colours:

4./JG 6	blue numbers
8./JG 6	blue numbers
12./JG 6	green numbers

Code	Aircraft	W.Nr.	Notes
blue 2	Fw 190 A-8	171697	8./JG 6, Königsberg, Lt. Löhr, 16 August 1944
yellow 1	Bf 109 G-14	785180	11./JG 6, Rangsdorf, Uffz. Hartig, 21 November 1944
green 15	Bf 109 G-14	784943	12./JG 6, Wesendorf, 26 November 1944
black 12	Bf 109 G-10	490719	10./JG 6, Uffz. Betz, 1 January 1945
<-+-	Fw 190 A-9	980543	Stab/JG 6, Obstlt. Kogler, 1 January 1945
black 13	Fw 190 D-9	211068	6./JG 6, Fw. Steu, 4 February 1945

Jagdgeschwader 7 'Nowotny'

It was intended that JG 7 should eventually comprise three Gruppen of four Staffeln each, but only the first three Staffeln of I./JG 7 and III./JG 7 were fully operational before the end of the war. These had the

following identification colours:

1./JG 7	white numbers
2./JG 7	red numbers
3./JG 7	yellow numbers
9./JG 7	white numbers
10./JG 7	red numbers
11./JG 7	yellow numbers

Code	Aircraft	W.Nr.	Notes
red 13	Me 262 A-1	130180	10./JG 7, Neuruppin, 14 January 1945
white 8	Me 262 A-1	110564	9./JG 7, Ofw. Schnurr, Mecklenburg, 23 January 1945
white 1	Me 262 A-1	130171	1./JG 7, Uffz. Werner, Kaltenkirchen, 15 February 1945
green 4	Me 262 A-1	111002	Stab/JG 7, Maj. Weissenberger, 17 February 1945
yellow 2	Me 262 A-1	500224	3./JG 7, Ofw. Schrey, Kaltenkirchen, 18 March 1945

Jagdgeschwader 11

When the three Gruppen of JG 11 were established in August 1944, the fourth Staffel adopted the following identification colours:

4./JG 11	green numbers
8./JG 11	blue numbers
12./JG 11	blue numbers

In addition, Jagdstaffel Helgoland, which was attached to JG 11, carried green numbers.

Code	Aircraft	W.Nr.	Notes
white 3	Bf 109 G-1/R	14093	4./JG 11, 17 May 1943
yellow 8	Bf 109 G-6/U4	20072	6./JG 11, 11 August 1943
green 4	Bf 109 T-1	7766	Jasta Helgoland, Jun 12, 1943
yellow 17	Fw 190 A-5/U8	1435	3./JG 11, Märk, Gef. Zimmler, 29 July 1943
white 3	Fw 190 A-4	5695	10./JG 11, Skagerrak, 18 November 1943
black 5	Bf 109 G-6	163797	5./JG 11, Uffz. Manke, 7 June 1944
green 21	Fw 190 A-7	642534	Stab/JG 11, Neuenkirchen, 31 May 1944
blue 13	Fw 190 A-8	732057	12./JG 11, Pazizme, Ofhr. Geise, 19 August 1944
green 2	Fw 190 A-8	173818	4./JG 11, Dedelstorf, 20 November 1944
blue 6	Bf 109 G-14	784176	8./JG 11, Worms, Fw. Trostmann, 30 December 1944

Jagdgeschwader 26 'Schlageter'

When a fourth Staffel was added to each of JG 26's three Gruppen in October 1943, this unit adopted the following identification colours:

4./JG 26	blue numbers
8./JG 26	blue numbers
12./JG 26	blue numbers

In addition, the 6. (later 7.) Staffel carried brown (RLM 26) numbers and some aircraft from the 3.Staffel had gold (RLM 04) numbers.

Code	Aircraft	W.Nr.	Notes
blue N+8	Bf 109 C-2		10.(N)/JG 26, 1939
yellow 3	Bf 109 E-4	3721	9./JG 26, England, Oblt. Ebeling, 31 August 1940

Code	Aircraft	W.Nr.	Notes
white 16	Fw 190 A-1	009	4./JG 26, Moorseele airfield, 9 September 1941
black 1	Bf 109 F-4	7211	8./JG 26, 6 November 1941
brown 3	Fw 190 A-4	656	6./JG 26, Uffz. Granabetter, 2 November 1942
gold 2	Fw 190 A-4	2386	3./JG 26, Antwerp, Lt. Kiefner, 17 August 1943
blue 16	Bf 109 G-6	16494	12./JG 26, Schweinefurt, 17 August 1943
black 2	Fw 190 A-6	470224	6./JG 26, Lünebach, Uffz. Hell, 20 February 1944
yellow 1	Bf 109 G-14	462676	11./JG 26, Mörfelden, Uffz. Tepperis, 12 October 1944
white 7	Fw 190 A-8	738134	1./JG 26, Herzhausen, Ofw. Freiberger, 10 December 44
brown 6	Fw 190 D-9	210086	7./JG 26, Fhr. Ahrens, 1 January 1945

Jagdgeschwader 27 'Afrika'

When a fourth Staffel was added to each of JG 27's four Gruppen in August 1944, this unit adopted the following identification colours:

4./JG 27 blue numbers
8./JG 27 blue numbers
12./JG 27 blue numbers
16./JG 27 blue numbers

Code	Aircraft	W.Nr.	Notes
white 9	Bf 109 E-1	4851	7./JG 27, Windsor, Oblt. Fischer, 30 September 1940
black 10	Bf 109 E-4	1603	8./JG 27, Kent, Oblt. Pointer, 27 October 1940
yellow 14	Bf 109 F-4./tp	9673	3./JG 27, Ofw. Marseille, 15 Sepember 1942
red 6	Bf 109 G-6	19870	11./JG 27, 13 August 1943
white 5	Bf 109 G-6	18470	10./JG 27, 18 September 1943
black 4	Bf 109 G-6	440654	5./JG 27, Uffz. Schröter, 5 August 1944
blue 2	Bf 109 G-14	780674	12./JG 27, Bonn, Ofhr. Reuter, Sep 21, 1944
red 11	Bf 109 K-4	330271	10./JG 27, Leuna, Hptm. Gobert, 2 November 1944
blue 9	Bf 109 G-10	490639	16./JG 27, Vechta, Fw. Czernehaus, 26 November 1944
green 6	Bf 109 G-10	490692	Stab II./JG 27, Rheine, Hptm. Hoyer, 21 January 1945

Jagdgeschwader 51 'Mölders'

When a fourth Staffel was added to each of JG 51's four Gruppen in August 1944, this unit adopted the following identification colours:

4./JG 51 red numbers
8./JG 51
12./JG 51 blue numbers
16./JG 51

In addition, the Stabsstaffel carried black numbers, and the 3. and 12. (later 15.) Staffeln carried brown numbers.

Code	Aircraft	W.Nr.	Notes
yellow 10	Bf 109 E-4	5587	6./JG 51, Ofw. Berck, England, 24 August 1940
brown 5	Bf 109 F-2	6665	3./JG 51, 23 June 1941
black 6	Bf 109 F-4	8932	11./JG 51, 30 June 1941

Code	Aircraft	W.Nr.	Notes
<<+	Bf 109 F-4	13332	Stab III./JG 51, 23 October 1942
white 10	Fw 190 A-3	0376	7./JG 51, Uffz. Bärmoser, Orel, 18 February 1943
black 13	Fw 190 A-5	7295	Stabsstaffel./JG 51, Lt. Lücke, 22 May 1943
blue 15	Fw 190 A-8	171015	7./JG 51, Uffz. Zechner, Alencon, 17 June 1944
yellow 12	Bf 109 G-6	411142	9./JG 51, Uffz. Busch, 26 June 1944
red 13	Fw 190 A-8	171151	4./JG 51, Uffz. Thienert, Erfurt, 21 November, 1944
<O+	Bf 109 G-14	491393	Stab III./JG 51, Ofw. Dietrich, 19 February 1945

Jagdgeschwader 52

Code	Aircraft	W.Nr.	Notes
red 14	Bf 109 E-1	3367	2./JG 52, Uffz. Zaunbrecher, 12 August 1940
black 1	Bf 109 F-4	7020	8./JG 52, 1 July 1941
white 14	Bf 109 F-2	8300	7./JG 52, 26 July 1941
<+	Bf 109 G-2	13476	Stab III./JG 52, 21 July, 1942
yellow 9	Bf 109 G-4	19242	6./JG 52, 25 May 1943
white 11	Bf 109 G-6	19961	4./JG 52, 22 July 1943
black 14	Bf 109 G-6	165041	5./JG 52, 29 June 1944
blue 4	Bf 109 G-14	510963	Stab/JG 52, 20 October 1944
black 6	Bf 109 G-10	610580	5./JG 52, Ofw. Mahr, 11 March 1945
black 9	Bf 109 K-4	333943	10./JG 52, Oblt. Klemens, Breslau, 10 April 1945

Jagdgeschwader 53 'Pikas'

When a fourth Staffel was added to each of JG 53's four Gruppen in August 1944, this unit adopted the following identification colours:

4./JG 53
8./JG 53 red numbers
12./JG 53 blue numbers
16./JG 53 blue numbers

Code	Aircraft	W.Nr.	Notes
yellow 2	Bf 109 E-1	3619	3./JG 53, Kent, Oblt. Haase, 15 September 1940
yellow 1	Bf 109 F-4	7375	7./JG 53, 10 April 1942
black 1	Bf 109 F-4/Tp	10278	8./JG 53, 19 June 1942
white 5	Bf 109 G-4	15073	1./JG 53, 25 March 1943
white 22	Bf 109 G-6/U4	440679	4./JG 53, Caen, 2 July 1944
blue 14	Bf 109 G-14	420219	12./JG 53, Uetersen, 18 August 1944
red 17	Bf 109 G-6	166304	8./JG 53, Metz, 11 September 1944
<<+	Bf 109 G-14	464201	Stab IV./JG 53, Stuttgart, Hptm. Müer, 2 January 45
yellow 13	Bf 109 K-4	331506	13./JG 53, Dasbah, 13 March 1945

Jagdgeschwader 54 'Grünherz'

When a fourth Staffel was added to each of JG 54's four Gruppen in August 1944, this unit adopted the following identification colours:

4./JG 54 blue numbers
8./JG 54 blue numbers
12./JG 54 red numbers
16./JG 54 blue numbers

Code	Aircraft	W.Nr.	Notes
white 4	Bf 109 E-1	6204	1./JG 54, 28 August 1940
yellow 10	Bf 109 F-2	9622	9./JG 54, 27 June 1941
black 10	Bf 109 F-2	9206	5./JG 54, 9 September 1941

Code	Aircraft	W.Nr.	Notes
white 2	Bf 109 G-2	10344	4./JG 54, 3 August 1942
brown 3	Bf 109 G-4	16138	9./JG 54, 4 March 1943
<-+-	Fw 190 A-4	1341	Stab I./JG 54, Maj. Seiler, 6 July 1943
yellow 5	Fw 190 A-4	0666	3./JG 54, Stfw. Jungbluth, 12 July, 1943
red 5	Fw 190 A-6	550483	4.(Jabo)/JG 54, Lt.Thies, 3 December 1943
red 2	Fw 190 A-8	730972	12./JG 54, St.Andre, Fw. Muders, 24 June, 1944
blue 5	Fw 190 A-8	732128	16./JG 54, Emmerich, Uffz. Egener, 29 September 1944
white 16	Fw 190 D-9	400616	9./JG 54, Hüblingen, Uffz. Koch, 13 February 1945

Jagdgeschwader 76

Code	Aircraft	W.Nr.	Notes
white 1	Bf 109 E-3	1304	1./JG 76, Bas-Rhin, France, 22 November 1939
black 21	Bf 109 G-14	460593	Stab III./JG 76, Hptm.Albrecht, 25 August 1944

Jagdgeschwader 77 'Herzas'

When a fourth Staffel was added to each of JG 77's three Gruppen in August 1944, this unit adopted the following identification colours:

4./JG 77	blue numbers
8./JG 77	blue numbers
12./JG 77	blue numbers

Code	Aircraft	W.Nr.	Notes
white 4	Bf 109 E-1	4448	1./JG 77, Lt. Petrenko, Navestock, 31 August 1940
white 1	Bf 109 G-2	13633	7./JG 77, 29 October 1942
<II+	Bf 109 G-14	413651	Stab I./JG 77, Eupen, 11 September 1944
yellow 7	Bf 109 G-14	460521	3./JG 77, Fhr. Schmid, Aachen, 11 September 1944
blue 14	Bf 109 K-4	330190	12./JG 77, Uffz. Michelink, 18 December 1944
red 10	Bf 109 G-14	512350	2./JG 77, Lt. Humitsch, Dortmund, 18 December 1944
blue 6	Bf 109 G-14	467172	4./JG 77, Ofw. Hagemann, Siegburg, 24 December 1944
<1+	Bf 109 G-14	512390	Stab I./JG 77,Westfalen, 24 December 1944
red 5	Bf 109 K-4	332565	10./JG 77, Uffz. Neufels, Bielitz, 3 February 1945

Jagdgruppe 200

Code	Aircraft	W.Nr.	Notes
white 15	Bf 109 G-6	440267	1./JGr 200, Fw. Bernhardt, 29 June 1944
red 7	Bf 109 G-6	162320	2./JGr 200, Uffz. Droese, 13 July 1944
yellow 1	Bf 109 G-6	162231	3./JGr 200, Lt. Hupfeld, 30 July 1944

Jagdgeschwader 300 'Herrmann'

Code	Aircraft	W.Nr.	Notes
white 12	Fw 190 A-6	550148	4./JG 300, Bremen, 19 September 1943
green 3	Fw 190 A-6	550453	Stab II./JG 300, Gummersbach, 22 October 1943

Code	Aircraft	W.Nr.	Notes
white 2N	Fw 190 A-7	340328	4./JG 300, Munich, 13 June 1944
red 1	Bf 109 G-6	412256	2./JG 300, Halberstadt, 7 July 1944
red 17	Fw 190 A-8	350180	5./JG 300, Leipzig, 7 October 1944
<<+	Bf 109 G-10	491233	Stab III./JG 300, Maj. Kemp, 31 December 1944
blue 1	Bf 109 G-10	151533	Stab III./JG 300, Hptm. Jenne, 2 March 1945

Jagdgeschwader 301

Code	Aircraft	W.Nr.	Notes
red 19	Fw 190 A-8	171058	10./JG 301, Rotenburg, 31 October 1944
blue 12	Fw 190 A-8/R11	176071	8./JG 301, Cleve, 21 November 1944
white 1	Fw 190 A-9/R11	206160	5./JG 301, Rethen, 26 November 1944
black 4	Fw 190 A-8	682027	12./JG 301, Lüneburg, 31 December 1944
green 9	Ta 152 H-1	150168	Stab/JG 301, May 1945

Jagdgeschwader 302

Code	Aircraft	W.Nr.	Notes
green 3	Fw 190 A-6	470212	7./JG 302, Odenburg, 1 March 1944
yellow 4	Bf 109 G-6	163537	3./JG 302, Hungary, 6 June 1944
white 9	Bf 109 G-6	411703	1./JG 302, Slovakia, 6 June 1944
red 11	Bf 109 G-6	441896	2./JG 302, Hungary, 1 July 1944
<<+	Bf 109 G-6	440285	Stab/JG 302, Hungary, Hptm. Lewens, August 1944

Jagdgeschwader 400

Code	Aircraft	W.Nr.	Notes
white 8	Me 163 B-1	440186	1./JG 400. Ofw. Straznicky, 2 November 1944
white 22	Me 163 B-1	191111	1./JG 400, Uffz. Schüller, 11 February 1945
yellow 15	Me 163 B-1	191659	II./JG 400, captured at Husum, May 1945
yellow 11	Me 163 B-1	191454	II./JG 400, captured May 1945, to Farnborough

Zerstörergeschwader 26 'Horst Wessel'

During the summer of 1944, the Me 410s of ZG 26 adopted conventional fighter markings, although these were applied to relatively few aircraft before the unit was redesignated JG 6 in August 1944.

Code	Aircraft	W.Nr.	Notes
black 3+–	Me 410 A-2/U4		6./ZG 26, Hildesheim, summer 1944

Fighter-bomber Markings

During the autumn of 1940, the Luftwaffe experimented with using the Bf 109 E as a fighter-bomber, hastily equipping it with a rack for a single 250 kg SC 250 bomb. The success of the operations led to the formation of a specialised fighter-bomber Staffel on 10 November 1941, under the designation 10.(Jabo)/JG 2. This unit was joined by 10.(Jabo)/JG 26 on 10 March 1942, the two Staffeln flying low-level sorties against rail installations, barracks, ships and factories on the British south coast. Eventually, in December 1942, the Staffeln were expanded to form a complete Geschwader under the designation Schnellkampfgeschwader (SKG) 10. The fighter-bomber Staffeln of JG 2 and JG 26 (and later JG 54) carried conventional fighter markings, with either black or blue numbers, but often with a white or silver diagonal bomb symbol, or a chevron and bar behind the fuselage Balkenkreuz.

Jabo Staffeln of JG 2, JG 26 and JG 54

Code	Aircraft	W.Nr.	Notes
blue 4+~	Bf 109 F-4/B	7626	10.(Jabo)/JG 2, Isle of Wight, 27 May 1942
blue 1+<-	Fw 190 A-3	0439	10.(Jabo)/JG 2, Oblt. Liesendahl, 17 July 1942
black 13+	Fw 190 A-2	2080	10.(Jabo)/JG 26, Eastbourne, 26 August 1942
blue 7+	Fw 190 A-3	2177	10.(Jabo)/JG 26, Lt. Eckleben, 26 October 1942
black 7+<-	Fw 190 A-5	0587	10.(Jabo)/JG 54, Oblt. Keller, 24 March, 1943

Schnellkampfgeschwader 10

SKG 10 was formed in December 1942 from various fighter-bomber and heavy fighter units. It was proposed that each of its three Gruppen should eventually have four Staffeln, but this last addition was never formed.

A directive issued by Ob. d. L. on 14 April 1943, set down a revised system of markings for the aircraft of the ground attack and fast bomber units.

> *Markings of the aircraft of the Schlacht- and Schnellkampfverbände.*
>
> *I. In addition to National markings (Balkenkreuz and Hakenkreuz) which are as before.*
>
> *II. Organization and schematic of unit markings.*
> *a) Staffel aircraft are to carry Latin letters from A to Z, i.e.*
> *The 1., 5. and 9. Staffel in white colour.*
> *The 2., 6. and 10. Staffel in black colour.*
> *The 3., 7. and 11. Staffel in clay yellow.*
> *The 4., 8. and 12. Staffel in blue with white border.*
> *b) The aircraft of the Gruppenkommandeurs carry a marking of a letter with a triangular section in black with white border. The Gruppen marking (I. no marking, II. horizontal bar behind Balkenkreuz, III. vertical bar behind Balkenkreuz) likewise black with white edge.*
> The remaining aircraft of the Gruppenstabes are to be marked similarly to the Gruppenkommandeurs, however carrying only the chevron without the triangular panel.
> *c) Markings of the Geschwaderkommodore and the aircraft of the Geschwaderstabes:*
> *The aircraft of the Geschwaderkommodore is to have an arrow in front of the Balkenkreuz with the remainder behind. Colour black with white edge. The remaining aircraft of the Geschwaderstabes carry only the pointed marking before the Balkenkreuz, without the arrow head marking. Colour black with white edge.*
> *d) Previous Geschwader emblems and ground-attack triangles are deleted.*
>
> *Dimensions and manner of applying markings for the Bf 109 and Fw 190 whereby the new markings of the Fw 190 have to be applied starting from the Balkenkreuz with spacing and size as for the Bf 109.*
>
> *Der Ob. d. L. 14. 4. 1943*
> *Az. 65a. 10. 12. Nr. 7428/43 (Genst. Qu 2 Abt./IIA).*
> *L. Bv. L. S. 425.*

Ground-Attack Unit Markings

The first Luftwaffe ground-attack unit to be formed was II.(S)/LG 2 equipped initially with the Hs 123 biplane. This formed the basis of the first Schlachtgeschwader, Sch.G 1, which eventually comprised two Gruppen of four Staffeln each. A second Geschwader was formed in 1942 with a similar establishment. Both units used very similar markings to those adopted by the fighter units, but with coloured letters replacing numbers. Sch.G 1 also used a black triangle marking, with the Balkenkreuz marking separating the letter and triangle from each other. There would seem to be no rule as to which was painted forward, and which aft. Deletion of the triangular marking appears to have been rapid upon issue of the instruction from Ob. d. L. of 14 April 1943.

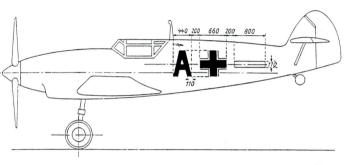

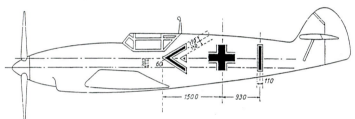

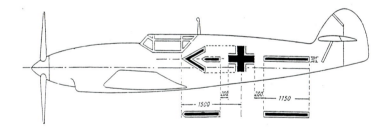

Schlachtgeschwader 1 (first formation)

Code	Aircraft	W.Nr.	Notes
D+blue H	Hs 123 A-1	2325	8./Sch.G 1, spring 1942
D+yellow E	Bf 109 E-4/B		2./Sch.G 1, spring 1942, southern Russia
yellow G+D	Hs 129 B-1		7./Sch.G 1, Schatalowka, Russia, May 1942
white P+-	Fw 190 A-5	5966	5./Sch.G 1, Ofw. Gläser, May 10, 1943
black S+-	Fw 190 A-5	1220	6./Sch.G 1, Lt. Rohnstock, May 10, 1943
D+white B	Fw 190 A-5	1226	2./Sch.G 1, Uffz. Götz, Bonezkij, May 23, 1943
red O+-	Fw 190 A-5	5962	6./Sch.G 1, Uffz. Weiss, 9 June 1943
yellow S+	Fw 190 F-3	670039	3./Sch.G 1, Uffz. Förster, 7 July 1943

ABOVE LEFT AND RIGHT: Two photographs that illustrate the positioning and size of the regulation white-edged, black triangle of the Schlacht force. The combination of letter and triangle were marked in the same order on both sides of the individual aircraft. The top photograph shows a Bf 109 E-4/B, 'Black H' of II.(Schlacht)/LG 2, during operations against Britain. The rudder and wing tips were painted white, dating the photograph to September 1940. The close-up view of Bf 109 E-4/B yellow 'C' of 6./LG 2, shot down at Hawkinge on 6 September 1940, illustrates that the Schlacht emblem was marked forward of the Balkenkreuz in most instances. This aircraft also had a white rudder and wing tip markings. The overall camouflage for both aircraft appears to have been standard 71/02/65, but with the 65-coloured side areas toned down with a thin sprayed application of 02.

LEFT: Hs 129 B-2, 'Yellow 3', W.Nr. 0350 of Pz.Jä.St./JG 51 photographed in the early spring of 1943. The streaky, pale nature of the 70/71/65 camouflage was the result of not having completely removed all traces of the temporary white winter camouflage colouring used in the previous months. Benzine was used for this task and it required much care to delete all traces. Note the change from the older style of ground assault markings, based on Kampfgruppen standards, to those of the Jagdgruppen.

RIGHT: Wearing tropical camouflage colouring of 78/79/80, this Stab machine, 'Blue 0' of 4.(Pz.)/Sch.G. 2, carried a fighter type chevron marking in white. The white fuselage band was approximately 900 mm wide and the same colour appeared beneath each wing tip, and also on the nose section. The spinners were divided into two-thirds white and one-third blue.

Schlachtgeschwader 2 (first formation)

Code	Aircraft	W.Nr.	Notes
< yellow O+	Hs 129 B-1	0310	4./Sch.G 2, North Africa, late 1942
white H+-	Fw 190 A-5	5940	5./Sch.G 2, Soukra-Ariana, 7 June 1943
yellow G+-	Fw 190 A-5	1274	7./Sch.G 2, Soukra-Ariana, 7 June 1943
green A+-	Fw 190 A-5	5919	Stab II./Sch.G 2, Soukra-Ariana, Jun 7, 1943
red A+-	Fw 190 A-5	5999	6./Sch.G 2, Pantelleria, 11 June 1943
black K+	Fw 190 A-3	0228	2./Sch.G 2, Uffz. Minuth, Jul 9, 1943
blue K+-	Hs 129 B-2/R2	0373	8./Sch.G 2, Apostolowo, Sep 1943

In October 1943, a complete re-organization of the Luftwaffe's ground-attack units took place, the old 'Stuka', 'Schnellkampf-' and 'Schlachtgeschwader' designations being changed to Schlachtgeschwader with the intention of eventually re-equipping them all with the Fw 190. The Ju 87s operated by the units retained the four-character code system, but the Fw 190s retained the coloured letter identification introduced by the original Schlachtgeschwader. Gradually, however, the letters were replaced by numbers making it difficult to distinguish day fighter units from ground-attack units.

Schlachtgeschwader 1 (second formation)

Code	Aircraft	W.Nr.	Notes
white 10	Fw 190 F-8	932318	4./SG 1, Ofhr. Thomader, 19 January 1945
yellow 3	Fw 190 F-8	931353	6./SG 1, Elbing airfield, 23 January 1945
black 11	Fw 190 F-8	586414	5./SG 1, Rahmel, 25 January 1945
yellow 13	Fw 190 F-9/R1	424145	3./SG 1, Uffz. Müller, 27 May 1945
white 8	Fw 190 F-9/R1	440319	1./SG 1, Fürstenwalde, 7 April 1945

Schlachtgeschwader 2 (second formation) 'Immelmann'

Code	Aircraft	W.Nr.	Notes
yellow 0	Fw 190 F-3	670427	6./SG 2, Russia, Uffz. Werner, 30 November, 1943
green 1	Fw 190 F-8	932589	Stab II./SG 2, 24 January 1945
yellow 2	Fw 190 F-8	933302	6./SG 2, Cottbus, 29 January 1945
black 9	Fw 190 F-8	428364	5./SG 2, Niemes-Süd, 18 April 1945
white 7	Fw 190 F-8/R1	931884	1./SG 2, captured May 1945, now at NASM

Schlachtgeschwader 3

For reasons unknown, SG 3 rarely recorded its operational markings in its loss reports to the Luftwaffe Quartermaster General's office. For this reason it has not proved possible to include examples of SG 3 markings.

Schlachtgeschwader 4

Code	Aircraft	W.Nr.	Notes
white H	Fw 190 G-3	160366	4./SG 4, Guidona airfield, 26 October 1943
black D	Fw 190 G-3	160389	5./SG 4, Capua, 20 November 1943

Code	Aircraft	W.Nr.	Notes
red H	Fw 190 G-2	180054	2./SG 4, Piacenza, 7 February 1944
yellow 5	Fw 190 A-6	470452	3./SG 4, Rome, Hptm. Strössner, 21 May 1944
black 10	Fw 190 F-8	586444	8./SG 4, Bastogne, 24 December 1944
green <2	Fw 190 F-9	420135	Stab II./SG 4 Ratibor, 1 February 1945

Schlachtgeschwader 5

The aircraft of SG 5 used the code sequence 'Q9'. See Chapter 9 for examples of these codes.

Schlachtgeschwader 9

Code	Aircraft	W.Nr.	Notes
white F	Hs 129 B-2	141973	10.(Pz)/SG 9, Uffz. Bayrle, Jul 16, 1944
red C	Hs 129 B-2	141837	13.(Pz)/SG 9, Uffz. Ruthmann, Jul 20, 1944

Schlachtgeschwader 10

Code	Aircraft	W.Nr.	Notes
green C	Fw 190 F-3	160619	Stab I./SG 10, Fw. Kruse, 8 December 1943
white H	Fw 190 G-3	160618	1./SG 10, Oblt. Siefert, 11 December 1943
black E	Fw 190 G-3	160099	5./SG 10, Ofw. Weiler, 12 December 1943
black 8	Fw 190 F-9	420711	5./SG 10, Ofw. Schopper, 29 January 1945
yellow 7	Fw 190 F-8	588449	3./SG 10, Oblt. Koratin, 4 February 1945

Schlachtgeschwader 77

Code	Aircraft	W.Nr.	Notes
+ white J	Fw 190 F-3	0773	1./SG 77, Uffz. Zschornack, 20 October 1943
<+D	Fw 190 F-3	670435	Stab II./SG 77, Hptm. Steinhoff, 19 December 1943
yellow 10	Fw 190 F-8	583072	9./SG 77, Laag, 17 January 1945
black 10	Fw 190 F-8	932666	8./SG 77, Frehaus, 20 January 1945
green <5	Fw 190 F-8	932601	6./SG 77, Prinkersdorf, 31 January 1945
white Z	Fw 190 F-9	428161	Stab/SG 77, Kamenz, 17 April 1945

Schlachtgeschwader 151

Code	Aircraft	W.Nr.	Notes
black 24	Fw 190 F-8/R1	586189	9./SG 151, 18 January 1945
white 36	Fw 190 F-8	584201	1./SG 151, Guben, 19 January 1945
black 11	Fw 190 F-3	670399	2./SG 151, Oels, 22 January 1945

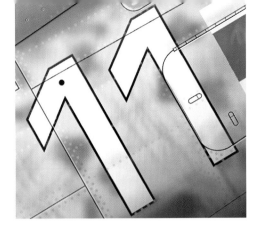

Tactical and Special Purpose Markings

his chapter endeavours to cover the entire range of special purpose markings seen on Luftwaffe aircraft from the 1930s to the end of the Second World War. *Tactical markings* are defined here as those markings specified for a particular theatre of war and used on a broad scale to distinguish German aircraft from those of the enemy. *Special purpose markings* were employed usually on a smaller, more localized scale, ranging from red disk markings used in pre-war military air exercises, red cross markings etc., to the tail and nose markings introduced by individual units for specific and often temporary purposes. (Both forms should be seen as distinct from the range of Geschwader and Gruppen Stab markings that persisted almost unchanged throughout). However the reader will find that the distinction between the two forms, tactical and special, sometimes blurred, and in some instances one form of marking lea to the broader establishment of another. To attempt to split the two forms empirically would be to repeat much overlapping detail and the following is presented in as near as possible a continuous account of those dual developments.

Luftwaffe tactical markings had their origin in the first war games that began on Tuesday, 24 September 1934. The 'defence's' HQ had been set up at Braunschweig-Warnemünde and the military situation was defined on the basis that the enemy had been attacking for the previous two days, approaching from the west, and was by then on the western bank of the Elbe. The enemy was designated as Red Force, the defenders Blue Force. In Pomerania ground troops were being organised to form a new army while the airports at Hildesheim and Braunschweig had been "destroyed" by the retreating Blue Force. These had been repaired by

Red force and air attacks launched that had 'destroyed' the harbour facilities at Stettin, making Warnemünde strategically important as the supply point from the Baltic. To complicate the exercise, the area over the Baltic Sea had been declared a neutral no-fly zone to either force. Intelligence reports had alerted Blue Force that two Kampfgeschwader of Ju 52 bombers were to attack Warnemünde in two waves. It was a complex scenario that also included fighter defences, reconnaissance aircraft, Flak and civil defence forces.

To distinguish the attacking force Balkenkreuze had been painted over with a red circle that just covered the marking. The paint used was a temporary semi-gloss lacquer and at certain angles to the main source of light the original marking could be just discerned.

These types of war games were repeated regularly up to the outbreak of war, the last being held in June 1939, and in later exercises opaque temporary paints were used as a single band of colour around the nose section of bombers of some (possibly all) of the defending force units. The only colours so far identified are yellow and blue for the bomber force, though it appears that green may also have been used. The fighter force is known to have used white and yellow.

BELOW AND OPPOSITE RIGHT: Use of temporary lacquers was employed to identify the attacking and opposing force in the annual German war games held from 1934 onwards. These two Ar 68 Es were damaged while attempting landings on soft ground during the 1937 manoeuvres. Both had had their Balkenkreuz markings overpainted with temporary red lacquer. Note that the wear to the lacquer was distinctly less on 'White 8' than on the markings of 'White 7'. This illustrates the very temporary nature of the finish, through which the underlying Balkenkreuz marking was just discernable at very close range. The abrasive nature of the airflow was enough to erode the finish over a short space of time.

BELOW: This air-to-air photograph of 54+F37, a Do 17 E-1 of III./KG 255, taken during the same war games, shows the semi-transparent nature of the red lacquer finish. (J. Radziwill)

ABOVE: The use of the temporary semi-transparent lacquer had changed by the time of the 1938 war games, the marking instead being applied as a band of opaque colour around the nose of bomber aircraft. The nature of this temporary finish, though similar to that of the previous red lacquer, was now a matt finish with no transparent quality. These two Ju 86s of 6./KG 254, were marked with a yellow band and the surface of the one on 42+C26, nearest the camera, indicates the rapid erosion of the temporary finish.

BELOW: The history of the use of temporary colour marking on fighter aircraft during these later manoeuvres is harder to trace, but this photograph of 'White 11', a Bf 109 E of I./JG 53 taken in 1939 during the last war games, shows the rear section of the aircraft painted in yellow.

ABOVE: During the war game manoeuvres of 1939, temporary white also was used. This Bf 109 E of 6./JG 26 used the temporary white finish for the same area of the fuselage, but with addition of the same colour to the wing tips inboard to the edge of the Balkenkreuz marking. Note the eroded surface of the white on the rudder. The use of at least yellow (see previous photograph) and white points to the change in the use of this form of marking, it being now employed for tactical formation work rather than just identification of friend and 'foe'.

ABOVE: Reputedly taken during the opening phase of the war against Poland, this Bf 109 E of 3.(J)./LG 2 wore an all-yellow engine cowling (with the name 'Peter' marked in white). If the dating is correct, it would indicate that some of the temporary markings adopted for the last war games were carried over into the opening phase of the war.

ABOVE AND BELOW: The use of special rapid recognition markings to identify the lead aircraft for other than bomber formations was a different form of markings system and had its origins much earlier than 1939. The unusual form of 'code' marking of 'A1', in the absence of any formal special visual marking at that time, possibly identified the Kommandeur of I./JG 132, which was just in the process of forming with He 51s at Berlin-Döberitz in March 1935. However, the two narrow black bands, with the grey-green background creating a three band system, was to prove closely related to the new system of rapid recognition markings that would be introduced at the beginning of July 1936.)

ABOVE: The presence of a white band on this Bf 109 E-1, also of JG 26 and photographed around the time of the 1939 manoeuvres, may point to a variable system of temporary markings for the war games that year.

Another form of marking employed pre-war was that of fuselage bands, initially it seems, to indicate aircraft of the Stab formation. Only one example has been noted, which occurred on a He 51 of Fliegergruppe Döberitz that had been renamed I./JG 132 in March 1935. Two narrow black bands, each approximately 15 cm wide and separated by a similar-sized gap, were painted around the rear section of the grey-green coloured fuselage. This aircraft was also marked with a Balkenkreuz in all six standard positions. Other aircraft in the unit still retained their civil registrations, indicating that this had occurred during the transition phase, Balkenkreuz markings having been promulgated for military aircraft on 15 September 1935, providing some approximate dating for the photograph. The particular aircraft also carried an unusual form of code marking, 'A1' in black, on each side of the fuselage.

The band marking was possibly a form of rapid identification, moreso than the distinctive 'A1'. Under battle conditions the band marking would have made the lead aircraft more easily identifiable. Use of the distinctive code may have been a trial as five-figure codes were introduced for the fledgling fighter force soon after, though that was to be relatively short-lived, a series of more distinctive markings replacing

BELOW: This form of rapid recognition marking seems to have survived the relatively short-lived implementation of specialised rapid recognition marking for fighter aircraft. This 2./JG 77 Bf 109 E, 'Red 1', had a series of bands marked around the rear section of the fuselage. Taken during the Polish campaign they point to the continued use of this form of marking for operational conditions. The purpose of the white circle is unknown.

the number/letter/number code structure in July 1936. Part of the suite of new markings did reflect the bands mentioned above, 2. Staffel aircraft being marked around the rear section of the fuselage with a 600 mm band divided into three, with white in the centre. It may have been coincidental, but the visual effect was the same.

As will be detailed further, the exclusive use by Stab aircraft of this form of marking appears to have been brief. Other variations of what has been termed by some writers as rapid recognition markings evolved, often peculiar to a single unit. A broader application occurred briefly during the air fighting over Britain in 1940 with temporary mass formation assembly markings for bombers, and a modified form of this concept was employed by transport units in 1941; both will be discussed later in the text.

With the introduction of the Bf 109 and full ground defensive camouflage of 70/71, the narrow rapid identification bands continued to

be applied, examples being recorded in black, white and red. The number of bands varied between one and two, spacing between the latter varying only to match the actual width of the band marking applied. Slight variation in bandwidth between different aircraft indicates that units did not adhere strictly to whatever regulation was set for such markings. Examples noted on Bf 109 Ds of J.Gr. 102 and Es of JG 77 seem to belie the suggestion that these markings were carried only by aircraft of the Stab formation. The odd one out was 'Yellow 12' of 3./J.Gr 102, which had two white bands around the rear of its fuselage. This combination of high number and two white bands would seem to refute the Stab suggestion. Further, the examples examined show no direct correlation between

ABOVE: Oblt. Robitzsch's Bf 109 E-1, W.Nr. 1257, 'Black 1' of 5.(J)/Tr.Gr. 186, which was shot down by a Dutch fighter on 10 May 1940. It wears 71/02/65 camouflage and a personal marking of 'Der Alte' in red beneath the cockpit. The white-edged black band is another example of operational use of this form of tactical marking. Note that the band appears to be wider at the bottom than at the top. Close examination shows that the black was painted over the white stripe by hand and this probably accounts for the variations in width. The aircraft carried the correct, revised style of Balkenkreuz markings, but still had the Hakenkreuz marked in the 1939 position. The Werknummer on this aircraft was only marked on the port side, in small numerals just above the horizontal tail plane, and included the prefix 'W.Nr.'. Camouflage was 71/02/65.

ABOVE: This Bf 109 D-1 of I./ ZG 2, a unit that distinguished itself during the Polish campaign, wears a form of white band marking, just visible on the right, but close examination of this photograph, and others of it, reveals that the white band was centred on a wider, very dark band, probably black.

LEFT: Heavy fighters and close-support aircraft all appear to have made use of a similar form of rapid recognition marking. This Ju 87 B, A5+AB, from the Stab of I./St.G 1 was photographed during the Polish campaign. The single narrow white band was not continued over the 65-coloured lower surfaces, perhaps because the contrast between the two was insufficient for practical purposes compared to the stark contrast when seen against the 70/71 finish.

RIGHT: The use of a white band marking extended also to the heavy fighter units as seen on Bf 110 C U8+HL W.Nr. 1372 of I./ZG 26, taken on 11 September 1940. The nose section of the aircraft had been painted with temporary white lacquer as a tactical marking used for a period during the air fighting over Britain as noted in the text. Close examination shows that it had been applied with a hand brush, producing runs of paint. (Kent Messenger).

LEFT AND ABOVE: During the Czechoslovak crisis of March 1939, JG 131 based at Berlin-Döberitz, introduced a radical set of rapid recognition markings for its Schwarmführer as seen in these pictures. The 'White X' and '?' markings applied to Lt Reifferscheldt's Bf 109 D-1, 'White 3' of 1.Staffel (left) prior to the occupation of Bohemia and Moravia on 15 March, were quite radical compared with the generalised form of tactical markings eventually adopted by the Luftwaffe for specific campaigns and theatres of operations. It is not known whether the same markings were applied to the lower surfaces.

either Staffel or Gruppe colouring and the colour of the bands. While this system of markings began to disappear from the Bf 109 force after the completion of the Polish campaign, a similar system of narrow bands, white being the predominant colour recorded, appeared also on Ju 87s and Bf 110s and continued to be seen until late in 1940.

Bomber aircraft utilized a similar system to that seen on Bf 109s but in this instance there was a correlation to Stab status in some instances. While narrow white band markings were recorded in use immediately behind the wing root trailing edge fairing on the Do 17s of KG 76 during the 1939-1940 period, Do 17 Zs of KG 2 used a diagonal band marking, usually in the Gruppe colour, around the nose section angled back to the belly of the aircraft. A similar type of band marking also was used by the Ju 88s of the Stab of KG 54 during the 1940 daylight campaign against Britain, a system seen also on the unit's He 111s in 1941. KG 3 also used a band of similar dimensions around the nose of its aircraft, again in Gruppe colour, during the 1939–1940 period. Again, both single and double white markings were used. The practice continued well into the mid-war period though it was more rarely seen. KG 54 was still employing it on its Ju 88s in 1942 as was KG 2 on its Do 217 E-4s. The Ju 87s appear to have retained this system longest of all with some machines being recorded as late as 1944 using narrow white diagonal band markings across the rudder. Of all the surviving photographic examples of this practice, it is perhaps significant that no more than two bands appear to have been used, indicating that the band markings, in white at least, were restricted to the Stab leader and his deputy.

KG 153 (redesignated KG 77) used wide bands of colour around the nose section of its Do 17 Zs pre-war, probably photographed during the annual war games. Photographs of two KG 153 machines, 3Z+BA and 3Z+DA, show each wearing a blue band, while a photograph of 3Z+BK shows a yellow band, but with the aircraft letter, in miniature, along side it in the Staffel colour of red. All codes were marked in black. While the Stab colour of blue was used, it appears that the main purpose of the bands was for identifying the force rather than being an air-to-air indicator of Staffel or Gruppe. That form of marking was used during the attack on Poland, but was painted out soon after completion of the campaign. This was the last known use of this form of marking dating back to the pre-war exercises. The next occasion when recognition markings were employed by bombers did not occur until the air fighting over Britain in August 1940, and took a much different form.

Battle of Britain

The adoption of recognition markings for bombers appears to have been directly linked to the decision to intensify the bombing campaign with massed formations protected by large numbers of fighter aircraft. 'Adler

Tag' ('Eagle Day') had been scheduled for 10 August 1940, but remained dependent upon weather conditions and as a consequence had been delayed until 13 August. However, introduction of temporary markings for bombers was preceded by the first use of what became established as more permanent tactical markings, these being added to the fighters.

Before moving to this topic, a brief digression is necessary since there is one well authenticated account, both in a written Intelligence report, plus ample photographs, of Oblt. Werner Bartels' aircraft, a Bf 109 E-1 (W.Nr. 6296F) of III./JG 26 which crash-landed at Northdown, Kent, on 26 July 1940. The rudder was painted yellow. This is sometimes shown in illustrations as the paler RLM 27 shade, but photographs taken at the crash site, from the nose looking aft, show the rudder to have a darker shade more consistent with 04. Whatever the actual shade of yellow, its appearance was the first time that this form of marking had been recorded during the air battle over Britain. As a III. Gruppe Stab pilot, it is most probable that the link was to the Gruppe colour (yellow). If so, then this premature appearance of rudder colouring as a 'tactical' marking was simply a form of rapid recognition of a Stab aircraft within the unit for means of air fighting tactics. As such, it presaged part of what was to come.

One other oddity needs special reference before continuing. Another variation on the system of tactical markings for single-engine fighter aircraft, and the only one that would be noted during the coming air fighting over Britain, occurred within JG 53. During the height of the Battle, the Stab and other aircraft were recorded using a wide red band around the engine cowling, the width of the marking varying slightly from aircraft to aircraft indicating that they were painted without use of a stencil. Precise dating is not possible, but examples of the marking are said to have appeared in July 1940 and were still in use in November. Several stories are extant as to the origins of the marking, but none has been confirmed. It might simply have been that, prior to the general adoption of an all yellow cowling marking as recorded next, it was a very effective rapid identification marking in dog fights where the approach of another single-seat aircraft needed quick identification. Significantly, when JG 53 adopted the all yellow engine cowling marking (see below), the red band was usually not over-painted, indicating further that it had a significance that warranted its preservation, perhaps purely as a unit marking in the mêlée that became more and more prevalent as the air fighting increased in ferocity.

ABOVE: The red band marking adopted by JG 53 is clearly visible in this photograph of a Bf 109 E-3 of II. Gruppe photographed at La Villiaze. The width and precise positioning of the red band marking varied slightly between machines. It replaced the unit's older 'Pik-As' emblem between August and October before itself being dispensed with in October, the original emblem being reinstated. Its use may have been simply for a pragmatic purpose – rapid identification of the unit's own aircraft in the intense aerial fighting of that period. The double chevron marking of the Gruppenkommandeur was black, thinly edged in white.

ABOVE: The temporary nature of the yellow tactical colouring can be seen in this photograph of a Bf 109 E-4 Jabo of JG 53 having its single 250 kg bomb loaded while mechanics carry out a final maintenance check. Most of the yellow colouring had worn away on the top section of the upper cowling. The red of the unit's band marking had been painted over in this instance, traces of it just being visible along the edges of the gun trough. (E. Mombeek)

LEFT: In this instance, the distinctive JG 53 red band marking had been retained over the yellow tactical colouring of the cowling. The 250 kg bomb in the foreground appears to have been painted in RLM 70 or a RAL equivalent. (See Appendix F)

The intensity of the air battle had continued to rise, and by the third week in August yellow (04) appeared for the first time as a form of rapid recognition aid on the Bf 109s. The earliest photographic record of this colour appears on a Bf 109 E-3 of 7./JG 26, though only a general date of August is known; however, it must have been somewhere around the second week of the month. The marking took the form of a relatively small, inverted wedge shape at the tip of the rudder.

ABOVE: The earliest form of tactical marking introduced for fighter aircraft during the Battle of Britain was the adoption of a yellow triangular wedge shape, as seen here on this Bf 109 E-3 of 7./JG 26.

While size and positioning alone would not appear to be very effective as a form of rapid recognition, in a rearward attack by another aircraft it may have achieved its limited purpose (that shortcoming would be addressed within two weeks). The first positive dating of this form of marking was on 18 August, on Oblt. Tiedmann's Bf 109 E-4, W.Nr. 1990, 'Black 13' of 2./JG 3, but by that date the coloured segment marking was already being used in combination with yellow applied to the tips of the horizontal tail plane and wings. A photograph of Hptm. Tietzen's 5./JG 51 aircraft, taken at his home airfield, shows the same array of yellow markings, but it must have been taken prior to 18 August as he was shot down on that day. Thus a fairly rapid progression of development must have taken place, possibly within two weeks at most and JG 3, JG 26, JG 51 and JG 53 were recorded with these markings by the third week of August. The areas chosen for the markings were logical; part of them would have been visible no matter what the angle

of the aircraft to the viewer. Oddly, other Bf 109s from JG 3, JG 26 and JG 54 were found to have carried no yellow markings at all between 24 August and the end of the month. That could have resulted from the intensity of air operations and serviceability factors not allowing time to add the new markings, though it seems very unlikely.

On 24 August, JG 26 lost an aircraft from 9. Staffel that had a changed array of yellow markings. Gone were the tip markings on the horizontal tail surfaces, and the rudder was now painted completely yellow, as was the entire nose section back to the leading edge of the wings. The official order for this change of markings has not been located to date, but it would appear that the wording possibly was slightly less than precise, because very soon other Bf 109s were seen with the yellow on the nose section taken back, in varying degrees, right to the front edge of the windscreen. The only other variation on this revised set of yellow markings involved the rudder, some aircraft marking only the rear half; but the general rule was the entire rudder surfaces were painted in yellow. Units positively identified using this combination included JG 2, JG 3, JG 26, JG 27, JG 51, JG 52, JG 53 and JG 77.

It might be assumed that the change of markings had taken place on the basis that the larger areas of colour were more effective, yet what seems to be a retrograde move was incorporated into a swift change to white that was first noted on 2 September. Yellow 04 had suddenly been replaced by white 21, in some instances the white being painted directly over the top of the yellow, which may indicate the urgency with which the change had been implemented. The additional oddity was that the very earliest example used the areas seen on the first yellow marked Bf 109s, i.e., a wedge of white at the tip of the rudder, tips of the horizontal tail surfaces and wing tips. By 5 September the markings had been extended by including the full rudder area, but at the expense of

ABOVE: An interesting photograph of cowlings lined up to have the 7./JG 2 Staffel emblem sprayed on them after being sprayed yellow. The stencil for the task can be seen on top of the mobile two-bottle compressed air tank unit. Spinners had also been assembled so that the tip of each could be painted white, the Staffel colour. The aircraft in the background appears to have an all-yellow fin and rudder, the demarcation line of the darker RLM 71 mottling of the fuselage side ending in a fairly sharp curved arcing line down to the base of the tail strut.

LEFT: A similar process in action, the cowling of another 7./JG 2 Bf 109 E-7 having its gun trough given a touch-up by being brush painted with yellow after overall spraying of the cowling. The Staffel badge can be seen on the side of the cowling, and the Gruppe emblem can just be seen below the cockpit quarter-light section.

deletion of the horizontal tail tips' colouring. No doubt the broader area of white of the rudder was deemed sufficient. The rudder was also subject to the same minor vagaries as when yellow had been applied, being restricted on some to the trailing half of the rudder alone, though on most, the entire rudder was painted. This may simply reflect those aircraft that had already been marked with just half the rudder in yellow, never having moved to the full rudder colouring, white being applied over the existing yellow section. One other variation was found at the crash of a 7./JG 53 machine north of RAF Manston on 6 September, that aircraft having white restricted to the rudder and nose section.

The entire period of utilization of white as a tactical colour for the Bf 109s appears to have been limited to around mid-September, and then only to certain units or parts of them. Analysis of aircraft that can be confirmed carrying some combination of the white markings reveals that all were from II./JG 2, JG 3, III./JG 27, JG 52, JG 53, JG 54 and LG 2.

While white markings had adorned most of the Bf 109 force during that period in September, other Bf 109s, those of JG 2, JG 26, I. and II./JG 27 and JG 77, had retained their existing yellow markings.

Use of white however had not been restricted to just the Bf 109s, elements of the Bf 110 force had also employed it; all three Gruppen of ZG 26, ZG 76 and Lehrgeschwader 1 had used white on the nose section of their aircraft during the same period as the Bf 109s. However, unlike the Bf 109s, they had continued using it until the last week of September, the last confirmed report being made on 30 September when a Bf 110 D of 4./ZG 26 crash-landed at Theville, Cherbourg. The significance of this brief shift to alternative tactical colouring is not clear and no Luftwaffe or RLM documentation has been found to clarify it. Elements within both Luftflotte 2 and Luftflotte 3 had been moved at the beginning of September, to cater for the changing tactics, and every aircraft, both Bf 109s and Bf 110s, known to have used the white markings had come under the control of Jagdfliegerführer 2 (Jäfu 2) at that time. However, so far no documentation has emerged to make a more definitive statement as to the significance of the month-long colour change.

At that stage of the war, German ground forces were the only ones employing temporary finishes (other than the temporary night black finish used for the Luftwaffe night bomber force) with an extended life, one of which was Warnecke und Böhm's Ikarin-A2515.21, a white-coloured paste (snow camouflage) that could be diluted and sprayed, or applied with a brush. It was this that was used on aircraft, in conjunction with an intermediate coat, which protected the original lacquer surface. It was semi-permanent but could be removed by washing with benzine.

As noted, fighter aircraft also used large areas of colour, yellow or white, on engine cowling, wing tips and rudder for a period of several months. To have used the lacquer employed for temporary night black by the bomber force, which had an eight day refurbishment cycle, would have been impractical to say the least, particularly at a time when daily battles were at their peak and maintenance crews pushed to their utmost. While reports of the nature of the finish clearly indicate that it was of non-permanent nature, it used different chemistry to that of the temporary night black finish. The very many photographs of rudders showing victory markings give a rich source of detail to examine and show the tactical colouring as a smooth finish rather than the coarser texture resulting from application by brush as was to be found with the special night black mentioned above.

The usual shade of yellow used for fighter markings was 04, described in contemporary intelligence reports as orange/chrome yellow, but some variation had occurred, possibly through decay of the finish, or poor mixing of the pigment before applying it. This is

illustrated by the Bf 109 E-4, W.Nr. 5178, 'Black 2', of 5./JG 54 brought down on 25 October 1940. The intelligence report states *"upper half of cowling yellow and lower half orange..."*, two colours distinct enough to prompt the intelligence officer to record it. Engine cowlings were exchanged between aircraft at times to keep aircraft serviceable – this seems to have been one such instance.

A system of coloured markings had also been adopted for bomber aircraft, but for a different purpose. Whereas the Bf 109s and Bf 110s had used their markings for rapid identification of friend and foe during the hectic air fighting, the bombers employed a system of coloured bar markings to assist with the mass formations composed of aircraft from different units. Individual aircraft situated in the lead centre position of these giant formations had markings applied to both sides of the vertical tail surfaces and on the upper surface of both wings, outboard of the engines. Other aircraft, dependent upon their position to port or starboard, carried similar markings but limited to the side of the aircraft that could be seen from within the formation.

These markings took the form of large oblong bars of colour in white and pink, use of pink, rather than red, appears to have been predicated by the superior visual observation range of the paler colour, strong toned red being difficult to distinguish at distance against the standard dark 70/71 camouflage. The oblongs were marked on wings parallel to the main spar on He 111s and Ju 88s; and vertically on tail surfaces, sometimes obscuring part or all of the Hakenkreuz marking. While triple bar markings were usually spread across both fin and rudder on He 111s, at least two examples show them confined to just the rudder. In some instances, both aircraft types are also recorded as having the markings applied to both sides of the rudder and on top of both wings.

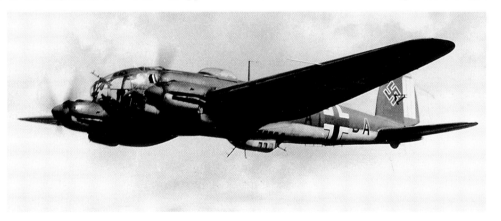

ABOVE: An He 111 H-2 from the Geschwader Stab of KG 53, coded A1+DA, illustrates the use of a triple-bar formation marking to just the rudder. The Stab letter 'A' was outlined narrowly in a pale colour. (B. Rosch)

ABOVE: This He 111, A1+BT, of III./KG 53, was also marked with a triple bar marking, but only to the starboard wing showing the error of trying to relate the number and placement bars to Gruppe or Staffel status within a single unit. Close examination of the bar marking shows that it was done with a large template, the over spray having left its mark on the outer and rear sections of the wing near the marking. (B. Rosch)

BELOW: This well-known aerial view of two Do 17s over West Ham speedway stadium in east London, taken on 7 September 1940, which date marked the opening of mass air attacks, shows more than one aircraft marked with a tactical formation marking. The Do 17 Z at the top of the picture has its individual code letter, 'G', visible on the port wing tip. It also has a horizontal stripe on the starboard fin and rudder, marked high up as in the previous photograph. The stripe on the starboard wing tip of each aircraft stands out clearly, illustrating the effectiveness of these markings. This confirms that within a single formation, markings were sometimes applied to only one side. In this instance these Dorniers would have been flying on the left side of the formation, their markings visible to the leading formation on the right. (RAF)

ABOVE: While of poor quality, this photograph shows two bars applied to the starboard side of the fin of this KG 26 He 111 H.

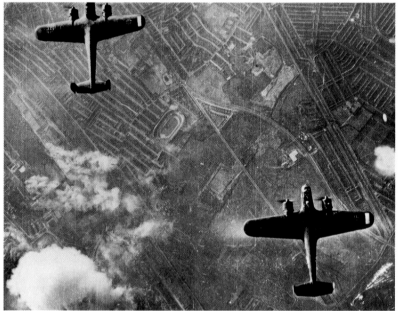

ABOVE: This Do 17 Z, 5K+DH of I./KG 3, had had its Balkenkreuz markings and code letter partly painted out with temporary black – strictly against regulations. There is some evidence that the aircraft also had had black applied over its entire upper surfaces, and then cleaned off only in parts. The white wing stripe on the starboard wing tip is evident even at this reduced angle.

RIGHT: The fin and rudder from the tail section of Oblt. Zehbe's Do 17 Z coded F1+FH of 1./KG 76 that crashed onto a building on Vauxhall Bridge Road, London, on 15 September with the rest of the aircraft falling on Victoria Station. The single pink bar marking across the fin and rudder can be seen in detail, the slightly ragged edges showing that it had been applied with a brush. The photograph clearly illustrates the problem of determining whether this marking was white or pale pink. It also illustrates the reason for the often incomplete records of such markings as the outer wing panels had become detached during the aircraft's death dive.

The Do 17 force however had employed wing bar markings parallel to the fuselage, and horizontally across both fin and rudder. The size and shape of the Do 17 fin and rudder assembly resulted in the trailing edge of the bar marking being slightly cropped, but it was applied carefully to strict dimensions, using a stencil. One Intelligence report quoted dimension on fin and rudder of two bands, each '12 inches wide', the nearest Imperial measurement equivalent to 30 cm. On Ju 88s, size varied from 135 cm x 45 cm for a single bar marking, to 90 cm x 30 cm per bar where multiple bar markings were used; in each instance the ratio of length to breadth remained constant at 3:1. Dimensions available for the vertical fin of the He 111 state 30 cm wide for each of the vertical multiple markings while single bar marking size appear to have conformed to those for the Ju 88, the same applying to the single bar marking across fin and rudder of Do 17s. This would follow the usual RLM style of using standard dimensions regardless of type and orientation of the marking. Where used, all wing markings were confined to the wing tip area, regardless of type.

The first photographic record of use of these markings coincided with the mass air raids launched against London on 7 September 1940, while the first intelligence report on a crashed aircraft – He 111 H-3, 1H+CB W.Nr. 5680 of the Stab of I./KG 26 – had occurred on 11 September. That machine revealed white stripes confined to the port side on both the wingtip and the vertical tail surfaces. Given the losses being experienced by the Luftwaffe at this time, it is unlikely that such unusual markings would have escaped the eye of British Intelligence had any been found prior to this date. (Unfortunately, as the battle progressed, Intelligence Officers did not always record the presence of these markings, or, more confusingly, not the complete disposition of such markings, as some photographs show.) This establishes a starting point for the first use of these markings though mass formation raids had been a feature for some time, the largest ever launched having occurred on 1 August.

After that initial massed attack, the few subsequent large-scale raids were spread over a number of targets. It was not until the change in bombing policy, with London's civilian population being targeted, that mass formations again returned to the skies over a single target. It seems logical, therefore, that the markings were introduced to assist with the formation problems that such large forces encounter, and the physical evidence also appears from that date. Timing over the target and turning points required precision, and formations were spread out over vast distances, the raid of 7 September had occupied an air space of about two and a half kilometres high and covered 1,300 square kilometres. The attack came in three waves, starting at a target time of 1800 hours (German Standard Time) for the first formations composed of I. Fliegerkorps with one Kampfgruppe of II. Fliegerkorps. These had been followed at 1840 hours by II. Fliegerkorps, with I. Fliegerkorps five minutes behind them. On the right were KG 30 plus II./KG 76, with KG 1 in the centre and I. and III./ KG 76 on the left. The formation heights had been set at 5,000 to 5,500 metres for KG 30, 6,000 to 6,500 metres for KG 1 and 5,000 to 5,500 metres for KG 76. By stepping the height of the central formation it allowed both of the flanking formations to see each other, as well as providing the central formation with a clear view of the tactical bar markings delineating the two lower formations. That was critical in the run up to the target and also in the process of wheeling about such a huge formation for the return flight. The value of easily discernible formation markings within each of the three parts of the mass formation is obvious. The three major elements of the mass formation were too far apart for the tactical markings to have any value, but the bold bar markings would have been clearly visible within the spread of aircraft contained within each of the three elements, as well as between the elements.

Between such operations the markings had been retained, and in some cases retained long after the end of the mass daylight attacks. A lone Ju 88 A-1 3Z+BB, W.Nr. 4136, of 7./KG 30 was one of two bombers shot down during daylight hours over England on 3 October. Bombing had been heavy and widespread during the previous night (where tactical bar markings were not of any use), but low cloud and drizzle had allowed a few sneak raids by individual aircraft during the day. The Ju 88 had a single white bar marking on the port side of the fin and one on the port wing tip. With daylight massed raids by then over, the marking had little use but had still been retained, pointing to the semi-permanent nature of the lacquer used. Nearly six weeks later, on 15 November, according to the British Intelligence Report in NA (PRO) *Air 266*, the badly mangled wreck of a Do 17 Z yielded up evidence of a large salmon-pink square (sic) on the starboard wing. Photographs show that the aircraft was destroyed almost beyond recognition, so much so that the unit codes could not be deciphered by the Intelligence Officer; but only one Do 17 Z had failed to return from that night attack; F1+BT, W.Nr. 2798 of 9./KG 76. Description of the shape of the marking, judging by photographs of the wreckage, had more to do with the fragmentary remains than a complete marking. The salmon pink colour was probably a product of the heat from the ensuing fire that had darkened the usual pink colouring. Use of pink markings accorded with earlier intelligence reports from 15 September on Do 17 Zs of that Staffel, F1+AT, W.Nr. 2184 and F1+DT, W.Nr. 3322, both of which had worn pink bar markings. The two-month gap between the dates attests to the fact that the lacquer used was definitely not the temporary eight-day life type mentioned earlier.

Physical evidence for how these markings had been allocated is extremely poor, and a summary of aircraft known to have used them is listed here only as a rough guide gleaned from records made from aircraft often badly damaged or partly destroyed, and also from photographic sources; so the range of markings for each type may have been more than recorded.

Date	Type	Code	Unit	Description of marking
15 Sept	Do 17	5K+CM	4./KG 3	pink bar wingtip and rudder.
15 Sept	Do 17	5K+JM	4./KG 3	pink bar wingtip and rudder.
Undated	Do 17	5K+EA	Stab/KG 3	pink bar across starboard fin and rudder.
Undated	Do 17	5K+DH	1./KG 3	pink bar starboard wing.
28 Oct	Do 17	5K+CH	1./KG 3	pink bar on rudder.
15 Sept	Do 17	F1+AT	9./KG 76	two pink bars on fin and rudder.
15 Sept	Do 17	F1+DT	9./KG 76	pink bar port wing and both rudders.
15 Sept and	Do 17	F1+FS	8./KG 76	pink bar on port wing both rudders.
15 Sept	Do 17	F1+FH	1./KG 76	pink bar across port fin and rudder.
6 Oct	Do 17	F1+FN	5./KG 76	pink bar on port wing and rudder.
15 Nov	Do 17	F1+BT	9./KG 76	large salmon-pink square
Undated	He 111	A1+DA	G/Stab KG 53	three vertical pink (?) bars port side of rudder.
Undated	He 111	A1+AB?	Stab I./KG 53	three pink bars port wing plus three vertical pink bars on starboard side rudder (style identical to A1+DA). White spinners. on starboard wing.
Undated	He 111	A1+BT	9./KG 53	three pink bars starboard wing.
Undated	He 111	A1+BY	III./KG 53	three pink bars on rudder

Date	Type	Code	Unit	Description of marking
Undated	He 111	A1+BT	9./KG 53	three pink (?) bars starboard wing.
15 Sept	He 111	A1+AN	5./KG 53	three vertical pink bars on both sides.
15 Sept	He 111	A1+LN	5./KG 53	three vertical pink bars on rudder.
15 Sept	He 111	1H+JH	1./KG 26	three vertical white bars, starboard side only on fin and rudder.
11 Sept	He 111	1H+CB	Stab I./KG 26	two white bars on port wing and rudder
26 Oct	He 111	1H+BL	3./KG 26	yellow stripe on leading edge tail plane
3 Oct	Ju 88	3Z+BB	Stab I./KG 77	white bar on port wing and fin.
18 Sept	Ju 88	3Z+E(D?)	Stab III./KG 77	number of white bars on various parts (sic) of aircraft.
18 Sept	Ju 88	3Z+DT	9./KG77	white bar on wing.
18 Sept	Ju 88	3Z+E(S?)	8./KG 77	white bar on wings (plural). A/c burnt out.
19 Sept	Ju 88	3Z+GH	1./KG 77	white bar port side of fin
Sept	Ju 88	3Z+HN	5./KG 77	white bar port wing and on port side of fin.
3 Oct	Ju 88	3Z+BB	Stab I./KG 77	white band on port wing and fin.

From the above small sample it is possible to discern that Do 17s and He 111s used pink markings (the references to 'white' for some of the He 111 examples in some undated sources results from interpretation of colour from black and white photographic sources, rather than from written accounts, and thus is questionable in view of the other written records for the type). The Ju 88s appear to have been restricted to white, though the latter may simply result from the poor information base. (Equally, with no real evidence of yellow having been employed, the entry for 26 October – He 111 1H+BL of 3./KG 26 – was probably a record of some other form of marking disassociated with the tactical

bar marking system under discussion.) Also, intelligence reports were recording analysis of wreckage, not always entire aircraft, and significant parts of airframes may have been missing, for example, the entries for Ju 88s of 8. and 9. Staffeln listed immediately above. One states a bar on one wing, the other a bar on both wings. Without knowing if both wings were sufficiently intact on both aircraft, the question of whether both had multiple markings is unclear. The analysis however does point to bar markings having been allocated on a Gruppe rather than Staffel basis. With the size of the mass bomber formations it would have been extremely difficult to have generated enough variations for a Staffel-by-Staffel, unit-by-unit basis; especially as Gruppen were employed mixed with others from different units. A further refinement analysis seems to verify this.

Do 17

Stab III./KG 3	single pink bar marking starboard side of fin and rudder.
II./KG 3	single pink bar marking wing tip and rudder.
III./KG 76	single as well as double bar marking both rudders.

He 111

I./KG 26	three vertical white (?) bars starboard side fin and rudder.
Stab/KG 53	three vertical pink (?)bars on rudder
Stab I./KG 53	three vertical pink bars.
II./KG 53	three vertical pink bars both sides of rudder.
III./KG 53	three vertical white bars both sides of rudder.

Ju 88

Stab /KG 77	single white bar port wing and fin.
I./KG 77	single white bar port side of fin.
II./KG 77	single white bar port wing and fin.
III./KG 77	single white bar on wing(s).

From such a limited sample, about all that can be ascertained with any certainty is that combinations of one, two or three bars had been employed on individual aircraft, either in white or pink. On an individual unit basis, KG 3 used single bar markings, KG 76 both single and double bar markings, KG 26 and KG 53 triple bar markings, and KG 77 single bar markings. The single anomaly presented by KG 76 machines, recorded with both single and double bar markings, raises caution about the extent of the bar markings vis a vis a single aircraft type. The fact that so far no evidence of use of two bar marking combinations within the He 111 and Ju 88 forces may simply reflect the paucity of surviving written and photographic records, rather than providing categorical proof that such combinations were not used.

Whether there was any connection between introduction of these bar markings and the sudden shift during the same period from yellow to white for fighter aircraft under the control of Jagdfliegerführer 2, remains enigmatic. The scant evidence for the bomber force points to only those aircraft under the control of Lutflotte 2, (the same HQ formation that controlled Jagdfliegerführer 2 during the same period), using the bar markings.

While the attrition rate and daily tactical changes in use of units would seem to favour temporary lacquer of the eight-day life variety mentioned earlier, the evidence of machines retaining their bar markings weeks after the

ABOVE: The Ju 88 force used vertical bar markings on its tail units, with horizontal bar markings on wings. The aircraft in the background show how well the fin marking stood out at distance. The Ju 88 A in the foreground, 3Z+HN, W.Nr. 7112, was amongst those shot down on the afternoon raid on London on 27 September, 1940. The aircraft's identifying letter 'H' was marked on the outboard section of both wing tips and the white tactical marking had been applied inboard of the Balkenkreuz, presumably so as not to obscure the aircraft identity.

close of the main battle negates this proposition. For practical reasons the markings do not seem to have been changed. (The same would happen when American and later, in limited form, British bomber forces introduced daylight tactical markings for their aircraft.) The existing allocation of markings would have been incorporated into the operational briefing on formation positions, rather than issuing instructions for physically changing individual markings on a daily basis. The latter would have required removal of the existing markings and then re-marking the new combination allocation. Given the number of aircraft in use, and the changing daily tactics involved, this would have presented an unacceptable, if not impractical workload for ground staff already fully engaged in daily maintenance under constant battle conditions. Both would have been time consuming.

The bar markings were applied either with a spray gun, or by brush, using a stencil in both cases. There is clear evidence of a soft film of over-spray on some markings, while others lack this telltale signature but exhibit paint runs at their lower edged in some instances. Depending upon the nature of the lacquer used, removal would have required some form of paint stripper, or over-spraying with the original camouflage colours. The evidence of the Do 17 remains mentioned earlier, where fire had ravaged the wreckage but not destroyed the bar marking (other than shortening of it through destruction of the adjoining panel), points to the lacquer used as being one of fairly permanent composition.

The Balkan Campaign

While the air battle over Britain was the main focus of the Luftwaffe in 1940, other battlefronts had also required the attention of German forces. Germany's Axis partner, Italy, had launched an attack eastwards from Cyrenaica on 13 September 1940. The initial thrust of General Graziani's forces had been halted three days later at Sidi Barrani where the campaign bogged down until the British counter-attack launched on 9 December. That would eventually drive the Italian forces back to El Agheila before being stopped on 8 February 1941.

Hitler had had no particular desire to enter the ground war in North Africa, though in his Directive Nr. 18 of 12 November, he had stated "...*employment of German forces will be considered, if at all, only after the Italians have reached Mersa Matruh.*"

His overall aim was to eliminate British forces from the Mediterranean pending the German assault on Russia. On 10 December, he undertook to send Luftwaffe units to southern Italy, for a limited period only, to assist in attacks on British shipping as it passed between Sicily and North Africa. The Italian Government had been requested to declare the area between Sicily and North Africa closed to avoid incidents with neutral shipping so that anything else could be attacked on sight. He was prepared also to extend its area of operations, if a critical situation developed, to the east as far as the Ionian and Aegean Seas.

To understand what had brought these moves into play we must go back to June 1940 when part of Rumania had been ceded to Russia under pressure from Germany. Further German pressure had resulted in territory being passed to both Hungary and Bulgaria, but at that point Germany had guaranteed Rumanian integrity for its remaining territory, moving some of its ground forces into the country so that the Rumanians could concentrate their forcers around their vital oil fields. This move annoyed Mussolini who felt, under the terms of the Axis agreement, that he should have been informed of Germany's intentions and movements. To show his displeasure he had Italian forces launch an attack on Greece on 28 October, expecting that it would prove to be nothing more than a bloodless action, similar to the German move into the Sudetenland in 1939.

The result was anything but simple, or bloodless. Hitler had been furious because German plans required a united, but pacified Balkans to suit the planned attack on Russia the following year. A week after the Italian attack commenced, and four days after the British occupied Crete

and Lemnos, Hitler had ordered plans for intervention in Greece from Rumania and Bulgaria.

Meanwhile he had been forced to give aid to the faltering Italian forces, who were ill equipped for the fighting, ordering the move of a transport unit to Italy to help provision the Italian ground forces via Albania. III./KG.z.v.B 1, equipped with 48 Ju 52 3ms had moved to Foggia at the end of November. They had remained there, carrying out supply flights to the battlefront until February 1941. It is unlikely that initially the German aircraft had carried any form of tactical marking as their Italian ally did not use any form of distinguishing marking. That had soon changed.

Italian problems protecting their shipping to North Africa had precipitated yet another concession from Hitler with the transfer of X. Fliegerkorps, from Norway to Sicily in December 1940, charged with responsibility for southern Italy, Sicily, south-eastern Sardinia and part of the North African coastline. The mixed force of some 257 Ju 88s, Ju 87s, He 111s, Bf 110s and Ju 52s had adopted a single white band marking, around the around the rear of the fuselage to indicate the Mediterranean Theatre of Operations. This was used both by German and Italian forces, which had required some form of distinctive identification given the presence of Greek and British aircraft in the region.

While the build-up of forces continued to be focused in the Balkans for the forthcoming attack on Greece, X. Fliegerkorps had been ordered to transfer part of its force to North Africa in support of the first German ground offensive, which was to be commanded by General Rommel who had arrived in Tripoli on 10 February. Initially, on 13 February, the entire Ju 87 and Bf 110 components (the Ju 87s of Gerschwader Stab and I./St.G. 1 and II./St.G. 2, plus a Staffel of Bf 110s from III./ZG 26) had transferred to Bir Dufan, some 150 km from Tripoli. The Stukas went into action the next day, St.G.1 losing its first aircraft in the fighting. No additional form of tactical marking, other than of the white fuselage band, had been carried at that stage.

Jugoslavia had avoided being drawn into the Italian-Greek conflict. During late 1940 and into 1941 its Government had negotiated with Germany, and Hitler urged it to sign the Tripartite Pact, promising no German forces would ever transit Jugoslav territory, something finally agreed to in Vienna and signed on the 25 March. The following night a coup d'etat occurred in Belgrade, the Government being replaced by a group that professed to remaining pro-German, but wanted Jugoslavia to remain neutral. Public display of anti-German sentiment did not reassure Hitler and on 23 March and he issued Directive Nr. 25 in which he stated his intention to treat Jugoslavia as hostile, and outlined his plan of attack to be incorporated into the proposed German assault on Greece. German forces would attack towards Belgrade and to the south from the Fiume-Graz area on one side, and from Sofia, in Bulgaria, on the other. The extreme southern portion of Jugoslavia would be cut off and form the base from which the German-Italian offensive in Greece could be continued. Bulgaria and Hungary however, remained reluctant to any attack on Jugoslavia. Three days later several Luftwaffe units had been ordered to transfer to the Balkans where they were to be placed under the control of Luftflotte 4. Some 600 aircraft, comprising five Kampfgruppen (three from France, one from north-west Germany and one from North Africa), six Bf 109 E Gruppen from France, and one Bf 110 Gruppe from north-west Germany were transferred in just 12 days; a most remarkable achievement.

On 3 April a Jugoslav delegation had arrived in Moscow to sign a mutual assistance pact, but instead had signed a "friendship and non-aggression" pact two days later. The following day, 6 April, Operation Marita was launched and German forces attacked Jugoslavia and Greece. Facing the 1,090 Luftwaffe aircraft were some 468 Jugoslav and 80 Greek aircraft. On 17 April Jugoslavia had capitulated; on 25 April German airborne forces attacked the Isthmus of Corinth with a force of 400 aircraft; by 30 April the last British troops had left or surrendered and hostilities in Greece ceased.

Luftwaffe Camouflage and Markings 1933-1945

ABOVE: Operation Marita, the opening of the Balkan campaign, saw a sudden flourish of yellow tactical markings. This Bf 110 D, from the Stab of III. Gruppe wore yellow on its engine cowlings and rudders. It is not possible to determine whether the elevators were also marked in yellow, which was part of the new tactical markings suite. The camouflage was 71/02/65.

LEFT: These two Bf 110 Ds, one from the Stab of I./ZG 76 marked M8+AB with the 'A' in RLM 24 blue, display the same range of tactical markings. Permanent lacquers were used for this purpose by this time. Camouflage was again 71/02 with mottling with both colours. (P. Malone)

RIGHT: The Ju 87s, which proved so valuable in the Balkan campaign of 1941, were also marked with yellow Balkan theatre markings. The full complement of markings can be seen on this formation from St.G. 77.

BELOW: This Do 17 Z was marked with the full set of prescribed tactical markings with yellow applied to engines, rudders and elevators.

campaign. It was that sort of short-term transfer that has lead to some confusion when assessing certain photographic evidence. Use of permanent 7120. lacquer for the application of tactical markings had been introduced either in very late 1940 or early in 1941, which required over painting in camouflage to 'remove' them.

The destruction of roads and facilities in Jugoslavia had thwarted the German schedule for the attack on Crete, which Hitler had directed had to be taken to ensure closure of the eastern end of the Mediterranean to protect the southern flank of the attack into Russia. The delays were finally overcome and Operation Mercury had been finally launched on 20 May, the subsequent savage fighting lasting for six days before the Germans could claim to have crushed all resistance.

While the Jugoslav/Greek offensive had been raging, events had occurred in Iraq in Germany's favour. Rachid Ali had seized power on 3 April, which directly threatened British oil interests in the Middle East; and also had

The campaign had been short and swift, the transfer of the large force of aircraft rapid. The Bf 109 Es from France had retained their existing yellow tactical markings. The remainder of the force had also been marked with yellow, confined to engine cowling, elevators and rudder on all classes of aircraft. For the engine cowling marking, Ju 87s had used the line of the rear edge of the radiator; Bf 110s had marked the yellow back to a similar point, while on Ju 52s, engine cowlings were completely yellow. The variation between the types points to an order that had not dictated precise dimensions.

North Africa and the Mediterranean

The Stukas of the X. Fliegerkorps transferred from El Machina in North Africa to support the offensive had retained their existing white band marking in addition to the yellow tactical markings applied for the new

produced a potential opportunity for the Axis control of oil from Iraq and Persia. In addition, it had offered a second line of assault on Egypt from a new direction for the Axis. Because of the events taking place in Greece and Jugoslavia, only a few He 111s and Bf 110s had been available to support the uprising, the latter operating from Mosul. All Luftwaffe aircraft had their German markings painted out and replaced with Iraqi markings – not exactly within the definition of tactical markings, but unique enough to have the matter recorded in this chapter. By the time that the Crete operation had been completed, the opportunity to support the uprising in strength had slipped away. British troops had occupied Baghdad on 30 May and Rachid Ali fled into exile. British forces had then occupied Syria (part of the Vichy French empire) by 14 July, aircraft from VIII. Fliegerkorps having been using the airfields to support the Iraqi rebels.

Luftwaffe Camouflage and Markings 1933-1945

ABOVE: Ground staff check the damage to the tail wheel of a Bf 110. Judging by the damaged port rudder, the aircraft may have been hit by flak rather than machine gun fire. The yellow tactical colouring to rudders and elevators can be seen, the relatively rough surface of the finish being just visible on the port rudder. The red oxide of the fabric primer can be seen in the damaged area.

ABOVE: The fighter force carried a full range of tactical markings for Operation Marita, as seen on these two 7. Staffel Bf 109 Es of III./JG 77. The same style and size of applications as used during the air fighting over Britain the previous year were used for the fighter force. The camouflage is 71/02 on wings and tail plane with what appears to be a darker colour used for the fuselage, though this is most probably the results of the poor colour balance of the photograph. The unit is known to have added its highly distinctive fuselage side-colouring before moving to the East, and black and white photographs show no clear tonal variation between wing and fuselage colouring.

RIGHT: The interpretation of yellow being applied to the engine cowlings was a mute one with the Ju 88-equipped units. Here the colour had been restricted to a very literal meaning.

274

RIGHT: Of the small number of German aircraft which went to Iraq in 1941, the triangular Iraqi national marking was added beneath the wings in the position normally occupied by the Balkenkreuze. Most of the aircraft still carried their white nose panel marking from the Staffel's previous deployment, along with the all-yellow engine cowlings. The long-range tanks were in 65-colouring with the exposed upper surface nose section matching the wing colouring. (M. Drewes via S. Santos)

BELOW: This overall view shows the positioning of the Iraqi markings on fuselage and vertical tail surfaces. The former comprised a black-edged, green triangle with a red outline 'double diamond on point' marking in the centre. The fin flash was, from the front, green, white, red and black. On this machine the white nose panel marking had been partly worn away. Camouflage on the Staffel's aircraft was standard 71/02/65. (M. Drewes via S. Santos)

Following completion of the Balkan campaign, Luftwaffe fighters stationed in the area had adopted the existing Italian combination of white fuselage band and yellow cowling markings. X.Fliegerkorps forces had returned to Sicily and had been ordered to make their main task the support of the Afrika Korps forces, 150 aircraft being concentrated in North Africa. The subjugation of Malta was to be accelerated (the first small scale German attack had occurred on 9 January) as it threatened supply lines to North Africa, and anti-shipping attacks were to be carried out, some 390 aircraft being moved to Greece, Rhodes and Crete. The latter group had been marked with tactical markings already in use by the Italian force, namely yellow cowling and a white fuselage band. All came under the tactical control of an ad hoc subordinate unit, Fliegerführer Afrika commanded by General Fröhlich.

No official instruction for application of the white band marking on Luftwaffe aircraft has been located, but judging by the dimensions shown on the various types of aircraft, size appears to have been 45 cm wide. This varied, probably for simplicity of application, on some

Bf 109 Es which had used the space between Frames 7 and 8, reducing size to 40 cm. On Bf 110s the band usually had been applied with the leading edge touching the rear edge of the fuselage Balkenkreuz marking but again there were variations with some aircraft marked further aft either between Frames 14 and 15 or Frames 15 and 16, the extreme rear of the fuselage. In a few instances some aircraft of III./ZG 26 had extended the marking from trailing edge of the Balkenkreuz to Frame 15 producing a single band approximately 90 cm wide.

Initially the white band marking had been absent on some Ju 87s, but on others it either was centred squarely behind the fuselage Balkenkreuz, front and rear edges coinciding with the extreme edges of the marking, or immediately aft of the trailing edge of the Balkenkreuz. On the Ju 88s the latter was also the more usual position, though again variations had occurred.

Initially, units operating in North Africa had used just the white band marking, but as the air fighting had increased the area of tactical marking colour had been increased to more rapidly distinguish friend from foe. On the Bf 109 E, white wing tips had been added by painting both upper and lower surfaces inboard for one metre. The range had then been extended with the introduction of the Bf 109 F series

RIGHT: Initially, fighter aircraft operating in North Africa continued to use just the white theatre band, marking around the rear part of the fuselage. This Bf 109 E, 'Red 3' of 2./JG 27, appears to have seen service previously during the fighting over England in the summer of 1940, the worn propeller blades attesting to considerable flying time. The camouflage of 71/02/65 had been slightly modified by using streaky narrow lines of 71 down the side surfaces. There is also evidence that the aircraft had had its original tactical number painted out with 02 and the new number applied over that. The engine cowling appears to have had 71 sprayed over most of its side areas.

LEFT: A Bf 109 F, 'White 7' of 9. Staffel, of an unidentified III. Gruppe stationed in Italy, carries the fuselage white theatre of operations band marking and yellow lower section engine panel colouring of aircraft operating in the Eastern Mediterranean. The camouflage is tropical 78/79 with the spinner divided into one third-white and two-thirds black. The manner in which the 79- camouflage colouring had been carried right down the engine cowling to the exhaust stub line was unusual. The aircraft behind had been painted in the same manner. (E.Mombeek)

BELOW: In the spring of 1943, II./ZG 1 was transferred from the Russian Front to Italy, where it operated between April and July, before transferring to France. Here, S9+AP of 6. Staffel shows its dual tactical markings – the white band of its Italian deployment around the rear section of the fuselage, with the yellow of its former Russian theatre of operations markings on the engine cowlings. Camouflage was standard 74/75/76 with the Staffel colour of yellow on the spinner tips. The striking Wespen emblem was perhaps one of the most colourful used by any Luftwaffe unit. Note the yellow filter on the landing light, a standard fitting for Bf 110s. Behind can be seen an Fw 190 and two Italian training aircraft, minus wings and empennage.

LEFT: Following the end of the campaign in the Balkans, Bf 110s of III./ZG 26 were transferred to the control of X. Fliegerkorps in December 1941, then to Fliegerführer Afrika, making their appearance over the desert in February, the yellow tactical markings of the previous deployment not disappearing immediately, as shown by this aircraft undergoing maintenance. This carry-over of tactical markings (especially where deployments were relatively short) on several types of aircraft has lead to some confusion about specific sets of tactical markings. Camouflage was 71/02/65 with heavy mottling in 71. The Staffel colour appears on the tip of the spinners.

BELOW: Like most of ZG 76's Bf 110s, 3U+ED had the width of its tactical marking extended to allow both of the last two characters of the fuselage code to be displayed. The aircraft also has yellow beneath the engines, having been transferred from the Balkan Front. It retains its European camouflage.

RIGHT; However, once the battle in North Africa became entrenched additional white markings were incorporated, on wing tips and around the front section of the engine, plus the spinner as shown on this Bf 109 F trop. Camouflage was 78/79 and the style strongly indicates that this was a factory-applied scheme. The rudder has two repair patches, doped with red oxide primer paint.

fighters to include a nose band and all-white spinner, but the Bf 109 Es in general had not adopted that change, possibly because the type was being phased out in favour of the newer model, something that had not completely occurred before the North African campaign came to a close. Unit hacks sometimes proved the exception to the general rule as in the case off a Fi 156 C-5 used by II./JG 27, which had a white band marked around the rear section of the fuselage and also the front of the engine.

Introduction of the Bf 109 F also appears to have coincided with production aircraft arriving painted in standard tropical finish (78/79 with no 80 mottling), complete with the extended range of white tactical markings. These comprised a 45 cm wide band around the rear of the fuselage, white spinner with a 30 cm wide band immediately adjoining it, and white wing tips marked on both surfaces inboard to the joint line adjoining the outer edge of the aileron. However variation had occurred even from that stable source, the fuselage band position varying in its precise location as before, and the white 30 cm nose-band sometimes not added. Italian fighters, which fought alongside the Luftwaffe units, appear to have added only the white spinner and 30 cm band marking on the nose of the fuselage to their existing fuselage white band marking, though some, but not all, MC 202s did use wing tip markings.

Bomber and reconnaissance aircraft, like their Italian counterparts, mostly had not adopted the extended range of markings, but some Ju 87s and He 111s in plain 78/79 factory finish did have white wing tip markings, (probably applied at point of production) in addition to the fuselage band marking.

Western Europe

By early 1941, back on the Western Front in Europe, day fighting had become largely a series of skirmishes by each side to probe strength. Luftwaffe fighters stationed along the French, Belgian and Dutch coastlines had retained their bold yellow tactical markings, with the entire engine cowling and rudder in yellow, but applied by then with permanent lacquer. This indicates that by that time the OKL had reached a decision to retain theatre of operations tactical recognition markings permanently, at least outside the Greater Reich Territory. That would change in due course.

The practice continued on the Bf 109 F series, but with the introduction of the G series in mid-1942 the area of yellow on the nose section was reduced to the section directly below the engine, ending on a line with the exhaust stacks. The Fw 190 had entered service with JG 26 in mid-July 1941, but used a similar reduced area of yellow for the engine cowling from the start.

In Holland, in 1941, white had been employed as the tactical colouring for both Bf 109 Es of JG 1 and Bf 110s of ZG 26. Why this sector should have been the subject of such a variation is unexplained, but the dated photographic evidence is unambiguous. It may have related to operational control considerations, though it is difficult to find the rational for that action as fighters to the North, along the Norwegian coast, were also using yellow. As on the French coast, the entire engine cowling had been painted as well as the rudder on the Bf 109 Es, but additionally the wing tips were also painted white on both upper and lower surfaces, extending inboard for one metre, reminiscent of the range of markings employed for Bf 109 Es during the height of the battle over Britain the previous year.

The Russian Front

The attack on the Soviet Union on 22 June 1941 employed large numbers of aircraft transferred from various theatres of operation. Fighters drawn from the Western Front retained their bold all-yellow engine cowling marking along with the yellow rudder, and to those had been added an additional marking in the form of a yellow (04) band around the rear fuselage. Fighter aircraft transferred from German home

ABOVE: Seen in full colour the effectiveness of the yellow tactical colouring against the greys of the contemporary fighter camouflage is clear. The aircraft belonged to an unidentified II. Gruppe based on the Channel coast.

ABOVE: Once the Balkan campaign had been concluded in April 1941, German forces readied for the plunge into Russia. Judging by the background, this Bf 109 F was operating from Balkan territory, windmills not being the sole prerogative of the Dutch countryside. The range of tactical markings had been revised to just yellow below the engine section, plus yellow wing tips and fuselage band. Camouflage was 74/75/76.

ABOVE: The opening thrust into Russia witnessed a carry-over of some of the range of markings adopted for the Balkan campaign. This Bf 109 F of JG 54 was photographed at Siwerskaja. The extent of the yellow was now applied right around the engine cowling, to each wing tip lower surface, and as a band around the fuselage. The 7. Staffel badge appears on the engine cowling with the Gruppe badge below the forward section of the cockpit. The camouflage is interesting, greens being used rather than the contemporary greys, but JG 54 was rarely to be seen in standard camouflage, as described in Volume One of this work.

Tactical and Special Purpose Markings

territory did not have these pre-existing yellow markings and employed only the fuselage band.

As was occurring in North Africa at about the same time, size and positioning varied from unit to unit. III./JG 53 used a band (and an all-yellow engine cowling) that extended from the rear-most edge of the Balkenkreuz marking aft to Frame 8 with its distinguishing jacking hole. 1./JG 53 and III./JG 51 used the section between Frames 7 and 8; the Stab and I./JG 3 employed a standard 45 cm band with its edge touching the rear edge of the Balkenkreuz marking; II./JG 54 placed its yellow band directly behind the Balkenkreuz marking with a narrow section protruding either side indicating a 90 cm wide band behind the standard 880 mm wide national marking. The Stab of JG 52 positioned its band marking immediately forward of the Balkenkreuz marking, touching its leading edge, a position also used by III./JG 54. However other aircraft within III./JG 54 used the aft-most position between Frames 7 and 8. By the following summer, Bf 109 Fs of I./JG 53 were seen using the very wide band noted on III./JG 53 the previous

ABOVE: This Bf 109 F-4, the mount of the Gruppen Adjutant of II./JG 53, had yellow over the engine cowling forward of the wing and yellow as a wide band aft of the Balkenkreuz. The positioning and width of the latter would vary from unit to unit and, as time passed and fortunes changed, it would be reduced in prominence. (H. Obert)

ABOVE: Another Bf 109 F-2 of JG 53, photographed during the first winter of the Russian campaign. Temporary white finish had obscured the upper area of the extensive yellow tactical colouring of the engine cowling, but the broad yellow band marking was left untouched.

ABOVE: Several Bf 110 Fs joined the Stab of I./St.G 1 on the Russian Front in 1941. These two, A5+HB and A5+EB nearest the camera, had their individual letter marked with blue for the Stab status. A wide yellow band was marked around the rear of each fuselage and below the wing tips of both aircraft. (F. Smith)

summer, while I./JG 52 aircraft were by then wearing their band immediately behind the Balkenkreuz marking.

The extent of the all-yellow engine cowling colouring also varied, though usually between two alternatives, both of which were noted on Bf 109 Fs of JG 52. One form had its rear edge in a vertical line at the end of the exhaust stack; the other extended back to the rear edge of the cowling producing a stepped vertical line.

Bombers, ground-attack aircraft, reconnaissance aircraft, seaplanes and transports also had been marked with the 90 cm wide fuselage band and wing tip lower surfaces in yellow. Again wide variation had occurred in the placement of the fuselage band, and size had also varied. No definite size also appears to have been set for the wing tip marking resulting in much variation, not just between units but also within them.

Initially few, if any, of the fighters had used the yellow marking on the lower surface of the wing tip, but that had changed by the first winter for much the same reasons that it occurred in North Africa – intensity of air fighting. The Bf 110-equipped units had used the same range of tactical markings as the single-engine fighter force, but appear to have marked their wing tip lower surfaces in yellow from the outset in accord with the directive applying to non-fighter types.

When Fw 190s had begun arriving in numbers, they followed the same erratic pattern of positioning for the fuselage band marking as had occurred with other types, but the coloured panel below the engine cowling was consistent as on the Bf 109.

By early 1943 the yellow rudder marking on the Fw 190 had been reduced in size, confined to the lower section with its upper extent on a line with the elevators. This no doubt had a direct relationship to the heavy counter offensive by Soviet forces, in as much as more care was being exercised with camouflage when seen from above and anything that compromised it was eliminated. To that end some units also sprayed over the upper portion of the tactical band marking along the spine of the aircraft.

ABOVE: This Bf 109 G, 'White 10' of 1. Staffel of an unidentified unit wears the 900 mm-wide yellow band around the fuselage, and tactical colouring to the engine bottom cowling. Camouflage is standard 75/75/76 with mottling in both colours to the fuselage side surfaces in almost perfect interpretation of the RLM-approved camouflage drawing for the type.

ABOVE: This view of 'White 5', from the same unit as the aircraft shown in the photograph above shows that the yellow tactical colouring was also applied beneath the wing tips. The division of the spinner into white and black was standard for the period.

Occupation of the Free French zone

On 11 November 1942, in response to the Allied landings in Algeria, Operation Anton (changed in May 1942 from its original name of Operation Attila in the contingency planning OKW Directive 19 of 1940) was launched as German forces occupied the Free French zone of metropolitan France that, until then, had been under the control of the Vichy regime. Little information has been found regarding the temporary tactical markings employed for this brief operation, but the following data has been compiled from the photographic evidence.

White band markings were marked chord-wise around the wings and a white band added to the rear section of the fuselage on some types, bomber, fighter and reconnaissance forces all being used during the action. The only fighter forces were the Fw 190s of the Stab, I. and III. Gruppen of JG 2 and 10.(Jabo)/JG 26 plus (at least on the basis of the photographic evidence) 3./JG 53 equipped with Bf 109 Gs. On these machines the wing and fuselage band markings were used, the former being applied so that they touched the outboard edge of the Balkenkreuz marking on the wing lower surface. That produced a small gap between the band and Balkenkreuz marking on the upper surface due to the regulation location of the national marking. Position of the fuselage band varied; on some of the Fw 190s it was marked hard up against the empennage join line and even followed the slight slope with the rear-most face in some instances. As both units had been serving on the Channel coast, they had been marked with the standard yellow 04 tactical colouring as a panel beneath the engine, and on the rudder. From the scant photographic evidence it appears that the yellow markings were retained when the new tactical markings were added, at least two Fw 190s exhibiting both sets of markings. The fact that the operation was intended to be of very short duration may explain that anomaly, though some of the fighter aircraft were

ABOVE: Aircraft operating in the support of the German occupation of Vichy France, Operation Anton, were identified by a white band around each wing and by a white band around the fuselage. This Fw 190 was photographed after landing at one of the Vichy French Air Force bases. (F. Grabowski)

ABOVE: A pair of Bf 109 Gs of 3./JG 53 preparing for take off on Operation Anton as German forces occupied the Free French zone of France. They wear white bands around wings and fuselage. 'Yellow 10' is in the background. The nearer aircraft still retains its rudder's yellow colouring. (S. Santos)

intended to move on to deployment in the Tunisian campaign on completion of Operation Anton.

One of only two known photographs of Bf 109s used in this operation shows the fuselage band applied to the last section of the fuselage. This machine also had a white spinner and white rudder and is thought to have belonged to 2./NAGr. 16, which, with the Ju 88 Ds of 1.(F)/33, were the only reconnaissance aircraft employed for the operation. NAGr. 16 had a mixture of Bf 109s, Hs 126s and Fw 189s at the time, but it is not known if either of the latter type was used for the operation.

Two of the identifiable examples of Fw 190s of 2./JG 2, show small numerals, approximately the height of the cross 'bar' of the fuselage Balkenkreuz marking, but this appears to have been a peculiarity of JG 2 and not related to Operation Anton.

On some, if not all the machines of the bomber force employed for the occupation, the band marking was used right around each wing, as the accompanying photographs of the Do 217 Es of KG 2 confirm. These aircraft also employed white for the lower half of each engine cowling as well as the fuselage band marking. Close examination of those photographs, highly enlarged, shows that unlike the Fw 190s and Bf 109s the band was painted centrally across the Balkenkreuz markings on wing upper and lower surfaces no doubt to make the nationality marking even more visible. The application in some instances appears to have been done with less care than usual, probably reflecting the haste with which the bands were painted for this surprise operation.

The width of the fuselage band on the wings of the fighter aircraft appears to have been about a half metre. This was a fairly standard

RIGHT: The bomber force was also marked in the same manner. This formation of Do 217 Es from KG 2 carry the markings adopted for Operation Anton. U5+BP of 6. Staffel and U5+CP of 7.Staffel each have a white band around each wing, as well as a band around the fuselage and white lower panels to each engine. Aircraft 'C' has the last group of its codes repeated on the fin.

LEFT: Being manhandled into position, this close-up view of U5+LS of 8./KG 2 allows more detailed study of the special markings. The band on the wing, centred over the underwing Balkenkreuz , had been with a sprayed application, the curve of the leading edge, no doubt because of its difficult shape, being done by brush. The engine panel in white was also a sprayed application. The last two digits of the aircraft's Werknummer, '62' had been stencilled on the nose section, something usually done at point of manufacture. The last two letters of the code group appear on the fin. The Hakenkreuz is difficult to see, being just an outline form that had been lightly over sprayed. The long metal wheel steering arm, being use don the tail wheel, was painted red and white.

measurement for this type of marking, though, as with many forms of tactical band markings, dimensions were often matched to a convenient structural element of approximately the same lateral dimension e.g., on a Bf 109, the width of the relative fuselage panel. For the larger, bomber aircraft the dimensions appear to be approximately double those used for the fighter aircraft.

For how long these markings were retained is not known, but at least one Fw 190 of II./JG 2 that subsequently transited on to the Tunisian campaign did retain the markings – at least temporarily. Given the hectic nature of that campaign it is not surprising that the markings were not obliterated more swiftly. By this stage of the war, tactical markings were normally applied with permanent lacquer, only brief campaign deployments usually providing the exception. In this instance however, it appears that the white band markings used standard lacquer – and that may also explain the reason why they had not been swiftly eliminated – a job that would have required painting them out with the appropriate range of camouflage colours.

ABOVE: Just visible in this photograph of 'White 3' of 7./JG 1, taken in late 1943, is the Reichsverteidigung band adopted by fighter forces engaged in the defence of the Reich. By early 1944 most fighter units would have their own individual set of Reichsverteidigung markings. The spinner on this Bf 109 G-6 was white at the front, with the rear section divided into two-thirds black and one-third yellow, reflecting both Gruppe and Staffel colouring.

The choice of white markings appears to have been dictated by the move south towards the Mediterranean theatre, where that was the current tactical marking colour. The ad hoc collection of markings, used for the occupation, appear simply to have been a short term expedient to prevent any possible confusion with the Vichy aircraft that may have opposed the action. Once permanently in place, Luftwaffe forces then adopted the standard tactical markings of the adjoining Luftwaffe commands that took control of the newly occupied areas.

Defence of the Reich intensifies

In the Reich, the intensity of air operations had increased dramatically by 1943 to counter increasing USAAF daylight bombing. JG 1, with its mixed force of Fw 190s and Bf 109s was ranged across the approaches from the North Sea through Holland and along the edge of the Ruhr.

There is no evidence of the source of the authority for adoption of any special form of marking, but in March, IV./JG 1 had begun marking the engine cowling of its Fw 190s all white other than for the standard tactical marking of a yellow panel below the engine. The earliest confirmed use was by 10. Staffel, but that may simply be a result of the fragmentary photograph evidence. This was an effective form of air-to-air recognition, especially with the mêlée that inevitably accompanied attacks against the American daylight formations.

On 1 April, JG 1 had been split to form a new Jagdstaffel; I. and III./JG 1 became, respectively, II. and I./JG 11, while IV./JG 1 was renumbered I/.JG 1. In May, a new III./JG 1, equipped with Bf 109s, had been formed at Leeuwarden. That change had been accompanied by adoption of distinctive cowling markings by the Geschwader and Gruppe Stab aircraft of JG 1, the white cowling marking obviously having been a success. The new Stab marking was distinguished by adoption of horizontal black stripes over the white background.

The former IV./JG 1 aircraft had retained their white cowl colouring after being re-designated I. Gruppe, and there is some photographic evidence that the practice was extended to the other Staffeln of the Gruppe; aircraft belonging to both 3. and 5. Staffeln also were recorded with white cowlings. Whether it was intended to expand this to a system of cowling colouring to match Staffel colouring (a logical enough process as a rapid recognition marking) is unclear. To confuse the matter, a photograph of a Fw 190 ('White 7' of 1. Staffel), appears to show an all yellow cowling. The possibility is that it was a 3. Staffel aircraft transferred to 1. Staffel; the 'White 7' marking had been applied over a patch of dark colour used to obliterate a previous marking. If so, then a possible re-painting the cowling had not taken place at the time the photograph was taken.

A further modification of the Staffel markings appears to have taken place in June 1943 with the adoption of a combination of Staffel colour and black cheques, of equal size, to replace the solid colour. Here the photographic evidence is more fruitful, photographs showing white and black, red and black and yellow and black in use.

ABOVE: The first form of tactical marking adopted for the home defence force – the Reichsvertiedigung – took the form of a wide red band. The exact size varied slightly, especially with some units equipped with Fw 190s where the angled frame line at the rear of the fuselage was used as an edge, as shown here in May 1944 on this Fw 190 A-8 of 6./JG 1 based at Störmede. (E. Mombeek).

RIGHT: A pair of Fw 190 A-4s of 1./JG 1 photographed at Deelen in the late spring of 1943, showing the white engine cowling marking adopted by the Staffel. The darker panel beneath the engine cowling was painted in the tactical yellow 04-colouring. (E. Mombeek)

LEFT: The striped engine markings in black and white were resurrected by 1./JG 1 at the same time as adoption of a red Reichsverteidigung band marking was introduced for fighter forces defending the Reich. This Fw 190 A-6 shows also that the yellow tactical marking beneath the engine cowling was also retained. Note also the white spinner with a narrow black spiral.

BELOW: The black and white-striped cowling markings adopted by I./JG 1 are seen here on one of the Gruppenstab Fw 190 A-4s at Deelen in April 1943; note that the yellow tactical marking beneath the engine was not compromised by the unit marking. The black and white bands were colour reversed on some aircraft. (E. Mombeek)

RIGHT: Fw 190 A-4, 'White 4', W.Nr. 0601, of 1./JG 1 shows the chequerboard-style of marking in black and white that was adopted by the unit. This accident happened on 25 June 1943 and thus provides a positive time marker for the markings. Note that the white areas of the fuselage Balkenkreuz marking had been toned down with a light over spray. Camouflage was 74/75/76 with a yellow 04 panel beneath the engine cowling area. (E. Mombeek)

ABOVE: Another accident to a JG 1 Fw 190 A-4, this time around the end of June or early July. Note that the black and white chequerboard pattern is reversed in sequence to the one shown in the previous photograph. The marking of a 'Yellow 6' on what was a 1. Staffel aircraft may have resulted from this aircraft being on transfer to 3. Staffel when the accident occurred. The front of the engine cowling ring had been left in the upper surface camouflage colour of 75. (E. Mombeek)

RIGHT: The red and black chequerboard pattern of 2./JG 1, is illustrated by these two aircraft, 'Black 2' and '3', in the early summer of 1943. (E. Mombeek)

While of consistent size the cheques were not always marked in the same sequence, colours being reversed on some aircraft. This probably arose simply from where the sequence was started when the ground staff commenced painting the cowlings. Following a tragic confusion with American P-47s, using similar coloured cowling markings, the cheques were dropped, the last known positive sighting being a photograph taken on 20 October 1943. The marking had then been replaced by adoption of the Stab marking of black stripes on a white cowling. Staffel identification had then reverted to the long-standing practice of painting the spinner in the appropriate colour. This appears to have taken place around November or December 1943. It did not last long though, any evidence for the stripes having disappeared around February 1944.

During that same period the Fw 190s of II./JG 1, and the Bf 109s of III./JG 1, had not adopted any specialised form of air-to-air recognition marking other than the standard yellow panel beneath the engine cowling common to all Luftwaffe aircraft on the Western Front. That appears to indicate that the other markings had been initiated at unit level, and not on authority from OKL.

It was to be common to aircraft defending the Reich, but only to those units along the northern approaches from England and the southern approaches through Italy.

A general defence of the Reich recognition marking of a wide red band (scaling suggests about 90 cm) had begun to appear in mid-1943 on Bf 109s of II./JG 11 (the former I./JG 1 based along the north German coast). Evidence for it on JG 1 aircraft however does not appear in the photographic record until November. At that time III. Gruppe was still based in Holland, (remaining at Volkel until February 1944). It did not appear until December on I. Gruppe; and then only until around February 1944, in combination with the white cowlings with black horizontal stripes. Deletion of the distinctive cowling markings may have been because the total combination compromised the camouflage of the aircraft too much. By then daylight air attacks on German occupied airfields had become increasingly serious; even draping full camouflage netting over the dispersed aircraft was proving less effective. The size and bright colouring of the Fw 190 cowlings may have proved too much of a risk.

Looking at locations of the various Staffeln of I. and II. Gruppen during that period, and comparing the timing of when each had adopted the red band marking, evidence points to the marking having been introduced on a Jagddivision basis. I. Jagdkorps covered all of Germany, north into Denmark, and west into Holland as far as the Belgian/French border at the north coast. The northern sectors were divided into 1., 2. and 3. Jagddivision and the band marking had been first introduced for the German sector, 2. Jagddivision (Jafü 2). By late 1943 the marking system had been extended west into 3. Jagddivison's (Jafü 3) sector that covered Holland and part of Belgium. Used in combination with the standard yellow panel beneath the engine cowlings, it had become the OKL's standard rapid identification marking; unit-developed markings were soon to prove a thing of the past.

To the south, Austria had by then become the other main entry point into Germany for daylight bombing attacks. The red band marking had been adopted by fighters of Jafü Ostmark, a subordinate command to 7. Jagddivision and II./JG 53, stationed at Wien-Seyring airfield, has been positively identified as using the marking in the autumn of 1943, though adoption of it may have coincided with its introduction in the northern German defence area.

Caution however needs to be taken in assessing distribution; II. and III./JG 53, wearing the red marking, were recorded at Hustedt in late summer 1944, but at the time were on transfer for rest and refitting. The movement of units did not always mean that such markings were immediately removed.

At the beginning of 1944 a white band marking had been introduced for both single and twin-engine day fighters within the 1. Jagddivision (Jafü 1) area of command. However, before pursuing developments that flowed from the introduction of fuselage band markings of different colours, it is necessary to pause for the moment and make a small detour back in time to explain an overlapping form of a more specialised marking, which ended up mixed with the band marking.

White empennage markings

In response to the confused and heavy air fighting, formation leaders found that they required something to rapidly identify them (and we have seen how JG 1 handled that need on a single Gruppe initiative). A broader scale approach, initiated by the RLM, had taken the form of white applied to the tail surfaces (usually from Frame 8 aft on Bf 109s, or the fuselage/tail section joint line of the Fw 190) on some single-engine day fighters.

The primary enigma attached to these markings is what distinction, if any, applied between the various sizes of Gruppe or Staffel formations. Some references suggest that the vertical tail surfaces of the aircraft of the Gruppenkommandeur were painted white up to a point just forward of the tail plane; the aircraft of the Staffelkapitan white only on the fin above the horizontal tail surfaces as well as the rudder, while the aircraft of the Schwarmführer used only a white rudder.

The scant photographic evidence however does not tally precisely with this breakdown. The tail unit of the aircraft used by Hermann Graf, while serving as Gruppenkommandeur of Jagdgruppe 50 on 6 September 1943, shows an all-white tail section forward to Frame 8 on his Bf 109 G. Taken the same day, of the same unit, is a similar photograph of Alfred Grislawski's Bf 109 G that shows enough to establish that the same section of the aircraft was painted white. With only one Gruppenkommandeur possible it would appear to invalidate the distinctions listed above.

However, ULTRA intercept VL 6122, dated 12 February 1944, does give clearer insight into those markings. [1]

> FURTHER TO CAMOUFLAGE RULES IN VL & VL FIVE NINE FOUR FIVE.) ADDITIONAL ORDERS OF TENTH FOR UNITS OPERATING IN DEFENCE OF THE REICH & REICH COLON ABLE. BAND BEHIND FUSELAGE TO REMAIN AS MARKING OF INDIVIDUAL GESCHWADER & GESCHWADER. BAKER. IN PRINCIPLE ALL KOMMODORE & KOMMODORE AND KOMMANDEURE & KOMMANDEURE FLY WITH WHITE FINS AND RUDDERS. CHARLIE. ALL FIGHTER AIRCRAFT OF LUFTFLOTTE THREE AND REICH & REICH TO HAVE BLACK AND WHITE SPIRALS TURNING IN SAME DIRECTION AS SPINNER, WIDTH ONE FIFTH OF DIAMETER OF SPINNER.[i]

This confirms that both a distinctive band marking and the white tail marking were used together. (The reference to the band marking will be dealt with later in the text.) It also explains the Graf/Grislawski duplication of markings. Often, as in this case, markings directives restated existing practices when adding further to them, in this case the spiral marking).

The earliest known example of the specialised marking appear in photographs of Heinz Knoke's Bf 109 G, taken around July 1943 when he was Staffelkäpitan of 5./JG 11. They show the white area restricted to the fin above the tail plane plus the rudder.

---

i VL 5945 was the intelligence decode message referring to changes in camouflage made by individual fighter and heavy fighter units. See Chapter 5 of Volume One of this work. Terms ABLE and BAKER were simply points 'a' and 'b'. Luftflotte 3 was part of I. Jagdkorps and covered western Belgium and all of northern France. Because Telex machines used only capital letters, with no additional keys for underlining or hyphens, repeating a word and use of a & sign, was a form of 'underlining' for emphasis.

ABOVE: A Fw 190 A-5, marked < - + - , from the Geschwaderstab of JG 1 that crash landed on 27 September 1943. The fin and rudder were painted white, only the square around the Hakenkreuz marking having been masked out when this was done. (E. Mombeek)

RIGHT: Lt. Berger of 1./JG 1 in front of the damaged rudder of Fw 190, W.Nr. 340016. The entire tail section of the aircraft had been painted white, illustrating the confusing nature of the evidence for this form of tail marking. It is possible that the aircraft was not Berger's usual machine; presence of a white band around the fuselage combined with the all-white tail plane was normally reserved for aircraft flown by a Gruppenkommandeur or Geschwaderkommodore.

ABOVE: The Bf 109 G-6, W.Nr.162764, relating to the incident in Switzerland on 29 March 1944 described in the text. The unusual, somewhat carelessly applied temporary overall finish of the aircraft can be seen, as well as the very dark areas of the lower parts of the fuselage. The white fin and rudder assembly is also evident, the slightly ragged application around the Hakenkreuz being visible. (JaPo)

The unexpected arrival of Bf 109 G-6, W.Nr. 162764, still wearing its Stammkennzeichen of RU+OZ, in Switzerland on 29 March 1944 provides some extra information about the actual application of some white tail markings. A combination of bad weather and low fuel had forced the pilot to land the aircraft at Samaden, near St. Moritz, during what had been a ferry flight from Erding to Osoppo airfield in north eastern Italy. Osoppo was a Platzkommando of Fliegerhorst-kommandanteur E 2 13/VII (Udine) and also the site of Flugleitstelle Osoppo that mainly served as a control centre for aircraft entering and leaving north eastern Italy. [2]

The aircraft had an overall finish in what appears to be temporary winter white applied to all upper surfaces – a very thin application that did not cover parts of the fuselage above the wing root or near the tail plane, nor the air intake on the engine cowling. The thinness gave the finish a distinctly off-white appearance. The lower area of the fuselage colouring was quite dark, as was the exposed area around the cockpit, which closely matched the 66-colouring of the canopy frame. The interesting feature was that fin and rudder had been painted in permanent white lacquer, the white having been sprayed fairly carelessly around the Hakenkreuz marking, obscuring the edge in places. The Werknummer had been stencilled in black on the rear fuselage, just forward of the horizontal tail plane, with the Überführungskennzeichen marking applied over it. The heavy exhaust staining showed that the aircraft had already accumulated some flying time, or had an over rich engine setting.

The fact that the flight had originated at Erding may explain some of the additions, since it was the home of a large Luftwaffe servicing depot. It is likely that the temporary white finish had been added there, along with the white tail markings. Other than applying standard theatre of operations markings (a norm from 1941 onwards), additional special markings were not the usual remit of aircraft manufacturing centres. The white band marking would have been applied at Regensburg. Erding was on the route to Italy and a logical location for the additional work, that centre having carried out many modifications from 1941 onwards for aircraft moving to Italy and North Africa.

A photograph of the tail unit of Anton Hackl's Fw 190 A, when he was serving as the Gruppenkommandeur of III./JG 11 in March 1944, again shows white restricted to the fin, above the horizontal tail plane, and the rudder. In this instance the white paint had been sprayed over the fin completely obscuring the Hakenkreuz, though it could still be detected at close range, indicative of the thinness of the white coat of lacquer. This marking, and the time frame, accords with the directive stated above. Photographs of Ernst Düllberg's Bf 109 G, taken at Wiesbaden-Erbenheim in Marz 1944 when Kommandeur of III./JG 27, again show white applied to the same areas; but the Hakenkreuz had been carefully masked out.

An undated photograph of Hptm. Friedrich Eberle's Fw 190 A-3 W.Nr. 518, 'White 1', taken when he was Staffelkäpitan of 10./JG 1, shows an all white tail plane marked forward to the fuselage join line. This probably pre-dates the issue of the directive quoted above, which reserved such extensive markings for only Kommodore and Kommandeure. Use by a lesser-ranked officer of such a distinctive marking (and there wcre other examples at this time) had probably brought the style of extensive marking to the attention of the RLM or OKL. Note the directive in the ULTRA decode of 12 February 1944 stated "*in principle*", thus leaving some leeway and indicating that the matter had not been finally resolved. The indecision may have indicated a move towards a more exclusive use of the marking.

A further dated example was that of Oblt. Klöpper, Staffelkäpitan of 7./JG 1, who had been forced to crash-land after the air fighting on 13 November 1943. Photographs of his Bf 109 G-6 show that the white was restricted to the fin above the tail plane and the rudder, (his aircraft also carried a red band immediately forward of the tail plane.) This matched Hackl's and Eberle's machines and status.

ABOVE AND BELOW: Oblt. Klöpper's Bf 109 G-6, 'White 1', W.Nr. 20272 of 7./JG 1, photographed after his crash landing on 13 November 1943. The entire tail unit was painted white. (E. Mombeek)

From these few examples it would appear that definition of who used the white tail marking was not as clearly defined as previously thought. What the dated photographs do establish is that the white tail markings were in use in Germany and on the Western front from July 1943 to March 1944, for Gruppe and Staffel leader aircraft. Logic points to the possibility of the time frame being extended at both ends, though by how much has not been established. The variation between the areas of white seems to have been more one of unit interpretation rather than two distinct forms meant to identify Gruppenkommandeur from Staffelkapitan.

There appears to be some evidence to corroborate use of white for the rudder of aircraft used by a Schwarmführer, though the sample base is much smaller. A photograph of Ofw. Herbert Rollwage's aircraft, a Schwarmführer with II./JG 53, clearly shows a white rudder. At the time there were 47 kills marked on it, the last one scored on 10 July 1943. Rollwage was wounded shortly after, which provides a fairly accurate timing for the photograph. A photograph of another Bf 109 G-6 of JG 53, a 6. Staffel aircraft flown by Schwarmführer and 'Experte' Ofw. Rudolf Ehrenberger, again clearly shows an all-white rudder, this time marked with 48 kills. The date was February 1944 when the unit was based in Austria at Wien-Seyring. In between those two dates is an example from November 1943 when 6./JG 27 were stationed at Wiesbaden-Erbenheim. Lt. Willi Kientsch, the Staffelführer, had the all-white rudder marking on his Bf 109 G-6, which carried also 42 victories.

The earliest date coincides with the use of the all white marking discussed earlier but, in the light of the distinction made in the ULTRA decode quoted earlier, how long it continued is not clear. Possibly it was phased out at the same time the white fin and rudder combination was eliminated.

Whatever the scope of its use, the marking had been employed at least by JG 1, JG 11, JG 26, JG 27, JG 52, JG 53 and J.Gr. 50. Some anecdotal evidence indicates that that form, if not colour, of marking for Gruppe or Staffel leader continued after the white markings appear to disappear from the record. Willi Heilmann, in his personal account of service with 10./JG 54 [3], makes reference to the 'Oberstleutnant's Fw 190' having a red painted tail unit, early in 1945. Retention of that singularly distinctive form of marking for the formation leader may only have been a unit initiative since there appears to be no photographic evidence to support a wider use; but that cannot be taken as irrefutable evidence.

The origins of that form of air-to-air rapid identification system were not new. A similar type, plus wing tip colouring, had appeared pre-war on a Bf 109 E of 6./JG 26 at Düsseldorf. The photograph, dated 10 August 1939, was taken during the last war games. Another photograph recorded an all-yellow tail plane, on a Bf 109 E of 1./JG 53, with both vertical and horizontal surfaces marked right up to Frame 8. Dating is uncertain, but appeared to be the second half of 1939, just before war broke out, so may have been related to the same last round of war games. The value of that form of marking obviously had not been discarded. Use of such rapid recognition markings on an aircraft not belonging to the Stab of the relative unit illustrates that the intention, at that time, was for a more broad-based application. As such it provides an interesting insight into the possible origin of both the tail markings and the more widely used wing tip markings employed during the 1940 campaign against Britain.

Expansion of the band marking system

To return to the discourse on the use of band markings, the original red marking had been employed as a general air-to-air rapid recognition marking of elements of the day fighter defence force. That system appears to have been expanded at the commencement of 1944, coinciding with the creation of Luftflotte Reich on 1 January, which had taken over responsibility for the Reichsverteidigung (the defence of the Reich).

The unified control had been created in response to the intensifying daylight bombing attacks, against which it had become necessary to

marshal greater formations of fighter units before launching a concerted attack against bomber streams (just as the RAF had had to do in 1940). A mass fighter formation was assembled over a convenient geographical point then vectored onto the enemy bomber formation, often more than one massed force being employed during the course of the battle. On the cusp of the change two new band markings had come into existence, however unlike the white marking, the second was, for the first time, unit specific.

ABOVE: Photographed during the winter of 1943/1944, 'Black 3' outlined in Red of 2./JG 1 displays its very visually effective, black and white striped engine cowling. (E. Mombeek)

At Dortmund on 1 January 1944, Sturmstaffel 1, (a special attack unit that had been created in October 1943), had 14 modified Fw 190s on strength. Each had been marked with a 90 cm fuselage band, divided equally into black/white/black, around the rear of the fuselage. The unit mounted its first operation on 5 January in concert with I./JG 1 (with whom it shared the airfield at Dortmund), and II./JG 27. This provides a conclusive instance of a unit specific band marking being employed in concert with the general red band marking in the same area, for the same operation by different units. Adoption of the distinctive band marking was probably a factor of the radical tactics being tested by that specialist unit as there is no evidence of any other unit specific markings from that early period.

The area of use of the white band marking needs examination as it confirms the general findings. The earliest photographic record occurs on the Bf 109 Gs of 7. and 9./JG 3 at Bad Wörishofen, 45 km to the south west of Augsburg, close to the Austrian/Swiss border. The Me 410s of ZG 26 also carried the marking, at least from around summer of that

year, when the Stab, I. and II. Gruppen were based at Königsberg-Neumark on the Baltic coast, on the eastern shore of the Gulf of Danzig.

With the Allied invasion of France in June, Luftwaffe fighter defences had been caught at low strength, II. Jagdkorps having only Stab and I./JG 2 plus Stab, I. and III./JG 26 to meet the onslaught. Some 200 additional single-engine fighters were flown into the area from Germany within the first 36 hours, followed by another 100 by 10 June, most having been taken from the northern defence sector of Germany. That emergency had temporarily shifted the focus away from the defence of the Reich, which in April had consisted of approximately 50 per cent of the single-engine day fighter aircraft, plus some 110 twin-engine day fighters – in all about 55 per cent of the Luftwaffe's entire day fighter force. The day before the Invasion the figure was slightly lower but still in stark contrast to approximately 170 fighters available for the defence of France and Belgium. The resultant rapid transfer of units had left only about 370 fighters for the Reichsverteidigung, of which approximately one third were based in the south to counter daylight bombing attacks on the oil industry.

The rapid transfers also had caused some random distribution of the band marking colours, producing a mixture that was never intended under the original system and allowing little or no time to remove existing tactical colour markings. However, some Allied intelligence reports ensuing from the new battlefront provide some additional evidence of the next stages of development of the band system.

Two significant references appeared in an October report [4] of Allied intelligence summaries of German aircraft abandoned in the wake of the invasion of France. Two III. Gruppe Bf 109 G-6, W.Nr. 163312 and W.Nr. 412736, respectively marked 'Black 2' and 'Black 12', had been found abandoned at the airfield at St. Andre-de-L'Eure, west of Paris. Each had a green band around the rear of the fuselage. The description was clear and the coloured bands had been distinctive enough to warrant specific mention by the Intelligence Officer in the wake of some 200 aircraft that had been examined in the previous week.

In fact both had been damaged and abandoned in August; the airfield where they were found had a range of damaged aircraft of various types, possibly signifying that it was, or had been, used as a salvage area for aircraft destined for repair. It would appear that the two aircraft had belonged to III./JG 27, that unit having transferred from Szombathely, almost due south of Wien and just over the border into Hungary. The Gruppe was designated Jafü Hungary, forming part of Luftflotte 4 which also controlled Jafü Ostmark. The latter comprised Stab, I. and II./JG 27 based in Austria, plus I./JG 302 and 7./JG 26 also in Austria, and Eins. Sta./JG 108 based at Voslau in Hungary. That same month, at Fels-am-Wagram in Austria, the Bf 109 Gs of II./JG 27 had been recorded in a colour photograph wearing what appears to be a green band of approximately 60 cm width around the rear of the fuselage. Collectively,

LEFT: On delivery to a front line unit, replacement aircraft required both their individual number and any relevant tactical markings to be applied as shown by this photograph (note also the stencil on the tail plane, used for the '7' marking). More importantly, it provides reliable evidence of a reasonably narrow time band for application of a white band marking. This Bf 109 G-6, W.Nr. 440117, was delivered to III./JG 3 at Bad Wörishofen early in 1944 and assigned to 9. Staffel. It was subsequently destroyed in a crash landing after intercepting some B-24s on 12 April 1944; so the photograph must have been taken prior to that date – and the snow points to March rather than April, and possibly even earlier. Camouflage is standard 74/75/76. The bucket seat section of the pilot's seat can be seen on the ground; a mechanic doing some small maintenance job to the interior of the cockpit.

Fw 190 A8/R8, W.Nr. 682204, 'Red 1' of 5./JG 300 in camouflage of 75/76 with heavy mottling in soft sprays of 75. Photographed in the winter of 1944, it wears the original style of Reichsverteidigung red band applied to the home defence force, however some controversy exists over the term 'red' in relation to this unit. Black and white film does not allow a conclusion as to whether this band was red or 'rusty-red' in colour. Eventually JG 300 would be allocated a blue/white/blue combination of bands.

the timing and origins would seem to corroborate the introduction of a green band marking by August 1944, at least on aircraft of JG 27.

A second intelligence report, concerning two JG 301 Bf 109 G-6/U2 Wilde Sau night fighters of 3./JG 301 that had landed by mistake at RAF Manston in the early hours of 21 July, provides another link in the expanding system. Camouflage and markings were detailed for W.Nr. 412951, which had landed undamaged. It was described as having a broad *brown* band, and photographs show what could otherwise be mistaken for the standard red band marking. All markings used for bands were drawn from the standard L.Dv.521/1 colour chart listing of designated markings colours – RLM 21, 22, 23, 24, 25, 26 and 27. No one could mistake the rich red of RLM 23 for a brown, so the evidence points to 26 being the colour.

Interestingly, a photograph of a Bf 109 G-10, of 2./JG 300 at Borkheide, some 20 km south of Potsdam, in Autumn 1944 [5], shows a wide dark band that could also be judged as red. However, the caption makes reference to the 'rust-red' band used by JG 300 at that time. Again 'rust red' was not a description that would fit RLM 23 – but it was a lot closer to the rich brown colouring of RLM 26.

Though the single-engine Wilde Sau force was still employed at night, there had been some sharing arrangements with some day fighter units in 1943 and on into 1944, the fighters being used by both units (e.g., II./JG 53 – II./JG 301, II./JG 1 – II./JG 300). However, this arrangement had been abandoned by mid-1944. Just why a band marking had been retained for what were night fighting aircraft is not clear, though the evidence of the band's retention is irrefutable. What is also clear is that when both JG 300 and JG 301 were finally withdrawn from Wilde Sau operations, and transferred to bad weather daylight interception duties, each eventually used band markings of different colours from those recorded earlier.

Despite the additional colours that had appeared, red had remained in use as a general marking until very late 1944 as a positively dated photograph of a Bf 109 K of 11./JG 77 shows [6]. That particular aircraft, marked with a wide red band, had been lost in air fighting on

27 November near its base at Neuruppin, some 20 km north west of Berlin. That provides a good time marker for a unit that eventually would have a band marking allocation comprised of two different colours.

The above instances reflect the gradual expansion of the system from the general to the specific. However, the physical evidence is very limited, both from the photographic record, and also from the intelligence records where the few examples stand out in reports amidst many others. It is not until around November/December 1944 that specific colour or colour combinations begin to appear in the record – and that timing comes closer to the only two OKL orders so far located specifying band allocations to individual units. Two ULTRA intercepts provide a time marker[7].

The first, BT 287, dated 24 December 1944, stated:

"JIG ONE ONE INSTRUCTION OF TWENTY FOURTH. AIRCRAFT OF JIG ONE ONE TO BE)) MARKED BY A YELLOW BAND NINE NOUGHT CM & CM WIDE ROUND FUSELAGE ABOUT ONE FIVE TO TWENTY CM & CM FROM FIN."

In simple language, JG 11 was to use a yellow band marking as per the instruction of 24 December. The second intercept, BT 630, dated 29 December 1944, was a similar instruction, but sent to JG 53.

"JIG FIVE THREE INSTRUCTION OF TWENTY EIGHTH, QUOTING OKL & OKL ORDER. FOR BETTER) DIFFERENTIATION IN THE AIR, FIGHTERS OF UNIT TO HAVE BLACK BAND ROUND FUSELAGE ABOUT 45 CENTIMETRES WIDE. ALL QUOTE ACE OF SPADES UNQUOTE MARKINGS INCLUDING THOSE OF M/T & M/T TO BE REMOVED. COMMENT, COMPARE YELLOW BAND ((FOR JIG ONE ONE, BT & BT TWO EIGHT SEVEN))"

There are three significant points to that intercept. First, the reason for adoption of the marking – for better air-to-air 'differentiation' (between enemy and Luftwaffe aircraft); second, removal of the 'Ace of Spades' (Pik As) unit emblem from both aircraft and all motor transport. Inclusion of the latter would seem to point to a decision to ensure unit identification was removed for security purposes, not allowing any correlation between the newly allocated band colours and an existing known unit identification. The third point was the size of the marking – approximately 45 cm compared with the more definitive 90 cm instruction included in the JG 11 directive five days previously. The latitude inferred by the term 'approximate' was probably only marginal, but it is interesting that the order did provide some minor latitude.

These two instructions are the only ones so far located that define introduction of specific unit allocations of coloured band markings. The earlier reference in the ULTRA intercept of 12 February 1944 had been reference to the limited band colours in use at the time, red and white.

However, there remains no absolute precise timing of the introduction of the unit specific allocations of colours, physical evidence of some colours being seen prior to the issue of the two December orders to JG 11 and JG 53 mentioned earlier. What appears to be clearly implied by the difference in dates of those two orders, is that allocation had not been done on a single day, en masse, to all existing day fighter units engaged in the defence of the Reich – nor is there anything to assert unequivocally that the two orders quoted were the first two issued. The photographic evidence, where the subject is reliably identified and date verified, supports the gradualist assumption of introduction from very late 1944, but with increasing frequency from early 1945.

The fact that JG 1 had been allocated red, and JG 3 white makes use of any dated material from those two sources unusable in terms of defining the transition period more definitively. Colours also had obviously been withdrawn and reallocated. The distinctive black/white/black bands of Sturmstaffel 1 had disappeared when that unit had been disbanded at the end of April 1944 to become 11.(Sturm)/JG 3, but had reappeared on JG 4 aircraft. (one of its Bf 109 G-10s had been photographed at Kleinhau on 18 December 1944 wearing the marking) [8]. Again the date was December, but the process may have begun a little earlier.

There are however some confusing records, such as a photograph of an 11./JG 53 Bf 109 K-4, photographed on 22 February 1945 "somewhere in Germany". Previously published information suggests that the mid-tone band marking was green, though it was more probably red (the tonal value being about the same for both colours) – but what ever its true nature, it was clearly distinguishable from black, which had been, presumably, by that date, allocated as the unit Reichsverteidigung band colour. The possibility is that either the aircraft had been transferred from another unit to JG 53, or the original red band marking had simply not been painted out with black. Either way, it demonstrated a lack of adherence to the changed marking system. The painting on or out of such markings was done at unit level, and that may account for some of the anomalies.

There was however another aspect to the Reichsverteidigung markings, namely a lack of any appearing in many photographs taken in 1945. Perhaps the most definitive illustration across a large number of aircraft of a single unit appears in a series of photographs of Fw 190s of I./JG 1. The entire Stab and all four Gruppen photographgraphed at Greifswald in December 1944 show a total lack of any band marking. If any unit could have been expected to have a clearly established colour marking, it should have been JG 1; it had been using the red marking since November 1943 and possibly had been allocated it as its specific band colour by December 1944 – and none of the aircraft in the photographs showed any sign of a painted out band marking.

That raises the question of how much importance had been attached to adding such markings. Bf 109 K-4s of III. and IV./JG 77 based at Neuruppin, just north west of Berlin in November 1944, also lacked any band marking. Taking an extreme view, it might be argued that they were aircraft delivered before allocation of a band colour, yet white was already in general use in that command area. Some of the Bf 109 K-4s of JG 3 seen in March and April 1945 also lacked any band marking, as did some of the Fw 190 D-9s of IV./JG 3 during the same period.

Reason for abandoning Reichsverteidigung markings in some instances may have resulted from the overwhelming ground attacks by Allied fighters. Several photographs do show aircraft wearing Reichsverteidigung markings with the upper section painted out, just as had occurred first in Russia, and later Italy when ground defence had become the prime requirement. Also there was probably an element of just not having time, or interest, in applying such refinements.

As had so often occurred, a system was approved and instituted before it ever reached general promulgation. In this instance, approximately two months had passed before the necessity had arisen (the ground fighting had by then entered German home territory) to inform German ground forces about the recognition system. The order had been promulgated on 20 February 1945:

"By order of the Reichsmarschall, and for the purpose of improving aerial recognition, Jagdgeschwader aircraft are to be marked by fuselage-encircling coloured bands as indicated in the appended enclosure. Attention of troops down to platoon level is drawn to these markings which should simplify the recognition and distinction of our own aircraft."

The bands were specified as having a total width of 90 cm, comprising either of a single colour, or two of 45 cm width, or three 30 cm wide. It is clear that the focus of the order were ground forces in this instance. Not surprising, given the almost total domination of the air by Allied aircraft, Flak crews and army forces in general had developed an understandable reaction to shoot first and identify later. Aircraft recognition standards, in the face of the influx of quickly trained recruits, had been a lower priority than in previous years.

ABOVE: A line-up of Ta 152s of JG 301 taken very early in 1945 when the unit had just begun to take delivery of this advanced fighter. The yellow/red Reichsverteidigung bands can be seen on the second aircraft. Camouflage was typical of the late production single-engine fighter type, with 81/82/76 finish. The Balkenkreuz markings are of correct form, but the Hakenkreuz markings also should have been outline form – this confusion of marking style continued to the end of the war.

As always, instructions never appear to have been quite precise enough to exclude 'interpretations'. Colour photographs show well enough that JG 301 had applied its yellow and red combination in two forms, one the reverse order of the other. A more puzzling mystery attends two other combinations; the first a green and yellow band combination which may have been used by JGr. 10, the other a white/red/white combination noted on an unidentified Fw 190 found north of Eindhoven in January 1945. [9] The latter may have resulted from misinterpretation when marking the allocated red/white/red sequence on a JG 6 aircraft. Unfortunately no unit identity is possible, as the report did not contain a Werknummer. Given the early date, the incorrect marking sequence theory may be plausible.

Eventually the colour system was extended in form, as well as in colour combinations, cheques replacing bands on on the Me 262s of KG(J) 6 (and their supporting Bf 109 s) and KG(J) 54; the former using a four cheque pattern each side of the centre line, the latter a ten chequered pattern either side of the centre line. Photographs have also been published showing Bf 109 Gs wearing a four square pattern with colours tentatively described as red and black. Cheques may have occurred because, by the time those units had become operational, further combinations of colours were considered lacking sufficient differentiation under battle conditions.

RIGHT: The blue and red Reichsverteidigung band on the tail of W.Nr. 500071, of 9./JG 7, the Swiss intelligence report on this aircraft recorded the width of the marking as 90 cm, conforming precisely to the RLM directive for such markings.

LEFT: The normal style Reichsverteidigung marking, using a band or bands of colours, was changed for the Me 262-equipped units. This wreck of a 9./KG(J) 54 machine shows the chequer marking of blue and white squares. The distinctive fin and rudder camouflage dates the aircraft to an earlier period. KG(J) 54 changed from bomber style to fighter style markings very late in the war.

BELOW: With the change to unit-specific Reichsverteidigung markings, bands of colour were composed of either a single 900 mm width, or two 450 mm bands, or three 300 mm bands. However, as noted, a few units employed a system of cheques as shown here on Me 262 A-1a, W.Nr. 501232, 'Yellow 5' of KG(J) 6, wearing bands of red and black or blue 24 cheques. (Compare the size of the cheques with those on the previous photograph.) The camouflage was 81/82/76 with the mid-line style of demarcation between upper and lower colouring areas. In plan view this broke up the solid dark mass of the airframe: note that some of the filler marks can be seen just forward of the 'Yellow 5' marking. The tip of the nose cone was painted in yellow (04), the Staffel colour. The undersurfaces of the fuselage were painted on this aircraft something unusual in so far as other aircraft from this production batch were left in bare metal, e.g., W.Nr. 500200 held by the Australian War Memorial. Also unlike the latter machine, the Werknummer was painted on both sides of the fin (note the slight misalignment of the last three digits). The Hakenkreuz marking was of obsolete form, a common feature of Me 262s despite the RLM reminders to industry. The underwing Balkenkreuz markings also were of incorrect style - a black centre cross with white surrounds - a style also found on Bf 109s and some Fw 190s.

Only one fighter unit had been left out of the band allocation – the hybrid JV 44, the nature of its formation and existence no doubt having put it outside the formalities of OKL consideration for any Reichsverteidigung marking.

The following is a summary of Reichsverteidigung markings issued under the 20 February 1945 directive, including some that have still not been positively resolved in terms of colour combinations, and also some that have been recorded only in Intelligence Summaries. (This listing is exclusive of the general markings employed between 1943 and late 1944).

JG 1	red
JG 2	yellow/white/yellow
JG 3	white
JG 4	black/white/black
JG 5	black/yellow
JG 6	red/white/red
JG 7	blue/red
JG 11	yellow
JG 26	black/white
JG 27	green
JG 51	green/white/green
JG 52	red/white
JG 53	black
JG 54	blue
JG 77	white/green
JG 300	blue/white/blue
JG 301	yellow/red
Jgr. 10(?)	green/yellow
JG (Unknown)	white/red/white
KG(J) 6	red/black (or red/blue) cheques
KG(J) 54	blue/white cheques

Tactical markings changes 1944-1945

Tactical markings had been a constant source of interest to Allied Intelligence and we must slip back in time to 1944 to take up this aspect. An intercept on 25 April 1944, KV 1979 [10], had alerted the Allies to the fact that some confusion was being experienced between Italian aircraft operating with the German forces and those then operating with the Allies:

"GAFSE & GAFSE ON TWENTYTHIRD ORDERED FOLLOWING)) RECOGNITION COLOURING FOR GERMAN AND ITALIAN AIRCRAFT OPERATING IN MEDITERRANEAN & MEDITERRANEAN AREA COLON UNDER PARTS OF ENGINE COWLINGS TO BE PAINTED BRIGHT YELLOW. ROUND THE FUSELAGE A WHITE RING ABOUT FIVE NOUGHT CM & CM WIDE BEHIND THE CROSS. CAPTURED AIRCRAFT TO BE PAINTED BRIGHT YELLOW. ITALIAN AIRCRAFT TO BE DISTINGUISHED (COMMENT DETAILS UNKNOWN)."

The reference that Italian aircraft were to be 'distinguished' was due to that growing confusion. An additional intercept, KV 2089, received the following day, had elaborated further on those markings: [11]

"COMMENT TO KV & KV ONE NINE SEVEN NINE COLON KNOWN THAT (ABLE) ORDERS WERE FOR)) CONTINUATION OF EXISTING REGULATIONS. (BAKER) IDENTICAL REGULATIONS EXISTED IN MEDITERRANEAN & MEDITERRANEAN IN DECEMBER ONE NINE FOUR ONE. (CHARLIE) IN NOVEMBER ONE NINE FOUR THREE CAPTURED ITALIAN AIRCRAFT TO BE USED ONLY WITH CROSS ON WINGS AND FUSELAGE, WHITE RING AROUND FUSELAGE, YELLOW PAINT ON WING TIPS ONE AND HALF METRES IN WIDTH."

Point (b) in the text refers to the fact that such combination of markings had been reported by intelligence sources as being in force since December 1941. In fact the marking combination had been implemented by April 1941, as noted earlier. It remained in force, technically at least, until the final ousting of Axis forces as shown by ULTRA decrypt KV 6434 dated 5 June 1944 [12] which contained an interesting comment on the problems of using bright coloured tactical markings. It read:

"REPORTED ON THIRD FLIFUE & FLIFUE CROATIA HAD ORDERED REMOVAL FROM ALL AIRCRAFT OPERATING IN HIS COMMAND; OF WHITE RING ROUND FUSELAGE AND BRIGHT YELLOW PAINT ON UNDERSIDE OF ENGINE COWLING. EXPERIENCE HAS SHOWN THAT DURING LOW LEVEL FLYING IN VALLEYS AND RAVINES; AND WITH CLIFFS AS BACKGROUND; THE SHINING OF THE WHITE AND YELLOW PAINT DESTROYED OTHERWISE SATISFACTORY CAMOUFLAGE EFFECT."

The message had originated on 3 June, and the term Flifue was an abbreviation for Fliegerführer. It is clear that OKL-dictated tactical markings could be deleted at the discretion of the area command authority. At that time the Balkans were a separate theatre of operations under autonomous control of Luftwaffenkommando Süd Ost and, as such, its permanent aircraft force were marked with yellow and white tactical markings appropriate to that area of operations.

Returning to the content of the signal, this decision and notification appears to have elicited enquiries to other units, because a further ULTRA decrypt, KV 7079, dated 9 June 1944, [13] again refers to some variance as to the value of tactical markings:

"AIRCRAFT IDENTIFICATION & IDENTIFICATION MARKS USED BY (ABLE) STRONG INDICATIONS FOUR FOX ONE TWO THREE; LOWER PART OF COCKPIT COVER AND SIDE FINS YELLOW; CROSS ON FUSELAGE AND WINGS; UPPER AND LOWER FUSELAGE BLUE IDENTIFICATION FIGURES.

(BAKER) WESTA FIVE ONE & WESTA FIVE ONE CAMOUFLAGE PAINT AS FOR SEA WITH CROSS AND LETTERS. PRESENT MARKINGS CONSIDERED SATISFACTORY BY BOTH UNITS ON EIGHTH. USE OF YELLOW PAINT NOT DESIRED (BY WESTA FIVE ONE)."

The first part of the message, which had originated on 8 June, referred to the Ju 88s of 4.(F)/Aufkl.Gr. 123. The yellow area "lower part of cockpit cover" and the reference to blue identification figures identified this as a Stab aircraft. They used yellow for the entire nose section back to the leading edge of the wing, which on the Ju 88 was the section below the canopy. Reference to "side fins" (which had to be a reference to more than one aircraft) is interesting, as normally even Stab aircraft had had yellow only on the rudder; in that instance the colour area may have been extended to the fin. Use of all-yellow empennage markings had been seen in the Balkans on Ju 87s of Stab status, so the description may have been accurate. The unit is believed to have been operating in the Balkans at the time and this style and extent of marking accords with that seen on the Ju 88s of the Stab of LG 1, which was in the same area of operations. This points to the more extensive Stab aircraft tactical markings being set by an official, possibly local, order, at least in that part of the war front.

The second part of the message referred to the aircraft of Wekusta 51 (Wetterkundungsstaffel – Meteorological Staffel), which operated a mixture of aircraft. The sea camouflage – 72/73/65 – would have been compromised by any form of tactical marking since these aircraft relied on camouflage for their lone sorties over the ocean.

Another air-to-air rapid identification had come about through the formalization of a practice that had, in turn, developed from the original Gruppe/Staffel markings applied to spinners. The factory practice of

ABOVE: Photographed over the Eastern Mediterranean, this Ju 88 A-4 of the Gruppe Stab of Lehrgeschwader 1, coded L1+BB, had the entire front section of the fuselage painted yellow forward of the wing leading edge. This somewhat liberal use of the tactical marking colour may have been to distinguish the unit's Stab aircraft during air operations. The camouflage was standard pattern 70/71/65 finish. (Helmut Stubert via L. Lyne)

Reference to the ULTRA intercept of 12 February [14] quoted earlier now clarified the fact that the spiral marking had been ordered for:

> "… ALL FIGHTER AIRCRAFT OF LUFTFLOTTE THREE AND REICH & REICH TO HAVE BLACK AND WHITE SPIRALS TURNING IN SAME DIRECTION AS SPINNER, WIDTH ONE FIFTH OF DIAMETER OF SPINNER."

(Note: Luftflotte Three covered France.)

The optical effect was quite dramatic and effective from whatever angle of visibility of the spinner (the same device is often seen on the spinner of modern passenger turbofan aircraft, for exactly the same reason). The oft-quoted purpose of the device to disorientate Allied air gunners is false; in fact the very opposite occurs as it made a very distinctive aiming point, but one that even the best air gunner would have had great difficulty of utilizing given the closing speeds and deflection aiming necessary in other than a head-on shot; and head-on the area exposed to fire was tiny.

dividing the spinner into two unequal parts, one third white with the remainder 70, introduced in 1941 had produced a modest optical effect when in motion; that may have been considered a useful adjunct during operations. Judging by factory production photographs of Bf 109 Gs that revised form of marking appears to have been modified in some instances with substitution of black for the base colouring of the spinner. However the official factory standard continued to specify 70 until at least the last issue of the official painting directive in 1944.

A further variation seen on some aircraft had the forward section of the spinner painted in white to form a spiral pattern, though that was probably a unit initiative. This pattern had been extended to the entire spinner by some units, the earliest officially sanctioned example positively dated from photographs appearing in March 1944. However it had possibly occurred even earlier; JG 3, JG 26, JG 52, JG 53 and JG 54 are known to have used this form of marking.

The Allied invasion of Western Europe on 6 June 1944 had been marked by addition of black and white stripes to the wings and fuselage of Allied aircraft as a means of rapidly identifying friend from foe. German response had been fairly rapid but opposite, reducing the range of markings that might cause confusion with Allied aircraft while retaining the distinctive spinner marking, which had been in force since February in Luftflotte Three. Two important ULTRA decodes help to confirm just how quickly the Luftwaffe responded. Document KV 9720, dated 25 June [15] contained the following:

> "ORDER FROM STAB JIG ONE TO SECOND GRUPPE JIG ELEVEN ON TWENTY FIFTH. WITH IMMEDIATE EFFECT AIRCRAFT TO BE MARKED ONLY WITH SPIRAL ON AIRSCREW SPINNER; CROSS; TACTICAL NUMBER AND GRUPPE MARK (BARS). ALL OTHER MARKINGS TO BE

ABOVE: A Bf 109 G-6 of IV./JG 3 photographed in southern Italy in 1943, displays the unit-initiated form of spiral spinner marking. However, not until February 1944 would this tactical marking become official policy.

ABOVE: A positively dated photograph, taken during the inauguration of III./JG 1 at Leeuwarden on 23 May 1943, shows Bf 109 G-6s wearing spinner markings of a very tight spiral of white on a base colouring of black. (E. Mombeek)

REMOVED. COMMENT; NOT KNOWN HOW WIDE APPLICATION. ON TWENTY THIRD JIG TWO SEVEN SUBMITTED PROPOSAL FOR AIRCRAFT MARKING TO FIVE JIG DOG." [ii]

What is interesting is that JG 27 had submitted a proposal for an unspecified form of marking on 23 June to 5. Jagddivision (which controlled Stab I., II. and III./JG 2) and two days later a message from the Stab of JG 1 had been intercepted ordering II./JG 11 to adopt specific changes, which included marking of a spiral on the spinner. Both units were under the control of 2. Jagddivision, but based in France for the time being. The normal relationship between the two units was close in terms of defensive actions along the northern coast of Holland and Germany.

Between 27 and 29 June, a further instruction had been sent out and intercepted, ULTRA decode XMO [16] read:

"NOW KNOWN THAT AIRCRAFT MARKINGS INSTRUCTIONS IN KV9720 APPLY TO ALL LUFTFLOTTE THREE AIRCRAFT. SPIRAL ON PROPELLER TO BE BLACK AND WHITE. ADDITIONAL IDENTIFICATION MARKINGS TO BE RETAINED EXCLUSIVELY FOR FIGHTERS, GROUND ATTACK; HEAVY FIGHTERS AND RECCE AIRCRAFT."

Those instructions, along with more detailed orders for different classes of aircraft, were promulgated in a more extensive document on 20 July 1944 and stated in part:

"With effect from today, the recognition markings of our own aircraft in the Western Area (Germany, France and Italy) will be changed as follows.

1 (a) Fighters, including twin-engine fighters, ground-attack and reconnaissance aircraft are to have a black and white spiral painted on their spinners.
1(b) All other operational aircraft, no special recognition markings.
2 (a) Captured aircraft, if flown operationally, to be marked as per 1(a) above."

(Flying captured enemy aircraft operationally was a reference to Italian aircraft used on the Italian front.)

As mentioned above, spiral spinner markings had appeared on all classes of aircraft well before the issue of the 25 June 1944 order, dating back to the early part of the war. In addition to the optical effect of the official one-third white/two thirds black (70 green), the spiral form marking may have evolved as a natural progression of the spinner rings of colour that units had adopted from around 1941 because of the visual value in air combat. The spiral effect was easily discerned from any angle and the combination of black and white provided the best possible visual identification range. Only yellow and black provide more contrast, but the problem of Staffel/Gruppe colours did not allow for that colour combination.

The white section of the marking was commenced at the centre of the spinner hub and wound down at a steady angle until it reached the bottom edge of the spinner. Close examination of many samples show that the spinner was probably mounted on a simple turntable and spun slowly around as the white was applied (trying to do the same thing when attached to the airscrew would have been impractical due to engine compression). At unit level, ground personnel were at liberty to apply the pattern as best they could, a relatively difficult task which resulted in wide variations.

On 9 September 1944, an extensive set of instructions had been issued covering the introduction of an additional range of tactical markings for several classes of aircraft. This was in direct response to the deteriorating air war situation. ULTRA intercept XL 9759, dated 11 September recorded the following. [17]

"ON NINTH TWO AND THREE AIRCRAFT FERRYING GESCHWADER ONE) AT MANNHEIM SANDHOFEN & MANNHEIM SANDHOFEN AND WEISBADEN ERBENHEIM & WEISBADEN ERBENHEIM INFORMED OF FOLLOWING AIRCRAFT MARKINGS. FIRSTLY IN AREAS OF LUFTFLOTTEN ONE AND FOUR. GAFSE & GAFSE AND GAF & GAF GENERAL HUNGARY & HUNGARY. FIGHTERS, GROUND ATTACK, HEAVY FIGHTERS AND RECCE AIRCRAFT, DEAD WHITE SPIRAL ON PROPELLER BOSS. BOMBERS AND COMMUNICATIONS AIRCRAFT AS ABOVE WITH YELLOW UNDERSIDES. SECONDLY, AREAS OF LUFTFLOTTEN TWO, THREE AND FIVE FIGHTERS, GROUND ATTACK, HEAVY FIGHTERS AND RECCE AIRCRAFT AS ABOVE, ALL OTHER AIRCRAFT NO & NO SPECIAL MARKINGS. THIRDLY, AREA OF LUFTFLOTTE REICH EXCLUDING HUNGARY & HUNGARY. FIGHTERS, GROUND ATTACK AND HEAVY FIGHTERS AS IN FIRSTLY. TRAINING AIRCRAFT, COMMUNICATIONS AIRCRAFT ETCETERA COLON UNDERSIDE OF ENGINE YELLOW. AIRCRAFT OPERATING AGAINST ALLIES TO HAVE TWO YELLOW RINGS FIVE NOUGHT CENTIMETRES BROAD ROUND MIDDLE OF FUSELAGE. FOURTHLY, AIRCRAFT OF STATES ALLIED TO GERMANY & GERMANY TO HAVE MARKINGS OF RELEVANT LUFTFLOTTEN. FIFTHLY, CAPTURED AIRCRAFT IN ALL LUFTFLOTTEN ABLE, WHEN OPERATING IN FIGHTING TO HAVE RELEVANT LUFTFLOTTE MARKINGS, BAKER NOT & NOT OPERATING IN FIGHTING, OUTER THIRD OF UNDERSIDE OF WING YELLOW, SEA RESCUE AIRCRAFT TO BE CONSIDERED AS ENGAGED IN FIGHTING. SIXTHLY, AIRCRAFT OPERATING EXCLUSIVELY BY NIGHT AS BOMBERS OR FOR TARGET PRESENTATION, NO & NO SPECIAL MARKINGS. SEVENTHLY, CIVIL AIR LINES IRRESPECTIVE OF TYPE, WHOLE ENGINE COWLING YELLOW, WHOLE UNDERSIDE INCLUDING ELEVATORS YELLOW, RUDDER YELLOW. ABOVE ORDERS IN FORCE (FROM TWENTIETH)." [iii]

The extent and range of the markings clearly indicates the seriousness of the prevailing air situation. The reference to adoption of a white spiral on the propeller boss for all classes of fighters and reconnaissance aircraft extended the existing practice as mentioned earlier. The old system of using the spinner to display both Gruppe and Staffel colouring also had remained in use until issue of the above order. A few random examples had later appeared amongst some units where the September instruction was adapted to allow continued display of Gruppe and Staffel colouring on the spinner in spiral form, the Staffel colour being retained in place of the 'dead white spiral' while the basic colouring of the propeller boss was painted in the Gruppe colour; but in general the new order marked the end of the old practice.

The above order came into effect on 20 September 1944, but on 25 September a new ULTRA intercept, HP 1207, [18] revealed a further set of tactical marking instructions.

---

ii. Stab Jig One was Stab JG 1, Second Gruppe Jig Eleven was II./JG 11, Jig Two Seven was JG 27 and Five Jig Dog, 5. Jagddivision.

iii. Reference to GAFSE and GAF above stood for German Air Force South East and German Air Force. The use of Able and Baker was simply a clear language form of (A) and (B).

"EARLY TWENTY SECOND LUFTFLOTTE FOUR APPRECIATED THAT ON RUMANIAN & RUMANIAN FRONT QUOTE THE ENEMY UNQUOTE WAS OPERATING GERMAN & GERMAN AIRCRAFT IN SOME CASES WITH GERMAN MARKINGS. IN ORDER TO IDENTIFY GERMAN AIRCRAFT WITH CERTAINTY ADDITIONAL RECOGNITION MARKINGS IN YELLOW PAINT ORDERED FOR ME & ME ONE NOUGHT NINE, FW & FW ONE NINE NOUGHT, JU & JU EIGHT SEVEN, JU & JU EIGHT EIGHT, JU & JU ONE EIGHT EIGHT, HS & HS ONE TWO NINE, HE & HE ONE ONE ONE AND DO & DO TWO ONE SEVEN. FOUR NOUGHT CENTIMETRE RING ROUND FUSELAGE IN FRONT OF WINGS. LOWER SIDE OF PORT WING, WHOLE WIDTH OF WING A VICTOR & VICTOR OPEN TOWARDS DIRECTION OF FLIGHT WITH ANGLE OF FOUR FIVE DEGREES AND ARMS TWO FIVE CENTIMETRES BROAD. THE ARMS OF THE VICTOR & VICTOR TO BE CARRIED OVER LEADING EDGE OF WING TO UPPER SIDE FOR DISTANCE OF SIX NOUGHT CENTIMETRES TO PERMIT REECOGNITION FROM ABOVE ALSO. COMPLETION TO BE REPORTED BY EARLY TWENTYFIFTH, FROM THEN ON ALL ABOVE AIRCRAFT NOT & NOT CARRYING NEW MARKING COULD BE FIRED ON AT THREE NOUGHT KILOMETRES DISTANCE FROM FRONT."

An additional order also had been issued a day later for Luftwaffe forces operating from Greece. ULTRA intercept HP1377 of 26 September 1944 [19] read:

"FLAK REGIMENT TWO NOUGHT ONE GAVE IDENTICAL INSTRUCTIONS FOR ADDITIONAL RECOGNITION MARKINGS YELLOW PAINT FOR GUARANTEEING RECOGNITION OF GERMAN & GERMAN AIRCRAFT IN SPHERE OF COMMAND OF GAFGE & GAFGE. ADDITIONAL TYPES MENTIONED WERE CR & CR FOUR TWO AND HS & HS ONE TWO SIX." [iv]

The speed with which ground staff had been required to apply these markings did not allow for absolute accuracy. When the Fw 190 F-8/R-1, W.Nr. 931884 was being restored by the National Space and Air Museum staff in Washington, the original tactical markings were carefully measured. The 40 cm regulation yellow fuselage band forward of the wing actually measured 37 cm. The Victor marking was found to be 28 cm wide, not 25 cm, and extended over the wing leading edge for 56 cm on the outboard section and 38 cm inboard, not 60 cm overall as specified. Not significant differences, and understandable under field conditions.

The final order contained in HP 1207 had remained in force until 7 March 1945. While the original OKL instruction has not been located, a copy of the new markings instructions was also promulgated to the Hungarian Air Force as part of a set of collected instructions, *M.kir. 1./II. (honvéd légvédelmi tüzér gyüjtöosztály paraucanokság*, dated 8 March. [20] Paragraph 8 read:

"An instruction for new identification markings for aircraft.
Order number 9 was issued on 8.3.45.
A.f.évi III. 8 – én kelt 9.sz.Biz.lgv.tu het.piég-I po
1.pontját teljtalmulag közlöm:
Az V.Flakkkorbs I.a.Br.B.Nr.689./45.geb. éz 696./45 geb.
o/10p.2.:/átiraira=:

Point 1 is issued in a full extract, as according to V Flakkorps. I. A. Br. B. Nr. 689/45geb/ and 689/45 geb/ep.2/

Regarding new identification markings of aircraft of IV. Luftflotte the following is advised.

1/ All aircraft, used in fighting during daylight (Bf 109, Fw 190, Ju 87, Hs 126, Ju 88, He 111, Cr 42) from 7.3.45) have to be marked with the following markings.
a) 50 cm wide yellow band around forward section of engine.
b) rudder is yellow.
2/ Older identification markings (yellow V on under surface of port wing and yellow band around fuselage) are cancelled for all aircraft.
3/ Night units: night reconnaissance aircraft remain unaltered, except headquarters flights of Luftwaffe which has yellow on side and under surface section of engine.
4/ Over painting of aircraft can take longer, for reasons of weather (rain or snowfalls). Due to these reasons some aircraft could still be flying with old form of yellow markings after 7.3.45."

Note that the order was issued a day after it was due to come into effect. No doubt the fact that this instruction had had to be passed on by OKL, and translated and promulgated to its Hungarian allies, may account for that delay. It is also clear that the implementation date, though stipulated, was flexible in view of weather (and no doubt battle) conditions. These factors were part of the reason for the non-conformity of style, or absence of the markings, on some aircraft photographed during this period. That order was still in force when the final surrender occurred; no further instructions for variation to tactical markings on the Eastern Front are known to have been issued.

As Russian forces advanced into northern Germany, units were pressed into attacks to try and stem the flow. The Fw 190s of III./JG 54 (II./ZG 76 having been re-designated as such), stationed at Müncheberg, just outside Berlin, were used to attack the enemy along the Oder River defence line. Surviving photographs show a white diagonal band

ABOVE: Heinz Schmidt's Fw 190 A-8 'Black 15' of III./JG 54, which was damaged by Russian Flak during a ground-attack sortie on 11 March 1945. The undercarriage mechanism had been hit and he crash-landed at München/Eggersdorf airfield at 1301 hours. He survived and continued operations until 27 March. As noted in the text, the significance of the white band tactical stripe marking is unclear, as also is the 'III' marking. A second Fw 190 that force-landed after the operation also carried the white stripe but not a 'III' marking. (H. Schmidt via R. Chapman)

---

iv GAFGE stood for German Air Force Greece East

RIGHT: The tactical markings instructions issued in September 1944 were repealed during the closing weeks of the war. On 17 March 1945 the yellow Victor marking and 40 cm fuselage band were deleted, being replaced with a 50 cm band around the front section of the engine, plus a yellow rudder. This 4. Staffel Bf 109 G, 'White 21', photographed at Munich in July 1945, was marked in accordance with those final instructions. (M. Olmsted)

ABOVE: These three Bf 109 Gs, photographed at Neubiberg at in July 1945, had also had their tactical markings changed to conform to the final instructions. The nearer, 4. Staffel aircraft, had had its unit badge painted out with what looks like 02, the remaining shape indicating that it had belonged to JG 53, possibly having been deleted in accordance with the RLM instruction detailed in the ULTRA decode message of 29 December 1944 (see page 289). The same colour had been used to paint out the old tactical band marking around the rear section of the fuselage, but a very dark colour had been used beneath the wing, presumably to paint out the V-victor tactical marking. Why such a dark colour was used is a mystery, unless it was all that was available. The rudder and nose section were marked correctly. The next aircraft, also a II.Gruppe aircraft, had had its fuselage band marking painted out with the same dark colour, which looks tonally darker than the black centre of the Balkenkreuz marking. It may have been 81 or 83, which, when applied fresh, might have appeared tonally darker than the older black of the marking. The third aircraft, in Hungarian markings, 'Red(?) 6', had a similar set of correct yellow tactical markings to the first one. Note that none of the aircraft carried a spiral spinner marking. (M. Olmsted)

RIGHT: Also photographed at Munich, this 6. Staffel Fw 190 G-8, 'Yellow 11', carried the correct combination of tactical markings. At first glance it appears to have two coloured bands around the engine cowling, but closer examination shows that the same colours appear both sides of the marking. The spinner on this machine conformed to the final order. (M. Olmsted)

LEFT: The striking effectiveness of the final official tactical markings is illustrated by this photograph of a Ju 87 D, W.Nr. 141255, surrendered at the close of the fighting. The dark camouflage provides a stark contrast to the yellow band around the forward part of the engine cowling and the yellow rudder marking.

marked, both sides, from the leading edge of the horizontal tail plane across the fin to the tip of the rudder. Some sources credit this marking to a joint force being used for these operations, but nothing else has emerged to support that broader application theory.

Some controversy has attended photographs of Fw 190 A-8s used by III./JG 54 in the closing weeks of the war. Fortunately, one of the surviving pilots, Heinz Schmidt, has been able to clarify matters, both from his personal account and also via his own documentation of the period. Despite the presence of a IV. Gruppe marking (in this case the flattened, more stylised form of the wave marking in use very late in the war by a few units), the aircraft were definitely being operated by III./JG 54 at the time. Further, while training and re-equipping with Fw 190s at Großenhain early in 1945, Fw 190s had been borrowed from SG 2 under the command of Major Rudel.

The suggestion has been put forward that the aircraft were originally intended for IV. Gruppe but ended up being used by III. Gruppe, something quite possible in the chaotic conditions of the very last stages of the war. However, even that is doubtful given that most of the pilots initially picked up their aircraft from various aircraft parks. Few were new and initially most retained the markings of their former users.

When III./JG 54 was disbanded in the closing weeks of the war, most of its aircraft were taken over by JG 51. At that late stage JG 51 made no attempt to remove the fin and rudder marking, which explains why a number of writers have claimed the so-called 'cancelled Swastika' to be specific to JG 51, which it definitely was not.

The presence of the white '111' marking on the rudder of Schmidt's Fw 190 is also unexplained. While it is tempting to make some connection between the marking and the fact that his aircraft was definitely operating with III. Gruppe, that was definitely not the case. It would have made little sense to add an elaborate and unconventional form of identification to just one aircraft, instead of simply painting out the IV. Gruppe marking. Nor did it have any connection with the narrow white tactical diagonal marking across both sides of the vertical tail surfaces. Schmidt has confirmed that his was the only aircraft to have such a marking in addition to the diagonal white line marking. He had ferried the aircraft from Großenhain to Eggersdorf of 17 February 1945, flew it operationally for the first time on 11 March, and crashed it the following day at Müncheberg/Eggersdorf at 1301 hours after a ground-attack sortie. Russian flak had damaged the undercarriage retraction mechanism.

While the style of tactical marking bears some similarity in size and angle to one seen on the rudder of two of the Ju 87 Ds of SG 2, Oberst Rudel's Stab aircraft, and one from 10.(Pz)/ SG 2, (part of a mixed force

of SG 2's Ju 87Ds and Fw 190s, which surrendered to the Americans at Kitzingen/Main airfield), the angle was reversed on the Fw 190s of JG 54. The marking appears to have been two narrow parallel bands of white, close together. This was a marking that had been used earlier in 1942-43 by the unit, sometimes marked as a solid stripe. It has been conjectured that it was a Stab marking, as it was most frequently seen on aircraft carrying the Stab letter 'A' or 'B'. However, the fact that it was in use on both a Stab and a 10. Staffel aircraft indicates that possibly it may have been some form of unit tactical marking, though perhaps restricted to the Ju 87s, as two of the accompanying Fw 190 s, one from the Stab, the other from II. Gruppe, both lacked the marking. Various coloured band markings for bomber aircraft had been in use from the opening days of the war, though not a widely used device.

Given the operational disposition of the two units III./JG 52 and SG 2 and the fact that they were under different command structures at the time, there is little likelihood of a connection other than for the general style of a marking, despite the earlier temporary connection between them at Großenhain.[21]

Transport units

Tactical and special markings had not been confined to just fighters and bombers. Returning to 1941 the Luftwaffe's transport units, which played such an essential part in the operational support role, had also developed a system of quick recognition markings. During the invasion of the Low Countries in early 1940, a white number in a white circle on the rudder was used by some of the Ju 52s. Just what the significance of the marking was is not known. A second form was narrow stripes, marked chord-wise across the engine cowling of all three engines. The only photographic evidence shows white, but all three Staffel or Gruppe colours may have been employed. A more sophisticated form consisted of repeating the KGr.z.b.V code in white on the top section of the rudder to which was added a simple system of coloured bands to indicate Stab or Staffel identity.

These early systems were replaced by one that incorporated a group of three symbols, marked on the rudder. This system arose out of the sudden need to form larger transport formations under a single control for special operations. Russia and its terrible operational conditions gave birth to this system, which is credited to a Lt. Wasserkampf, the Technical Officer of Transport Einsatzgruppe Kupschus. His idea was to introduce a simplified and unifying temporary code system that allowed flexibility because using each transport unit's codes was a logistical nightmare. Its success brought about its wider adoption in other

BELOW: Another example of the temporary collective unit code system is seen on this Ju 52 of 15./Kgr.z.b.V 1, seen over Russia during the winter of 1942/43. The aircraft's individual and Staffel letters 'FZ' were marked in a small (permanent colour) white panel at the tip of the fin in black (though the 'F', narrowly outlined in black, was in yellow on the fuselage), with the tactical codes 'D3 F' marked in black on the rudder. The 'D' identified IV./KGr.z.b.V 1; the '3', 3. Staffel and the 'F' was the aircraft letter. The overall finish of the aircraft was winter temporary white, while the darker coloured band behind the last letter of the code was the 04 yellow tactical band marking, the upper sections having been painted over with temporary white. The wing tip lower surfaces were also painted in 04-colouring. (M. Jessen)

ABOVE: This Ju 52/3m offers a feast of markings features. 4V+AT, W.Nr. 6518, was on the strength of 1.Staffel of I./KG.z.b.V. 172 before ending its days on this aircraft dump in North Africa in 1943. The rudder markings are explained in the text. In this instance the white letter/number combination gave the following information - the letter 'T' identified the unit (KG.z.b.V. 172); the number '1' was for 1.Staffel while the 'J' was the aircraft's identification letter within IV./TG 3, the parent body. This code had no direct relationship to the normal unit code carried by the aircraft. The significance of the '0' superimposed on the fuselage Balkenkreuz marking is unknown. The overall camouflage appears to be a monotone finish, suggesting a 78/79 scheme. The different colour scheme on the rudder (patches of faded 80 over 79) appears to indicate that it had been cannibalised from another aircraft prior to having the formation tactical identification markings added to it. The background star-shaped marking of the KG.z.b.V. 172 emblem was marked on the nose, forward of the cockpit, but close examination shows no sign of this Transport Geschwader's famous pig emblem. (J. Crow)

theatres of operation, and in May 1943 the Transport Gruppen were reorganised into five Transport Geschwadern. The larger KG.z.b.V. formations were incorporated into the new parent structure, while smaller units were redesignated Transport Staffeln or Gruppen depending on their size.

The markings were applied to the rudder and consisted of a pair comprising a letter and number (or an 'S' if a Stab aircraft) with a single letter below the pair. The first letter identified the parent unit, the number identified the temporary Staffel that had been created within that unit, while the last letter was that of the individual aircraft within that formation. This form of abbreviated marking, which used the simple single first letter as a form of shorthand code to indicate the unit, rather than applying the actual two part alpha-numeric code, was visually effective, especially for aircraft which usually operated in bomber style fixed formation. The usual range of Theatre of Operations tactical markings were also carried by the aircraft. The Ju 52s were, of course, not the only transport aircraft to employ this system of rapid identification markings, the Me 323s of I./KG.z.b.V 323 also used it as did the aircraft of the marine transport units. As always there were

oddities amongst the system; KG.z.b.V 1 was recorded using just two letters in a white circle near the top of the fin, the first was the aircraft letter, the second was the code for the Gruppe. At other times, some units simply used the same system within their own structure as a quick recognition feature.

Ambulance aircraft markings

The markings peculiar to ambulance aircraft are included with this section of the work because their unique nature accords more with the rational of the type of markings discussed above.

The earliest example is of an unidentified Ju 52/3m finished in 61/62/63 camouflage with the abbreviation 'San. Flz 2' (Sanitätzflugzeug 2 – 'Ambulance aircraft 2') in white, marked on both sides of the fuselage and also upper and lower surfaces of both wings. It wore a mixture of markings and the old style camouflage, positioning of the military Hakenkreuz overlapping fin and rudder (the red banner and white disc markings having been painted out), and the old style Balkenkreuz markings, indicating that it was taken pre-war. The odd markings point to this being a form of interim identification used prior to the introduction

LEFT: The standard form of ambulance registration markings, after replacement of the 'D' prefix with 'WL', is seen here on WL++AHEP. The Balkenkreuz marking was still positioned ahead of the larger Red Cross marking on the fuselage and both markings were displayed on each wing. An overall colouring of white, other than for the engine cowlings and the exhaust stain area behind each engine, was also retained. (M. Jessen)

of all-white ambulance aircraft wearing civil registered markings. The fact that the abbreviation has a figure '2' after it indicates that this was one of at least two such aircraft. The fuselage Balkenkreuz marking was moved forward of the white markings, almost over the wing root trailing edge, with the red cross in a white circle marked forward of that again. The same arrangement appeared on the wings where the extreme outboard position of the old style Balkenkreuz marking accommodated the white markings and Red Cross symbol.

On 1 January 1939, ambulance aircraft, in common with all second line military aircraft, had the 'D' for Deutschland prefix element of their civil registration replaced with 'WL' (Wehrmacht Luft). However, after the outbreak of war the civil 'D' prefix was reinstated, no doubt to ensure the non-military status of the aircraft. This may have occurred with effect from 8 October 1939 when the revised form of Stammkennzeichen was introduced and blocks of these codes were allocated to all existing second line Luftwaffe aircraft. This replaced the 'WL' prefixed civil registrations then in use. (The exception appears to have been some classes of gliders.)

By 1940 all German ambulance aircraft were painted white overall with a red cross marking replacing the Balkenkreuz in the six standard positions. The vertical tail surfaces were marked with the Reichsdienstflagge (State Service Flag), comprising a black, vertically oriented, Hakenkreuz superimposed on a white disc. The disc was superimposed centrally on a red field marked chord-wise across fin and rudder. On each side, near the top forward corner, a white stylised Luftwaffe eagle was painted on the red background. Aircraft were marked with civil registrations, the hyphenated first two letters of which were placed to the left of the Red Cross marking. The civil registration was repeated on both surfaces of the wing, above the top and below the lower in the case of bi-planes. Most Ju 52/3ms retained their black painted engine cowlings, a common feature on this type at that period.

Use of the Reichsdienstflagge and white-painted ambulance aircraft came to an abrupt end in July 1940. During the initial stage of the air war against Britain, He 59 seaplanes carrying this form of tail marking and wearing civil registration, were constantly engaged in the rescue of downed aircrew. However, despite the number of normal Luftwaffe reconnaissance flights already being flown over shipping lanes and British ports, doubts continued about their neutrality because of frequent sightings of these rescue aircraft near convoys during attacks. (In hindsight, it made sense for them to be summoned to such actions for obvious reasons, but this does not appear to have been considered. If it was, then the subsequent decision disregarded this factor.)

The first He 59, D-ASAM of Seenotflugkdo. 3, had been forced down on 1 July 1940, by Spitfires of No. 72 Squadron, the crew being rescued unhurt by the Royal Navy. A second machine, D-ASUO of Seenotflugkdo. 1,

was forced down by a Spitfire of No 54 Squadron on 9 July, and towed ashore by the local British lifeboat crew. Five days later, on 14 July, the British Government instructed RAF Fighter Command to order all pilots to shoot down enemy ambulance aircraft encountered in areas where fighting was in progress; a decision ratified by an Air Ministry Order No. 1254 of 29 July 1940.

While the He 59s continued to operate in their humanitarian role, retention of the all white finish and black markings ceased in the face of continuing losses, all Luftwaffe ambulance aircraft adopting standard camouflage and Stammkennzeichen markings of second line aircraft. The Red Cross marking was retained in place of the Balkenkreuz in all six positions, applied as per the following instruction in the 1941 edition of L.Dv. 521/1.

Marking for the identification of ambulance aircraft

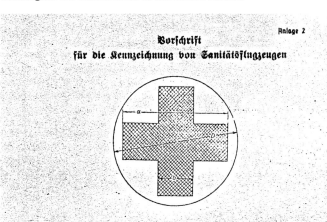

Anlage 2

Vorschrift
für die Kennzeichnung von Sanitätsflugzeugen

Die Kennzeichnung der Sanitätsflugzeuge wird ab sofort wie folgt festgelegt:

1. Die Flugzeuge behalten den für das jeweilige Baumuster vorgesehenen serienmäßigen Tarnanstrich.

2. Das Seitenleitwerk erhält das Hoheitsabzeichen (Hakenkreuz) wie bei Frontflugzeugen.

3. Anstelle der Balkenkreuze an den Flächen und am Rumpf ist das rote Kreuz in weißer Kreisfläche aufzubringen. Das Verhältnis Kreisdurchmesser (D) : Balkenlänge (a) des roten Kreuzes : Balkenbreite (b) = D : a : b = 7 : 6 : 2. Es sind lediglich folgende Maße anzuwenden:

D =	52	70	87	105	122	140	157	175	192	210
a =	45	60	75	90	105	120	135	150	165	180
b =	15	20	25	30	35	40	45	50	55	60

Alle Maßzahlen in cm.

Der Durchmesser der weißen Kreisfläche ist unter Anwendung obiger Maße so zu wählen, daß er das Balkenkreuz (der Frontflugzeuge) umschreibt. Sodann ist das rote Kreuz einzusetzen. Kennzeichenfarbe nach LDv. 521/1.

RIGHT: This close-up view of D-A+SUO shows that the civil registration marking was divided by the rearmost Red Cross marking. Note also the 23 red stripe across the front of each float with PROPELLER marked in white block letters across it. This is interesting as the German word is 'luftschraube' - indicating that rescue was intended to include RAF aircrew perhaps, or why else use the English word? The upper surface inboard sections of the lower wing retained the original 72/73 finish, as this was walk area for engine maintenance. The usual red rubber tips to the floats have been removed, but the exposed area had not been over painted with white. (Syndicate International)

ABOVE AND BELOW: Two views of D-ARYX. The placement of the additional Red Cross marking, in the middle of the civil registration, and lack of any military markings was typical of these aircraft until action by the British Government brought to a close their special humanitarian status. Interestingly this machine lacked the stylised Luftwaffe Eagle emblem on the Reichsdienstflagge marking across the fin and rudder.

RIGHT: After the International controversy over the neutral status of air ambulance aircraft in July 1940, with few exceptions ambulance aircraft reverted to standard camouflage as shown by this 70/71/65-camouflaged Ju 52/3m. Red Cross emblems however were retained in place of the military Balkenkreuz markings to fuselage and wings; only the Hakenkreuz emblem – which was the National Socialist Party political emblem, not the national emblem – was retained from the normal suite of military markings, declaring the aircraft's 'civil' status. In this instance, the last two letters of the Stammkennzeichen had also been retained, though why the first two had been deleted is unknown.

LEFT: This low angle view affords a look at the large diameter Red Cross markings beneath the wings on ambulance Ju 52s. As with the fuselage marking on the aircraft shown in the previous photograph, the diameter of the marking was the largest possible, whether on fuselage or wing.

RIGHT: The size of the Red Cross markings is vividly illustrated in this view of RQ+AC, the marking being used, as with the military Balkenkreuz, to divide each pair of the Stammkennzeichen letters.

301

The identification of ambulance aircraft will be carried out in accordance with the following:

1) The aircraft are painted in standard camouflage scheme applicable to the particular model.

2) The national marking (Hakenkreuz) on the fin is the same as carried by operational aircraft.

3) The Balkenkreuze markings on wings and fuselage are replaced by a red cross on a white disc. The proportions of the circle diameter (D) width (a) of the red cross: stroke width (b) = D : a : b = 7 : 6 : 2. Dimensions as specified in the accompanying table have to be strictly adhered to.

D=	52	70	87	105	122	140	157	175	192	210
a=	45	60	75	90	105	120	135	150	165	180
b=	15	20	25	30	35	40	45	50	55	60

(All dimensions in centimetres)

The diameter of the white disc according to the table is to be large enough to cover the Balkenkreuz (of operational aircraft). The red cross is then applied. Markings colours are in L.Dv.521/1.

The paints to be used are:

for spray painting : 7160.21 and 7160.23
for brush application : 7164.21 and 7164.23

While all aircraft engaged on air ambulance duties used the revised markings, as instructed above, at least one example has been noted where a civil registration, and the all-white finish, was retained (long after the original instruction was sent out in 1940), plus the standard Reichs und Nationalflagge marking across the vertical tail surfaces. This was D-EMAW, a Fi 156 photographed in southern Italy in 1941. The odd combination may relate to use by the German Red Cross organization (as indicated by the civil registration). That body had lost its private status to the jurisdiction of the German State in the late 1930s. Normally, in place of the civil registrations, ambulance aircraft had by then reverted to their Stammkennzeichen.

ABOVE: As described in the text, this example of an Fi 156 D-0 used for air ambulance work, possibly in Italy, included some interesting anomalies. Even the placement of the Red Cross markings on the wings was unique.

Another odd example was a Ju 52/3m wearing a hybrid combination. Its standard black Stammkennzeichen marking, BJ+YJ, was divided by a Red Cross marking as large as the original Balkenkreuz marking. The side surfaces only of the fuselage, from trailing edge of the wing back to the leading edge of the horizontal tail plane, were painted white over the standard 70/71 camouflage. Standard Red Cross markings appeared on the wings, with the Hakenkreuz marking on the fin, The aircraft carried the 04-coloured tactical markings applied for Operation Marita in April 1941. It may have been photographed during the period when the change to ambulance markings occurred.

Another oddity was a Fi 156, finished white all over, bearing the Stammkennzeichen CI+QZ, with oversize red cross markings lapping the full wing chord, as well as being marked as large as possible across both fin and rudder. The latter position was not normally used for such markings. In addition, a tiny black Hakenkreuz marking appeared near the leading edge of the fin, just above the fin/fuselage junction. While no date is known, the fact that the Stammkennzeichen were marked in the reduced size introduced for the first two characters of military codes, indicates that it was around mid-1943 or later. Stammkennzeichen were not required to be marked in that manner and this aircraft carried not a single marking that was applied correctly, indicating that they had been applied at unit-level. Lack of any Theatre of Operations markings indicates also that it might have been operating in Italy at that time.

1 Dr. J. H. Kitchens research.

2 L. DeZeng research.

3 Alert in the West, William Kimber and Co. Limited., London, 1955.

4 Crashed Enemy Aircraft Report No. 257, Dated 25th October, 1944.

5 Messerschmitt Bf 109 F, G, & K Series, Prien & Rodeike, Schiffer Publishing Ltd., USA 1993, page 157.

6 Op Cit, page 170.

7 Dr. J.H. Kitchens research.

8 Broken Eagles 2, Bf 109 G/K part 1, page 5.

9 AIR40/45

10 Dr. J.H. Kitchens research

11 Ibid

12 Ibid.

13 Ibid.

14 Ibid.

15 Ibid.

16 Ibid.

17 Ibid.

18 Ibid.

19 Ibid.

20 G. Punka via T Poruba.

21 Heinz Schmidt and R. Chapman correspondence.

Night Fighters

The first tentative night fighter exercises were carried out in May 1936, near Berlin, using aircraft from II./JG 132. Further independent trials were then conducted in 1937, using II./JG 132, JG 134 and I./JG 137, the results being collated and passed to the OKL in November 1937. The perception however remained that night fighters would be only a support to the considerable flak and searchlight defences of Germany. The results of these initial trials however were inconclusive, and while sufficient interest was raised to permit some units to continue with modest trials, the OKL showed little real interest until 1 February 1939 when 10./JG 131 was activated as an experimental night fighter Staffel. On 1 June, 10./JG 132 was added to this meagre force, and other small detachments were added over the next few weeks; but in July the idea was soundly rejected at a conference of service chiefs – Germany would rely on its considerable Flak forces for defence and existing Luftwaffe units were returned to the control of day fighter units. To that point the Ar 68 had been the main type used for the experiments, though a few Bf 109s had also been tested in the role. For the Ar 68s, no change from their prevailing RLM 63-finish had been deemed necessary until the political crisis of 1939 resulted in hasty camouflaging of many second line aircraft viewed as being potentially useful for front line duties. At that point some Ar 68s were given upper surface camouflage of standard 70 and 71.

In the interim, Ar 68s had become the first Luftwaffe aircraft to be tried operationally in the night fighting role since the end of the 1914-1918 war. In 1938 three Ar 68 E-1s of 5./J.88 had been based at La Cenia from where they had flown a few night interception patrols over Castellon during the Spanish Civil War; however, lack of opposition had deprived them of any chance of success or indeed, the development of tactics. Like their home-based counterparts, the three aircraft had retained their overall 63-colouring, no specific camouflage being deemed necessary for their role. However, they had been marked with standard Condor Legion form of coding, with solid black numerals '9●1', '9●2' and '9●3'.

ABOVE: Two of the Luftwaffe's first three night fighters. Coded 9●1 and 9●2 these two Ar 68 E-1s were attached to 5./J 88 in Spain. Colouring for both aircraft was standard 63 overall finish to which Spanish Nationalist tactical markings had been added. (D. Vincent)

The RLM lack of interest in developing a night fighter force continued until the first RAF bombing raid on the night of 15/16 May 1940, when 99 aircraft were sent to attack industry and railway targets in the Ruhr, with another 12 sent to attack communications targets in Belgium. While good weather favoured the bombers, intense ground haze robbed the Flak defences of their anticipated effectiveness. No British bombers were shot down though one crashed, through weather conditions, in France. Damage to German targets was light; but the effect had been alarming.

The subsequent onset of British night bombing attacks, despite the sporadic accomplishments, resulted in reactivation of the night fighter concept, though still in very limited form, obsolescent Bf 109 Cs and Ds and Ar 68 Fs being employed, all of which retained standard 70/71/65 camouflage. The Ar 68s had been repainted in standard 70/71 splinter pattern, but unlike the Bf 109 Cs and Ds (which had been modified to the new fighter standard with raised demarcation line on the fuselage side surfaces) the upper surface greens extended right down the sides of the fuselage. Furthermore as a unique point amongst the fledgling night fighter force, permanent black 7160.22 nitro-cellulose was sometimes applied over the 63- or 65-coloured lower surfaces. This exclusiveness may have resulted from a decision to retain full day camouflage for the Bf 109 C and D aircraft in case they were needed for daylight operational sorties.

When the German night fighter command finally came into being in July 1940, no specialised night fighter scheme existed for its Bf 110 and Ju 88 aircraft. Unlike the bomber force, theirs was a dedicated, not intermittent role, and an overall finish in permanent black was adopted in place of the temporary 7120.22 finish. That was done with lacquer 7160, the nitro-cellulose finish used for Hakenkreuz and Balkenkreuz markings, distinguishable by its very smooth texture, which produced a very slight sheen. As noted above, the Ar 68 F aircraft diverted to this role employed that lacquer. Photographs of Ju 88s and Bf 110s of this early period are distinguished by an overall low sheen finish that shows no distinction between the general finish and that of the black area of the Balkenkreuze. This extremely smooth 7160.22 finish also produced less drag, and under cover of darkness did not compromise the aircraft as it might have done under daylight conditions. However, use of 7160.22 gradually disappeared during 1941 as replacement aircraft were received, camouflaged in permanent black 7124.22 at point of manufacture. Unit codes were usually applied in 77-colouring.

A letter written by Wolfgang Falck in answer to questions raised about the evolving night fighter camouflage of that period makes interesting reading:

> *"… Our first reaction, when we were converted from Zerstörer to night fighter, was to paint our birds black, because we thought that then they would be difficult to see. We changed the colour several times, according to experience of the crews. There couldn't be an order from the 'green desk' [Headquarters], because they had even less experience, not to say none at all! So we changed the moment when we believed that we had a better solution. I can't remember at which time that happened and which colour followed the other. Very soon, we came to the*

ABOVE AND RIGHT: An Ar 68 F serving with 10.(Nachtjagd)/JG 72, in south-western Germany in 1940, converted for night fighting using camouflage of 71/02 with black applied to the under surfaces. The gloss on the black tail wheel cover indicates that this was a nitro-cellulose finish in permanent paint. The splinter pattern is close to standard for the period. (H. Obert)

LEFT: Ageing Ar 68 Fs were supplemented by Bf 109 C and Ds, this group serving with 11.(N)/JG 2 at Vaarnes, near Trondheim, in Norway in 1940. Camouflage was the revised form in 71/02, but the 65-coloured side and under surfaces had been retained rather than utilizing black as with the Ar 68 F in the previous photographs.

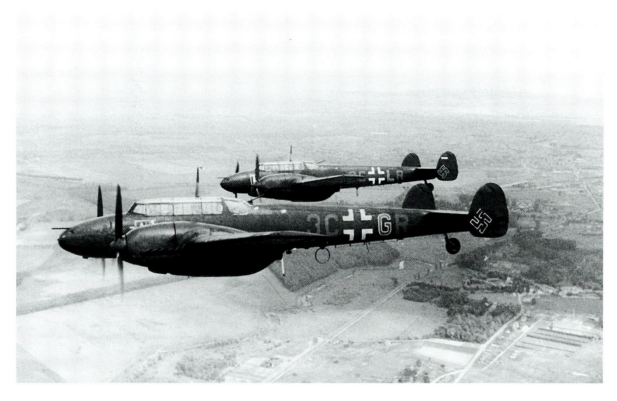

LEFT: All-black finish, which came into use in 1940 when a night fighter force was established, was still in force when these Bf 110 Es of 7./NJG 4 were photographed in 1941. The slight sheen produced by the nitro-cellulose finish is just discernible on the engine cowling and forward fuselage. Code letters were in 77 grey with the aircraft letter outlined in white. The aircraft in the background, 3C+LR, has a line of white kill marks near the top of the fin.

ABOVE: Under duller light conditions the sheen on the nitro-cellulose finish was less noticeable, as seen here on this Bf 110 C, L1+BL of Stab I./NJG 3. The grey code letter 'B' was outlined in the Staffel colour of yellow. Note that the fuselage Balkenkreuz had had its white areas slightly toned down, with a patchy wash of black. In the background is Bf 110 C, L1+LK and a Ju 88 nightfighter.

RIGHT: A less than perfect colour photograph of a Bf 110 of NJG 1, showing the black overall finish with the aircraft code letter 'D' marked in yellow on the tip of the nose cone. The sunlight had caught the yellow filter attached to the landing light fitted in the leading edge of the port wing, the yellow acting as an aid in restricted visibility landings. (J. Crow)

opinion, that the paint colouring [SEEN] from above should be dark, so no cdifference [WAS MADE] to the colour from above, but the view from the ground shouyld be light[ER]. However the view from the ground should be light. It is certain, that early on no order about the camouflage schemes existed, but it is possible, that later, after more we had more experience and so many new night fighter units were created, that then the colour of the camouflage was ordered from the big bosses..." [1]

This makes interesting reading when trying to ascertain the precise period in which the Luftwaffe changed over from its all black finish to the lighter greys for its night fighter force.

The accompanying photograph shows a Do 217 J in an overall pale finish which illustrates another step in this developmental process. Major Günther Radusch, Kommandeur of I./NJG 3 reasoned that a pale finish would make an aircraft more difficult to detect at night and, after discussing his idea with Oberleutnant Hans-Joachim Jabs of NJG 1, they decided to put the theory to the test. They had a Do 217 painted in a very pale overall finish, although the precise colour is not known, but with the exception of the underside wing tips which were left yellow, the finish was definitely a smooth textured temporary paint that had been sprayed very thinly over the entire airframe including the gun barrels, radar antennae and even the engine cooling fan blades. While 76

would seem to be the logical colour choice, the overall tone is much brighter, closer to an off white – and 76 was not available as a temporary colour at this period of the war. RLM 77 was available in temporary finish, and also had a smooth finish, but the shade shown is too light for that colour, at least at full strength. While a very thin application, as shown here, could influence the tone, the finish more likely may have been a mixture of temporary white and 77. For the trial flight the modified Do 217 J was flown by Radusch, with Jabs flying an all black Bf 110. The two men related the account to Eddie Creek in 1968, at which time he was also given the photograph. Radusch flew his Do 217 so close to Jabs' aircraft, without being detected, that it scared Jabs when finally he saw it; as the latter remarked, the Do 217 was not exactly a small aircraft.

The all-black finish for night fighters continued in use until early 1942 (though some isolated examples were still to be seen a year later, probably awaiting their major overhaul for any repainting) before being superseded by greys 74, 75 and 76. The night sky is rarely black, and greys provided better concealment, as the RAF also discovered. Camouflage directive D. (Luft) T 2217 N-1 issued on 23 February 1943, for the painting of the Do 217 N-1 night fighter, contained a mixture of colours. It was similar to that of the day fighter force, with 74/75 upper surfaces, but restricted to the plan view only, and applied in straight-edged standard splinter pattern form as for the bomber version. Sides and under surfaces were to be finished in 02 or 76 with patches in 74 and 75. Those patches were much larger than the usual mottling, probably being adopted because of the larger size of the airframe compared to that of a single-engine fighter.

Why both 02 or 76 were listed for use on sides and under surfaces is not explained in

BELOW: The revised form of night fighter colouring was in stark contrast to the all black finish, as shown by this Do 217 N-2, PE+AW, awaiting delivery. Camouflage was 76 overall, with mottling in 74 and 75 restricted to the plan view. The inside face of each of the fin and rudder assemblies was however given a network pattern of both colours, with the darker 75 predominating here. The 74-colouring also was used as the background for the revised style of Balkenkreuz marking, the RLM directive calling for the darkest colour of the camouflage to be used, as shown here. The radar array for the Lichtenstein BC 'Maratzen' had not been fitted at the time that the photograph was taken. (D. Vincent)

ABOVE: Experimentation with night fighter finishes continued for some time, before the final shift from the all black to day fighter colouring took place. This Do 217 J was used to test a very pale overall finish, thinly sprayed over the entire airframe, including the propeller blades, cooling fans, gun barrels, radar array, code letters (Satmmkennzeichen?) and national markings. On the original print it was just possible to detect the Balkenkreuz marking and the two letters 'CK'; the thinness of the application, and its liberal application, point to the finish being a temporary one. The precise colour is unknown, but may have been either 76 or possibly 77, though the tone looks too light for the latter. The presence of yellow wing tip markings and the dent in the nose section, indicate that this was an operational aircraft, rather than a factory issue test machine. The aircraft was flown for the trials by Major Günther Radusch, (see text).

ABOVE: A rare bird; an Fw 190, G9+XV from 11./NJG1 with the unit emblem marked on the engine cowling. The small size of the unit code identifies the date as after mid-1943. III. Gruppe used Fw 190 As at one stage of its operational career. The camouflage appears to be a solid application of a single dark colour (75?) over 76' with mottling confined to the fin and rudder. Note the blade aerial beneath the port wing. (M. Jessen)

ABOVE: An unusual camouflage scheme for the He 219 VO+BC was this 82-finish with soft mottles of a slightly darker colour, not 81 judging by the mottles that were extended down onto the 76 surfaces. The tone of the mottle colouring, judged against both the pure black of the Balkenkreuz and the very pale whitish-grey of the 76-colouring point more to 83 rather than 81 having been used. Note the incorrect form of Balkenkreuz marking, just the solid black centre being retained. The choice of this ground defensive scheme was becoming more common amongst night fighters during the closing weeks of the war. (S. Coates)

any document so far located; it was not intended to be part of the mottling process as patches of 74 and 75 were specified for that purpose. Eventually 02 would be used to tone down the 76-colouring on nightfighters, but that process had not appeared at the time under discussion. While inclusion of 02 disappeared fairly swiftly from the painting specifications, the main colours of 74/75/76 continued in force until 1944, albeit with distinctive variation in style of application, though 74 already was being dropped from some schemes by late 1943. The improved Do 217 N-2 model had entered service late in 1942 in the same basic scheme, but mottling had been removed from the sides of the fuselage whilst being retained on the inside faces of the fins and rudders above the tail plane. Retention of the mottling in this area was logical as it blended with the segmented upper surfaces when the aircraft was viewed at an angle.

By March 1944 black had reappeared on the few He 219s in service, some Bf 110s and occasionally on Ju 88s. Application was restricted to the lower surface of the starboard wing and the engine nacelle, though not always where the nacelle projected beyond the wing surface. The Balkenkreuz marking was left unobscured and stood out against the black background. This was a visual aid marking for searchlight and Flak crews defending metropolitan areas. The earliest documented example was that of Bf 110 G, W. Nr. 5546, 2Z+OP of 6./NJG 6, which landed in Switzerland on 15 March 1944. The starboard wing under surface was painted black, ending in a soft, slightly wavy line just short of the wing leading edge. The black was also applied to the external fuel tank below this wing. A second example turned up in Switzerland on 28 April, another Bf 110 G, C9+EN of 5./NJG 5. It too had its starboard wing lower surface painted black in the same distinctive manner, ending in a wavy-edged finish.

Interestingly, a Do 217 N-2, 3C+IP, W.Nr. 1570 of 6./NJG 4 also landed in error in Switzerland, on 2 May 1944. It had a camouflage of 74/75/76 with the greys applied heavily to the upper surfaces and the side surfaces aft of the wings, but lacked any black marking beneath the starboard wing. It is known that use of the black, single wing marking was brief, and this example may provide an approximate time marker for closure of that practice. The earliest dated example, mentioned above, is equally unlikely to provide a definitive date indicator for introduction of the marking, which could have occurred in the preceding weeks. In the absence of any OKL order, all that can be definitively stated from these examples is that the marking was in use from March to May 1944.

Use of the 74/75/76 scheme continued on some Bf 110 night fighters, but a general change had occurred around the end of 1943/early 1944 with adoption of soft sprayed mottling, only in 75, on

the upper surfaces of the overall 76-coloured surfaces on the He 219. This scheme was in broad use before the August 1944 total withdrawal of 74 was officially promulgated and gives an indication of just how early the reduction in colours by the RLM had been implemented in its quest to conserve resources, at least amongst this class of fighter. The fact that it seems to have been implemented on night fighters, well before applying the change to day fighters in general, may have been influenced by the purely nocturnal role, where removal of one grey from a pair of greys was not such a radical shift in terms of camouflage and offered a savings both in materials and labour at a time when such savings were becoming ever more critical.

The solid application of 75 alone was applied in strict plan view form, over the otherwise overall finish of 76, a scheme seen mostly on Bf 110 G night fighters, though a similar style of a solid application to wing and horizontal tail surfaces also occurred amongst the handful of Me 262 two-seat night fighters that entered service in 1945. Alternatively, 75 was used as a mottle over the 76, though some applications show that the procedure was reversed, with 76 being sprayed over a solid application of 75, producing an open net-style of finish that broke up the solid 75-finish very effectively.

ABOVE: An abandoned Bf 110 G-4 night fighter that had crash-landed, due to collapse of the starboard undercarriage. It had been abandoned well before the occupation of the airfield by USAAF forces judging by the weathering stains on the camouflage beneath the cockpit. Camouflage was 74/75/76, which also identified it as an aircraft built before early 1944. The tubular mounting rod fitted to the nose was for a FuG 212 radar array.

ABOVE: The He 219 V 33, DV+DL, photographed during the summer of 1944, wore standard 76 with 75-coloured mottling, the latter applied as a very soft sprayed application. Note that the Balkenkreuz marking beneath the wing had been applied only as the central solid black portion. The fuselage marking was of the obsolete form, retaining its black centre, though this may have resulted form the fact that the overall camouflage offered no strong areas of dark colouring, for use as the centre to the white outline of the marking.

ABOVE: Use of black beneath the starboard wing commenced around March 1944, but its employment was relatively brief, spanning perhaps only two months. This Bf 110 G-4, C9+?? of NJG 5, appears to have extended the use to the upper cowling of the starboard engine judging by the remaining section near the wing leading edge. General camouflage was 74/75/76 and the black area of wing marking ended in a straight line, following the front spar line.

ABOVE AND RIGHT: On 28 April 1944, Oblt. Johnen's Bf 110 G-4/R3, C9+EN, of 5./NJG 5 landed in Switzerland following engine failure during a night interception of a Lancaster. A new aircraft, it was fitted with FuG 212 and FuG 220 radar. Camouflage was 76 overall with small patches of 75 mottled over this finish, which covered all upper and side surfaces including the spinners and even the exhaust pipes. Its starboard wing lower surface was painted black; ending in a wavy-edged finish. The tail fins carried a tally of 17 kill markings transferred from Johnen's previous aircraft. (Museum der Schweiz via Grp Cpt. Richardson)

RIGHT: During the mid-war period, night fighter camouflage adopted the 'Arabesken' form of overspray using the lower surface colour over the upper surface dark colouring. This close-up view of a Ju 88 shows this type of modification, which often included also the spinners, as seen here. The radar array is for a FuG 220 SN-2 installation.
(Royal Danish Air Force via M. Jessen)

ABOVE AND RIGHT: Two views of Ju 88 G-7, W.Nr. 620643, 3C+PN of 5./NJG 4, showing the other method of producing a mottled pattern. This time 76 has been sprayed over a solid application of 75 on the extreme upper surfaces. Compare the solid 76-coloured fin and rudder on this aircraft with the tail of the machine on the left, W.Nr. 714759. The latter has 75 sprayed in mottles and streaks, over the 76- finish, which was continued as a dense mottle pattern on the fuselage, engines, wings and tail surfaces, but was not continued beyond the wing leading edge.

LEFT: Ju 88 G-7a, W.Nr. 623185, showing the manner in which the 75-colouring had been applied as a very dispersed, ragged mottle pattern on the fuselage upper surfaces as well as the fin and rudder, but as much larger forms of mottles on the starboard wing and starboard horizontal tail surfaces. In distinct contrast, the 75-colouring had been applied in linear fashion on the port wing and horizontal tail surfaces. As the aircraft carried no front line markings, and marking of Stammkennzeichen had been forbidden since August 1944, it is probable that this was a new machine captured when awaiting delivery when captured. Thus the eclectic painting of the camouflage probably resulted from pre-painting of components and then failure to match the parts up at final assembly, possibly the result of damage to component stocks at the assembly plant. (J. Crow)

BELOW: Compare this photograph of another new Ju 88 G-7a night fighter, W.Nr. 622891, taken from approximately the same angle. The finish again was, 76 overall with mottling in 75 on the fuselage and horizontal tail surfaces, but in this instance, both wings had an almost solid application of 75. As in the previous photograph, the stark whiteness of the late war 76-colouring stands out well, On both aircraft the Balkenkreuz and Hakenkreuz markings were correct for the period. Note the Schräge Musik installation of two 20 mm MG 151 cannon. (J. Crow)

310

In view of the RLM directives reducing labour times and materials, this seems to have been a somewhat profligate form of application, but it was also to be found on some Ju 88 night fighters. It may have arisen as retrospective modification to a batch of aircraft that had initially been finished with a solid application of 75 to the upper surfaces, and 76 to the remainder. The crossing lines of 76 would have been the simplest and quickest manner of breaking up the solid area to form something more akin to the preferred mottling in 75. Alternatively, the process may have arisen to compensate for the ever-whitening appearance of the late production 76-coloured lacquer. Given the very thin nature of the lacquer applications by that period of the war, applying the darkest colour first would help to tone down the rather stark paleness of the 76, much in the same way that some Me 262s and Ar 234s appear to have used 81 as the overall base colour with 82 sprayed over it in segments, producing a lesser degree of contrast (see Chapter 6).

While Ju 88 night fighters followed the same main trend, 75 being applied as a mottle, none appear to have adopted the solid 75-coloured upper surfaces seen on some late production Bf 110s. A few Bf 109 Gs were also employed in the night-fighting 'Wilde Sau' role, but they retained daylight camouflage applicable to late production versions of this type. The few units involved were usually in an aircraft-sharing role with a day fighter unit at the same base, which explains why day camouflage had been retained.

Because of the late date, a Ju 88 G-6 night fighter shot down by fighters over Broek-Sittard on 29 November 1944 revealed an interesting example of what appears to have been the elusive green-blue colouring. 4R+RL W.Nr. 620055, was described in an Intelligence report [2]: "...*camouflage was duck-egg blue with dark mottling sprayed on the upper surfaces, with 'A' painted in black on the nose*." The NJG 2 code '4R' had been painted 13 cm high with 'RL' in large black letters. A Roman 'IV' appeared under the Werknummer, which was painted on the fin. The date, and the description of 'duck-egg blue', a common colour description for green-blue colouring is indicative of another instance of that elusive late war colour. As noted in other parts of this work, 76 had become a washed out very pale blue, often described as a grey-white colour by that stage of the war, something unlikely to be confused with this description of green-blue.

Colouring for night fighters had become more variable as ground protection needs exceeded those of the air. NJG 101 had been operational on the Eastern Front and slowly forced to retreat to the West. Among the Bf 110s surrendered at war's end was 9W+BO, which wore a base coat of 76 with a slightly thinned application of 81 sprayed over all upper and side surfaces in a dense network of lines, a far remove from the highly simplified 75/76 scheme to which night fighters, in general, had been reduced in August 1944.

Another interesting machine to surrender, to the Swiss, was Ju 88 G-6, W. Nr. 623211, of 7./NJG 5, which landed at Dübendorf airfield on 30 April 1945. Again, for what was a pure night fighter, its camouflage was unusual

ABOVE: Ju 88 G-6, W.Nr. 623211, C9+AR of 7./NJG 5 which landed at Dübendorf airfield in Switzerland on 30 April 1945. The entire upper and side surfaces were finished in a dense mottle of what the Intelligence report described as moss green with olive spots, (82 with 81 mottle). Density of the application almost entirely obscured the overall 76-colouring. Note the line of 76-colouring on the leading edge of the flap, which is partly lowered. The markings, painted out by Swiss personnel, were white outline Balkenkreuz, solid white Hakenkreuz, white codes and Werknummer.
(Museum der Schweiz via Grp Cpt. Richardson)

ABOVE: Photographed at the end of the war, this Ju 88 G displays the last form of production camouflage for the type – 76-colouring overall with mottles of 75 to break up top and side surfaces. Note the addition of spiral markings to the spinners, in accordance with the mid-1944 directive for aircraft based in Western Europe, though this was only of value to daylight operations. The starboard wing under surface appears to have a black finish aft of a line running parallel to the wing leading edge, just forward of the Balkenkreuz marking, but whether this was another example of the limited temporary marking adopted by night fighters is unknown. The propeller blades appear also to be in black rather than the standard RLM 70. Balkenkreuz and Hakenkreuz markings are of the correct, late-war form.
(Royal Danish Air Force via M. Jessen)

– a base coat of 82 with a dense mottle of 81. Lower surfaces were recorded as "*light blue*", which was probably 76. Code letters C9+AR had been applied in solid white with the first two 1/4 size, as per the regulations. National markings were also strict regulation variety in style with white outline Balkenkreuz markings on fuselage and wing upper surface, and black outline form below the wings. However, the Hakenkreuz markings, like the codes, had been applied in solid white, as was the Werknummer at the tip of the fin. Use of 81 and 82, while dark, would have sufficed as a night fighter camouflage, whilst more importantly also doubling as a good daylight ground dispersal defensive scheme.

On first consideration the solid white national markings on the upper and side surfaces seem an anomaly for both roles. However, camouflage nets over the national markings, standard practice since the first day of the war, would have been adequate during static parking of the aircraft in daylight hours, and at night the distinctive national markings would have been an aid to the Flak crews. The original overall 76-colouring on the upper surfaces could be detected where the flaps were partly depressed, and close examination of photographs shows small areas of 76 just visible where the base coat of 81 had been thinly applied. There is no sign of regulation 75-colouring on the upper areas of the airframe. Why this scheme was utilised for an aircraft built specifically as a night fighter, and issued to a night fighting unit, remains an enigma, but the reality was that night fighters, like all aircraft, were most at risk while at dispersal during daylight hours in the last weeks of the war. The change from its overall 76-colouring, detectable as noted above, was probably done post-production by a maintenance unit where such non-standard changes were effected.

By the late war period, the night fighter force comprised principally Bf 110s and Ju 88s. It was with these two types that the force would finish its war despite the promise of such new designs as the He 219, which only became operational in very small numbers, and the Ta 154 which failed to enter service in this role other than in token, test numbers. The Me 262 was also tried in the role but again only seven had been delivered to 10./NJG 11 before the war ended, and only four of them radar-equipped two-seater machines.

The Me 262 B-1a/U1s displayed camouflage application variations not dissimilar to the Ju 88 described above. The two-seater night fighter conversions had been carried out at the Deutsche Lufthansa airframe and engine repair facility at Berlin-Staaken, and it was there that the mixture of camouflage schemes applied to those few conversions had originated.

The historical record is fortunate in that Mr Ronald Belling has left an eye-witness account of W. Nr. 110305, 'Red 8', as he first saw it in June 1954 in South Africa in its original state. His record of that time was later presented in an *Air International* [3] magazine article in April 1975 accompanied by some fine artwork prepared by himself; it was, in short, a very clear and unequivocal reporting of what he saw. However, the 1975 article had one disadvantage – Belling's original examination relied on colours he had actually seen, significantly, described by him as a variety of shades of 'green', with no mention of a distinct brown. In the article he had appended RLM numerical designations that subsequently had been published in the intervening 20 years and considered to be correct at that time. Given the lingering controversy about 81 brown

violet and the confusion of the written description 'dunkelgrün' for 81 in a Do 335 document, it is more reliable to rely on his original visual colour descriptions. That is not a criticism of the accuracy of his report, but rather a factor of the confusion to which all of us have been exposed until more recent times.

BELOW: This line-up of Ju 88s, mostly night fighters from several units gathered for disposal at war's end, accords a good selection of prevailing camouflage schemes. W.Nr. 620542, nearest the camera, had the very abbreviated 76/75-colouring as seen in the earlier photographs. The next, W.Nr. 620818, had the same factory finish, but with scribbles of 75 added, post-production, to the side surfaces. The next machine is a Ju 88 S, 4D+BW of 12./KG(Erg.)30, which had 82 sprayed in three large segments between the cockpit and the fin, leaving the overall 76-finish in between. The 82 was taken down the sides of the fuselage to about the line of the wing root, with 02 sprayed as a snaking series of lines. The sides of the fuselage, and parts of the fin and rudder assembly, had had 81 added (note that the black 'W' of the code is darker than the 81-camouflage). The '77' painted in 04 across fin and rudder identified that it was used for training. The tip of the fin and rudder were painted blue 24, the IV. Gruppe colour. The fuselage white band marking had the code '4D' marked in reduced-size characters, as per standing instructions introduced in mid-1943; however, the reason for the white band is unexplained. The next two, W.Nr. 620407 and W.Nr. 730144(?) coded 'D5' were both from NJG 3. The nearer wears a finish of 76 with 75-mottle modified on the side surfaces, and scribbles of two colours, probably 74 and 75. The next machine has a similar overall finish, but on the sides of the fuselage the darkest colour had been used to form a sharp-edged pattern, reversing the tonal effect seen on 4D+BW. Behind that is an intriguing finish. Under strong magnification the aircraft has a solid application of a dark colour (83) over the rear fuselage upper and side surfaces and vertical tail surfaces with a very dark colour (81) used as short snaking lines. However, the engine cowlings retained their 76-overall finish with 75-coloured mottle. The radar aerials on the nose confirm that it was a night fighter.

ABOVE: This rear view of Me 262 W.Nr. 110305, 'Red 8', shows the solid application of a single colour to the wing (and horizontal tail plane) as described in the text. Ronald Belling's detailed description of the camouflage preserved the best-documented notes on these rare two-seat night fighter variants. Judging by the Halifax C.Mk.VIII in the background, this photograph appears to have been taken at Farnborough, before this Me 262 was transferred to the Fighter Interception Development Unit at Ford, in July 1946.

Belling described the aircraft as having 76-coloured side surfaces lightly sprayed with thinned-out 02, which softened the colour, producing a warmer tone, (this was consistent with camouflage applications to Bf 110 night fighters of the period). The fact that 76 was, by then, a much paler shade of blue, tending to a whitish-grey, the use of a fine spray of 02 was advantageous. Over that a mottle of a variety of shades of "green" had been applied – which can only have been 82 and 83. Those had been sprayed in a "fine but irregular" pattern with some disparity in style of application between the port and starboard sides (the normal disparity that resulted from two painters, one each side of the aircraft). The port side had a fairly regular style of mottling, but the starboard side also showed some short strokes and lines. The positioning of panels and fairings were quoted as having had some influence on the distribution of the application, 83 being the dominant colour and more concentrated in some areas.

The entire upper surfaces of the wings and horizontal tail plane were 82, (there can be no confusion over the RLM numerical description used by Belling for that colour). Use of a solid application of colour was consistent with the prevailing night fighter camouflage application of a single solid colour (though normally that would have been 75). He then described the upper cowling section (between wing leading edge and engine cowling), as having a different shade of green which blended more gradually into the black of the under sides (i.e., from a mid-green to a black). He had subsequently ascribed the RLM designation of 80 to the colour; however, use of 80 was extremely unlikely as that was a tropical colour issued to depots where aircraft from such battle areas were either maintained or converted. The likelihood of 80 having been issued to the DLH workshop at Berlin-Staaken is virtually zero. A very close match to 80 was 83, and other than use of 83 for mottling, no solid application of the colour had been in evidence elsewhere on the airframe. His own description of the mottling had been of a "fine application", so he may not have recognised a larger, solid application of the same colour; a colour shift was often significant between the two styles of application. Using 83 to blend the solid application of mid-green 82 into the black makes colour sense.

The only other green that might – just might – have been used was the darkish green that has also been found on a number of Messerschmitt airframes, used as a coating between fuselage and wing, and horizontal tail plane attachment surfaces on a Bf 109 G and a Bf 110. That was one of the internal colours that remain without a known RLM numerical designation. The same colour was used for some internal equipment and for seat and equipment frames. On balance, looking at black and white photographs of the aircraft, the use of 83 was the more probable. While such subtlety would appear to have had no value in night operations it would have aided ground defensive purposes – the same reason that had shifted some very late war night fighter colouring from the usual greys to the same colours by then in use for all aircraft.

Adoption of black for the under surfaces was an anachronism produced by 10./NJG 11's specific role for the defence of Berlin, where raging night fires produced illumination on a vast scale, sufficient at times to be detrimental to the attacking bomber force as some RAF Bomber Command accounts attest. The very pale 76-finish of the Me 262s would have made them stand out like moths in a spotlight, both to bombers and the accompanying Mosquito night fighters. The black however was not the temporary night finish of 7120.22, the evidence of the neat stencilling in 23 red over the black precluding that type of application. Also the sheen on the black surfaces, discernible in some photographs, contrasts with the flat finish on the rest of the airframe, so it was probable that 7160.22 nitro-cellulose black had been used rather than the permanent 7124.22 finish, which had a matt finish. If so, it was ironic, night fighter colouring having gone full circle.

The restoration of this aircraft in the early 1970s shows areas of 81 braunviolet, despite lack of any reference to brown in Belling's original report. Significantly, when describing internal colouring, he had stated 66 had been used for everything except "...*the sub-dividing radar console and seat frames which had been sprayed Dunkelgrün 81*." This may explain why 81 braunviolet, ended up as part of the restoration, reliance being placed by then on the RLM number identification rather than Belling's written colour descriptions. Other than for instruments, equipment casings in Luftwaffe aircraft were consistent in their colouring, a dark green being used from at least 1937 to 1945. Seat frames had used the same colouring - and Belling had described his colours as 'greens' from the start. The unfortunate confusion that reigned for so many years over written descriptions of 81 incorrectly described as "dunkelgrün" (in a single Dornier document) was still holding sway when the restoration was done – using Belling's notes and it seems, his subsequently appended (partly incorrect) RLM number designations.

W.Nr. 110306, 'Red 9', had been finished differently in parts. This aircraft, for which multiple photographic views exist, shows a finish of 76 on upper and side surfaces to which soft, thinned down, mottles of 02 had been applied along with darker mottles of full strength 75. Again each side of the fuselage exhibited variation from the other; on the port side elongated strokes were used while on the starboard side soft patches were applied, again the usual normal consequence of two painters at work at the same time. Upper surfaces of wing and fixed tail plane were finished in a dense overlapping mottle of two dark colours with very small patches of the 76 base coat showing through along the trailing edges. What the two dark colours were has not been recorded. In view of the fact that all four of the aircraft of 10./NJG 11 available in the photographic record had been modified at the same depot, the likelihood that 81 had been introduced into the scheme is extremely doubtful. With only 75 in use as a night fighter 'standard' colour it points strongly to 82 and 83 having been used. The upper portion of each engine nacelle appears to have had a solid application of 83, or the slightly cooler green mentioned above. Lower surfaces were in black.

W.Nr. 110635, 'Red 10', also retained standard night fighter camouflage of 76 overall with mottling in 75 on its upper surfaces, flanks and engine cowlings. Style of application of the 75 again varied between port and starboard sides of the fuselage; on the port side short dense strokes of colour, while the starboard side had more elongated strokes, which had resulted in a thinner application of colour. Although the wings matched the same style of application as the fuselage, oddly 76 was combined with a 75 mottle rather than a solid application, while the horizontal stabilizer had an almost solid application of a dark colour that appears to match the 75 on other parts of the aircraft. Under surfaces were finished in black. Why this one aircraft should have retained the more conventional night fighter colours is unexplained, though given the chaos of the final weeks of the war anything was possible. There is also no record of in what order the four aircraft were converted. 'Red 10' may have been the first, and as such the

subsequent change in upper surface camouflage may have been a consequence of paint stocks or revised instructions.

W.Nr. 111980, 'Red 12', had a dense, fine mottle of 75 sprayed over the 76-coloured upper and side surfaces, the mottle forming a snaking line effect in some places. Upper surfaces of the wings and tail plane wore a solid application of either 75 or 83, most probably the latter judging by the very dark tonal match of the leading edge areas, in particular the inboard slat section, and the horizontal tail plane and starboard engine top section. Lower surfaces were black, which also covered the entire nacelles and extended to the upper surface of the wings in line with the leading edges.

These four machines provide a good example of the variation that could occur during the repainting processes which were undertaken at maintenance depots. Given the fact that all four machines were converted within relatively close time proximity, the variation is a good benchmark for late war conversion depot painting standards.

LEFT: W.Nr. 110306 'Red 9', wears 76-overall on the fuselage with dark mottles 75 and softer patches of very thinned down 02. Upper surface of the wings and horizontal tail surfaces were painted in a dense mottle of 82 and 83 with a few very small areas of the original 76 finish visible, mainly along the trailing edges. Lower surfaces were 7160.22 black. The next aircraft in line, 110165, an Me 262 A-1a, wears a solid 75-finish on the extreme upper surfaces with mottling in the same colour on the 76-coloured side areas and no black on lower surfaces and engines. The remaining aircraft, also single-seaters, have a dense camouflage of 81/83 with 76 lower surfaces.

RIGHT: Me 262 B-1a/U1, W.Nr. 111980, 'Red 12' of 10./NJG 11 which was employed in the night defence of Berlin. Camouflage is 76 overall with a heavy mottle of 75 over all upper and side surfaces and a dense application of either 75 or 83 on the wings and tailplane horizontal surfaces. Lower surfaces were finished in permanent black 7160.22, the slight sheen being visible on the engine cowling. The external fuel tanks are also finished in the same lacquer. Note that the starboard engine cowling is a replacement item with its lower and side surfaces in 76.

1. Letter from Wolfgang Falck to Morten Jessen, 11 May 2004.
2. Crashed Enemy Aircraft Report No. 260 dated 11 December, 1944.
3. Air International, April 1975.

Ground-Attack Aircraft

German pre-war strategy planning envisaged close cooperation between air and ground forces, the idea ultimately resulting in development of the Sturzkampfflugzeug – the dive-bomber. A two-stage development program was initiated, the first phase in 1933 calling for an interim design. The Hs 123 design won the contract and the prototype appeared in early 1935. With introduction of a camouflage scheme using colours 61, 62, 63 and 65 early in 1936, the overall 02-colouring of the prototypes was replaced by the multi-coloured finish on production aircraft when Luftwaffe deliveries began in the summer of 1936. Anxious to test the dive-bomber concept under battle conditions, five Hs 123s were shipped to Spain for field evaluation in December 1936. Those, and subsequent deliveries of the type, retained their 61/62/63/65 scheme.

The Legion Condor's Chief of Staff however was more interested in testing the aircraft's potential in the Schlachtflugzeug (close-support) role, a concept he was developing, but which had, at that time, no official status. By sheer persistence he was able eventually to convince the Commander in Chief of the Luftwaffe of the concept, resulting in issue of a specification for a more advanced design of Schlachtflugzeug in Spring 1937. Thus another important category of aircraft was introduced to the Luftwaffe inventory.

The Hs 123 was re-categorised as a close-support aircraft and in 1938, in line with the general change to the new camouflage scheme of 70/71/65 for all land-based aircraft, new production aircraft rapidly began to appear in that finish. Some of the older machines however continued on in their original 61/62/63/65 finish, there being no reason to repaint them before their next major overhaul. The type occupied a very active role during the Polish and French campaigns, some still wearing the old 61/62/63/65 camouflage in many instances, possibly the last front line aircraft to do so in numbers in the Second World War. It then saw little further service until the opening of the war against Russia in June 1941. There the Schlachtflieger formations became all important in a war more attuned with German tactical concepts than those fought so frustratingly at arm's length against Britain.

The single-engine fighter had also been tested in the role by a part of Lehrgeschwader 2 during the Battle of Britain. The three Staffeln (4., 5., and 6.) of II. Gruppe had been equipped with Bf 109 E-4s and E-7s, and commenced ground-attack duties in July 1940. With them came a new emblem, a 920 mm-sided, solid black triangle, sometimes outlined very thinly in white. The code structure was also something new, following that of a conventional Kampfgeschwader for unit identification, but combining it with a single letter to identify the individual aircraft. The size of the Bf 109 fuselage did not lend itself to displaying the full aircraft code as well as the Schlacht emblem, so instead the process was reduced to just the aircraft letter, plus the Schlacht emblem, separated by the fuselage Balkenkreuz. While the order remained the same on both sides of a particular aircraft (i.e., letter diametrically opposite letter, etc.) the order of presentation varied from aircraft to aircraft.

The first example recorded in Intelligence reports was an E-7, W. Nr. 5567, flown by Fw. Gottschalk, which crashed on 6 September 1940. It had a yellow 'C' forward of the Balkenkreuz with the Schlacht emblem aft. Rudder and wing tips were white, though the earlier tactical colouring of yellow could be discerned. The spinner was blue with white and black rings, while the general camouflage was described as "…two shades of grey on the upper surfaces and …standard duck-egg blue lower surfaces." [1] The 6. Staffel emblem of a cat bearing a lantern and a sword was also carried.

The next 6. Staffel machine recorded in detail was Fw Pankratz's E-4, W. Nr. 3726 which fell on 5 October. This time the aircraft letter, a yellow 'M', was aft of the Balkenkreuz marking. The black triangle marking was again outlined in white and had an additional vertical black bar (outlined in white) just forward of it. The spinner was pale blue with a white tip, while the engine cowling, wing tips and rudder were yellow, the period of white tactical markings having been restricted to September; the 6. Staffel emblem was carried on the engine cowling. Camouflage was 71/02, with soft-sprayed areas of both colours taken right down the fuselage side surfaces.

The wide variation in camouflage between these two aircraft from the same Staffel is interesting. There may be a clue in that a 3. Staffel Bf 109 E brought down on 15 September had also exhibited a

BELOW: Three Hs 123s in formation from 2./St.G.165 illustrate the near absolute conformity of application of this early form of geometric three-colour sequence camouflage pattern. Nearest the camera is W.Nr. 969, 52+B13, with W.Nr. 970, 52+C13, and then 52+A13. Note also the precise positioning of the code markings.

ABOVE: In addition to its fighter role, the Bf 109 E was also used as a Schlachtflugzeug during the Battle of Britain. Ofw. Harmeling's W.Nr. 5593 was one of four LG 2 aircraft lost as a result of action on 29 October 1940, (an E-7 of 3. Staffel which crashed in France because of battle damage, two E-4s, including Harmeling's, from 4 Staffel and another E-4 of 5. Staffel). Luftwaffe loss returns cite the code for Harmeling's aircraft as '3X+N' but as the photograph shows only the aircraft code letter, a white 'N' with thin black edging, was used. ('3X' was sometimes used as a form of shorthand in German documentation for 'dreieck', which means triangle). The black triangular Schlachtflieger emblem was thinly edged in white. Camouflage was 71/02 with a thin spray of 02 over the entire spine of the aircraft. Side surface 65-colouring had been softly mottled in 02. (M. Payne)

rudimentary grey camouflage scheme. This aircraft had not worn the Schlacht emblem and used the conventional fighter identification of a numeral, in this case a brown '2'. Camouflage was described in the Intelligence report as *"… cloudy grey on fuselage, wings battleship grey upper surfaces and light blue lower surfaces."* [2]

Use of greys by 3. Staffel and conventional fighter coding had occurred at the same time, when 4., 5., and 6. Staffel were commencing their specialised role. There is a possibility that Gottschalk's aircraft was one transferred from 3. Staffel to 6. Staffel, such exchanges not being uncommon, and LG 2 had only a relatively small holding of Bf 109 Es at this time.

The descriptions of the shades of grey are also interesting; "cloudy grey", "battleship grey" and the even less definitive, "two shades of grey". It must be remembered that Intelligence Officers, who examined each aircraft wreck for technical details, were faced with a considerable workload during this period of high attrition for the Luftwaffe. Their principal focus was on technical innovation, construction details, new variants of existing designs etc.; unit codes were a source of intelligence in terms of enemy strength, but camouflage, while of interest, was very much of minor importance, as illustrated by the brief, often too brief, descriptions recorded. Thus trying to match a known colour value to the very loose colour descriptions recorded is purely speculative when it comes to the burgeoning non-standard camouflage schemes of the late summer of 1940. The greys described are indefinable in terms of actual shades of grey, but the general descriptions point to a mixture based either on RLM 66 with white added, or just a black and white mixture using 7109.22 and 7109.21 rather than the black and white lacquers used for the national markings. The latter were nitro-cellulose based lacquers and produced a slight sheen, something that would not have been acceptable for the general camouflage.

The next positively identified sample was Uffz. Morschel's 4. Staffel E-4, W. Nr. 5566, brought down on 7 October. Again the aircraft letter, a white 'F' this time, was carried aft of the Balkenkreuz with the white-outlined Schlacht emblem forward. Tactical markings were a yellow

engine cowling and spinner, and yellow wingtips and rudder. Traces of the Stammkennzeichen KB+IF could still be discerned on the fuselage.

The Hs 129, winning design for the subsequent Schlachtflugzeug specification of 1937, was slow to enter service but finally did so in 1942, wearing standard camouflage of 70/71/65. In November 1942, 4.(Pz)/Sch.G.2, the first full Staffel of the newly formed Schlachtgeschwader 2, transferred its Hs 129 Bs to North Africa in support of the failing Axis campaign. Arriving on 8 November, their tenure however was to be very brief.

Re-camouflaging of these aircraft had taken place in Poland when the unit was working up at Deblin-Irena. Staffelkapitän Hptm. Bruno Meyer recorded that the aircraft had been repainted in yellow and brown with a light overspray of violet. [3] These colour descriptions are unusual at first examination, the yellow being 79 but, at first evaluation, the brown does not appear to accord with any of the usual camouflage colours. However, it is now known that this time the pre-war RLM colours of 61, 61 and 64 were being evaluated on the Eastern Front. The brown then appears to have been either 61 (later to be reissued under the designation of 81) or alternatively, it may have been 80. The latter was issued to front line units for use in conjunction with 79 – and Meyer's description does speak of a "yellow" – while photographs show a colour scheme consistent with 79 and 80, with the latter used as small, closely spaced spots. If a thin misting of 61 (cum 81) were used over the top of the 80 it would produce a definite brown where over the 80, with a definite violet tinge to the general finish. The violet tinge to 61(81) is apparent when the original RLM colour chip is viewed under some light conditions. In the absence of any violet colour in the RLM range, or in the RAL range used by the ground forces, it would seem most likely that the colour involved was 61(81).

The colour description by Meyer is none the less corroborated by a British A.12(g) Crashed Enemy Aircraft Report filed on 'Blue A', W.Nr. 0296, which recorded the colours as greenish-brown (which would be 80) mottled with 'purple' on upper surfaces and light blue on the underside. The colour description of violet and purple is not far removed from each other in colour terms and under the circumstances described can be taken as a description of the same colour in both cases, possibly a lighter shade in the first instance because of the fine misting technique used as opposed to the denser "mottles" in the second.

After only three days of operations the Staffel was forced to withdraw to Misurata for repairs. By early January 1943, due to the hopeless supply situation, none of the aircraft were operational and the sole survivor was withdrawn to Tunisia.

But other Hs 129s had already reached North Africa, the first two aircraft from 5./Sch.G 1 arriving at El Aouina in the Tunisian bridgehead on 29 November 1942. Re-camouflaging took two distinct forms. One employed a soft-sprayed application of 79 over the existing 70/71 camouflage, leaving green areas to break up the sand colour. This was done either by covering most of the upper airframe with 79, leaving small irregular areas or spots of the original two greens, or using more widely spaced continuous wavy lines of 79. The other used the base camouflage of 70/71 over which wavy lines of 79 were added and then broken up with short strokes of 80.

One of two damaged machines, found abandoned near the harbour when the Allies had entered Tunis on 23 February 1943, wore a different scheme. The one coded 'Red K' had had 79 applied using closely spaced, wide, oblong strokes that almost obscured the existing 70/71 camouflage on the sides and upper surfaces. This was a brush application that had left slightly ragged, hard edges to each stroke, three types of broad brushes being available in the standard painter's kit at factory/maintenance facilities (see Volume One, Chapter 2).

The Fw 190 had also been employed, very successfully, in this role, but had rarely adopted a specialised colour scheme for its task, more usually retaining the 74/75/76 fighter scheme. The Fw 190 F-2 had been built specifically for the task and entered service in the spring of 1943. A few had found their way to Tunisia and were re-camouflaged in tropical colours. Style of application varied, as again these were schemes applied at maintenance unit-level. In some instances the 79 was restricted to the upper surfaces of the fuselage, leaving the side surfaces in 78. More elaborate applications involved a close mottle of 80 over a solid application of 79 on all upper and side surfaces.

The only other distinctive variation seen amongst subsequent ground-attack aircraft occurred on the Eastern Front with the creation of a night ground-attack force in December 1942. The Nachtschlachtgruppen were equipped with obsolete, former second line aircraft, composed of Ar 66s, He 45s, He 46s, He 50s and Go 145s. These retained whatever colour scheme they were wearing at time of their transfer, but their lower and side surfaces were resprayed in permanent 7124.22, their role being one of permanent night operations. As with other aircraft types operating in winter, the upper surfaces of some machines were resprayed in 21 temporary white, which was gradually removed as the spring thaw exposed a mottled terrain of browns and white.

ABOVE: Found by Allied forces at Tunis, this Hs 129 B-2, 'Red C' of 8.(Pz)/Sch.G.2, wears its original 70/71/65 finish with snaking lines of 79 sprayed over its upper and side surfaces. The port spinner was original to this machine and had been camouflaged with an over spray of 79, but the starboard spinner was a replacement in 71-colouring.

ABOVE: An abandoned Fw 190 A-5 trop, 'Yellow O' of SG 4, photographed at Catania aerodrome, Sicily, in 1943. It wears a finish very similar in tonal value to the Macchi 205 fighter to the right, possibly 79 and 80 on the upper surfaces with 78-coloured side and lower surfaces. The side surfaces additionally had had a soft mottle, in original factory style, added in those two colours with a dense patch of 80 below the cockpit windscreen quarter light. White tactical markings have been added as a band to the rear fuselage and under the wing tips. (F. Smith)

RIGHT: A line-up of factory fresh Fw 190A-5 aircraft delivered to II./SG 1, which had already added the individual aircraft letter to each, as well as marking the unit emblem on some. Camouflage was 74/75/76 with 04-coloured tactical markings to the rear of the fuselage, wing tip lower surfaces and the underside of the engine cowling; all of which had been applied at point of manufacture. The black triangular Schlacht emblem is thinly outlined in white. Note the near uniformity of camouflage application. (P. Malone)

1. AIR 22/266.
2. Op. Cit.
3. Martin Pegg research.

LEFT: The Ju 87 G-1 was fitted with 3.7cm BK cannon for ground-attack work. This abandoned machine wears standard 70/71/65 scheme with 04-colouring on rudder, wing tip under surfaces and also as a band around the engine nacelle. The fitting of the long flame-damping exhaust pipe indicates that this aircraft was used for night attacks. (Hans Obert)

BELOW: Support aircraft for front line units were usually drawn from obsolete former first line aircraft, but occasionally a current type was employed, as here with this He 111 H-6 used by the Stab of SG 3. Careful examination of the original photograph does not show the unit code of 'S7', just the aircraft and Stab letters of 'FA', the blue 'F' thinly outlined in white. Photographed at Nurmoila in Finland in 1944, the camouflage was the type seen on some other He 111s serving on the Eastern Front at that time. The base camouflage of 70/71 had been oversprayed with 65-colouring using a soft mottling-style effect that ran to ragged ribbons of colour in places. This was more effective camouflage for the type of countryside being fought over on that Front. (Valtonen via M. Jessen)

LEFT: With a less intense finish of temporary white, 'Black 9' an Fw 190 F-8 of SG 2, wears a mixture of obsolete tactical markings – an 04-coloured band around the rear fuselage, beneath the wing tips and on the lower section of the engine cowling. These were superseded in September 1944 by a combination of a single yellow band and 'V' marking. This provides a clue as to the nature of the aircraft's camouflage, which was probably not an 81/82 finish given the dates involved. (H. Obert)

ABOVE: Gathered together at Ceské Budejovice airfield at the end of the war, this collection of aircraft includes several Fw 190 Fs of SG 10, wearing a very dark overall finish. The camouflage on these was 81 and 82, which can be detected on 'White 2' in the immediate right foreground, and on 'Black 4' above and behind. Two more of the units' Fw 190s are just discernable to the left of the photograph, with the starboard wing upper surface of the nearer one visible, again showing the very dark two-tone finish. All wear the final tactical markings standard of a yellow band around the nose and a yellow rudder. The engine cowlings on 'White 2' were replacements. The contrast with the more standard colours worn by the Bf 109s and other Fw 190s is quite apparent.

ABOVE: Other obsolete aircraft were also used for night ground attacks. These Go 145s of the Latvian manned Erg. Nsgr. Ostland retain the original 02 overall finish of their former role as training aircraft (note the painted out emblem below the interplane struts, the shape, size and positioning indicating FFS A/B 72). The unit code of '6X' had been applied by stencil in white, using the background colour to fill in the marking, but the remaining two characters of the code are solid black. Note that this section of the code, while reduced in height, has been marked at approximately three times the regulation height. (B. Rosch)

Bombers

German bomber development paralleled that of fighter aircraft during the 1930s. Subject to the same conditions of service, initially they employed the same basic 02-overall finish, then changing to colour 63 until introduction of a four-colour camouflage scheme for all bombers and dive-bombers. The first to wear the multiple-colour scheme appears to have been the Ju 86 A-0 series, which began leaving the production lines in this scheme in February 1936.

This camouflage scheme took the form of a complex splinter pattern using 61, 62 and 63 for all upper and side surfaces, with 65 for the lower surfaces, providing a good ground defensive camouflage, the splinter pattern breaking up the outline of the aircraft when viewed from any angle. It was less effective as an air-to-air camouflage, but German assessment of its strength, vis-a-vis its potential combatants to the west, was such that it assumed that an air superiority role would be gained within a short time of commencing an attack.

The Spanish conflict was used to assess the technical aspects of bomber and dive-bomber types. Early deliveries of Ju 52s retained an overall 63 finish, as did some of the 30 He 111 Bs that arrived in March 1937. However, from the start, the Ju 86 Ds and Do 17 Es were seen in camouflage of 61/62/63/65, but the earliest example of this multiple-colour scheme had appeared on five Hs 123 dive-bombers that arrived in December 1936. The same camouflage scheme was also used for their subsequent successors, the Ju 87 A and B models, which were also tested in Spain. With each subsequent delivery of bomber-types the four-colour camouflage became more established amongst the bomber force, supplanting the older, plain 63 finish. There is no evidence that aircraft delivered in overall 63 finish were repainted during their period of operation in Spain.

As noted above, deliveries of the Ju 87 A-0 model in late 1936 were made in the 61/62/63/65 scheme, but by mid-1937 the multi-colour scheme was abandoned for all but the heavy bomber force, colours 70/71/65 replacing the old colours on dive-bombers. For the latter group, that situation however was to be short-lived following the

Munich crisis of August 1938. In September the old four-colour camouflage was abandoned completely and the simplified 70/71/65 scheme instituted for all classes of military aircraft. As with the previous scheme, the demarcation point between upper and lower surfaces occurred at the lowest point on the fuselage sides, on a 35 degree tangent from the lowest point on the centreline.

While the four-colour scheme had been abandoned for front line aircraft, during the opening phase of the war a few older aircraft were seen still wearing it, and even the superseded code system (see Chapter 8). That situation was brief, a combination of the result of the change over period and also the use of aircraft from the strategic reserves. Luftwaffe bombers fought the first eleven months of war in the 70/71/65 scheme before battle tactics brought about another change to camouflage – the adoption of temporary black finish for night operations.

The war situation dictated not only changes but also new products, some specifically for use by field staff. Because the Luftwaffe was principally created as a day bombing force, it lacked resources for a permanent, separate night bombing force, though it had been anticipated that some night bombing operations would be carried out. The use of temporary paints was the solution, allowing maximum utilisation of the existing force.

In June 1940, 11 Kampfgeschwader were moved into place in France and Belgium while others were deployed in Denmark and Norway. Night training sorties were begun over Britain where it had been anticipated, correctly at first, that crews would encounter little or no effective opposition other than from searchlights.

The temporary lacquer 7120.- , with the specific desired colouring pigment added to the base formula was used in conjunction with an isolating lacquer IS 238 (produced by Gustav Ruth). This lacquer had been developed not for issue to industry, but strictly for use by front line units to enable them to responsed to tactical situations encountered. The extent of its employment was limited initially, and correct utilisation of this finish was slow to be implemented within some units judging by the order issued by the Oberbefehlshaber der Luftwaffe [Genst. 6. Abt. (IIIB), Nr. 7797/40 geh.] on 16 July 1940. The document restated the regulations previously promulgated for using the temporary black finish, with the final paragraphs noting again that previous Order relating to camouflage.

> *"Already at 16. July 1940 the commander-in-chief of the Luftwaffe (General Staff 6th division (IIIB), Nr. 7797/40 geh.) has ordered the application of a night camouflage paint:*
>
> *For obtaining a largely camouflage [effect] against the searchlight effect by application of a night camouflage paint [to] the lower sides of the wings, the lower sides and the flanks of the fuselage and the tail plane inclusive, the markings applied there have to be overpainted completely with night camouflage paint.*
>
> *Only the Balkenkreuze on the top surfaces of the wings are to be left visible to show the nationality of the aircraft. Furthermore it has to be guaranteed, that the overpainted Balkenkreuze are again recognizable after washing off of the night camouflage paint.*

ABOVE: The effectiveness of the 61/62/63 camouflage may be judged by this photograph of a Ju 87 A-1, one of three St.G.163 machines sent to Spain in late 1937 to develop dive-bombing tactics under operational conditions. The visual qualities of the Nationalist markings, seen against the landscape are quite apparent.

Bombers

LEFT: A beautiful in-flight photograph of 33+A25, an He 111 P-1 of 6.Staffel, II./KG 253. The painted-out red background and white disc of the Hakenkreuz marking confirms that the photograph was taken after January 1939. Note that no attempt was made to match up the background colour segments of the 61/62/63 camouflage pattern, a single colour (62) being used for the purpose. (R. Chapman)

RIGHT: The positioning of the palest colour segment of the 61/62/63 camouflage pattern could produce quite striking effects, depending upon which type of aircraft and the angle at which it was viewed. At this angle, the He 111 P-1, (25+E33 of III./KG 152), gives the impression that it has an overall dark finish with just the nose section in a pale colour. In this instance, the Hakenkreuz marking had been applied in the correct (post-January 1939) position. The photograph was taken before May 1939 as by that date, this Gruppe was re-numbered III./KG 51. (R. Chapman)

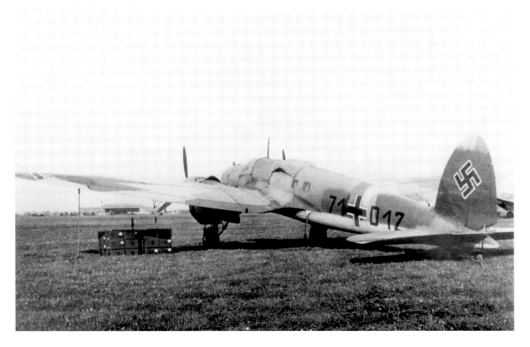

LEFT: An He 111 F, photographed at Braunschweig in the spring of 1939, something validated by the painting out of the red band and white disc marking, which sets the time as after January 1939. The overall camouflage finish was standard 61/62/63/65, but note the relatively rough manner with which the vertical tail surfaces had been repainted. The code, 71+D12, identified the aircraft as belonging to I./KG 157, a unit under the control of Luftkreiskommando VII, which had come into being on 12 October 1937, absorbing parts of adjacent Luftkreiskommando areas of control. The first two elements of the code marking, '71', had been painted out but the remainder of its code was retained. This fits with the fact that KG 157 had formed from KG 154, part of Luftkreiskommando IV, with Gruppe and Staffel order being retained, in which case the first two elements of the previous code must have been '41'. (R. Chapman)

LEFT: This Do 17, photographed from another of its unit, illustrates the reason why the 16 July 1940 additional instruction, relating to the application of temporary night black finish, was needed. The temporary night finish has been taken right over the fuselage upper surfaces, wings (leaving only the outboard sections) and tail plane horizontal surfaces. The original instruction's ruling about ("Only the Balkenkreuz on the upper surfaces of the wings are to be left visible....") had been taken out of context. Interestingly, the type of Balkenkreuz marking used on the wings was also incorrect, this being the form approved only for the wing lower surfaces and the fuselage.

RIGHT: A He 111 P being prepared for night operations provides yet another example of how the original order, relating to application of the temporary night finish, was misinterpreted. Once again the black finish was being applied over the top of the fuselage. Note that in addition to the large paint tin (standing on the tail plane), two standard issue metal buckets were being used for the 7120.22 temporary black finish, illustrating how the mixture had been prepared in bulk, rather than being applied directly from the tin. The man working on the fin and rudder assembly was using a fairly large brush that was not part of the standard painter's kit.

LEFT: An He 111 P of I./KG 55 has its engine covers removed. The starboard spinner is finished in 25 green but the port one is half 04-yellow and half 22-black making unit identity an undecipherable mixture, one of them being a replacement part. Camouflage is 70/71/65.

As far as the aircraft used for night sorties [that] *are not yet camouflaged with night camouflage paint in the above described manner, this has to be accomplished quickly. Attention has to be given to the application of a primer with isolation paint before the application of the night camouflage paint."*

Clearly, the only perceived threat to the proposed night attack force was from searchlight detection and anti-aircraft batteries. The potential for night-fighter attacks, correctly for the time, was estimated to be of little consequence. Instructions for use of the isolating lacquer IS 238 were issued in a special RLM order. (Some references show this product identification as JS 238, but this is simply a result of the confusion caused by the occasional use of the old written Germanic form of 'I', where the letter looks more like an English 'J'.) To be completely effective, the surfaces to be sprayed with this substance had to be carefully cleaned with lacquer thinner 7238.00, all oil and dirt first being removed with benzine. Instructions forbade the use of IS 238 on any of the dark-coloured camouflage areas. The IS 238 was then sprayed on, using cross-hatch strokes at 90 degrees to each application, to ensure total coverage of the surfaces, and then allowed to dry for about six hours. This set up a temporary coating between the permanent camouflage and the temporary night finish.

Lacquer 7120, with 22-colouring, was then to be applied by large ceiling (distemper) brushes and/or brooms, in strokes running parallel to the line of flight, to all under surfaces finished in the colour 65, as well as to the engine cowls and propeller spinners. The entire under surfaces and all protrusions were to be covered. Wings and horizontal tail surfaces were to have the 7120.22 taken over the upper surfaces to a point half a metre past the leading edge. The sides of the fuselage were to be painted up to a point in line with the top edge of the Balkenkreuz. The fin and rudder assembly was also to be painted over, as were the Hakenkreuz and the Balkenkreuz markings on the fuselage sides and wing under surfaces.

1941 Diagrams showing areas painted RLM 22 black, for night camouflage

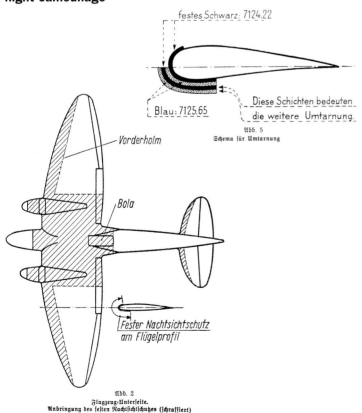

The 16 July order indicates that initially Balkenkreuzen were simply to have the temporary black washed off until the outline was again visible, but in some instances ground staff outlined the markings with white lines, allegedly using chalk for the purpose. While there is no documentary evidence to support the use of chalk, it does appear the most likely substance based on appearance, availability and ease of removal, (this situation would eventually be improved, in 1941, by introduction of a new pale grey colour, 77. When this came into use the outer white angles of Balkenkreuze were re-applied using 7120.77, thus not compromising the night camouflage. The accompanying instruction stipulated that no other colour except 77 was to be used for this purpose. For daytime flights over Germany the white portions of the Balkenkreuz markings were to be stripped back for easy identification).

The temporary black finish had a limited life and had to be removed no later than eight days after application. Rubber scrapers were to be used except in places affected by oil, wooden scrapers being used for those areas, followed by thorough cleaning with benzine. Wherever possible this was to be carried out with the wind from behind to protect the ground staff from becoming covered in the paint and fumes.

It is noteworthy that careful examination of all the available photographs of Luftwaffe bombers in temporary night camouflage, including those of wrecks shot down during the official period of the Battle of Britain (i.e., to 31 October 1940), and those referred to in British intelligence reports of the period, reveal none to have been using the 7120.77 application over the Balkenkreuz markings. There are several instances recorded in the intelligence reports that state that the aircraft had its under surfaces and markings over painted in black, something confirmed by contemporary photographs. The last for which an intelligence extract is available occurred on the night of 15/16 November 1940. Lt Svatha's He 111 H-2, W. Nr. 5509 coded A1+LN of KG 53, had its code and the Hakenkreuz marking blacked out. Had 77 been available it would have been in use during this period. All other machines, a variety of He 111s, Ju 88s and Do 17s, were recorded as having black on their under surfaces and over the markings.

This points to introduction of the additional colour 77 at a much later date. As discussed in Volume One of this study, colour identification numbers were issued in strict sequence indicating that 77 did not come into use until at least the same time period as the switch to the 74/75/76 fighter scheme of around May 1941. (Although the colours later identified as 74 and 75 were field-tested in June 1940, the significant point is that they were not approved for use, mass production and issue until early the following year. Issue of 77 before 74, 75 and 76 is unlikely, and there is no physical evidence that this occurred.) Positively dated photographs that show 77 in use all point to May 1941 as the point where this colour became available. This also connects with the issue of 74, 75 and 76 – and also 78, 79 and 80 – but the latter three were the product of much different circumstances as noted in Chapter 5 of Volume One of this work.

This process was improved in 1941 when lacquer 7124.22 was introduced as a permanent night camouflage for both bombers and night fighters. L.Dv.521/1 stated that where weathering would necessitate continuous repainting of the temporary 7120.22 finish, 7124.22 would be substituted. This was restricted to lower surfaces only. The underside of the fuselage was painted from the wing root trailing edge forward to the nose of the aircraft. Lower surfaces of the wings, plus engine cowlings, were painted completely to a point just outboard of the engines, continuing along the leading edge to a depth of no more than one metre on the lower surfaces and a half metre on the upper surfaces. Horizontal tail plane surfaces were treated in a similar manner, but with depth being restricted to half a metre maximum on both surfaces. Two sprayed coats were used for this application. 7124.65, could be used in conjunction with 7124.22 to allow rapid change from day to night camouflage and back again. The 7125.65 was only painted over the 7124.22 black-coloured area and vice versa, (SEE DIAGRAMS LEFT). Removable temporary night black 7120.22 was

ABOVE: Three He 111 Hs of 2./KG 27 illustrate the eclectic mix of stages of finish that accompanied the use of the 7142.22 smooth, permanent night black (which was restricted to specific areas as explained in the text) in combination with 7120.22 temporary finish. The aircraft in the centre of the photograph, 1G+GK, (the 'G' was red, thinly outlined in white), and the one to the left (1G+BK?) had the permanent black applied according to the diagram that accompanied the official order. The aircraft on the right of the photograph had had only the areas that normally showed heavy exhaust staining painted in 7142.22. Possibly the pressure of operations prevented the additional areas along the wings and tail plane being completed. All three aircraft carry standard Eastern Front yellow markings beneath the wing tips and as a band around the fuselage. The upper and side surfaces were covered with temporary white. (H. Obert)

applied to the remaining two-thirds of the undersides. The new paints made it possible for a far quicker change between the day and night scheme, something necessary for the changed tactical requirements of the Luftwaffe forces by then fighting on the Eastern Front.

Where exhaust fumes and oil soiled the camouflage, ground staff had found that painting them permanent black made maintenance of the surfaces easier. However the RLM objected to the increasing size of such areas, which compromised the camouflage. The practice was forbidden and instead the affected areas were sprayed with two coats of isolating material IS 238.

Middle East and Italy

The transfer of Luftwaffe units into North Africa early in 1941 had caught the German aircraft production centres un-prepared, such had been the swiftness and extent of German involvement in varying war fronts. Until

then, the air war had taken place over predominantly temperate climate areas, where existing camouflage colours had sufficed. Luftwaffe units had first appeared in the Eastern Mediterranean in 1940 when elements were transferred to assist the Italians, Ju 87 and Ju 88 formations moving to Sicily where they were employed very effectively against British shipping in the Mediterranean, and also against Malta. Despite the over-water operations and the climatic conditions, no change had been made to the camouflage of the Ju 87s, but some of the Ju 88s had introduced mottling and short, wavy lines of 70 and/or 71 to the 65-coloured lower surfaces at the front of the aircraft, effectively breaking up the stark pale colouring that formed a distinct break between the aircraft and the surface of the sea.

Transfers to Libya had begun on the last day of February 1941, followed by further units over the next couple of months. Early arrivals included the Ju 88s of II. and III./LG I and the Ju 87s of I./St.G 1, II./St.G 2 and Stab/St.G.3. Prior to supplies of 78, 79 and 80 becoming available, (starting with the original colour forms of 78 and 79 as discussed in Chapter 5), for the first two to three months aircraft were forced to operate in their European camouflage scheme.

After stocks of tropical colours became available from around late April, re-camouflaging of the Ju 87s was made in a variety of styles, indicating that each Gruppe specified to the repair/maintenance depot(s) what form the changes were to take. I./St.G.1 adopted a tight mottle of 80-coloured spots over a base coat of 79, with 78 for the under surfaces, upper surface camouflage being taken right down the sides of the fuselage. II./St.G.2 machines used a very open application of 80-coloured green segments over the sand base colour, in a manner not dissimilar to that of contemporary RAF camouflage. In contrast I./St.G 3 adopted a much looser application of 80-coloured spots over the sand base colour or, in some instances a scribble-style of 80, achieved by using a narrow spray gun setting.

Those variations underscore the fact that no standard camouflage pattern incorporating 80 had been issued with the stocks of the newly

ABOVE: Ju 87 B-2 trop, T6+AN, of 5./St.G. 2 in North Africa displays the style of unit-applied 79/80 camouflage peculiar to this unit. The fact that each of the Ju 87 B units displayed a distinctive style of modified camouflage points to each having access to a particular set of maintenance support facilities.

ABOVE: A Ju 87 R-2, of St.G. 1, fitted with a 300 litre drop tank and bomb in place, illustrating this unit's preferred style of camouflage. (Ian Primmer)

introduced tropical colours. The replacement of the entire camouflage was done through a process of rotation of aircraft through one or more of the major base facilities, for practical reasons most probably in Sicily or Italy, open-air painting being totally impractical, especially in desert conditions. The individual style of the 80-application, Gruppe by Gruppe, was however, consistent enough to identify individual ownership.

In August 1942 the Bf 109 E-7 and Me 210 fighter-bombers of III./ZG 1 were transferred to North Africa to support the Jabo Bf 109 Es of III./JG 27 and III./JG 53, which had taken on bombing attack duties in a manner similar to that of the fighter units on the Channel coast. The Bf 109 Es wore standard 78/79 camouflage with upper surface colouring taken right down the fuselage sides, but the Me 210s retained their European colour scheme of 74/75/76.

The war in North Africa had ebbed back and forth with the land battles, and the rate of attrition was high for both sides. Maintaining Luftwaffe strength proved very difficult and was only achieved by shuffling transfers of aircraft from the Balkans and Eastern Front, producing an influx of temperate camouflage schemes and 04-coloured tactical markings amidst the desert camouflage colours (usually combined with the white markings in use on that battle front.) North African-based Ju 88s and He 111s wore the factory finish of overall-79 upper surfaces with 78-coloured lower surfaces, the demarcation line being as for the 70/71/65 scheme. Like the deliveries of fighters already camouflaged in desert colours, there was to be little variation to this scheme. Such variation as was seen came, as noted above, from the influx of bombers from other theatres of operations.

Replacement Ju 87 B and R aircraft received late in 1941 had been pre-painted in tropical camouflage of 78 and 79 at point of manufacture. However, with few exceptions, the small number of Ju 87 Ds that eventually entered the action retained their European 70/71/65 camouflage. The exceptions appear to have been confined to the few new replacement aircraft delivered in factory finish tropical camouflage of 78 and 79.

Sicily had remained a useful base for anti-shipping operations in the Mediterranean and, as noted above, the Ju 88s of the Kampf-geschwadern engaged on these duties added small areas of mottling or lines, usually in 70 or 71, to the engine cowlings and front fuselage where they were painted 65. This broke up the

ABOVE: The Bf 110 was used to good effect in the fast bomber role on various battlefronts. This Bf 110 E of SKG 210 had a finish of 71/02 with its 65-coloured side surfaces toned down with a fine spray of 02, which produced a yellowish-green tinge, depending upon light conditions. The white of the spinner tips was the Staffel colour, though which Gruppe is not known.

ABOVE: The wreckage of an He 111, 6N+GG, W.Nr. 7060 of Stab V./KG 100 in full tropical camouflage of 79 upper and side surface, with 78 lower surfaces (though they appear to have been painted over in permanent black). The marking of the code group is unusual. Despite its Stab status, the marking was all in black with the last two letters of the code group repeated on the fin in white. The area behind the code group on the fuselage appears to have been painted out, either indicating a change of ownership, or simply painting over of the Stammkennzeichen marking. The white band was the standard Mediterranean theatre of operations tactical marking. (S. Coates)

solid pale areas that otherwise compromised the aircraft during low-level shipping and harbour strikes. The process was later taken further with a series of almost continuous wavy lines of 65 over the 70/71-coloured upper and side surfaces, the lines being continued onto the 65 lower surfaces using 70 or 71 in counterpoint shading (following Abbott Thayer's principles – see Volume One). As land-based bomber units, paint stocks were 70, 71 and 65 rather than the 72 and 73 of the land-based maritime units. LG 1 carried out most of its operations in the Mediterranean,

operating from Sicily, but had sent I. Gruppe to North Africa for about eight months in 1941. Some aircraft, but not all, had been repainted in the two-colour tropical scheme of 79 on top and side surfaces with 78-coloured lower surfaces. When they returned to operate from Sicily they retained their sand-coloured upper surfaces, but adopted 22 black-coloured lower surfaces for night operations.

Amidst this loose conformity of colours must be mentioned the Ju 88 described in Volume One, which had used an overall dark blue finish

ABOVE: A damaged Ju 88, L1+EH of 1./LG 1, found crashed in the Libyan desert in December 1941. It wears the overall 79-colour scheme on upper and side surfaces with 78-coloured lower surfaces. The use of 04 tactical markings beneath the wing tips and around the rear fuselage as a band was not correct for the North African theatre of operations, but this Gruppe, on temporary transfer, had previously been serving in the Balkans where such markings were in use.

ABOVE: LG 1 also used a mottled form of camouflage on its Ju 88s as this photograph of Obf. Isachsen's L1+RH shows. It was shot down near Tobruk on 17 January 1942. Camouflage is 79, heavily mottled with 80 and a paler colour, possibly thinned out 02, on upper and side surfaces. (M. Shippard)

with lines of black over that on upper and side surfaces, and then lines of pale sand colouring over that. The possible origins of that unique colour scheme have been discussed in Chapter 5, but odd colouring was not confined to just that one aircraft.

When Allied forces reached Foggia in late 1943, Intelligence officers examined the mass of aircraft abandoned on the Italian airfield. Amongst the subsequent reports were several relating to Ju 88s found at the No. 1 and No. 3 satellite strips of the main airfield. The colours attributed to them raise some interesting variations on standard finishes of the time.[1]

In addition to a training establishment, Ju 88s from LG 1, KG 1, KG 6, KG 30, KG 54 and KG 76 were found and described. It should be noted

that many of the aircraft had been burned out, blown up or badly damaged, so full descriptions were not recorded. From IV./LG 1 W.Nr. 3277, L1+BY had mottled green and blue upper surfaces with green below. KG 6 had two aircraft, W.Nr. 144721, (identified only as being originally S1+YS, possibly from the compass card marking), which was mottled green and blue on top and dark green below; the second, W.Nr. 3998, 3E+AH, had identical camouflage. W.Nr. 300203, 4D+FP (PG+IW), of KG 30 also had the same camouflage description.

What is noteworthy is the consistency of camouflage description across LG 1, KG 6 and KG 30 – all of which had dark green lower surfaces. The green and blue upper surface mottling description could have been 70/71 mottled or lined with 65, but the verification of a base overall blue scheme for so many Ju 88s from different units stationed at Foggia points more realistically to blue overall colouring mottled with a green. As recorded in Chapter 5, comments by Joachim Siebers of KG 76 confirm that some of the Ju 88s at Foggia were finished in dark blue, the monochromatic-scheme having been modified by adding snaking lines ('Arabesken') of pale colour once they arrived in Italy from München.

A secondary counter-check on the accuracy of the consistent identification of a dark green is verified by the description of W.Nr. 3562, V4+GM of KG 1, which had light blue upper surfaces and black lower surfaces (not dark green) and W.Nr. 0880 140541, B3+ER (ML+ED) of 7./KG 54, which had an identical scheme. Black and green both were clearly identified. The description of dark green lower surfaces does not fit with any prevailing standard, and most probably had been added once the aircraft were in Italy.

The nature of the dark green is speculative, but logically most likely one of the normal upper surface colours of 70 or 71, (or even 80, though this is less likely). Using lines or mottles of dark green over the pale blue finish recorded on some aircraft, simply reversed the darkish blue/pale lines counter-shading effect seen on some of the KG 76 machines (and on *some* KG 54 machines as confirmed by the Swiss report).

Some caution is required regarding the terms 'light' or 'pale' blue in some instances – but not all. Siebers's eyewitness record of a 'dark Royal blue' colour on the KG 76 aircraft is beyond question, yet from his own unit W.Nr. 300058 had been found wearing what was described by the Intelligence officer as a 'pale' blue overall scheme. The ever-present greyish-white clouds of dust at the airfield complex, which coated everything, may have accounted for a perception of a paler shade of blue on some aircraft remains. The pervasiveness of the dust is attested to by Siebers:[2]

"The Foggia area was notorious for its heavy greyish-white dust. All aircraft were so thickly covered with it, that one could hardly tell what colour lay underneath, several aircraft taxying together would blow up such clouds of dust, that we could see nothing more, and usually had to turn on our formation lights."

Credibility has to be given to the presence of two shades of blue – the dark one described by Siebers, and either 65 or, perhaps less likely, the contemporary lighter shade of the 78. The few reliably identified photographs of Ju 88s taken in Italy in 1943 all show a darkish upper and side surface finish, with lines of a pale colour snaking over it, more consistent with Siebers's description and the Swiss record of the Ju 88 of KG 54. Photographic evidence for a paler blue finish with green added to it remains elusive at the time of writing.

LEFT: Full tropical camouflage for bombers seems to have been confined almost exclusively to the North African area, though transfers of units to Italy and Tunisia did produce a sprinkling of tropical colours in those locations. This Sicilian-based Ju 88 A-4, 4D+DR, of III./KG 30, wore standard 70/71/65 camouflage with the 7. Staffel colour used for the aircraft letter, and also as a band around the spinners. The white tactical band marking around the rear of the fuselage denotes the aircraft's Mediterranean theatre of operations disposition.

RIGHT: The variation in the style of the 79-coloured 'Arabesken' seen in this group photograph of five Ju 88s taken from an unidentified 8.Staffel aircraft operating over Italy, illustrates the random nature of this form of camouflage modification. Added at a maintenance depot, the application was very much at the whim of the painters involved with each aircraft. As noted in Volume One, Chapter 5, it is difficult to determine what the base camouflage colour was for many of the Ju 88s operating out of Italy. The addition of 79-colouring as thin snaking lines, in combination with non-tropical camouflage colouring produced an effective compromise for Mediterranean operations.

LEFT: This Ju 88 of KG 77 shows a different style of additional lines over its base camouflage. Note that the Balkenkreuz and Hakenkreuz markings had been painted over with temporary black for night operations.

The units listed had all participated in coastal attacks around the Mediterranean where blue and pale lines, or a paler blue and green finish would have been advantageous over water. That operational environment probably explains also the use of dark green rather than black for under surfaces; a black finish for the lower surfaces would have been less advantageous during daylight attacks at low-level over water, since the surface of the sea is dark greenish-grey and at a distance, the dark green blended better than stark black. However, for night attacks the dark green would have served just as adequately as black.

A small adjunct to the general system of unit markings was detailed in part of Joachim Siebert's descriptions mentioned in Chapter 5: [3]

> "... on most of the aircraft of KG 76, the first letter of the code was repeated on the rudder. This helped crews to find their aircraft which stood partially hidden by camouflage nets in their revetments."

The Ju 88 equipped units had rapidly disappeared from Italy by 1944; KG 77 had disbanded at the turn of the year, KG 54 had transferred to Norway early in 1944, LG 1 and KG 30 had departed in June, while KG 1 had disbanded around the same time. With their departure the unique camouflage schemes disappeared from the Mediterranean.

Russia and the Western Front

Amongst bombers on the Eastern Front little variation in camouflage had occured since the opening offensive in July 1941; Ju 88s, He 111s, Do 17s and Ju 87s had all continued to wear the prescribed 70/71/65 scheme. Only in winter was there variation, and then only in the manner in which temporary white 21 was applied, ranging from random blobs to fairly solid applications over all upper and side surfaces.

With transfer of the main bombing force to the Eastern Front in mid-1941, bomber camouflage had also remained in a static state in the West, fighter-bombers taking over the main role with hit-and-run nuisance raids, until the heavy attacks against German cities prompted the institution of retaliatory bomber attacks against British cities in April 1942. These had been mounted by a relatively small force of Do 217s, Ju 88s and He 111s, the small-scale night raids continuing into 1943, augmented by the fighter-bombers. Not until December 1943 had IX. Fliegerkorps, which controlled the bomber force based in northern France, received reinforcements from the Mediterranean, starting with II. Fliegerkorps, which had controlled all tactical air operations in Italy. In early March X. Fliegerkorps had followed, taking over command of anti-shipping units based in western and southern France. Anticipation of the Allied landings in Western Europe had shifted the priorities to that theatre of operations.

By 1943 the bomber force in the West, and much of that on the shrinking Eastern Front, had been forced over to night bombing, daylight operations being far too costly. Units of IX. Fliegerkorps, based in northern France and in the Low Countries, carried out sporadic attacks against Britain. From March 1943 Generalmajor Dietrich Peltz had taken over responsibility for directing the attacks, rapidly recognizing the deficiencies in training of many of his aircrew. To counter that weakness he had ordered the formation of specialist pathfinder crews to assist with navigation and target marking.

These crews were equipped with the new Ju 188, which had made its service debut with the Stab of KG 6 at Criel in May 1943. Subsequently I./KG 6 became the first Gruppe to be equipped with the type, and operated them as the route and target marking

ABOVE LEFT AND LEFT: Two views of a most unusual finish, applied to a Do 217 E-4 of II./KG 40. Note that the overall pale finish, which even extended to the propellers and engine cooling fans, had a slight shine to it, ruling out that this was winter temporary white finish. The slight exhaust staining also shows that the shine was not the result of freshly applied paint. The Balkenkreuz and Hakenkreuz markings can just be discerned, showing the pale colouring had been very thinly applied. At the time, II./KG 40 was engaged in anti-shipping sorties, and this may possibly be the pale green-blue colouring also reported in the encounter with the BV 222 wearing an overall 'duck-egg blue' (see Volume One, page 120). That encounter took place over the Atlantic, the same general area and conditions under which KG 40 was using its Do 217 E-4s for shipping attacks. The RLM's E-Stelle field-tested a number of camouflage colours with front line units during the war.

Beleuchtergruppe (Illuminator Group) under Luftflotte 3. The camouflage style adopted for much of the force (KG 2, KG 6, KG 26 and I./KG 66) reflected that of the night fighter force – with both types operating on night sorties it had been a natural progression from the 70/71/65 day camouflage. Upper surfaces were a mixture of either 70/71 with snaking lines of 65 or 76 applied over them, or simply 76 with 75 applied as snaking lines or mottling. The prevailing system of painting part of the lower surfaces in permanent black 7124.22, with the remaining 65-coloured areas finished in temporary black 7120.22 had been adopted, though there had been little chance that the flexibility of the system of changing back and forth between 7124.22 and 7125.65 would be used, at least on the Western Front. In the East, some use of that system still prevailed in 1943, but not for much longer.

The bomber operations had been a mixture of small raids on land targets mixed with mine-laying in estuaries and along the coast, but pressure from Hitler to mount a sustained bombing campaign against Britain (London in particular), had finally culminated in the commencement of Operation Steinbock on 21 January 1944. The bombing force of the previous year had been expanded by the influx of KG 30, KG 40, KG 66 and KG 100, and the pathfinder duties had shifted to just I./KG 66, by then equipped with a mixture of Ju 188 E and Ju 88 S aircraft. The latter were finished in standard 70/71/65, but subsequently had had their camouflage modified for their pathfinder task. Upper and side surfaces remained in 70 and 71, but lower surfaces were finished in black 7124.22. The entire airframe, including the black-painted sections, had then received additional camouflage of 65 (or 76) as soft-sprayed wavy lines over top, sides, all lower surfaces, and including the propeller spinners.

Other units engaged in the campaign had followed suit and had the camouflage of their aircraft either modified or replaced. Painting had varied; in some instances a solid coat of 75 on the upper surfaces oversprayed with 76 to produce a soft mottle of the darker colour; others simply relied on just a scribble pattern of 76 over the existing 70/71 camouflage. Others used dot-like patches of 76, spaced fairly evenly, in a close pattern over the 70/71 upper and side surfaces. Some units had applied the black finish only in patches, breaking up the solid colour. Balkenkreuz and Hakenkreuz markings also had been reduced to minimum form in most instances, just outline forms being very common.

One well-documented aircraft example was provided by a Do 217 M, U5+DK W. Nr. 56051 of II./KG 2, which landed by itself after the crew had baled out during an operation on the night of 23/24 February 1944. Upper surfaces had been oversprayed with 76 to produce patches of dark greens from the original 70/71 camouflage. The sizes of the darker areas varied from narrow winding strips to more rounded, mottle-like areas and extended to the inside face of the vertical tail surfaces. The external faces were in solid black, as was the rest of the airframe, extending up the side surfaces to a line just above the wing root trailing edge. Code letters were all in miniature characters, including the aircraft letter, (which was unusual for that item), and all had been over painted in 77 grey. The Werknummer was marked in white near the top of the fin with a large white '2' occupying approximately one-third of the fin, with the full code repeated in white as two characters either side of it. Oddly, the rudders remained in 71 green, but that may have resulted from these being replacement units. Two narrow white bands encircled the end of the fuselage, where it protruded beyond the tail plane; possibly some form of tactical unit marking. It did perhaps accord with the aircraft's 2. Staffel status; but what purpose it served on a night bomber is unknown.

The force, despite strenuous efforts, was too small, and by May had achieved little for a loss of some 60 per cent of the original numbers employed in January. No force could sustain such attrition, and the raids petered out.

The final actions of the Kampfgeschwader in the West occurred with the Allied push into Europe and much of the force was disbanded, the bombing role shifting from strategic to purely tactical. From a peak of about 550 heavy bombers produced in late June 1944, production had rapidly fallen to about 300 in October; rose briefly to just under 400 in December and then plunged steeply to approximately 100 in February 1945, before trailing away to zero.

Expansion of the defensive forces for protection of the Reich had been achieved at the direct expense of the bomber arm. Between January and September 1944 at least 25 Kampfgeschwader had been disbanded, 80 per cent from July to September. That action, and the meagre final production run of bomber aircraft, had coincided with the introduction of the replacement camouflage colours of 81, 82 and 76 for such aircraft. As a result, few of the older types had ever worn the revised colour scheme. The conversion of the Me 262 for this role has been well documented before and more accurately falls into the category of fighter-bomber. The Ar 234 testing and production cycle had lapped the change from one scheme to the other, the early test machines and some early production aircraft using the old colours 70 and 71, but the majority of the production airframes had the revised colours; KG 76, being the principal, if limited, user of the pure bomber version.

In the East, the front had shrunk rapidly in 1945 as units were withdrawn to try and stem the tide of the Allied push from the west. Stab, I. and III./KG 4 had been subordinated to Transportfliegerführer Lfl. Kdo. 6, and pressed into service to deliver supplies to German troops surrounded on the Eastern Front, operating from Hradec Králové airfield in Czechoslovakia. II. Gruppe had operated from Greifswald in northern Germany as part of Gefechtsverband Helbig, formed to attack bridges and Russian positions on the Oder and Weser rivers. The He 111s of KG 4 had retained their 70/71 finish, but modified it with large pale areas sprayed with what probably was 76. Colour 65 had been withdrawn in August 1944 though its use cannot be discounted judging by the few photographs of He 111s of KG 53 equipped to air-launch Fi 103s, one at least of which used the modified camouflage style. That particular aircraft must have dated from the second half of 1944 at the latest.

Under surfaces of the KG 4 machines were black for the most part, probably 7126.22, a single layer of permanent camouflage that had been

ABOVE: He 177 A-5/R2, 6N+DN, of 5./KG 100 illustrates another of the style of finishes that were used by He 177s. The basic camouflage appears to be 70/71/65 over which an intense network of 'Arabesken' had been applied using a colour lighter in tone than the 65 of the lower surfaces, possibly 76. As usual with this large aircraft type, the code letters were spaced further apart because their size and spacing was based on the ratio of the Balkenkreuz marking. The latter was reduced to just a thin outline version on many He 177s, as shown here.

LEFT AND BELOW: Two views of Ju 188 A, 3E+HK, of 2./KG 6 found abandoned at Melsbroek airfield, showing one camouflage variation used by the type. The side and lower surfaces were painted in permanent black with the upper surfaces in a dark camouflage, most probably 70 and 71 as the type was being phased out of production at the time the new colours of 81 and 82 were being introduced (see Volume One). What appear to be large areas of 76 (it is too pale in tone to be 65) were used to create the 'stone wall' effect on upper and side surfaces. Interestingly, the entire code appears to have been applied in red, the 2.Staffel colour. (F. Grabowski)

RIGHT: Generally, camouflage for the He 111 was more conservative throughout the war, few showing the flamboyant styles seen on other types. This wrecked He 111 H-16, 5J+DL of 3./KG 4, had a base camouflage of 70/71/65 over which large swatches of 65-colouring had been applied using a fan setting on the spray equipment, allowing the painter to use broad sweeping strokes. Thin lines of the same colour had been added in places. The effect was quite striking, breaking up the solid bulk of the aircraft's shape. The under surfaces on this machine were black. Other He 111s of this unit exhibited differing styles of application, from soft lines, wavy lines to spots, using the same colour. All were deliberately destroyed at the end of the war rather than let them fall into the hands of the Russians, who occupied the Czech territories from where KG 4 carried out its last operations. (J. Crow)

LEFT: The Ar 234
development programme
was slow to come to
fruition, and the more
advanced prototypes,
such as the Ar 234 V21
seen here (either PI+WZ
or RK+EK), straddled the
changeover from the old
bomber colours of
70/71/65 to the new
81/82/76 colours. The
Ar 234 V21, the first
genuine C-3 variant, made
its maiden flight on 24
November 1944, so the
colours were more likely
to have been 81/82/76.

RIGHT: The first
example of the
Ar 234 B-2 to fall into
Allied hands crash-
landed at Siegersdorf
on 22 February 1945.
F1+MT, ('Yellow M')
W.Nr. 140173 of
9./KG 76 wore
camouflage of
81/82/76, but the
unit had modified this
finish by spraying
large areas of 76 over
the 81/82 of the side
surfaces. This
obscured part of the
Hakenkreuz marking
as well as the
Balkenkreuz and code
markings. The aircraft
is seen here at
Farnborough during its
subsequent technical
examination.

RIGHT: This view of the fuselage,
taken during disassembly, shows
clearly how thin was the application
of the 76 sprayed on the side
surfaces, individual spray lines
being visible on the centre portion
of the airframe.

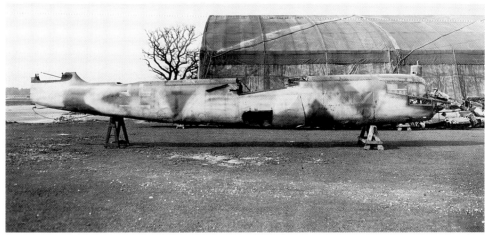

ABOVE: Abandoned by its hangar, which was disguised as a house, this Ju 188 wears camouflage far removed from the old 70/71/65 scheme. The airframe has been finished overall in 76-colouring, heavily spotted with a colour close in tonal value to that of the 70 of the propeller blades, probably 81. The Hakenkreuz and Balkenkreuz markings are the prescribed white outline type with the former almost lost beneath the camouflage. Even the Werknummer at the tip of the fin had been over sprayed with the dark mottle. The lower surfaces were painted in temporary black.

introduced in August 1944 to replace the existing 7124.22 permanent night finish. Its main advantage over the earlier lacquer was the rapidity with which it could be applied over fresh undercoat lacquer. As always,

old stocks of the 7124.22 had had to be exhausted before employing the new finish. But old or new, the finish looked identical.

In some instances the pale colouring formed elongated patches loosely linked by finer lines of the same colour; on others, a simpler application had been made in a more regular spot pattern, or in some instances simply snaking lines of 76 had been used, but in a very diffuse manner. On some, the application of 76 formed an intense net of lines, reducing the base dark colouring to a spot effect. The wide variety of application indicated that several people had been used for the work at whatever repair/maintenance depot had carried out the work. These were the last camouflage variations for Luftwaffe bombers in the Second World War – all made post-production.

1. Martin Pegg research

2. J. D Gallaspey research.

3. Ibid

Maritime Aircraft

Between 1933 and 1935, like all the other paramilitary aircraft, an overall 02-finish had been used for maritime aircraft, changing to 63 in 1936 with the shift to the new range of camouflage colours. Where aircraft were equipped with metal floats, and also seen on hulls of seaplanes, 7107.02 was used above the water line and 7108.02 below, the latter extending up to a point 10 cm above the high water mark; this was a waterproofing measure, but there was no visual difference to be seen. If wooden floats or hulls were used then 7145.04 was used above water and 7162.04 below to ensure the integrity of the finish above water level. A 3 mm wide line, painted in 28 weinrot, marked the division between the two lacquer types. While the official factory standard clearly stipulated the 02-finish, this was not followed in some instances, 7102 translucent zinc chromate finish being used instead, leaving the floats on some types with the appearance of bare metal. Upper surfaces of wings (in the case of biplanes, only the top wing surfaces) were painted 04. Use of yellow for floats, parts of hulls and wing upper surfaces was intended to act as a visual safety aid when the aircraft was operating over the sea. Ship-borne aircraft also exchanged their previous grey finish for 63-colouring.

When a number of He 59s were transferred to Spain for active duty, in order not to draw undue attention to the aircraft, the wing upper surface yellow colouring was replaced by 63. However, yellow continued in use on some home based aircraft until 1939 when, in conjunction with a decision by the E-Stelle Travemünde, the RLM issued instruction LC 2 Nr. 2890/39 (VI) geh. Az 70 k on 24 May [1], withdrawing permission for continued use of the 04-coloured lacquers for wing fabric and floats. That coincided with the introduction of 72/73/65 for the Ar 196 A seaplane camouflage and provides an insight into how long the process took for replacement of the overall 63-finish, common to seaplanes, with the new maritime camouflage colours.

Colours 72 and 73 were introduced for upper surfaces of maritime aircraft (sea planes and flying boats) with issue of the 1938 colour card in L.Dv.521/1, and were applied in standard splinter pattern, with 65 for lower surfaces. All maritime aircraft in service, other than for those with training establishments, were gradually repainted in these colours, including land-based machines. The exceptions were aircraft of those Kampfgeschwadern seconded to anti-shipping duties, which more usually retained their existing 70/71/65 scheme.

However, some further experimentation with sea camouflage was undertaken; II./KG 40 had formed in March 1941 specifically for anti-shipping duties in the Atlantic, equipped with Do 217 Es. The photographs on page 328 (Chapter 14) show one of the unit's Do 217 E-2s is intriguing as it shows a very similar pale overall finish that included everything from spinners and cooling fan blades to propellers blades. The very pale finish would have worked well against the skies of the Atlantic. This forms an interesting comparison with one of the BV 222 Versuchs machines (either the V 2 or V 4), which was recorded on 8 October 1943, over the Bay of Biscay, wearing a pale green-blue overall colour; possibly it may have been part of 1.(F)/See-Aufklärungs-Gruppe 129. (See Volume One, Chapter 5). Existing photographs of the BV 222 V2 and V4 show them in a 72/73/65 scheme, so this appears to have been a field test of a new colour. This dual occurrence may signal that there had been an ongoing experiment for a camouflage that worked better against the vast ocean skyscape, with its strong division between the dark sea and light sky, and especially the softer lighting occurring at the sea/sky boundary. The colour description also matches the under surface colour identified from paint samples taken from remains of Fw 190s of JG 5 when based in Norway for coastal patrol work. [2]

Kampfgeschwadern operating over the Mediterranean from Sicily and Italy in 1942/1943-period added patches of 70 or 71 to the

LEFT: A Do 15 Militär-Wal 33, 60+I12 of 2./Kü.F.Gr.106 (formerly Fliegerstaffel (F) List). It wears the Luftwaffe's original military finish of 02, which was applicable to all military types of the 1935 period.

ABOVE: The He 60 C was a deceptively large aircraft as this photograph of D-IVKA shows. The overall colouring was 63 for the main airframe, with the floats left in treated bare metal and anti-fouling paint for their under-water surfaces. The civil registration and presence of the National Socialist Flag on the starboard side of the fin and rudder were changes introduced on 15 September 1935, this photograph being taken at Bug am Rügen in July 1936. (B.Ketley)

LEFT AND INSET: Two views of Ar 196 A-2, T3+HK, of Bordflieger Staffel 196, in standard 72/73/65 camouflage. The unit's sea horse emblem can be seen on the forward fuselage. The aircraft letter 'H' was repeated in black beneath each wing tip. (D. Vincent)

BELOW: Ar 95 A-1, 7R+DL, of 3./SAGr. 125, wearing the standard sea camouflage colours 72 and 73 on upper and side surfaces. Lower surfaces were in 65 colouring.

ABOVE: Another maritime design from the Heinkel stable was the very useful He 115, PP+AX being seen here. The camouflage for the type was standard sea colouring of 72 and 73 with 65 for the under surfaces. Serving with the Küstenfliegergruppen, the type gave valuable service in the patrol and mining roles at the outbreak of war, but had become obsolescent by 1941. Its last major operational activity was taking part in torpedo attacks against the PQ convoys travelling through Arctic waters. (H. Thiele)

LEFT: The perennial workhorse of long-range operations, a Do 18 G-1, M2+?K, of 2./Kü.Fl.Gr.106 in 72/73/65 finish but, when photographed still lacking allocation of an individual aircraft letter.

TOP AND ABOVE:
Two views of the fifth production Fw 200 C-1, BS+AJ, W.Nr. 005. Freshly painted, the good lighting conditions and an application of DKH Wetterschutz protective finish produced the appearance of a high contrast for the finish. Land-based maritime aircraft normally used standard maritime camouflage colours of 72/73/65, but these two photographs would lead one to suspect, perhaps incorrectly, that the finish was 70 and 71. (C. Cole)

ABOVE: Lighting conditions can produce quite distinct differences to the appearance of camouflage. The second production Fw 200 C-1, W.Nr. 002, is seen here under a low sun angle, which has highlighted the slightly less matt finish of the unit code F8+EH (applied in enamel lacquer) as well as showing up the original Stammkennzeichen marking of BS+AG. The appearance of the two camouflage colours is quite different from that in the previous two photographs. The finish now looks more like the regulation 72/73. This aircraft was serving with 1./KG 40 at the time, and was shot down north of Ireland on 20 July 1940. It had been in service for a little over a month. (C. Cole)

65-coloured under surfaces in an attempt to break up the starkness of the pale colouring, which was detrimental during low-level shipping attacks. This had been taken a step further with adoption of what appears to have been in most cases, wavy lines of 65-colouring added to the upper surfaces and, in some instances, extended as wavy lines of 70 onto the 65 coloured areas of the lower surfaces of the forward fuselage and engine nacelles. As described in Chapter 5, some Ju 88s of I./KG 54 serving in the Mediterranean adopted some similar-looking, but very unusual camouflage. How extensive was the use of the deep blue overall colouring, plus black and sand coloured lines, or the pale blue upper, and dark green lower colouring, is unknown.

While sea-based aircraft retained a 72/73/65 scheme for the remainder of the war, other than for application of 7126.21 temporary white for those operating amidst the ice flows of the far north, land-based maritime aircraft continued to exhibit some changes. Operating over the Bay of Biscay, early in 1944, the He 177s of KG 100 adopted a distinctive camouflage of a dark colour applied in a broad-stroke-style network, creating islands of a pale colour. There seems little doubt that the pale colour was RLM 02 rather than 65, as in some photographs the lower surfaces show a colour that is clearly different and paler, and the greenish component of the 02 colouring would have favoured the camouflage effect over the sea and against sky. The combination is consistent with 65 lower with 02 on side and upper surfaces. Also noticeable on some aircraft is the very soft, sprayed edge where the darker ribbons of colour meet the lowest line of the fuselage. In contrast, aircraft that had retained 65 for their lower surface colouring had a sharp demarcation line between the dark ribbons of colour and the 65-colouring.

The nature of the darker colour however is less easily determined. Close examination of the available photographs does not reveal which of the two upper surface colours had been applied first, but judging from the angles of the arcs of darker colouring created against the paler colour, and applying the logic of using the palest colour first (which was normal practice at that time), it was the 02. The darker colour does not appear to have the depth of tone associated with 70 or 72, no matter which photograph is examined, and in every case it was definitely paler than the standard 70 seen on the large propeller blades. It would seem then that either 71 or 73 had been used; the maritime environment in which the aircraft were operated possibly favouring 73.

While the style of application remained fairly consistent, naturally there were variations in each case in what was essentially a random pattern. On some aircraft the lower surface 65 colouring was absent as noted above, just 02 base colouring being used. It may be then that these aircraft had been delivered in their basic 02 primer coat to a Luftwaffe conversion depot or maintenance unit for completion of their specialised camouflage. Close up detail of the bomb bay area, on one of the aircraft using 02 as an overall base colouring, clearly shows the four-line stencilling and arrow markings relating to the bomb bay doors. This supports the conclusion that the aircraft had been delivered in the overall basic colouring.

A more conventional form of camouflage modification appeared later on He 177s of KG 100, the dark upper surface two-tone camouflage of 70/71 being broken up with the usual snaking lines of a paler colour. The latter, where it overlapped the existing 65-colouring, shows that it was 76 (a colour that also gradually became more prevalent on bombers used for the late war bombing attacks against Britain).

Do 217 Ns, found in Norway at the end of the war, exhibited a broadly similar approach to maritime camouflage. In the most 'conventional' form, the basic dark colouring of the upper surfaces was sprayed with a weaving line of a pale colour that appears to be 65. A more radical form appeared on others, using large segments of what looks like 02 over the basic dark green upper surface camouflage. The latter form of application also appeared on some of the Ju 188s based in that theatre of operations.

An example of this camouflage for land-based maritime aircraft is illustrated by the following. At 1352 hours on 2 May 1945, a Ju 188 made a wheels-down landing at Fraserburgh airfield in Scotland where its crew of four surrendered to the Allied forces. The subsequent A.I.2 (g) Crashed Enemy Aircraft Report Serial No. 270 of 11 May contains some interesting information.

> *"The machine shows no outstanding points of interest, but certain details are welcomed as this is the first completely intact Ju 188 which we have had since the outbreak of war. The aircraft has been flown to RAE,* [Royal Aircraft Establishment] *Farnborough, where flying trials will be carried out."*

The report went on to detail that the aircraft carried W.Nr. 190335 marked on the fin and repeated on the aircraft data card in the cockpit, while on the lower section of the fin '5465' was marked. This was a machine of 9./KG 26 marked 1H+AT, with a small '1H' in black (12.5 cm high), the 'AT' standard size in black with 'A' outlined in the Staffel colour of yellow. Camouflage was quoted as *"…greenish-grey on both upper and lower surfaces with white mottling"*, which would indicate an overall base coat of 02 with white mottling. The latter may have been either temporary winter white, still in use in the far north even at that time of the year, permanent white or a very pale application of 76, by then being described as greyish-white in most Intelligence reports.

A second Ju 188 A-2, 1H+GT, W.Nr. 190327, from the same Staffel was flown to Farnborough on 8 August 1945 and allocated the Air Ministry number AM113. That aircraft had '0327' stencilled in white on the fin while on the rear most part of the fuselage, stencilled in smaller white numerals, was '5366'. The elevator obscured the latter when it was in the neutral position. A photograph taken when the aircraft was at Lübeck airfield shows a very dark base colouring in two colours, either 72 and 73 or 70 and 71, over which pale coloured snaking lines with soft edges had been sprayed. The thinness of the spray application allowed the base camouflage greens to discolour the paler colour. Given the eye-witness account of white being used on the other Ju 188 described above, from the same unit, the pale colour appears to have been white rather than 65.

What is interesting is that these two aircraft, which display such a dramatic change in camouflage, were only eight airframes apart in the production cycle. The Stammkennzeichen marked on the data card in the cockpit of W. Nr. 190335 was KQ+GH and a quick calculation based on sequential allocation of these temporary ferry markings shows that W Nr.190335 was the eighth machine in a new block allocation:

190327	??+??
190328	KQ+GA
190329	KQ+GB
190330	KQ+GC
190331	KQ+GD
190332	KQ+GE
190333	KQ+GF
190334	KQ+GG
190335	KG+GH

W.Nr.190327 did not fall into the same block, which may also indicate a change point in the factory applied camouflage scheme. Acceptance date for W.Nr 190335 is quoted in the report as "July 1945", obviously a typing error for the year should have been 1944. It has been suggested by some writers that some aircraft, in keeping with unique duties or location, were given "special" camouflage during production that were outside the standard variations allowable at production centres. Aircraft were certainly allocated in advance to various theatres of operation, information essential when producing, as in this instance, maritime versions of land bombers; or aircraft requiring tropical camouflage colouring. However the suggestion that the recipient unit of individual aircraft was known and influenced the camouflage scheme to such an extent that a totally unique application was made at point of manufacture would not seem to stand up to scrutiny in this instance. Given that both machines were still operational within the same Staffel and were surrendered at the end of the war, the difference in camouflage is quite marked.

Significance of the two other numbers '5465' and '5366', found on these aircraft is uncertain. They were 100 apart in sequence yet the Werknummern, allocated to each entire airframe, were only eight apart, and the two aircraft were probably produced within a day or so of each other. The second number sequence probably related to individual airframe sub-component manufacture, tail units being a complete sub-unit in themselves produced at a dispersed location. The sub-contractor would have no way of knowing what Werknummer would be applied to

any completely assembled machine, but would require markings to keep a record of the tail unit production cycle. In past times such a marking would have been painted over at final assembly stage, but with sub-units arriving already painted, and with the restrictions on paint stock use, it is not surprising that the marking was left visible.

As with other production types, the sub-contract system had also produced some hybrid schemes, tail units delivered to the main production centre where final assembly of Ju 188s arrived camouflaged in 81 and 82, some ending up on those allocated to maritime duties, something confirmed by an Air Ministry report on yet another 9./KG 26 machine found in Norway. As noted in Chapter 5, Ju 188 final production took place at the main manufacturing plant, and the main plant never used the 81/82 camouflage scheme as stocks of existing 70 and 71 greens were sufficient to see out the last of the production run. But sub-contractors had their own paint stocks.

ABOVE: This eclectic mix of camouflage finishes on the Ju 88s and Ju 188s of KG 26 illustrates the vast variety that emerged via the post-production system of units having their aircraft camouflage added to by maintenance depots. KG 26 had commenced anti-shipping duties from Norway in the spring of 1944, having exchanged its He 111s for Ju 88s and Ju 188s. The full spectrum of finishes is shown, starting with the dark 72/73-camouflaged Ju 88s in the middle line. Forward of them is a Ju 188, 1H+K?, which had just short lines of 65 applied over its dark 72/73 camouflage. In contrast, the Ju 88 behind, IH+NM, had a very intense application of 65-coloured snaking lines, producing a quite pale effect overall. Compare that with the Ju 88 A, 1H+EF, on the left of the photograph, the pale 65-coloured lines being used frugally in a more linear style, producing a stone wall-like effect. However, the aircraft right at the front of the photograph has the most complex pattern of any in view. The pale base colouring appears to be more consistent with 02, over which soft-sprayed strokes of 65 and a mid-tone colour, possibly 72 or 73, were added to break up all the surfaces.

ABOVE: Another view of the collection of Ju 88s and Ju 188s of KG 26, photographed at the end of the war. The aircraft in the foreground, 1H+KV of 11./KG 26, wears standard 70/71/65 finish but the other Ju 88s and Ju 188s have had a scribble pattern of 65 applied to the dark camouflage. Close examination reveals not only the random nature of the scribble application, but also the style. One of the Ju 188s had not had the scribble markings applied to the engine nacelles. On the extreme right are two more Ju 88s in standard 70/71/65 finish, one of them, coded "ZV", suggesting that perhaps 11. Staffel machines were left with unmodified camouflage.

However, that process had not been responsible for the great variation in general camouflage form noted on some aircraft within a single unit. Why the variation should have been so relatively extensive is not clear. Individual crews were not usually in a position to request a specific change to camouflage, something that was more possible on a Staffel scale. The likelihood exists that aircraft in general were transferred between Staffeln, or even between units after general refurbishment, or major repairs after battle damage. This could produce a general mixing of schemes that were outside those specified in the type's standard camouflage schedule.

When the later versions of the Ju 290 began to reach operational status in the maritime role in 1944, they wore standard 72/73 colouring, but restricted to the strict plan view, with 65-under surface colouring extended up the side surfaces to include the vertical control surfaces. This helped to break up the bulky profile of this large form of aircraft when seen against the sky. Adoption of this form of camouflage largely addressed the problems that had beset the huge BV 222 aircraft with their dark colouring, and in doing so was probably adopted as a simpler alternative to the green-blue colouring that was tested on several types, as noted earlier. By the time the Ju 290 was entering service in this role, the austerity measures were moving rapidly to a very reduced range of colours.

Like their land bomber counterparts, the maritime bomber and torpedo bomber force fell rapidly into decline. The turning point had been in the early months of 1943 and the debacle that had overtaken the Luftwaffe in the Mediterranean Theatre of Operations. The force never recovered from that, and numbers of torpedo bombers in particular had fallen away steadily from then on.

RIGHT: The Fw 200 served to the end. This machine, F8+FR of 7./KG 40, was photographed in Norway at the end of the war. It wears an intense scribble pattern of 65-colouring over the base camouflage of 72/73. The 65 of the under surfaces look slightly darker than the scribble, but the latter was a more recent addition and probably fresher paint. Why the scribble should have been applied so intensely is a mystery, but may have related to where the aircraft had been operating. (D. Wadman)

LEFT: The Ju 52 served in a great variety of roles throughout the war, amongst them the semi-maritime duty of mine-sweeping. Fitted with a large metal ring that generated a magnetic field they worked to explode magnetic mines in the main shipping lanes and canals. This example, found at Bøtø airfield in Denmark at the end of the war, had standard 70/71/65 finish. The last two letters of either its code or Stammkennzeichen were 'GH', marked also beneath the wing in white. A white '53' marked below the cockpit reinforcing flutes, ws probably part of its Werknummer. The two vertically mounted tubular brackets and the angled one, mounted beneath the central engine, held the ring fitting at the front of the aircraft. (Royal Danish Air Force)

RIGHT: In this rear view of the same Ju 52, the large magnetic ring fitting can be seen on the grass in the foreground. It was also attached beneath each wing and to the rear section of the fuselage. The splinter pattern, though worn, is still quite distinct. The rudder had been removed, along with the propellers, after the surrender. The red ribbon hanging off the tail plane was attached to the elevator gust lock. (Royal Danish Air Force)

1. M. Ullmann research.
2. Dr. William Berge research and paint samples.

Reconnaissance Aircraft

Reconnaissance had always been recognised as a vital role for the German armed forces and a variety of aircraft had served this purpose in the close-, medium- and long-range duties. The He 45 long-range reconnaissance aircraft began flight trials in the spring of 1932 having been preceded late the previous year by the He 46 short-range reconnaissance aircraft, with which it was being evolved in parallel. Both types then entered service in 1934 wearing an overall 02-colour scheme; that colouring still was to be seen on some He 46s as late as 1937. Initially, the colour had been chosen simply because it was used as a standard colouring for the paramilitary aircraft of the clandestine military forces; however, it also proved useful as a sky camouflage, ideal for the lone operating nature of reconnaissance aircraft, which probably accounted for its retention until 1937. By late autumn 1934, the He 70F-1 had entered service, that sleek, fast machine combining both reconnaissance and light bomber duties – a trend in multi-purpose roles which was to grow. Like its stablemates, 02-colouring was used as an overall finish, but with addition of the black, stylised surround to the engine and fuselage.

Accompanied by six He 45 Cs, 18 reconnaissance He 70 F-2 aircraft of Aufklärungsstaffel A/88 were sent to Spain as soon as the civil war there started. Both types were delivered in either 02 or 63-overall finish, depending on the production age of each machine as the shift to 63 had occurred very early in 1936. However, that colour was soon replaced on some machines; some of the He 70s were given a locally applied camouflage comprising a base coat of 62 green with a disruptive pattern of 61 brown segments that had a soft-sprayed edge to them. Lower surfaces were in 65. A small number of the He 45s were given a more elaborate scheme, using all three upper surface camouflage colours, 61, 62 and 63, applied as relatively small angular patches in roughly square and triangular shapes, and using 65 for the lower surfaces. While effective, it was a quite complex application, and most were given the more simplified 61/62 style of camouflage as applied to the He 70s. When the first of the Hs 126s arrived to replace the aging He 45s, they also received camouflage of 61/62/63 applied in small angular patches. That indicates that the machines had arrived in basic 63-colouring as the angular style of camouflage patches was a localised form of camouflage style. In Germany, standard pattern camouflage in 61,62,63 and 65 had been used briefly for the type until superseded by new camouflage colours of 70/71/65, as worn by later deliveries of the type to Spain.

Night reconnaissance had fallen to the He 46, which, because of its nocturnal role, appears to have retained a 63-overall finish for the few aircraft that saw service in Spain.

The Do 17 F-1 succeeded the He 70 F-2 in the long-range role and these machines arrived in Spain in the contemporary, factory-applied 61/62/63/65 camouflage scheme. Early deliveries of the F-1's successor, the Do 17 P-1, initially retained that scheme, but later deliveries changed over to camouflage of 70/71/65.

Back in Europe, Do 17 Ps generally wore the 70/71/65 camouflage scheme, but there were variations. A Do 17 P of 1.(F)/123, shot down by F/O Kain of No. 73 Squadron RAF, on 8 November 1939, produced some media attention. The aircraft had dived into the ground vertically from 6,000 metres, impacting close to a small French village, and leaving little evidence of itself for examination. *Flight* magazine had one of its correspondents, H. F. King, visiting the area at the time and he recorded that he had found parts of a wing, the fuselage, tail and other items. However, his most significant comment related to the finish: *"A curious point was that the Dornier seems to have been coloured a sort of pastel blue, probably to render detection more difficult, though it must be remembered that, what ever the colour of the aircraft, it appears from a distance as a dark silhouette."* [1]

The accompanying photographs to the article make it clear that not many large portions of the airframe had survived for examination, though the tail cone appeared to be relatively intact, providing both upper and lower surface colouring for comparison. The section beneath the tail plane shows four roughly circular dark mottles, all of very similar size. The colour appears to be similar to the original dark camouflage colouring. The term pastel blue is not one that could be mistaken for anything other than the normal bright shade of 65. It is possible then that the aircraft had been finished overall in 65 as a form of sky camouflage. The fact that all other known reference photographs of Do 17 Ps of Fern.Aufkl.Gr. 123 show camouflage of either 61/62/63/65 or 70/71/65 finish makes it difficult to judge whether this was a one-off finish, or whether other Do 17 Ps of the Staffel had been similarly painted 65-overall. Why small patches of the original darker colouring had been retained on the aircraft is unknown.

A different form of monotone sky camouflage turned up on another reconnaissance Dornier on 13 January 1940, when a Do 17 S-2, W.Nr. 2502, of I. Aufkl. Gr (F)/Ob.d.L. was forced down behind French lines by Curtiss Hawks of GC 1/4. It wore an overall finish of 02, but this had been sprayed quite thinly, over the original dark camouflage, which could just be detected at certain light angles. The wing upper surface area immediately behind each engine had been left in its original dark 70/71 colouring, presumably because of the dark exhaust staining; the only other variation to colour were the solid black 'T5+FH' code markings. National markings were all correct for the post 24 October 1939 revisions with the exception of the positioning of the Hakenkreuz markings, which overlapped both fin and rudder, indicating that the aircraft had been in service prior to Az. 19 d 10 Genst. 2. Abt. (III B) being promulgated on 15 December 1938, effective from 1 January 1939. That instruction included the details for removal of the red banner and white circle from behind the Hakenkreuz marking. This aircraft was one of three specially constructed Do 17s for use by that unit, which was also designated Kommando Rowehl. The style of finish was relatively rare however and appears to have been confined to that unit, which also operated four similar Do 17 R aircraft. Those differed only in camera installations and crew arrangements. When a small number of Do 215 B-0 and B-1 aircraft were added to the unit strength, some, if not all, were given the same overall finish of 02 over their existing camouflage, again leaving the dark greens of the original camouflage of the wing behind each engine.

Dorniers from the main units operating in the reconnaissance role normally wore conventional camouflage. Some minor variations occurred later, during the air war over Britain, when a heavy mottle of either 70 or 71 was used on the sides and under surfaces of the engine nacelles, and the forward section of the fuselage on some aircraft. That seems to have been applied in an effort to break up the pale blue lower surfaces to assist when the aircraft approached Britain at sea-level,

LEFT: One of the most widely used types in the fledgling Luftwaffe was the He 45. Here a formation from Aufkl.Gr.(F)/124 shows off the deceptive size of this aircraft. In the centre is 40+C11. The finish appears to be silver, but it would be unusual for that colour to be used for front line aircraft in the Luftwaffe of that period, 63 being the standard. It may be that the gloss was caused by moisture. (B. Ketley)

RIGHT: The He 60, although originally developed for shipboard duties, spent most of its operational life land-based. The prototype, D-2325, is seen here in 1933 with the staff of the E-Stelle Travemünde lined up on front of it. Finish was what would become known in RLM parlance as 02, but it was still identified at that time by the paint manufacturer's house code designation. (B. Ketley)

LEFT: The Do 18 played a significant role in sea reconnaissance duties, its long-range capabilities making it a valuable tool. This Do 18 D, 60+B42 of Kü.Fl.Gr.406, wears the ubiquitous overall pre-war finish of RLM 63. Airscrew blades were bare metal with the old-style tip band marking in the national colours of red, yellow and black. The staffel emblem of an armoured glove on a brown background, with a blue segment at the top and a yellow one below, is marked on the side of the engine cowling. Note the camera sighting lines on the fuselage, just forward of the sliding cockpit window. The observer would lean out of the window with a hand held camera, and use the lines for taking his photographs. Angles were critical to the subsequent photo-analysis.

Luftwaffe Camouflage and Markings 1933-1945

LEFT: He 70 F, 10+G12 of 2./Aufkl.Gr.(F)121, illustrates the practice of sometimes retaining the gloss black Heinkel company civil livery for the forward part of the fuselage, with the sweeping cheat line taken aft to the tail. This was only modified to allow for the placement of the military codes and Balkenkreuz marking. Overall finish was 63, that colour being used also to outline the lightning bolt marking against the black of the nose section. The unit codes were marked also on the wings. The aircraft's weights and loading table can be seen marked just forward of the tail plane. The Balkenkreuz is of the later variety, with thin black edging to the white angles, dating the photograph to 1936 or later (2. Staffel having formed in October 1936). This unit adopted a practice of replacing the company name 'Heinkel' (normally marked on the engine cowling) with German place names marked in white. This particular machine bore the name 'Gumbinnen', visible on the section of engine cowling on the ground by the wheel. Where the Heinkel black livery was deleted, the names were marked in black. The spinners on 'plain' machines within 2. Staffel appear to have been painted red. (B. Ketley)

ABOVE: The Hs 126 proved to be a versatile, sturdy reconnaissance aircraft, used on all war fronts. The first prototype had flown in late 1936, with two more Versuchsmachinen flying the following year. Ten pre-production examples were completed before the end of 1937, D-ODBT being one of them. This A-0 series was camouflaged in 61/62/63/65, but by the time the first production A-1 models were ready in early 1938, camouflage had changed to 70/71/65. (D. Wadman)

LEFT: The Hs 126 A-1 in its natural element, carrying out relatively low-altitude reconnaissance. This machine, H1+FH from 1./Aufkl.Gr (H)/12, had standard pattern 70/71 upper surface camouflage with the aircraft letter repeated in black at each wing tip. Note the rearmost camera angle guideline, running down and forward from the rear cockpit. (R. Chapman)

ABOVE: Aufklärungsgruppe Ob.d.L was established in January 1939, shedding the clandestine cover of its former civilian status. This Do 17 S-2, W.Nr.2502,T5+FH, crash-landed at Les Hemmes in Belgium on 13 January 1940, shot down by two French Air Force Hawk 75s of GC I/4. The camouflage was standard 70/71/65, overpainted with a very thin coat of RLM 02, which acted as a good sky camouflage. The thinness of the 02 coating was such that the original splinter pattern could be seen at some light angles, but the exhaust areas behind each engine were left in their original colouring.

ABOVE: This view of T5+NC, from Aufklärungsgruppe Ob.d.L, shows the upper surfaces with their monochrome 02 finish and the wide area of original camouflage left behind each engine. The angle of the rudders gives the false impression of a light-coloured finish.

something done on occasions for low-level reconnaissance sorties to evade the British radar coverage. The use of 02 did however linger on, as will be noted later, being almost identical to the old 63-colouring, it proved to be a good high altitude finish.

The Bf 110 C-5 entered service during the battle over Britain, operating alongside the Do 17. One of the first examples brought down wore a 71/02/65 scheme with 65-colouring taken up to a high demarcation line along the fuselage, and patterned with a heavy mottle of 71 and 02 right down the fuselage sides, a style which matched that of the contemporary fighter version. The Bf 109 E-5 model entered service in May 1940 in the pure reconnaissance role, but it too wore only standard day fighter colouring of 71/02/65.

Short-range tactical reconnaissance duties were filled by the Hs 126, a type that had entered service in late 1937 wearing contemporary camouflage of 61/62/63/65. With the changeover to 70/71/65 camouflage in 1938, later deliveries adopted that scheme. The Fw 189, which eventually replaced the ageing Hs 126 in most units, used the same colours; close-range reconnaissance work required no specialised camouflage.

Not until the North Africa campaign did any major variations to camouflage on Bf 110s and Hs 126s occur. The mixed complement of Bf 109s, Bf 110s and Hs 126s of 2.(H)/14 had arrived in March 1941 before any German-produced tropical colours were available. Like their bomber counterparts, initially they continued to operate in their existing European camouflage until stocks of the Luftwaffe tropical colours became available to re-camouflage them. The Bf 110s then used 79 as the base colouring for sides and upper surfaces, oversprayed with 80 in a loose net-like system of soft-edged strokes; lower surfaces were painted in 78. The Hs 126s were also repainted with a base coat of 79 to which was added a fine, soft spray of random mottling in 80. The sprayed pattern was very thinly applied in places; lower surfaces were again in 78. Repainting had probably been carried out in Sicily, or even Italy, utilising facilities made available to the Luftwaffe at a number of locations.

When replacement Bf 110s arrived in 1942, some were finished in two forms of standard factory finish tropical camouflage, with 79-upper and side surfaces, taken right down to the lowest point and 78-colouring restricted to the under surfaces; alternatively the upper and

ABOVE: France 1940 - Do 17 P-1, 6M+TL of 3.(F)/11, in standard 70/71/65 finish with some solid, irregular-shaped elongated patches of a dark colour added to the under surfaces. The colour is lighter than either 70 or 71 camouflage, or the 66 of the wheel hubs, possibly a unit-mixed colour of blue or blue-green, such minor additions being within the capabilities of front line units. Do 17 P-1, 4N+TL of 3.(F)/22, in the background had had its colour demarcation line raised and short lines of 70 and 71 sprayed on the 65-coloured side and under surfaces of the fuselage and engine cowls. The raised demarcation line mimicked the fighter camouflage of the period and was more practical for the photo-reconnaissance role of these aircraft. (Hans Obert)

ABOVE: This Do 17 P also had had 70-colouring added as a mottle on its under surfaces, but applied as soft-edged individual patches. The wing root leading edge fairing had been repaired and undercoated with 02. The unit badge was still incomplete at the time, only the shield-shaped background having been sprayed on in what appears to be 04. The shape is the only clue to unit identity and this may have been a machine of Aufkl.Gr.(F)/10. The fuselage Balkenkreuz marking was the 1939-style. (Hans Obert)

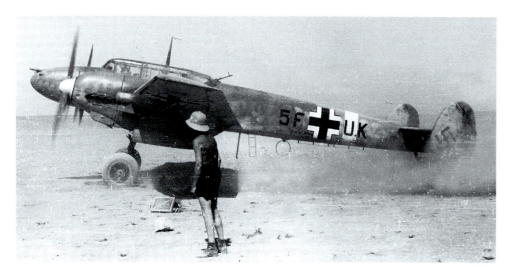

ABOVE: Aufklärungsgruppe (F) 14 also served in North Africa. This Bf 110 F-3, 5F+UK, still retained its European 71/02/65 camouflage, with heavy mottling in both colours, mostly eliminating the 65-coloured side surfaces. It is possible to detect that the mottling had been used to extend the individual segments of camouflage colour down the side surfaces. There is also some evidence of repainting in 02 behind the '5' of the code. The rudders had been heavily mottled in 71, with both fins mottled in 02. The spinners had one-third marked in white and only a single white band tactical marking (the norm for the Mediterranean theatre of operations) had been added to the fuselage.

lower colours met along the horizontal mid-line. The ultimate successor to the Bf 110 in this role was the Me 410, and a few saw tropical service in Sardinia with 2.(F)/Aufkl.Gr.122 but were not re-camouflaged, instead retaining their factory applied 74/75/76 scheme consistent with the overall category of the type as a heavy fighter.

Unit hacks, second line aircraft that were the workhorses of the fighting units, were also re-camouflaged in most instances, producing some interesting variations. 1.(F)/123 used the ubiquitous Ju 52, adding broad, full chord-wise, wavy segments of 80 to the 79 colouring on the wings, and repeating them at a slight angle across the fuselage.

Maritime reconnaissance duties were divided between land- and sea-based aircraft, the Fw 200 providing long-range capabilities from the start of the war. Camouflage was officially prescribed as 72/73/65 despite being land based, the same as worn by the perennial Do 18s, which, with Fw 200s, did much convoy shadowing duty. Ju 188 D-2s eventually joined the land-based maritime reconnaissance force; camouflage was possibly 72/73/65 rather than the standard 70/71/65 of the bomber version, with upper and side surfaces broken up with continuous snaking lines of 65.

High-altitude reconnaissance sorties had been conducted between 1940 and 1943 by specially modified Ju 86 P-2 aircraft operating at very high-altitude over Britain, Russia and the Middle East/Mediterranean. Initially camouflage colouring was 70/71/65, but an overall 02-finish, a colour that worked well for high-altitude work, replaced it. That appears to have received further refinement at some stage in 1941 when the camouflage was changed to 77 grey. Use of 77, with what appears to have been 76 rather than 65 for the lower surfaces in some instances, continued until 1944 when the type was finally withdrawn, but the colouring continued to be employed on other types. A high-altitude reconnaissance version of the Bf 109 G, possibly a G-5 since it had to have had a pressurized cockpit, was intercepted and shot down during a sortie at 12,000 metres over Scapa Flow on 21 February 1944.[2] It wore the same style of colour scheme as the Ju 86 P-2s described above. The intercepting pilots remarked that it was pale grey above and blue underneath and appeared to have no nationality markings; the latter were probably all marked in white as part of the high altitude camouflage system and not easily seen during the engagement. Reference to blue underneath indicates that 76 was still being retained for lower surfaces on high-altitude aircraft.

The Luftwaffe had taken on charge the first of a batch of ten Ju 388 L-0 aircraft, the pre-production version of this high-altitude reconnaissance aircraft, in August 1944. Camouflage for these first machines was 76 lower and side surfaces with upper surface colouring in a slightly darker shade of grey that is hard to detect in some photographs where the light is direct and strong. This appears to have been 77, which was confined to the extreme plan view other than for the engine cowlings, forward of the wings, where it was taken slightly further down the side surfaces. (This style of scheme matches that reported on the Bf 109 G-5 mentioned earlier.)

Given the move to simplify paint production and deliveries, the use of 77 may well have given way to 75 on later production aircraft as the austerity campaign reduced the range of colours to a few standard shades. RLM 76 was prescribed as the only under surface colour from August and that may have been the rationale for any change. Deliveries of the production version, the L-1, began in October 1944 and carried a more definitive camouflage style. Colours by then appear to have been 76 with 75 for the upper surfaces, but the latter was now applied in full strength and brought down from the upper surfaces to a line level with the horizontal tailplane. The 76-colouring of the vertical fin and rudder surfaces were broken up with a fine soft mottle using varying strengths of 75-colouring. On other machines, the vertical tail surfaces were treated with a more solid application of 75 in the form of streaks and spots.

On 10 September 1944, the first Ar 234 to make an appearance over Britain (the V-7 W.Nr. 130007 T9+MH) did so on a high-altitude photo-reconnaissance sortie over the Thames Estuary and London, flown by veteran reconnaissance pilot, Oblt. Erich Sommer. This followed the first operational flight of the type, also by Sommer, over the Allied beachhead at Normandy on 2 August. The extreme height and speed of the Ar 234 had made a specialised camouflage for the type redundant. In March 1945, Sommer moved with a detachment of three Ar 234s to Italy, where he conducted the only jet aircraft operations flown in that country. One of those machines, W.Nr. 140142 T9+DH, was shot down on 11 April, the subsequent report by No 1 Field Intelligence Unit in May 1945 describing

ABOVE: The BV 138 was another in the maritime forces' inventory. Never deployed in large numbers, it nevertheless proved a valuable and reliable asset. This example, from SAGr.125, appears to have been marked only with the aircraft letter 'P', in yellow. The narrow white bands around the tail booms are indicative that this machine was deployed in the Mediterranean at the time that the photograph was taken. (D. Wadman/M. Jessen)

LEFT AND BELOW: This Ju 88 A trop, 7A+GH, of 1.(F)/121, wears a maintenance unit-modified form of camouflage of 78/79, repainted with broad 'seams' of 80 over the 79-finish. Also, a full set of North Africa theatre of operations white tactical markings had been added to the wing tips as well as to the fuselage.

LEFT: 7A+BH shows a style of additional 80-colouring used to break up the factory finish of overall 79-colouring; evidence of the work having been done at the same maintenance depot as the aircraft shown in the two previous photographs. The lower surfaces were painted black. (D. Wadman)

BELOW: While changes to the main camouflage of aircraft were handled by maintenance facilities, minor additions, such as random mottling in a paler colour as seen here, were sometimes done at unit-level when facilities or access to a maintenance unit, was limited. This Ju 88 of 3.(F)/Aufkl.Gr.33, based in Sardinia, had lines of 'Arabesken' added while parked in the open, using unit equipment more normally employed for markings changes. While this made for poor adhesion, any flaking-off of the additional random lines of the very thin colouring would not be detrimental to the underlying overall camouflage finish, nor to the random nature of the extra lines of colour. (D. Wadman)

ABOVE AND BELOW: The Fw 189 was another versatile reconnaissance type that saw widespread use. These two views of Fw 189 A, SI+EG, were taken at a factory in October 1941. The base camouflage is difficult to determine, careful examination of the original photographs show no evidence of a splinter pattern beneath the wandering lines of the paler colour. The finish appears to be 78/79 with 78 used for the lines. Lack of any tactical markings (which by that time were marked by the manufacturing company where aircraft were pre-allocated to a specific battle front) gives no definitive clue as to where the aircraft was to be delivered. The addition of the wavy lines at what appears to be a factory setting was unusual, though some production companies also had dedicated maintenance refurbishing facilities, where both standard and non-standard camouflage finishes were accommodated. Alternatively, this may also have been one of the major Luftwaffe maintenance depot settings. (H. Redemann)

RIGHT: Ageing Ju 86 airframes were given a new lease of life with conversion for high-altitude reconnaissance work, operations beginning in 1942. The P variant was derived from the D model as seen here. This machine had had its standard 70/71/65 camouflage oversprayed with 02, a colour found very suitable for high-altitude camouflage purposes. Note however, that the 02 coating was flaking away along the fuselage joint lines, possibly a result of spraying under poor control conditions and exacerbated by the effects of the metal contraction and expansion due to the high-altitude work.

RIGHT: T5+PM, a Ju 86 R of Höhenflugkommando Beauvais, had a more unusual form of camouflage, with a thin-sprayed mottling of a darker colour over the base 02-colouring. The poor quality of the original photograph makes it difficult to determine what the colours were, for there are two shades of mottling. Given the nature of the operations, the darker colours were possibly 74 and 75, though this is speculative.

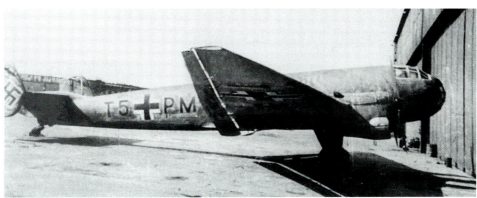

LEFT: The Bf 110 continued to serve in the reconnaissance role for most of the war. This example, a Bf 110 D-3, had camouflage typical of the type in the mid-war years, with upper surface colours blended into the pale side surfaces with very soft mottling in both upper surface colours. Note the open 'network' effect on the nose cone – the faint over spray form the mottles subtly altering the base colouring. The nose emblem appears to be a derivative of that worn by aircraft serving with Nahaufklärungsgeschwader 1. The white spinner tips and the white code letters indicate that this was a 4.Staffel aircraft.

These four photographs of a Bf 109 G-6 trop (or G-8 trop) of 2./NAGr. 12 show a very unusual camouflage scheme. The photographs were taken in Albania in 1944 and the scheme had been applied, presumably, to fit with local conditions over that rugged terrain. There are three colours on the upper surfaces; a base pale colour, with streaked applications of two dark colours of fairly similar tonal value. The paler colour is not 76, something confirmed by close examination of the wing leading edge area visible in two of the photographs. It is paler than the under surface 76 colour. The two darker colours were possibly 74 and 75, or two greens, though the latter are less likely. Breaking up the two darker colours into more fragmentary form apparently provided a better disruptive form of pattern for the terrain.

the camouflage as "dark olive drab". While only the tail unit and parts of the port wing remained after the wreckage was burned by German troops, photographs clearly show that the starboard side of the fin and rudder, where they were not heat effected, retained their splinter pattern camouflage. What the Intelligence Officer saw was a combination of 81 and 83, which produced a dark brown-green finish and his assessment obviously referred to the overall colour effect produced, rather than individual colours. Photographs of reconnaissance Ar 234s of 1.(F)/Aufklr.Gr. 33 also show a very dark overall finish consistent with use of 81/83/76 rather than 81/82/76, a combination of colours that appear to have been used on late production aircraft of this type.

ABOVE: The Ar 234 was the ultimate Luftwaffe long-range reconnaissance aircraft. Kommando Sperling was established to exploit this role and T9+HH, W.Nr. 140153, shows the 81/82 finish employed by the type. The unit code 'T9' was applied in white with the letters 'HH' in black.

The first Ar 234 to fall into Allied hands, F1+MT W.Nr. 140173 of 9./KG 76, force-landed at Siegersdorf on 22 February 1945. It was carefully examined after being shipped back to RAF Farnborough; its camouflage was described as a splinter pattern of green and brown-green with pale grey underside, patches of which also covered the fuselage sides. Several good quality photographs of the aircraft show a contrast level between the two colours more consistent with 82 and 83 than 81 and 82 and that is supported by the colour description used in the report. The green was definitely 82 and brown-green is a reasonable description of 83. Had 81 been used, the second description would not have referred to brown-green, but rather to a distinct brown; 81 exhibiting no green characteristics. The subsequent report also stated:

> "…that the external finish, particularly of the fuselage, was very smooth, a heavy coat of plastic filler being spread over the joints and rivets and subsequently polished. In contrast to this, construction of the various sub-assemblies suffered from poor workmanship."

This reference to a plastic filler and polishing has nothing to do with the external surface of the camouflage finish. As recorded earlier, the practice during construction was to fill all joints with filler paste and to smooth (polish) them to remove any surface irregularities. The remark about the sub-assemblies is noteworthy; such items coming from external production sources where factory controls were less rigorous at that late stage of the war. By that stage most able-bodied men were being used for the fighting, their places being filled by forced or semi-skilled labour.

The Me 262 was also produced, in small numbers, in a reconnaissance version. In March 1945, elements of NAG 1 and NAG 6 were advised that they were to be re-equipped with the Me 262A-1a/U3

variant. The first photo-reconnaissance aircraft, W.Nr. 170006, had been flight tested at Lechfeld, an extensive test regime starting in late July 1944. However, delivery of Me 262s to the reconnaissance units had been slow, and it was not until 10 March 1945 that the General der Aufklärer had reported the equipping of parts of NAG 1 and NAG 6 was to take place. In the event, very few machines reached these units.

The Me 262 A-1a/U3s delivered to NAG 6 at Lechfeld carried a non-standard style of camouflage, but did exhibit a degree of consistency of application and style, having been produced at the same centre. The nose section, a sub-manufactured component supplied in 02 finish, had 76 on the lower surfaces, but upper and side surfaces were finished in a thinned-out application of 82 with a dense network of soft-edged lines of 83 sprayed over that in a loose netting style. On at least one example patches of very thinned out 81 had also been applied over the 82, approximating the normal areas of 81/82 camouflage segments, before the network of 83-colouring was sprayed on. Lower surfaces were a mixture of 76 and treated bare metal.

The helicopter, a radical innovation for its time, also saw service in the light reconnaissance role, albeit in very small numbers and often in the form of pre-production test machines. For the latter reason, while numbers were small, the varieties of camouflage and paint finishes were not.

Of the two types to reach production status the Flettner Fl 282 was the smaller. The initial prototypes were left unpainted although probably receiving a clear coat of lacquer 7171.00 for the wooden parts, and later given a pale overall colouring (probably 02 or 65). However, several were later painted in standard 70/71/ 65 using a modified splinter pattern, the shape and size of the machine making a standard pattern application impractical. Examples used by the Kriegsmarine, such as the V6, which was flown for convoy protection duties in the Aegean Sea, possibly used a 72/73/65 scheme, though the 70/71/65-colouring would have been just as effective and it is impossible to differentiate between the two colour schemes in photographs. The rotor blades, technically rotating wing surfaces, were treated as such and camouflaged with one of the greens, photographs favouring the paler of the two colours.

The Focke-Achgelis Fa 223 was a larger helicopter, intended for land-based work, but few had been produced. Having been completed by mid-June 1944, several had seen service with Lufttransportstaffel 40, the few photographs indicating that a standard 70/71/65 finish had been applied to them. One additional machine was completed just before the end of the war. If it was camouflaged, then possibly by then it would have had an 81/82/76 scheme.

Not so the tiny Fa 330 gyro-kite, designed for convoy spotting work and flown behind a surfaced submarine. Other than for the rotors and vertical tail surfaces the structure was composed of metal tubes, all of which had been painted in a pale colouring, probably 65 rather than 02, but either would have worked well as sky camouflage.

ABOVE: Originally designed for Deutsche Lufthansa, the Fa 223 V2 first flew on 20 April 1942 and retained its original 02-colouring, civil markings and registration during its early test programme.

1. Flight and The Aircraft Engineer, November 16, 1939
2. The Big Show, Pierre Clostermann, Chatto and Windus, London 1953, page 103.

RIGHT: This colour photograph of an Me 262 A-1a/U3 taken at Lechfeld, illustrates just how softly the base colours of 81 and 82 had been sprayed. The 83-application had been applied by using the spray gun at an angle, so that one edge was sharper and the other diffused. Note carefully the distinct lines of 83-colouring immediately forward and aft of the Balkenkreuz marking - the design is freehand and thus unique. Note the single 30 mm MK 108 cannon with which only some of these reconnaissance aircraft were armed.

ABOVE: Bf 109 G-10/R2 W.Nr. 770269, 5F+12 of NAGr 14 was camouflaged with an interesting mixture of colours. The fuselage aft of the cockpit was in 75/82, but the engine cowling area was a mixture of 75 and 83, as also was the rear section of the fuselage where it met the empennage. The fin was heavily mottled with 83, all but obscuring the underlying 76-colour, while the horizontal tail surfaces were in a solid application of 83. The 76-colouring of the fuselage sides had disappeared beneath the mottling and a soft application of 02, leaving just small areas of the original colour showing through. The positioning of the Werknummer across both fin and rudder, with just one figure marked on the fin, followed the final RLM directive eliminating Stammkennzeichen markings. This was a Wiener Neustadt Flugzeugwerke-built aircraft, as shown by that company's distinctive form of marking for the MW 50 filler point, a red/white/red triangle. The yellow tactical markings had been changed to accord with the final RLM 1945 directive, but remnants of the previous 04-yellow fuselage band marking were still visible behind the miniature '5F' marking in black, total removal of the yellow in that area being too difficult without having to repaint the code. The fuselage side area beneath the cockpit showed heavy exhaust staining. Note also the light colouring of the wheel hubs, possibly a coat of 02-colouring having been used.

ABOVE AND LEFT: Two views of the damaged remains of the experimental DFS 228 V1, rocket-powered extreme-altitude reconnaissance aircraft. The DFS 228 was to be launched from a Do 217 K at 10,000 metres, then climb to 23,000 metres. Using its rocket power in short bursts it was anticipated that it would stay at that altitude for 45 minutes. The high gloss RLM 05 finish can be seen more clearly in the rear view of D-IBFQ.

BELOW: This view of the DFS 228 V1 mounted on a Do 217 K (V3) provides a good impression of the very simple, clean lines of this highly advanced reconnaissance aircraft. Note that the DFS 228 appears to have an emblem of a 'Narwhal' painted on the nose. The civil registration had not been added at this stage.

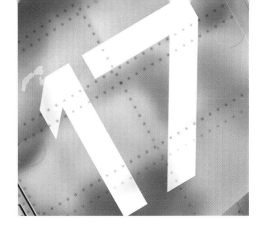

Civil Registrations, Überführungskennzeichnen and Stammkennzeichnung

by J. Richard Smith and Tom Willis

The Treaty of Versailles, which came into force on 10 January 1920, prohibited Germany from retaining any flying units, and left her with just residual land and sea forces. Three months later, on 9 April, the army Chief-of-Staff, General von Seeckt, at the request of the Ambassadors' Conference then in session in Paris, ordered the disbandment of the few remaining air force units.

At first, no restrictions were placed on the manufacture and use of civil aircraft but, in 1922, certain limitations were placed on their size and performance. The Paris Air Agreement of 1926 withdrew these restrictions, and from then on Germany began to develop a number of military aircraft under the guise of civil "mail planes" or the like.

Until 1934, all German civil aircraft were identified by the national letter 'D', (for *Deutschland*), and a consecutive number sequence beginning with '1'. This system was imposed on Germany by the Paris Treaty on Aerial Traffic of 13 October 1919; an intentional ploy by the Allies to keep a check on aircraft production and procurement.

The first German civil registration, D-1, was issued to a Junkers F 13 (W.Nr. 531) named "Nachtigall", owned by Bayerische Luftlloyd GmbH in Munich. Photographic evidence appears to indicate that initially there were some repeated registrations, e.g., Ju 50 A registered D-3 and an He 70 also shown with the same registration. This apparent anomaly however resulted from retention of the registrations for use as temporary markings applied to aircraft while under air testing at their point of manufacture, or for their delivery flight, and was a limited to the first nine registrations. The Ju 50 A registered D-3 was manufactured around 1921, while the He 70 first appeared on the civil register in June 1933 as D-2537. The D-3 registration had also been used for a Sablantig P 1. Why these few remained in use for this purpose is not known, but from the D-10 registration onwards, none were issued twice, while the first nine were obviously kept in circulation as the significant time gap between the Ju 50 A and the He 70 examples show.

One of the most important stimuli to the re-establishment of military flying in Germany was the formation, in 1925, of the German Airline Pilot's School, Deutsche Verkehrsfliegerschule (DVS) at Berlin-Staaken. Although ostensibly formed to train commercial pilots, it was not long before it began the training of military aircrew. Soon the organization began to expand its facilities, opening two new schools in 1927 at Schleissheim (near München), and at Braunschweig. A naval school was initiated at Warnemünde on the Baltic coast, and later a fourth land-based school was established at Würzburg. The DVS schools were equipped with a large variety of aircraft but all used the civil registration system described above.

The last known numerical registration was D-3463, issued to a BFW M 35 b light plane (W.Nr. 627) in March 1934, and owned by the Deutsche Luftsport Verband (DLV) in Berlin.

On 20 March 1934, the system of the national letter 'D' followed by a numerical sequence was replaced by the letter 'D' followed by a combination of four letters. The first letter of this combination identified the aircraft's specific class or category based on the number of people carried, flying weight, landing run and number of engines. The six categories employed vowels as the prime letters together with 'Y', which was used for ultra-light aircraft. These category letters were as follows:

Landplanes

Registration	Class	Crew	Flying weight	Landing run	Eng.
D-YAAA - D-YZZZ	A1	1 to 3	up to 500 kg	up to 300 m	1-2
D-EAAA - D-EZZZ	A2	2 to 3	up to 1000 kg	up to 450 m	1-2
or		1 to 2	500 - 1000 kg	300 to 450 m	1-2
D-IAAA - D-IZZZ	B1	1 to 4	up to 2500 kg	up to 450 m	1-2
or		1 to 3	up to 1000 kg	over 450 m	1-2
D-OAAA - D-OZZZ	B2	up to 8	2500 to 5000 kg	over 450 m	1-2
D-UAAA - D-UZZZ	C1	over 6	over 2500 kg	over 450 m	1
D-AAAA - D-AZZZ	C2	over 6	over 2500 kg	over 450 m	multi

Seaplanes

Registration	Class	Crew	Flying weight	Eng.
D-YAAA - D-YZZZ	A1	up to 2	up to 600 kg	1
D-EAAA - D-EZZZ	A2	up to 3	up to 2000 kg	1
D-IAAA - D-IZZZ	B1	up to 3	up to 3500 kg	1
D-OAAA - D-OZZZ	B2	up to 6	up to 3500 kg	1
D-UAAA - D-UZZZ	C1	over 6	over 3500 kg	1
D-AAAA - D-AZZZ	C2	over 6	over 3500 kg	multi

LEFT: Each of the first nine registrations in the new system were recycled through several different aircraft. This Ju F 13 W.Nr. 531, seen here are Tempelhof airfield circa 1928, was the first civil aircraft to wear the newly introduced D-series' registration. It is seen here finished in pale grey with black trim of Luft Hansa, the company name being marked on the engine cowling. Constructed in 1919 and fitted with a single BMW IV in-line engine, it was originally registered to Luftlloyd G.m.b.H at München, passing to Deutsche Luft Hansa AG in 1926 who eventually added the company fleet name 'NACHTIGALL'. With the change in the civil registration system in 1934, it was re-registered as D-OJOP.

RIGHT: He 70, W.Nr. 403, was the third aircraft to wear the civil registration D-3. It was operated by Luft Hansa, re-registered as D-2537 and then as D-UHUX under the revised civil registration system as noted in the text. It wore the DLH pale grey finish with the characteristic black trim and lightning bolt sign with the names Blitz and Luft Hansa marked on the engine cowling. Note the abbreviated form of the national tricolour marking which was confined to the rudder. (Lufthansa)

LEFT: This airborne shot provides a clear view of the positioning of the registration on the under surface of the wings as well as showing how the black cheat line extended along the under side of the fuselage back to the tail wheel. The clear cover over the landing light, set into the lower surface of the engine cowling, can also be seen. (Lufthansa)

BELOW: Registrations were allocated sequentially, regardless of size, engine numbers or all up weight. This Dornier Do 8t Wal, W.Nr. 185, was built in 1931. Bearing the name 'PASSAT', it displays its registration, D-2068, which was marked in black on both sides of the fuselage and both the wing upper and lower surfaces. The shiny surface of the black-painted registration below the wing produced a mirror-like finish from the reflected glare on the water. (Lufthansa)

LEFT: This Ju 60 ba, W.Nr. 4201, registered in May 1933, was allotted the registration D-2400. Operated by Luft Hansa it was painted in their traditional finish and carried the name 'PFEIL' (arrow). It was later re-registered as D-UPAL. (Lufthansa)

RIGHT: The ubiquitous Ju 52/3m,; W.Nr. 4019 was registered in May 1933, as D-2468. This gives some idea of the pace at which registrations were being created at that time. Christened 'JOACHIM VON SCHRÖDER' it eventually became D-AFIR. (Lufthansa)

LEFT: This Fw 44 E, W.Nr. 340, differed from the main production variants in being powered by an Argus As 8 B in-line engine. Delivered to the DVS, it had an overall finish of silver with either black or dark blue trim, and marked with the civil registration D-3174, issued in April 1934. Note the overlap in time with the revised 'D-alpha' registrations that came into force on 20 March 1934.

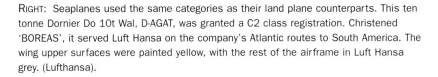

ABOVE: The new system required aircraft to be registered in specific classes. Christened 'EMIL SCHAEFER', this Ju 52/3mho, W.Nr. 4045, was fitted with Junker Jumo engines; it was granted a class C2 registration as D-AJYR in 1934. It wore standard Luft Hansa paintwork, plus the German tricolour marking across fin and rudder on the starboard side. (Lufthansa)

RIGHT: Seaplanes used the same categories as their land plane counterparts. This ten tonne Dornier Do 10t Wal, D-AGAT, was granted a C2 class registration. Christened 'BOREAS', it served Luft Hansa on the company's Atlantic routes to South America. The wing upper surfaces were painted yellow, with the rest of the airframe in Luft Hansa grey. (Lufthansa).

LEFT: This view of D-AKER, 'TAIFUN', being catapulted from its mother ship in the South Atlantic, shows how well the black registration letters showed up against the yellow of the wing surfaces, a safety feature for over water operations. (Lufthansa)

LEFT AND BELOW: Two views of Fw 44 C, D-EVOH, illustrate the incorrect interpretation of the placement of the civil registration markings. The registration had been marked on the underside of the top wing, instead of the underside of the bottom wing in this instance. The tricolour fin and rudder marking dates the photograph to between July 1933 and April 1934. (S. Santos)

BELOW: The Junkers W 34 was a versatile type that gave both civil and military service for well over a decade. This example wearing a B2 registration, D-OJOH was in service with Lufthansa, and named 'CASTOR', one of a series of names chosen from celestial groups. Marked in white on the black cowling was 'HANSA FLUGDIENST' ('Hansa Air Service').

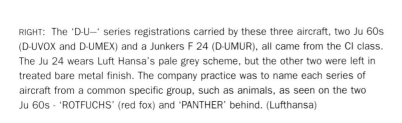

RIGHT: The 'D-U—' series registrations carried by these three aircraft, two Ju 60s (D-UVOX and D-UMEX) and a Junkers F 24 (D-UMUR), all came from the CI class. The Ju 24 wears Luft Hansa's pale grey scheme, but the other two were left in treated bare metal finish. The company practice was to name each series of aircraft from a common specific group, such as animals, as seen on the two Ju 60s - 'ROTFUCHS' (red fox) and 'PANTHER' behind. (Lufthansa)

ABOVE: The Fw 200 V2, powered by 720 hp BMW 132 G-1 radials was given a civilian class C2 registration of D-AETA. Note how the registration was treated on this large aircraft, with lettering only outboard of the engines on the wings and in much smaller size both on wings and fuselage with the name 'WESTFALEN' being given prominence. The black engine trim and cheat line look paler where the sunlight is more direct. Note the prominent display of the manufacturer's name and the aircraft designation on the fin. (Lufthansa)

(**Note**: *The sequence D-IAAA – D-JZZZ was actually written with the letters D-JAAA. While many writers have stated that this was an incorrectly applied marking, the simple fact is that in the German style of script in use at that time the capital letter 'I' was sometimes written as, what to English speaking people, appears to be a 'J'. The same use was still being made of this form of the letter as late as the mid-war years as shown by part of a stencil on the wing slat of one of the Me 262 prototypes, marked JNNEN, despite the fact that by then it was more usually written as INNEN.*)

Instructions for application of the revised civil registrations were promulgated in Luftverkehrvorschrift 1 (Air Traffic Ordinance 1) of Air Traffic Ordinance of 21.8.1936 (Reich Government Gazette 1936 Part 1 s. 675 and 691 of R. F. L. 1936 S. 638 and 657). These were published in the Reichsgesetzblatt of 29 August 1936 under the title Encl. Nr. 1 to Paras 4, 12 and 75 of LuftVo Reichsgesetzblatt of 29 August 1936. The relevant sections read as follows:

"German aircraft and airships carry the letter "D" as national marking followed by a four-letter registration. The Reich Air Minister may permit non-standard registrations for airships.

On aircraft the national identification "D" and individual registration is carried on both sides of the fuselage, in the space between the wings and the vertical stabilizer, on monoplanes also on upper and lower surfaces, biplanes under the lower and on top of the upper wing.

Airships carry the markings on both sides of the hull, at the point of its largest diameter, in such a manner as to be visible from the side as well as from the ground, also on top of the hull at right angles to the fuselage markings and equidistant from both.

Markings are to be applied either in solid black characters on light background or in light characters on dark background in wipe-resistant lacquer, always to be kept clearly visible. The national letter "D" is separated from the registration by a hyphen of a length similar to the width of a letter. The area covered by the markings has to be in the form of a rectangle, taking care that it is not obscured by engines, struts, undercarriage or floats.

On aircraft the minimum spacing of the lettering from the leading and trailing edges at the wing's narrowest point

is to be at least one-sixth of the size of the letter. On airships the size of the hull characters should be one-twelfth the circumference measured at the largest diameter of the hull but no larger than 2.50 m.

Registered and licensed air trailers [towed gliders] carry the national letter "D" and registration in a similar manner to aircraft, the characters to be underlined.

Sailplanes, if flown outside of gliding fields, carry the national letter "D" as stated above for powered aircraft.

Free balloons carry the national letter followed by the individual name in the same form as that applying to airship lettering."

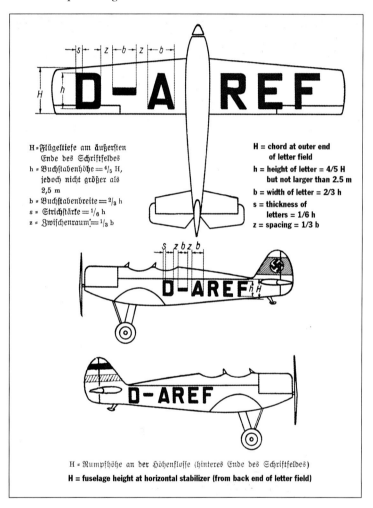

H = Flügeltiefe am äußersten Ende des Schriftfeldes
h = Buchstabenhöhe = 4/5 H, jedoch nicht größer als 2,5 m
b = Buchstabenbreite = 2/3 h
s = Strichstärke = 1/6 h
z = Zwischenraum = 1/3 b

H = chord at outer end of letter field
h = height of letter = 4/5 H but not larger than 2.5 m
b = width of letter = 2/3 h
s = thickness of letters = 1/6 h
z = spacing = 1/3 b

H = Rumpfhöhe an der Höhenflosse (hinteres Ende des Schriftfeldes)
H = fuselage height at horizontal stabilizer (from back end of letter field)

The diagrams shown above accompanied the instructions.

A single anomaly to subsequent changes in registration form was D-2600, which was reserved for the personal aircraft used by the Führer. This practice continued, both on his Ju 52 and subsequently his Fw 200, from the time of Hitler's election as Chancellor in 1933 until 1945. Aviation historian, Dr. Karl Kössler, has stated that Hitler's former personal pilot, Hans Baur, told him that the call sign D-2600 had been retained as it was known to every air traffic controller in Germany and instantly identified the Führer's aircraft, ensuring priority in all circumstances and at all locations. After the change to civil registrations, when a four-letter combination was introduced, there ensued a long struggle between Baur and the authorities to retain the original distinguishing registration. Eventually, permission was forthcoming and when the Ju 52 was replaced by the Fw 200 V2, (W. Nr. 2891 named 'IMMELMANN III'), the anomalous registration was retained. The only other changes that occurred were during 1939, when the prefix 'WL' replaced the 'D' temporarily (see below), and later, when the marking was given pseudo-military form as 26+00. (This aircraft was eventually destroyed at Schleissheim by air attack.)

The 20 February 1939 issue of *Luftwaffen=Verordnungsblatt* contained a revised ordinance dealing with the introduction of temporary ferry codes (Überführungskennzeichen – see below), which effected both civil and military aircraft, but contained only the following brief reference to civil registrations.

"Civil markings may only be ordered from the manufacturer (and only with the authority of the manufacturing control inspectorate) when it is certain that the specific aircraft will retain that registration and will not, at a later date, be replaced with a military marking.

R. d. L. u. Ob. d. L., 13.2.1939,
Az. 38P48 L. B. II , 8
Nr. 8105/39"

Einteilung der Flugzeuge / Signale / Hoheitszeichen

a) Einteilung der Flugzeuge in Deutschland

1. Nach der Zulassungsklasse

Klasse	Zeichen	Personen		Fluggewicht
A—1	D—Y...	1—2	bis	500 kg
A—2	D—E...	1—3	„	1000 kg
B—1	D—I...	1—3	„	2500 kg
B—2	D—O...	4—6	„	2500 kg
C—1	D—U...	über 6	über	2500 kg
C—2	D—A...	„ 6	„	2500 kg

2. Nach der Verwendungsgruppe

H = Höchstleistungsflugzeuge
G = Güterflugzeuge
P = Personenflugzeuge (gewerbsmäßig)
R = Reiseflugzeuge (privat)
S = Schulflugzeuge (nur Klasse A—2)
K = Kunstflugzeuge.

Flugzeuge der Luftwaffe WL— statt D—.

3. Nach der Beanspruchungsgruppe

1	sehr gering
2	gering
3	normal
4	hoch
5	sehr hoch

Beispiel: Ein Flugzeug der Klasse B—2 (Bezeichnung D—OVIP) ist zugelassen für G 4 und P 3, das heißt für Güterbeförderung mit hoher oder Personenbeförderung im Verkehr mit normaler Beanspruchung.

b) Signale und Zeichen im Flugbetrieb

Eine rote Leuchtkugel: Gefahr, Landebahn nicht frei.
Drei rote Leuchtkugeln: Höchste Gefahr. Nur im äußersten Notfall landen.
Drei Rauchpatronen (tags): Landeaufforderung.
Drei grüne Leuchtsterne (nachts): Landeaufforderung.
Eine weiße Leuchtkugel: Hebt die vorherigen Zeichen auf. — Landebahn ist frei. — Nachts: Hier ist der Platz!
Roter Ball am Signalmast: Startverbot.

The above table shows the civil aviation instructions, including 1 January 1939 revision for second line military aircraft markings.

When front line aircraft adopted the system of revised military codes, the majority of second line units and para-military organizations, such as the Nationalsozialistischen Fliegerkorps (NSFK), continued to use civil registrations. Between 1 January and 24 October 1939, however, all military aircraft carrying the letter 'D' for Deutschland prefix were instructed to replace the 'D' with 'WL' for Wehrmacht Luft (Armed Forces Air). However, there is ample photographic evidence that compliance with this instruction was slow and a mixture of both forms of marking were seen for an extended period. For existing powered training aircraft of the A/B Schulen, modification of the civil registration was not always effected with consistency, producing variations to the distribution of the markings that now also had to include the addition of military markings at the same time. Sometimes the existing horizontal black bar, separating the 'D' from the remainder of the registration, was utilised as the horizontal stroke of the Balkenkreuz.

This was obviously adopted only as an interim measure as it was soon realized that a more permanent and better method of identification would be needed should hostilities begin. This system would be used, not only for visual identification, either from the air or on the ground, but also as radio call sign letters.

Sailplane and Glider Markings

In March 1933, the DLV had been established to promote German public interest in gliding, ballooning, powered flying and aircraft modelling. Two years later the DLV divided administrative control of all civil flying into 16 Luftsport-Landesgruppen, (later increased to 17 after the Austrian Anschluss in 1938), one for each separate region of Germany, plus Austria. To identify gliders within each area, they were to have their fuselages painted different colours. When two colours were specified, the first named would be used for the front part of the fuselage, the last named for the rear and tail. Where two regions used the same combination of colours the order was reversed for one regional group to distinguish ownership from the other. Sailplanes and gliders were marked with a 'D' registration, followed by the number of the Landesgruppe plus an individual number, e.g., the Rhönbussard D-15-1067 seen at Dettingen airfield in June 1939. The registration identified it as the 1067th glider registered within Luftsport-Landesgruppe 15, Stuttgart. Registration codes were painted (in most cases) on either side of the fuselage and above and below the wings. The letter 'D' and the first two letters would be painted above the port and below the starboard wing, with the remaining number on the opposite wing in each instance. For some gliders, such as the SG 38 for example, it was impossible to paint the registration on the fuselage because this comprised simply an open steel tube structure. In this case the marking was painted, in very small characters, on the bottom half of the rudder.

The 17 administrative regions and the colours allocated were as follows:

No	Area	Headquarters	Colour
1	East Prussia	Königsberg	white
2	Nord (Pomerania)	Stettin	light blue
3	Nordwest	Hamburg	black
4	Prussia	Berlin	black and white
5	Sachsen	Halberstadt	light green
6	Silesia	Breslau	yellow
7	Elbe-Saale	Dresden	white and green
8	Mitte (Weimar)	Eschwege	green and white
9	Weser-Elbe	Hannover	white and red
10	Westfahlen	Dortmund	white and black
11	Hessen-Westmark	Darmstadt	red and white
12	Niederrhein	Essen	black and white stripes
13	Main-Donau	Nürnberg	white and blue
14	Bavaria Süd	München	blue and white
15	Schwaben	Stuttgart	red and black
16	Südwest (Danzig)	Karlsruhe	brick red
17	Austria	Wien	(not relevant)

(Region 17 was added after the date of the creation of the NSFK).

The multi-coloured paint schemes for gliders were applied only until October 1937 after the DLV had been replaced by the NSFK on 17 April 1937, a branch of the National Socialist Party designed to promote an interest in flying in boys from 12 years of age upwards. The NSFK ordered that all gliders should be painted cream overall, but the marking system of letters and numbers described above was retained. Gliders and sailplanes under Luftwaffe control (e.g., at A/B Schülen) utilised the same marking system but with the distinction that the Arabic numerals were replaced by Roman numerals. The NSFK retained the 17 area division system, broken first into Standarte, then into Sturm formations, these distinctions being marked on gliders as two sets of small numerals divided by a vertical slash. The boundaries of some of the original areas appear to have been revised during the transition. The listing of Gruppen areas was then as follows. ([1])

No	Area
1	Ostland (East Prussia)
2	Nord (Ostsee, Baltic)
3	Nordwest (Hamburg)

RIGHT: The revised form of civil registration marking applied to second-line military aircraft between January and October 1939 is seen here on this fully militarised Do 18. The registration WL-ADBA was applied to both upper and lower surface of the wings as well as the fuselage.

ABOVE AND RIGHT: Two photographs taken at a Luftwaffe training airfield in the summer of 1939. Both the Go 145 A, WL-ISKO, seen in both photographs, and the Ar 66 C, WL-ILQO, are marked correctly for the period with the paramilitary version of a Class B1 registration. (H. Obert)

4	Berlin und Mark Brandenburg (Berlin)
5	Wartheland (Posen and Warthegau)
6	Schlesien (Breslau, Silesia)
7	Elbe-Saale (Dresden)
8	Mitte (Eschwege)
9	Weser-Elbe (Hannover)
10	Westfahlen (Dortmund, Westfalia)
11	Westmark/Moselland (Frankfurt am Main)
12	Niederrhein (Essen)
13	Rhein-Donau (Nürnberg, Danube)
14	Hochland (München/Alpenland)
15	Schwaben/Württemberg (Stuttgart)
16	Südwest (Strasburg, Alsace)
17	Ostmark/Donau (Alpenland Wien)

Despite changes to newly manufactured military aircraft, as explained below, existing training aircraft continued to retain their D-type civil registrations until 1 January 1939, when the 'D' prefix was replaced by the 'WL' code on Luftwaffe controlled aircraft of the A/B Schulen, although the remainder of the original marking was retained until replaced by the Stammkennzeichen system in June 1943

ABOVE: Aircraft impressed into the Luftwaffe were treated in the same manner in terms of registration, as shown by this Avia F 39 (licence-built Fokker F IX M), marked WL+AHSQ. Note the manner in which the registration was split up, with a single Balkenkreuz marking displayed to divide the two elements. (M. Clayton)

ABOVE: Incorporation of a Balkenkreuz into the 'WL'-prefixed registrations often presented a problem for space on some types. In some instances the problem was solved by careful, sometimes innovative positioning of the Balkenkreuz as shown here on this Fw 56, WL-IBE+Y. What solution was used on the port side remains unknown, most probably the 'WL' portion being split from the remainder by the military marking.

Introduction of the Überführungskennzeichen (temporary ferry code) markings

With effect from 23 September 1937, all new production military aircraft had their civil registrations replaced by a four-letter ferry code (Überführungskennzeichen) for identification purposes. Up to this time, all new aircraft had been required to carry a normal civil registration. This was proving both time-consuming and inefficient for military aircraft, as the civil markings were immediately replaced on delivery to a Luftwaffe unit, and the original civil marking returned to the civil register for re-issue. Delays, or failure by Luftwaffe units to notify the removal of the civil markings, restricted re-issue of the registration and the rising production cycle of military aircraft threatened to place a severe strain on the civil registration system.

ABOVE: A Do 17, DO+JY, provides an example of the Überführungskennzeichen system introduced in September 1937, consisting of two letters to identify the manufacturer and two allocated to each airframe. In this instance 'DO' identified the manufacturer as Dornier and 'JY' the individual aircraft. (M. Ullmann)

The new four-letter code system markings were applied to both the fuselage and under surface of the wings and stayed with the aircraft until it was assigned to a flying unit. The letters were to be applied in pairs, immediately inboard of the Balkenkreuz marking beneath each wing. Each block commenced with a consonant, with the first two letters identifying the aircraft manufacturer (and in some cases the licence builder), though with the added subtlety that they identified different production plants where firms had multiple facilities e.g., BÜ for Bücker; BY for Bayersichen Flugzeugwerk Regensburg G.m.b.H.; DO for Dornier's Oberpfaffenhofen plant and DF for their Friedrichshafen factory; FI for Fieseler; FO for Focke-Wulf's Bremen plant; HA for Hamburger Flugzeugbau (which changed its name to Blohm und Voss in due course); HE for the Heinkel Rostock-Marienehe works; JB for Junkers production at Bernberg and JU for the parent plant at Dessau; WE for Weser Flugzeugbau, et al.

Initially, two blocks of double letters were to be placed only on the wing under surface (as shown here in the first diagram), washable black lacquer being stipulated for what was to be a temporary marking. However, very soon the code marking also began to appear on fuselage side surfaces and this change was incorporated into the revised instruction of 1939. The example shown in the diagram is an actual temporary ferry marking, used by ATG-Machinen G.m.b.H. As the new system did not allow use of a vowel for the first letter the 'A' was dropped in this instance, (given the three letter combination of this company identification, one would have had to be deleted, probably the last had not the first been a vowel).

BELOW: A Habicht, operated by the Deutsche Luftsport Verband, wears the style of registration used by that organization from March 1933 until 1939. Marked D-4-1722 both beneath and above the wings, as well as one each side of the fuselage, the number '4' shows that it was operated within the administrative area of Prussia, the HQ of which was in Berlin. (P. Selinger)

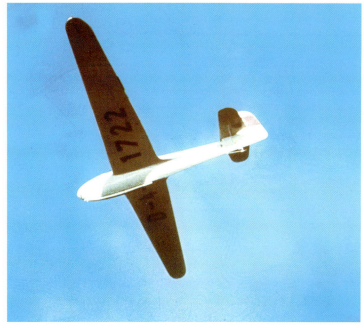

ABOVE: In this view of the same Habicht, the style of presentation of the registration on the fuselage can be clearly seen. (P. Selinger)

LEFT: A pair of Habicht gliders, with WL-XI-243 in the foreground. Luftwaffe-controlled flying groups employed a Roman numeral, in place of an Arabic numeral, for the middle section of the registration marking. (P. Selinger)

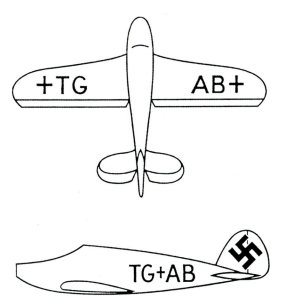

The 23 September 1937 Überführungskennzeichen instruction diagram.

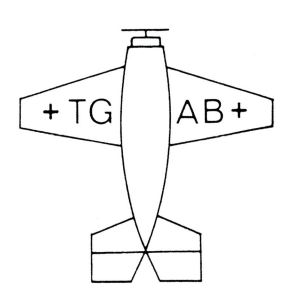

The 13 February 1939 Überführungskennzeichen revised instruction diagram.

The new code system followed the existing civil registration process in so far as the allocations were intended to be re-used. A quick calculation of the available range shows that it would have been exhausted fairly quickly had this not been so. The last two letters of the new code consisted of a consonant and a vowel and progressed alphabetically, commencing with the vowel letter of the sequence, regardless of whether it was the third or fourth letter in the four-letter sequence. Where two vowels appeared simultaneously in a running sequence, e.g. +EE, the sequence continued with the principal vowel in sequential use, e.g., +EB, +EC, +ED +EE, +EF etc.

A detailed instruction was promulgated on 13 February 1939, which reiterated the general instruction regarding changes to temporary ferry marking regulations. It read:

"Ferry Codes for Military aircraft:

The lifting of regulations relating to military aircraft transfer codes as set down by L. C. II Nr. 10451/37 II8 of 23. 9. 1937 (V. Bl. 1937 S. 542 Nr. 1279 and S. 583 Nr. 1380) and Az. 38P48 L. B. II, 4 Nr. 4909/37 of 25. 9. 1937 as well as the only single department of the RLM which issued order Az. 38 e 45 L. C. 3 Nr. 195/39 (3V) will take effect from 16. 1. 1939.

I. General.

Aircraft that have not yet received final military markings will receive for ferrying from the manufacturer, repair works, aircraft departments or air parks of the Service Headquarters before they are moved, ferry markings (Balkenkreuz and number or WL and four letters).

The ferry markings on the underside of the wings (on biplanes only on the lower surface of the bottom wings) and on both sides of the fuselage will be in addition to the Balkenkreuz in appropriate size, form and colour. Also on the fin and rudder the Hakenkreuz will be marked according to Luftwaffe regulations.

II. Style and positioning of the ferry markings.

The style and spacing of the ferry markings which will be of four letters will be in accordance with the following diagram marked on the underside of the wings (on biplanes only on the lower surface of the bottom wings) and on both sides of the fuselage.

Size and spacing and colour of the letters accords with para 4 of the original document 1 of Air Traffic Ordnance of 2.8.1936 (Reich Government Gazette 1936 Part 1 s. 675 and 691 of R. F. L. 1936 S. 638 and 657).

The colouring of the ferry codes must be removable on aircraft with fixed weapons, but the Balkenkreuz is not to be removable.

III. Validity period.

After delivery at its [the aircraft] destination the markings are to be immediately removed. The Service Headquarters department which takes over the aircraft must notify the aircraft manufacturer, transferring agency etc., of the aircraft department or air park within 3 days after which the markings can be re-issued.

IV. Traffic regulations.
For aircraft with the described ferry markings, for

transfer to the Service Department [the markings] are the same as those [used] for military marked aircraft.

V. Radio operations.

Radio contact of aircraft with ferry markings are the same as for aircraft with military markings. The call sign of aircraft with ferry markings are to use the markings with the letter D in front (example the ferry marking "TGAB" will use the call sign "DTGAB"). Calls signs like that are differentiated from civil marked aircraft in so far as the first letter after the D is not a vowel (A, E, I, O, U, Y), it is always a consonant.
VI. Issuing of ferry markings.

The ferry markings are issued from the RLM- L. B. II 8 - to constructors, construction department and air park authorities. All those places are required to record the ferry markings. Issuing of these ferry markings is to be registered through all departments so that at any time the appropriate authority can trace which aircraft were so marked and by whom it was transferred.

Civil markings may only be ordered from the manufacturer (and only with the authority of the manufacturing control inspectorate) when it is certain that the specific aircraft will retain that registration and will not, at a later date, be replaced with a military marking. The ferry markings which have been allocated to the manufacturing control inspectorate are to remain unchanged. The ferry markings for construction departments and air parks will be issued through a special edict.

R. d. L. u. Ob. d. L., 13.2.1939,
Az. 38P48 L. B. II , 8
Nr. 8105/39

It is clear from "*III. Validity period*" that the markings were to be re-used. Luftparks (air parks) did receive special allocations, (the letters 'LP' being used for the first two in each four-letter sequence) for aircraft that were kept permanently on the strength of an individual Luftpark for ferry pilot and training purposes. This allocation sequence was an exception to the existing vowel plus consonant rule. Note the specific reminder that civil registrations were not to be issued to military aircraft, yet anomalies continued; aeroplanes from such second line units such as the Luftfeldpost Staffeln (mail carrying units), for example, retained 'D' series registrations. Technically they were para-military aircraft, but were kept under the civil registration system. Why this was done is not known.

Replacement of the Überführungskennzeichen system with the Stammkennzeichen system

On 24 October 1939, coincidental with the revised positioning of wing Balkenkreuz markings, a modified version of the four-letter factory code was introduced which, for security purposes, no longer identified the aircraft's manufacturer. Positioning of each pair of letters was also changed, the Balkenkreuz marking being used to separate each pair. Most significantly, the new system extended the possible combination of codes at a time when military aircraft manufacture was expanding rapidly, putting a strain on the existing four-letter system sequence.

This new Stammkennzeichen code sequence was intended not only for factory-built and repaired aircraft, but also to incorporate all *Luftwaffe* aircraft assigned to second line status. The codes were now

RIGHT: He 111s under construction at Hienkel's Oranienburg plant, probably in 1940. The aircraft are fully camouflaged and have their Stammkennzeichen applied in white in accord with the RLM regulation, which stated that such markings could be applied as dark on light or vice versa. However, the more common practice of using black lettering prevailed at most production centres. In addition to 'DJ', white applications of sequences commencing CI, CK, DL, GD, NO, PB and TE have also been recorded for He 111s, CA for He 115s and DL for He 177s. While not a common practice, Arado sometimes also used white for markings, sequences commencing DF and OU having been noted. Dornier is also known to have used white on occasions. Some impressed aircraft were also given white Stamm-kennzeichen markings, e.g., Avia F 39 TF+BO. (via D. Vincent)

LEFT: Aircraft of the transport units sometime retained their Stamm-kennzeichen as shown here on this 61/62/63/65-camouflaged Ju 52/3m, BB+RY, of KGrzbV 105, photographed at Fürstenwalde on 25 May 1940. Ju 52s were allocated a range of Stammkennzeichen sequences from the 'B' series blocks, including BB, BC, BJ and BV. (M. Jessen)

ABOVE: While registration markings on training school aircraft were changed over to the new system, they usually retained their existing overall finish in accordance with RLM instructions. This Fw 44 C, BB+XD, retained its original pre-war 01 silver finish despite the wartime setting. (I. Primmer)

ABOVE: Blocks of the new form of Stammkennzeichen were allocated to units with a holding of aircraft at the date of the changeover to the new system. The distribution of a portion of any given sequence thus ended up shared across an eclectic collection of types. Here the Ar 66 C on the left and the Junkers W 34 of the same school have markings beginning with 'DB'. The former retains its pre-war finish of 63 while the other has standard camouflage of 70/71/65. (I. Primmer)

LEFT: The debate over whether vowels were used for the first letter of the new system has been clarified to some extent by photographs appearing to show that at least some vowels were definitely used. This photograph of a line-up of brand new Bf 109 F-4s in 78/79 finish, possibly aircraft supped to III./JG 77 when it was transferred from the Eastern Front to North Africa in October 1942, gives a tantalizing glimpse of the use of 'IA' as the opening pair of the Stammkennzeichen used for at least one of these aircraft. On the edge of the right-hand side of the photograph the rear section of the first Bf 109 F clearly has the letters 'IA' marked. The aircraft immediately behind it comes from another block marked V(?)+KA. In the background are an Hs 129, a Ju 88, a Ju 52/3m and an Me 323 transport. (H. Obert)

RIGHT: This photograph of a Bf 109 F-4 trop in camouflage of 78/79, fresh from the factory, provides a rare glimpse of the use of decals for marking Stammkennzeichen on first-line aircraft when III./JG 77 received a batch of new machines after its to North Africa in October 1942. The very temporary nature of this form of marking can be seen by the scratching out that had already taken place during the delivery flight. Note also the difference in surface texture compared with the slightly gloss finish of the black enamel-based paint of the Balkenkreuz and Hakenkreuz markings. This form of temporary marking was useful where it was certain it was to be removed immediately, saving the time and material needed to paint out the old marking and then restore the camouflage pattern. For how long this innovative form of marking was utilised is unknown, but references to decals for Hakenkreuze have been noted towards the later part of the war. (H. Obert)

LEFT: This group of production Bf 109 G-6 trop aircraft at a factory airfield, illustrates the sequential allocation of Stammkennzeichen, all four being from the KG+?? batch. KG+QM and KG+QN can be identified, but there is no guarantee that either of the remaining two aircraft were from the same sub-sequence as gaps were often left in blocks for security reasons. Camouflage was 78/79 with the division between the colours along the horizontal centre line of the aircraft. Note the differing spinner colouring; 'QM' and 'QN' have what appear to be yellow tips to their spinners, with the standard one-third/two-thirds division of the rear portion of each as seen on the aircraft on the extreme right; the remaining aircraft has a white tip to its otherwise standard form of spinner marking.

ABOVE: A Do 217 displays its markings DD+LF set out in regulation style beneath the wings, out board of the engines for multiple-engine aircraft, and on the side of the fuselage.

issued with the intention of their being used, at least by second line aircraft, on a long term basis, usually staying with an aircraft for its working life. Only when such aircraft were written off was the relevant Stammkennzeichen made available for further use on a new aircraft.

Unlike the previous four-letter system, the last two letters of the combination progressed alphabetically from the last letter, e.g., ??+AA, ??+AB, ??+AC, etc., moving to the first letter of the combination as the second letter sequence reached 'Z'. The new code blocks, at least initially, were restricted to beginning with a consonant; however, as the war progressed this restriction appears to have been eased, perhaps because of the large numbers of aircraft being produced. Certainly documented evidence of blocks beginning with a vowel had appeared by 1941.

Initially there appeared to be anomalies that flouted this 'consonant' rule. Codes beginning with the letter 'A', for example, appeared to have been allocated mainly to captured ex-civil multi-engine aircraft from Italy. However, it seems that these codes were originally civil registrations that had been militarised by adding a Balkenkreuz to separate the letters. There are no photographs to authenticate these codes, all known examples being extracted from contemporary documents. It was common practice amongst Luftwaffe pilots and personnel to militarise civil registrations in this way in their personal documents. This was clearly the case with codes beginning with the letter 'E', but in the 'I', 'O' and 'U' ranges there are photographic examples of production codes, e.g., IY+YF seen on an He 114, OU+AR on an Ar 196 A-2 and UA+IK on an He 60. While these examples are all float planes, there is no special connection, as the accompanying photograph of a Bf 109 F, marked with 'IA', shows. All other instances of codes falling within the restricted ranges are clear mistakes made at the time by both German documentation and Allied intelligence sources.

The issue and control of all Stammkennzeichen codes was undertaken by a new department, entitled GL Prufstelle für Luftfahrtzeug, based at Berlin-Adlershof. This authority also held the title of Chef Luftwehr L.B.2 IIID.

Code blocks were deliberately issued in random order for security purposes - in other words they did not begin with AA+AA (which would have been disregarded under the vowel rule anyway) and work through to ZZ+ZZ as might have been expected. A good illustration of the random issue of blocks, within the manufacturing industry, is shown by the record of 100 Do 24s constructed by Dornier. ([2])

ABOVE: FW 190 F-3 W.Nr. 160022, DN+FV, reputedly photographed at Montecorvino in Italy. The Theatre of Operations band marking (white in this instance) was sometimes applied at point of manufacture where RLM advice on allocation had been advised prior to final construction phase.

ABOVE: From the same Stammkennzeichen block allocation, DN+FR should have had the W.Nr. 160018 if the sequence had been allocated without interruption, However, while the Werknummer on the fin is blurred, the last number can be identified as a '7' indicating that there had been a shift in Werknummern allocation within the alpha-sequence. (I. Primmer)

W.Nr.	Stammkennzeichen	Number Constructed
1-25	unknown	25
26-34	CH+ER - CH+EZ	9
35-44	CH+JA - CH+JJ	10
45-60	CM+JK - CM+JZ	16
61-74	VH+SA - VH+SN	14
75-100	DJ+ZA - DJ+ZZ	26
101-109	DM+RA - DM+RI	9
4155-4162	DM+RJ - DM+RQ	8
4196-4200	DM+RR - DM+RV	5
4211-4213	DM+RW - DM+RY	3

Note the jump in sequences, even within blocks commencing with the same two letters, e.g., the CH+EZ block was not followed by the sequence CH+FA, but CH+JA, a jump of five letters. The introduction of the 14-group long alpha-sequence commencing VH is a more radical shift. The last block, while running sequentially from DM+RA to DM+RY also illustrates the random allocation of Werknummern blocks within the industry, with the jump from W.Nr. 109 to W.Nr. 4155. These random shifts in both four-letter sequences, as well as Werknummern blocks shows how effective this process was as a security measure, ensuring that very little intelligence information could be gleaned about production runs for any type of aircraft.

Some extracts from early Fw 190 production illustrate the point further. Data on the pre-production Fw 190 A-0 series is not complete, but still has enough information to observe a random pattern:

0008-0020	KB+PJ - KB+PV
0021-0027	SB+IA - SB+IG

Between 0028 and 0036 a block using an SK+J? sequence was used, ending at 0036 SK+JS, then changing immediately to almost the end of another completely different sequence.

0037-0041	CF+OV - CF+OZ

With the commencement of the production series of Fw 190 A-1 aircraft, the original SB sequence was resumed, this time in a complete 26-letter alphabetical run. Note also the shift back to a three digit numerical sequence for the Werknummern.

001-026	SB+KA - SB+KZ

Special code blocks

As detailed in Chapter 9, all first line units, with the exception of fighters and ground-attack aircraft, were given a special number/letter or letter/number prefix code that would identify it with a particular unit. It has been suggested that it was also possible to identify to which second line unit an aircraft belonged by its Stammkennzeichen marking. This may have had some relevance with the first mass issue block of the new markings system, but only because the burgeoning Luftwaffe was awash with second-line unit aircraft. In the first instance units were issued with sufficient sections of code blocks to mark all existing holdings of aircraft, regardless of type, and for that reason one can see sequences that were common to a particular second line unit. But this first cohesive picture soon evaporated as replacement aircraft were issued, particularly in training units where attrition produced a constant turnover of aircraft holdings.

The issuing authority employed at least two distinct methods of assigning special combinations and sequences of code blocks. Whether these were employed at the same time or one superseded the other is unknown. Most likely, it was an internal policy change in order to integrate and simplify a very complicated system. These were then assigned to the units, which would then apply them to their existing

aircraft on strength. It appears that some Flugzeugführerschulen (Training Schools) applied these special sequence blocks to just one or two individual types.

A/B Flugzeugführerschulen & Flieger-Ausbildungs-Rgt.
FFS A/B 4 - Prag-Gbelly
Code allocation:

PF+J?	Fw 44 & He 72
PF+K?	Bu 131 & Kl 35
PF+L?	Ar 66 & Go 145
PF+M?	Ju W 34
PF+O?	Fw 58 & Zlin 212
PF+Q?	Fw 58

FAR 21 - Magdeburg-Ost
Code allocation:

CB+Q?	Praga E 241
CB+S?	Praga E 241
SE+N?	Fw 44
SE+O?	Praga E 241
SE+P?	Praga E 241

ABOVE: An interesting example of an Arado Ar 68 E in service with a fighter training unit, camouflaged in 71/02. The Stammkennzeichen marking of DA+PX is hard to see, despite the letters each being outlined thinly in white.

FAR 31 - Heiligenbeil
Code allocation
CA+A?   Go 145 & Ju W 34

Blindflugschulen
Blindflugschule 3 – Königsberg-Devau
Code allocation
NG+V?   Ju 52/3m
NG+W?   Ju 52/3m, He 111 and Do 17

Flugzeugführerschulen C
FFS (C) 4 – Sprottau
Code allocation
DB+Q?   Ju 52/3m
DB+R?   Ju 52/3m & Ju 86
DB+S   Do 23 & He 111

Flugzeugführerschulen (See)
Fl.Waffenschule (See) 1 - Parow
Code allocation
DA+H?   He 115
DA+K?   He 60
DA+L?   He 60
DA+M?   He 59 & He 115
DA+N?   He 115

In this way it is possible to identify some of the code blocks assigned to these units between late 1939 to early 1940. After these dates, however, it becomes more difficult because of, as stated, the high attrition rate and movement of aircraft within the training system.

The second method was slightly different and used only the first letter of the code before and after the Balkenkreuz. This seems to have been assigned to units that had large numbers of aircraft on strength or their handling and movement of aircraft was very high. Special cases included the following:

Erprobungsstelle der Luftwaffe
Erpr.Stelle Rechlin
Parent code   G?+A?   (Misc.types)
Erpr.Stelle Travemünde
Parent code   T?+H?   (Misc.types)

The following blocks are known to have been issued up to October 1939;

TH+HA to TH+AZ
TI+HA to TI+HZ
TJ+HA to TJ+HZ
TK+HA to TK+HU

A/B Flugzeugführerschulen and Flieger-Ausbildungs-Rgt.
FAR 31 - Heiligenbeil
Parent code   T?+N?
Code allocation:
TW+N?   Fw 44
TX+N?   Ar 66 & Go 145
TY+N?   Fw 58, He 46, He 70, Ju W 34

Luftkriegsschulen
LKS 2 - Berlin-Gatow
Parent Codes (1939/40) B?+N?,
                           C?+A?,
                           C?+B?,
                           T?+H?

Code allocation
BS+N?   Bu 131
BT+N?   Bu 131 & Fw 44
BV+N?   Fw 56
CF+A?   Fw 44
CG+A?   Fw 44
CH+A?   Bu 131
CH+B?   Ju W 34
CG+B?   Fw 44
TP+H?   Ar 66 & Bu 131
TQ+H?   Ar 66

Luftnachrichten Schulen
LNS 1 – Nordhausen
Parent Code   T?+H?
Code allocation
TS+N?   Fw 58 & Ju 86
TT+N?   Ju W 34

Fallschirmschulen
Fallschirmschule 1 - Wittstock-Dosse
Parent Code (1939)   T?+B?
Code allocation
TM+B?   Ju 86 & Fw 58
TN+B?   Ju 52/3m
TO+B?   Fw 58

Kampffliegerschulen
Gross Kampffliegerschule 1 - Tutow
Parent Code (1939)   R?+N?
Code allocation
RB+N?   Ju 86 & Fw 58
RC+N?   Fw 58
RF+N?   He 111
RG+N?   Fw 58
RI+N?   He 111

It should be noted that not all of the total available combinations were used, these being re-assigned to other units at later dates.

A further instruction was issued in June 1943, pertaining specifically to gliders:

"Marking and Authority for Glider aircraft.

1. All gliders have a registration existing of four digits which are recorded in the aircraft log book. For gliders operated by the Luftwaffe, the Balkenkreuz marking is to be used between each pair of letters and on civil gliders a dash, e.g.

Luftwaffe	*XY + AB*
Civil	*TZ - XR*

The additional sign of a letter D civil aircraft operated within Germany is void for the duration of the war when the aircraft is flown in Reich territory or German occupied territories.

2. Gliders of the Luftwaffe and of the civil authority (for the duration of the war when flying within the Reich territory and occupied areas) and of the aerodynamic stressing group (Bgr.).2 and construction regulations for gliders (BVS) are to carry the national marking of a black Hakenkreuz on the fin.

ABOVE: One of the ex-Luftwaffe Grunau Baby II B gliders taken over by Czechoslovak forces at the end of the war. The style of the Stamm-kennzeichen LN+PC is a little unusual in that the 'C' had been applied with a stencil, leaving cut-outs in the letter. Overall colouring was 05. (JaPo Publications)

3. *The new markings* [registrations] *are – same as for powered aircraft – are being distributed by the R. d. L. and Ob. d. L.. Control for Aircraft LB 2. Berlin- Adlershof; the same authorities handle the register of gliders.*

4. *The R. d. L and Ob. d. L. Control for Aircraft LB 2, issues the change of markings as well as registration procedures and necessary instructions.*

Notice
Air Traffic Regulation instructions will not change until further notice.

* *The instructions are in accord with para 4 of a special edition to Nr. 6 issue of - Airman's Notices - 1943 issue. These can be obtained through R. d. L. and Ob. d. L., Control for Aircraft/LB 2, Berlin-Adlershof, Rudower Chaussee 114/116.*

5. *These work instructions take effect from 1 July 1943.*

All other instructions are now void.

R. d. L. u. Ob. d. L. 25. 6. 1943.
Az.38p48 Nr. 1800/43 (Gen. Qu. 2.Abt. (IIA)/LB 2 II)"

Mention needs to be made of an additional exception that relates to the above change in registration style. Special code blocks appear to have been set aside, commencing with the letter 'L' for sailplanes of all classes. Allocation of these blocks commenced from 1 July 1943 when both styles of the existing three-part code system used for sailplanes was withdrawn. The following examples have been identified.

LA-AC	Horton Ho IV W.Nr. 26 (ex D-10-1452)
LA-AD	Horton Ho IV W.Nr. 25 (ex D-10-1451)
LA+FT	Grunau Baby (Luftwaffe)
LA-HH	Stumme Habicht (NSFK)
LF-JZ	Grunau Baby (NSFK)
LF-KI	Grunau Baby (NSFK)
LF+KG	Grunau Baby (Luftwaffe)
LF+VO	DFS Olympic-Miese, W.Nr. 227 (Luftwaffe)
LG-TR	Grunau Baby (NSFK)

ABOVE: The diminutive SG 38 primary glider lacked any significant structural members on which to mark the Stammkennzeichen, making it necessary to mark the registration in miniature at the base of the rudder as shown here on LM-RT. This former NSFK machine was in use by a Czechoslovak flying school in the immediate post war period, but retained its wartime camouflage of spots of 81 and 82 on the side below the tailplane, and possibly still also on the wing upper surfaces. (JaPo Publications)

LG-WZ	Akaflieg München Mü 13 A (NSFK)
LH+FT	Grunau Baby (Luftwaffe)
LK-EB	Stumme Habicht (NSFK)
LK-KC	Grunau Baby (NSFK)
LN+PC	ex-Luftwaffe
LN+SS	Grunau Baby (ex D-IX-46) (Luftwaffe)
LN+ST	Grunau Baby (ex D-IX-47) (Luftwaffe)
LZ-NC	Grunau Baby (NSFK)

It has been stated in the past by many researchers that there were two distinct types of Stammkennzeichen codes in use at the same time; in effect a two-tier system. The one applied to newly built production aircraft and the other issued to aircraft in the field. Because of the many instances of aircraft with the same code, it is easy to assume this to be the case. However, the authors' research over many years, during which they have amassed a very substantial number of codes, has shown that an altogether different picture emerges. This is that a simple single-tier system existed similar to that employed by the operational units. When an aircraft was destroyed or re-assigned then the code or block would be re-used at a later date.

To illustrate this, a few examples are listed below in which the first three allocations in the BC+W?-range were issued to different aircraft.

BC+WC	Gladiator 9/5 457 10Erg.(S) 1, crashed 15 April 1942, 45 per cent damaged.
BC+WD to BC+WZ	Bf 110 F-2 4554 to Bf 110 F-2 4576 built by Luther Werke.

The Gladiator was either an ex-Latvian or Lithuanian aircraft captured in July 1941. These aircraft were shipped back to Germany for repairs and through the Chef AW organisation were assigned as towing aircraft for DFS 230 gliders with the Erganzungsgruppe (S) 1 at Langendiebach in early 1942. Therefore the code was issued on that date. The production of the Bf 110 F-2 was re-commenced in February 1942; the dates then match up with the allocation of the rest of BC+W? block to the Bf 110 F-2 production batch (W.Nr. 4554 to 4576) built by Luther Werke.

As with the previous example, this next one also illustrates the allocation of codes to individual types with the rest of the sequence being assigned to the production program.

THIS PAGE: Chaos in the system. These three photographs illustrate the complete confusion that obscures the origin of the markings found on some aircraft at the end of the war. Fw 190 TS+MA, W.Nr. 5753, carries what appears to be a normal Stammkennzeichen. On its own, it might have been a marking received prior to the 1 July 1944 directive, forbidding further use of such markings. However, the use of TS+MB on a Bf 109 is cause for puzzlement as the odds on two aircraft with sequential allocations surviving from before 1 July 1944, are extremely unlikely. The point is made more dramatically by the photograph of a Bf 110, marked with the same registration, TS+MB. As noted in the text, there were even more bizarre examples. Interestingly, all these anomalies so far found involve 'TS' allocations. (J. Crow)

DE+IM	Ar 66, 1247, FFS A/B 117, crashed 18 September 1940, Kamenz	
DE+IN to DE+IW	Bf 110 D-0, 3411 to Bf 110 D-0 3413 built by Messerschmitt, Augsburg	

The Bf 110 D-0 series appeared from early 1940. As the Ar 66, Werke Nr.1247, crashed on 18 September 1940 at Kamenz it is highly likely that it received its code earlier in the year.

When codes were allocated to production aircraft, whole blocks from 'A' to 'Z' were often assigned and sometimes would run consecutively to include three or more ranges. The Ar 96 B-1, for example, used three blocks at the end of the DC range:

W.Nr. 1071 to 1096	DC+WA to DC+WZ
W.Nr. 1097 to 1122	DC+XA to DC+XZ
W.Nr. 1123 to 1148	DC+YA to DC+YZ

Other examples were the Fw 190 A-8s built by Focke-Wulf at Bremen:

W.Nr. 170120 to 170140	GU+PA to GU+PU
W.Nr. 170301 to 170305	GU+PV to GU+PZ
W.Nr. 170306 to 170331	GU+QA to GU+QZ
W.Nr. 170332 to 170357	GU+RA to GU+RZ
W.Nr. 170358 to 170383	GU+SA to GU+SZ

Note that once again there is a sudden jump in the Werknummern block, but no corresponding gap in the Stammkennzeichen sequence, making it difficult for Allied Intelligence sources to track production numbers of aircraft types.

Although this may have been a general rule, there were exceptions. For example, the first three Ju 252 Versuchs (prototype) aircraft were assigned civil registrations under a test programme to meet Deutsche Lufthansa requirements but, by 1942, the needs of the Luftwaffe's Transportverbände (Transport Units) had grown to far outweigh those of the civil section. Consequently, it was planned to produce a military prototype, plus ten production aircraft for the Luftwaffe. These 11 aircraft were then allocated a batch of Stammkennzeichen that completed a code series already allotted to a series of Fw 190 A-2s being built by the Fieseler company at Kassel. Thus:

DF+BA to DF+BO	Fw 190 A-2, 7006 to 7020 built by Fieseler at Kassel
DF+BP	Ju 252 V4 production prototype
DF+BQ to DF+BZ	Ju 252 A-1 Ten production aircraft (also known as Ju 252 A-1, the Ju 252 V5 to V14).

Once issued, the code would stay with the aircraft even if it were transferred to other units, as long as it kept its second-line status. If assigned to an operational unit, the aircraft would be re-coded accordingly. Occasionally, aircraft would operate with both codes. This was more a case of operational pressures of not over-painting underwing codes than that of military policy. Stammkennzeichen were used as radio call signs when a military aircraft entered civilian airspace, as per the instructions set out in the RLM document above. A.I.2.(g) intelligence reports on captured aircraft in Europe list examples of Stammkennzeichen markings taken from the individual aircraft data card or marked on the internal structure, usually at the radio operators position where such personnel formed part of the crew. The aircraft data card stayed with an aircraft throughout its life and was unique to that aircraft, containing such items as air speed corrections, established during the factory acceptance check flights, and compass deviation markings. The following examples illustrate this.

LeO 451	G6+BX	DL+ZI
Ju 188 A-2	3E+KS	DM+NM
Ju 88 G	4R+QP	SW+DH
He 111 H-20	S3+LL	BU+AG
Bf 110 G-4/R-7	G9+BZ	RR+LF
Bf 110 G-4/R-6	G9+LS	EN+YO
Bf 110 G-4/R-6	G9+ES	CQ+GW
Bf 109 G	14+ -	TT+ED

Once the large numbers of second-line aircraft had received their codes (between 1939 and 1940), the bulk of the system was employed to identify aircraft coming off the production line. This system then remained in use until the end of the war despite the changing situation and setbacks on the war fronts. An order issued in Sammelmitteilung of 1 July 1944 stipulated that marking of Stammkennzeichen on aircraft airframes was henceforth forbidden for security reasons. Their replacement was to be a prominent application of the aircraft Werknummer, without additions, in 25 cm high digits on both vertical tail surfaces. For larger aircraft, such as Ju 88s, this was feasible, but for Bf 109s and Fw 190s, the size was relatively large and no examples have been found with this size of Werknummer marking. Most appear to have a vertical size range of about 12 to 16 cm.

The only other compromise to this instruction occurred on some late production Bf 109 Ks, marked on the rear section of the fuselage with the last three digits of the Werknummer, but in much larger size. This temporary identification was retained during transfer to front line units. However, this was simply an extension of the existing practice that had been in force at the Messerschmitt production centres since the late 1930s. Usually, a coat of camouflage lacquer eventually obliterated the marking. While it served the purpose *de facto*, it was not what was stipulated in the order mentioned above. The one consistency arising from the order was the disappearance of the Stammkennzeichen markings after about August 1944.

Having said that, the appearance at the end of the war of some aircraft, all of which wear what appears to be a Stammkennzeichen marking – in some instances duplicate markings - has created a mystery that appears to counter what has been stated above. Photographs show the same four-letter code, TS+MA, applied to several aircraft, Bf 109s and Fw 190s, at different locations and in the same time period; in a second instance a single sequence, TS+MB, is repeated on each individual Bf 109 G in a line-up of five; in another instance a Fw 190 A and a Bf 110 were each marked TS+MB, totally destroying any relevance in terms of identifying individual aircraft under the Stammkennzeichen system. The reader is warned that no explanation for these glaring anomalies, if they are such, has been found amongst contemporary German documentation. Indeed, it is difficult to think of any rational explanation, particularly as such markings were forbidden from July 1944 onwards, and most, if not all these aircraft had been produced after that date, and at different manufacturing centres judging by the different types listed.

---

1 Norbert Schuchbauer article, Luftwaffe Verband, page 27, Issue Number 30, April 2002

2 D. Vincent research.

Civil, Commercial and Military Transports

Transport aircraft were a vital component of the Luftwaffe; the first, and most lasting occupant of this role being the Ju 52, which had begun its working life as a commercial airliner for Deutsche Lufthansa (DLH), the German state airline, as well as in service with several overseas airlines. It served alongside the elegant He 111, which also had first appeared in civil guise, though its real role was barely disguised. The sleek He 70 also had started its service life with the airline, joined later by the Ju 160. All four types were finished in DLH's light grey company colour with black trim added around the engine areas and bore names of German cities or prominent Germans, as well as animals, plus their civil registration, in black. Other types carried the names of winds, storms and seas, celestial bodies, wild animals of the European countryside, and German mountains. The Fw 200 joined the ranks of Lufthansa in 1938, but in very small numbers, wearing the same style of finish as for the rest of the fleet. An alternative 'bare metal' finish of a translucent coat of 7120 zinc chromate, with silver on fabric surfaces, but retaining the usual black trim, appeared on some aircraft, such as the Ju 160, Ju 86 and Ju 90.

Paints used by the DLH for its fleet of aircraft were extensive and were supplied by the principal German paint manufacturing companies. A painting schedule for DLH aircraft, titled *Zusammenstellung* (Consolidated situation), issued 1 November 1936,[1] listed all types operated by the airline and provided a detailed description of all paints used both on airframe and engines. The colours employed were those peculiar to DLH, probably matched directly to the huge RAL range, but with a few RLM colours in special instances. The latter may have been brought about by the fact that DLH aircraft were considered as an emergency resource for the Luftwaffe during the tense political times of the mid-1930s, when Germany's ambitions were expected to have raised more opposition.

A precis of extracts from the painting schedules for DLH will better illustrate the range of lacquers:

> *Junkers Ju 52 – External finish DKH Ölgrund, hellgrau (Dr. Kurt Herberts & Co oil base coat light grey) and finished with Ölüberzugslack DLH-grau (oil coating lacquer). The Ju 52 Rb used the same lacquer sequence tinted Rb-grau (Rb grey). Ikarol Aluminiumlackfarbe streichfertig (Warnecke und Böhm Ikarol aluminium lacquer, brush finished) was also used as a base coat.*

> *Dornier 10, Dornier to Wal and Dornier Do 18 flying boats - External finish above water Cellesta Überzugslack DLH-grau (Cellesta coating lacquer DLH grey). Below water Ikarol - Decklack silber (Ikarol base coat silver) followed by Ikarol Überzugslack silber (Ikarol coating lacquer silver). Upper surface of the wings Cellesta Überzugslack hellgelb (Cellesta coating lacquer light yellow). Final sealing finish was Cellesta Überzugslack farblos (Cellesta coating lacquer clear).*

Use of light yellow on the wing upper surfaces was a safety feature for over-water operations, the company colour scheme of light grey making it difficult to spot an aircraft forced down on the surface of the sea. Use

of this colour is not always easy to determine from contemporary black and white photographs because under certain lighting conditions tonal response of the light grey and yellow appear very similar. In an extract from an article in the April/May 1937 issue of *Die Dornier=Post* [2] titled, *"With the Dornier-flying boat Do 18 'Zephyr' over the North Atlantic"*, Flugkapitän Joachim Blandenburg records his description of the Do 18s colour scheme during a flight in September 1936:

> *"With its decoration, grey fuselage and yellow wing surface colouring, under the fluttering flag of the Hakenkreuz, the Lufthansa house flag and the national standard of Portugal..."*

Yellow, however, had been in use on the Do 18 before this date though; Do 18 'AEOLUS', sister aircraft to 'ZEPHYR', had flown non-stop for twenty and a half hours between 27-28 May 1936. Photographs of the aircraft clearly show the yellow, which covered the entire upper surface of both wings other than for the black painted walk area either side of the centrally mounted engines.

The same colours later were used on the Do 26 and Ha 139 aircraft operated by the company. On the Ha 139, yellow was applied to the V3 D-ASTA and also to the V1 D-AMIE later in its career. Possibly the same retrospective addition also was made to the V2 D-AJEY. The yellow panel-marking was applied only to the outboard section of each wing, from the main joint line outwards, and did not include the ailerons. The exact shade of yellow is not specified but from its description of 'pale yellow' it more closely matches the shade of yellow that appeared on DIN L 5 regulations for safety markings. In which case it possibly was RAL 1012 (zitronengelb).

ABOVE: This view of D-AJEY,' NORDWIND' being prepared by ground staff shows the addition of the yellow panels to the upper surface of each wing outboard of the inboard engines. This was done for safety reasons as an aircraft was more easily seen if it was forced to land at sea en route; a practice also used by pre-war Luftwaffe maritime aircraft. The wing and float walkways were painted in black, with the rubber-block tips of the latter painted red. Colours used were from the RAL standard. (Lufthansa)

Heinkel He 70 – External finish - DKH Nitro-emaille lack grau (DKH nitro-enamel lacquer grey).

Heinkel He 111 – External finish metal parts DKH Nitro-emaille lack, duralgrau (Nitro-enamel finish dural grey). Fabric surfaces Cellesta Überzugslack DLH grey (Cellesta coating lacquer DLH grey).

(As photographs show, this finish allowed the panels of the metal skinning to be seen through the finish under certain light conditions. The fact that there is no visible difference between the colour of the fabric-covered ailerons and the main structure indicates that the dural grey finish was to DLH colour standards.)

New lacquers being introduced for the Ju 52 (with exceptions for specific materials) included Ikarol Zwischenlack I grau (Ikarol intermediate coat lacquer I grey). An experimental lacquer Ikarol-Einschichtdeckfarbe DLH-grau (Ikarol single coat base colour DLH grey) was tried on the exterior of the Ju 160 and later the Ju 52. Another was Ikarol Decklack RLM-grau (Ikarol surface coat RLM grey); this had an additional note stating that it was a special lacquer for government (military) aircraft (this was RLM 02).

Engine cowlings were painted with DKH Nitro-emaille lacquer schwarz (DKH nitro-enamel lacquer black), which was a heatproof finish. Engines, such as the Junkers Jumo, had the motor body and cylinders in DKH Nitro-emaille lack silber (DKH nitro-enamel lacquer silver). On in-line engines, body and cylinders were finished in Einbrennlack schwarz halbmatt (single coat fireproof lacquer semi-matt black).

Ikarol-Einschichtdeckfarbe DLH-grau (Ikarol single coat base colour DLH grey) was used internally for the cabin area in the Ju 160, Ju 86, Ju 52 and He 111. Onboard toilets were finished in Lackfarbe weiss Schliefemaille (Lacquer colour white polished enamel). Instrument panels were finished with Wermalin-Spritzlack grau matt (Wermalin sprayed lacquer matt grey). Polished grey or black finish, in the same lacquer, were used for the instrument surrounds.

Additional finishes used both for engine areas and other sections were Elastodurlack schwarz glänzend (polished black elasticised lacquer) used on the forward section of the engine cowling, parts of the undercarriage framework (e.g., Ju 52), and for lettering. The same finish, in halbmatt (semi-matt), was applied only as an anti-dazzle panel to the Townend ring and NACA cowling fitted to each of the Ju 160s. The inside of the cowling ring was painted Lackfarbe grau (lacquer colour grey). Undercarriage sections were in Lackfarbe blau (lacquer colour blue – possibly RAL 5009) as was the Lackfarbe gelb (lacquer colour yellow, possibly RAL 1012) used for the lettering on undercarriages.

The Hoheitszeichen (state flag emblem) was applied in DKH-Öllackfarbe rot (DKH oil lacquer colour red). Markings were applied with Kennzeichnungsfarbe (marking colours) chromgrün (chrome green), chromgelb (chrome yellow), braun (brown) blau (blue) and rot (red).

The Zeppelin of First World War fame had also made the transition into the civil aeronautical field, though in a more refined form, offering passenger comfort on a scale not possible with conventional aircraft of the period. That ascendancy was to be abruptly ended with the *Hindenburg* disaster and the remaining Zeppelin eventually found its way into military service on radar calibration trials. The metal frames of these giant machines were painted with DKH Kobaltblau Lasurlack (cobalt blue transparent lacquer), the fabric covering being sealed with a lacquer, named Worwag, from Atlas Ago. The latter was released under the trade name Cellon and was colourless. For the Zeppelins it was tinted with Eisenoxyd (iron oxide giving a reddish-brown colour) and Aluminiumpulver (aluminium powder). The iron oxide tinted coat was applied first and was listed as Lichtstrahlen-Schutzstoff (ultraviolet protection coat), followed by the final silver-coloured coating.

Twenty Ju 52s had been sent to Spain within a week of the opening of hostilities in the Civil War, their initial task being to air-lift troops from Morocco to Seville, interspersed with bombing operations. The capacious interior of this aircraft was to serve many roles throughout the following years, moving supplies, troops and heavy equipment. These aircraft had been left in 63-colouring overall finish, but later deliveries wore the more practical full camouflage of 61/62/63/65. A small number of Ju W 34hi aircraft were used as light transport and initially they retained their 63-overall colouring with some later given a rudimentary camouflage of 61-coloured 'ribbons' over a base coat of 62 on upper and side surface, with 65 for lower surfaces. This form of improvised camouflage followed a standard also established for some other types in use by the Legion Condor.

Success of the Ju 52 in the airlift subsequently lead to the type being used for the newly formed paratroop force, which had formed in the autumn of 1937. The Ju 52 was being phased out of its alternative bomber role at the time, and IV./KG 152 was transferred to troop transport duties. The aircraft retained their 61/62/63/65 camouflage scheme, but subsequently this was replaced by the 70/71/65 camouflage colours which, with rare exception, the Ju 52 was to retain until 1945. It remained the single most important transport type throughout the subsequent years.

The Ju 52's intended successors, the Ju 90, and its ultimate development the Ju 290, Ju 252 and Ju 353, were never produced in large numbers. Other than for the few machines serving on sea reconnaissance duties, which employed 72/73/65 or simply 75/76, most retained a standard 70/71/65 colour scheme. A singular oddity, was a Ju 290 serving with KG 200, a special duties unit, which possibly accounts for its radical camouflage change. Upper surfaces had been repainted 75, restricted to a plan view, with a heavy mottle of 74 on the sides, and under surfaces in permanent black. Another attempt to find a suitable replacement for the Ju 52 resulted in the Ar 232; however, only but despite promising performance, the type never entered series production. The Ar 232 V-1, VD+YA, first appeared in plain RLM 02 overall but after it, and the V-2 (VD+YB) were handed over to the Luftwaffe to fly supply sorties into Stalingrad they received standard 70/71/65 camouflage, upper surface colouring being taken right down to the lowest line of the side elevation. The same camouflage colouring was used for the remaining aircraft produced and put into operational service, though one, or possibly more of the four Ar 232 B-0 and the Ar 232 V 2 aircraft used by the Ergänzungs-Transport Gruppe, used black for side and under surfaces.

The DFS 230 troop-carrying glider had entered service in 1938, the production version exchanging the 02-colouring for standard 70/71/65 camouflage. Upper surface colouring ended on a line extending fore and aft from the wing root. As with the Go 244 type, on many machines the 65-coloured side surfaces were heavily mottled with one or both of the upper surface greens in a soft-sprayed application Even when based in Italy, and transferred in small numbers to North Africa, European camouflage was usually retained, although one exception has been photographically recorded wearing 79-base colouring with patches of 80. It was probably not the only one, though total numbers of the type were relatively small.

The Go 242 transport glider, which entered service in 1942, also employed a 70/71/65 scheme, usually with the 65-coloured deep side areas broken with a soft mottle of one of the greens. First operational use of the type occurred in North Africa and some effort had been made to give some of the aircraft a form of desert camouflage. Like the Hs 129 camouflage conversions mentioned in Chapter 13, this was achieved by a fairly crude application of 79 over the existing 70/71 scheme on the wings and upper side surfaces. In some instances camouflage netting had been laid over the 70/71-coloured surfaces to act as a simple stencil to break up the 79-sprayed colouring.

However it was on the Eastern Front that the most innovative schemes appeared on the Go 242. Precise identification of the two contrasting

RIGHT: The first three-engine version of the Ju 52 was the modified seventh airframe, W.Nr.4007, fitted with a trio of uncowled Pratt and Whitney Hornet radial engines. It first flew in April 1931. In 1932 DLH received its first two Ju 52s, W.Nr. 4013, D-2201,'BOELCKE' and W.Nr. 4015, D-2202, 'RICHTHOFEN'. The latter is seen here in standard DLH livery. (Lufthansa)

LEFT: First revealed to the public at Berlin-Tempelhof at a press gathering on 10 January, 1936, the ten-seat He 111 C-0, 'KÖNIGSBERG', D-ABYE seen here outside the DLH office was delivered in the autumn of 1936. Like all DLH aircraft, it was christened with the name of either a famous German personality, city, celestial body, wind, mountain or animal. This aircraft was in standard finish with W.Nr. 1831, marked under the Reich- und Nationalflagge and the DLH emblem marked near the tip of the fin. (Lufthansa)

BELOW: Tempelhof was a busy hub by 1939. There are 22 aircraft in view, most DLH machines. In the foreground is D-AREV, 'BROCKEN', the Ju 86 V4, W.Nr. 4904, in treated bare metal finish with DLH markings. In more usual company trim are the Ju 86s immediately behind the Douglas DC 2, SP-ASK, D-AHAL, 'OTTO BERNERT', D-ADEK, 'ANTON SCHULZ', the Fuhrer's personal aircraft D-2600, D-AVAU, D-ALAV with OL-LAM in the far distance. Starting at the nearest aircraft in the row to the right are D-AKIY, 'WILLIAM LANGANKE', D-AMYY, 'WILHELM SESERT', D-AHIH 'RUDOLF KLEINE', D-ABOQ. On the far right D-AMIT O. 'VON BEAULIEU-MARCONNAY' stands in front of D-AUJG, 'HANS WENDE' which has its fuselage registration marked in smaller letters set further aft. Note the slight variation in the width of the black wing trim extending aft from the engines. Like D-AREV, Ju 52s D-AUEK and D-ALAV lacked the usual black trim.

LEFT: The Ju 90 V3, serving under false colours as a transport during the Axis inspired Syrian revolt. The rudder colours, from front to rear, are green, white, red and black. Overall colouring appears to be 02 but the black engine trim of the aircraft's former employer, DLH, had been retained. (H. Obert)

BELOW: A most unusual subject, this Do 17 Z was used for transport of Stab personnel in Italy in 1942. The overall camouflage was 78/79. The white painted rim to the engine cowling, and spinner were possibly a mixture of tactical and Gruppe markings, since it was unusual to see the Italian or North African tactical white marking applied to engines on multi-engine aircraft. The white spinners probably identified I. Gruppe rather than a Staffel.

BELOW: The ubiquitous Ju 52 was at home on water as well as land. This example, 1Z+MN of LTSt(See) 1, formerly 5./KGr.z.b.V 1, was operating from the Aegean when photographed. Its 70/71/65 camouflage had been overpainted with temporary white other than for the rudder, possibly a replacement part. All the cabin windows had been painted over other than for one at each end of the row. An 04-yellow tactical band marking was painted around the rear section of the fuselage, the colour undoubtedly being repeated beneath each wing tip. From the Aegean these aircraft were able to operate into the southern Russian sectors and Balkans. (M. Jessen)

LEFT: Wearing very weathered temporary winter white over its standard 70/71/65 finish, this Ju 52, G6+EZ of 15./KGr.z.b.V 105, was operating over Russia, the harshness of the landscape and weather making flying difficult for these workhorse aircraft. The temporary white finish was left off in an oblong around the unit markings, only the yellow 'E' being easily seen. The standard array of yellow tactical markings was painted beneath wing tips and around the rear section of the fuselage. The unit badge - a winged canister in white with the Staffel number between the wings - can be seen on the nose of the aircraft. The narrow horizontal banner beneath the marking carried the words 'Narvik-Kreta', commemorating the unit's participation in those two major airborne assaults. (M. Jessen)

ABOVE: This DFS 230, LH+1.8, captured intact in North Africa, had mottling in 70 and 71 very sparingly applied to the side surfaces. The pale patch behind the Balkenkreuz on the fuselage is the original 65 colouring, indicating that the rest of the lower surface areas of the fuselage have been lightly sprayed with a colour to reduce the paleness of the 65-colouring, possibly a very thin application of 02. Note overpainting of the unit badge on the nose below the cockpit. (When based at Comiso in Italy, this was a long oval-shaped badge with a cartoon of an elephant pulling a glider past a palm tree). This has been done with 02, which blends with the background colouring to the mottle. In this instance a Balkenkreuz was marked below the wings, but only in reduced size, as on the fuselage.

ABOVE: DFS 230 gliders were sometimes utilised as unit hacks to transport personnel and equipment. This one, coded S7+?K, indicates that it was used by 2./St.G.3. Camouflage was 70/71 with mottling in both colours on the 65-coloured lower side surfaces. (F. Smith)

upper surface colours remains contentious, but the darker of the two, applied as broad stripe-like patches, was possibly 71 (or 80?). The lighter base colouring of the sides and upper surfaces was too dark for 02 and possibly might have been a colour similar to that employed by some of JG 54's fighters, 79 sand brown. On others, the combination appears more consistent with a base colouring of 02 applied as patches surrounded by 70-coloured 'seams'.

The Me 321, designed as a medium-range transport glider, appears to have maintained a consistent 70/71/65 camouflage scheme throughout its service life, only application of temporary white during winter providing any variation. However, unlike its contemporaries the upper surface greens had been taken right down the sides of the fuselage; possibly the sheer size and slow speed of this aircraft had made it more practical to disguise it against the natural ground colouring, rather than the sky. The powered conversion of this large troop and equipment-carrying glider, the Me 323, had produced no change from the standard camouflage.

The ubiquitous He 111 had also been converted for transport duties, a few of the older machines retaining their 61/62/63/65 scheme into the opening stages of the war, but most retained the standard colour scheme of 70/71/65. An interesting example was exhibited at Farnborough in 1945, an He 111 H-20, W.Nr. 701152, with top turret removed and finished overall in matt black. The origins of this aircraft are not known, but it had been captured by American forces. Its relatively unarmed state may account for the night finish.

VIP transport aircraft belonging to the Regierungsstaffel, mostly Fw 200 Cs, initially had been left in their existing colours of 72/73/65 or 70/71/65 depending on the source of their original units. Late in the war, the upper surface camouflage of the aircraft used by Reichsführer-SS Himmler (and later Grand-Admiral Dönitz) had been repainted. The original splinter pattern was retained for colour division and from the description of the colours used (dark green and dark grey), and photographs of the aircraft, that combination appears to be the darker of the original greens (either 70 or 72) with 75. The former would appear to be the most logical candidate. The aircraft of this Staffel also had retained their original Stammkennzeichen, and each was marked with a numeral on the upper section of the rudder; GC+AE W.Nr. 176 had a white '5', GC+SJ W.Nr. 0181 a white '8', D-ASVX W.Nr. 0111, an ex-DLH machine, a white '1'. The undersides of the engine cowlings of GC+AE were yellow, thus partly according with the required markings changes introduced in September 1944.

1 M. Ullmann research

2 Ibid

LEFT: The Go 242 was used extensively on the Eastern Front. This machine, marked LB+2.1, had the first two characters reduced in size as per the revised RLM instruction of mid-1943. The fuselage Balkenkreuz (of reduced size) was usually marked on the extreme rear of the fuselage on this type as seen here. Camouflage was standard 70/71/65 with mottling in the two greens. The 04-coloured band applied around the rear of the fuselage usually was also accompanied by 04-colouring painted below the wing tips. (D. Vincent)

RIGHT: Awaiting conversion to Go 244 configuration at Stendal in mid-1942 these two Go 242 A gliders had standard camouflage with the addition of 04-colouring painted below each wing tip and as a band around the rear fuselage. The cockpit covering on SN+BE has Go 242 RD+TV painted in white on its 70-coloured surface and belongs to the machine, RD+TV, on the left. The cover over the rear of the fuselage however belongs to the machine, being marked Go 242 SN+BE. This form of marking was a common practice for all categories of Luftwaffe aircraft. (H. Jonas via D. Vincent)

LEFT: Airborne the Go 244 B-1 was an impressive, if ungainly sight. This example, RH+GL had standard 71/71/65 camouflage with mottling in both colours over the pale side surfaces, a thin spray of 02 having been used to subdue the 65-colouring on the side areas. The small size of the Balkenkreuz markings can be seen. The wing tip lower surfaces, inboard to the outermost letter was painted in 04-colouring, a band of the same colour appearing around the rear of the fuselage.

RIGHT: A very special transport, Fw 200 C-4/U1, CE+IB, W.Nr. 0137, which was the Führer's personal aircraft. It is seen here finished in temporary winter white over its 70/71 upper surfaces and marked with a yellow tactical band. Built in 1942, it was probably being used somewhere on the eastern borders of the German occupied territories (P. Jarrett)

LEFT: This VIP Fw 200 transport, its 70/71/65 paintwork immaculate, was the personal transport of Grossadmiral Dönitz and bears the Kriegsmarine Abzeichen, with the word ALBATROS III underneath, painted in gold colouring. The black eagle's head in a white wreath has the letters FDF at the bottom and a Hakenkreuz marking at the apex. (D. Vincent)

Training, Liaison and Light Aircraft

lying in Germany had seen a small resurgence in 1922 when gliding was established as a legitimate sport, the early machines being left in the colouring of their natural components of plywood and fabric and simply clear varnished. In 1933 the first nationally organised flying association came into being with the formation of the Deutsche Luftsportverband (DLV) - (German Sports Flying Association). As described in Chapter 17, in 1935 it was decided to divide administrative control of all civil flying into a series of Luftsport-Landesgruppen. Gliders within those regional areas were to be identified, in addition to the civil 'D-registration' markings, by a combination of two colours specific to each region. These were to be displayed on the fuselage, addition of colours to the wings remaining an option. Prominent use of regional identification colours however seems to have been relatively short lived; most examples appear to have been confined to the 1935 to 1936 time frame. However, the colour allocations remained in force when the Nationalsozialistisches Fliegerkorps (NSFK) came into being on 22 October 1937, absorbing the DLV glider system in the process. From then on, all gliders were to be painted a uniform light colour, described as a cream beige, possibly RAL 1001, though given by then the general State control of all flying, this may well have been the RLM finish of 05 elphenbein, that colour only ever being used for unpowered aircraft. While the NSFK was not military organization, boys from 12 years of age upwards joined to learn about flying; its purpose was to produce a ready pool of Luftwaffe pilots.

The gliders used were painted to a consistent standard as proscibed by the official standard that had been promulgated. Titled Farbentafel für den Anstrich von Segelflugzeugen – (Colour chart for the painting of gliders), it contained six colours; elfenbein FAS 1 (ivory), hellblau FAS 2 (light blue), braun FAS 3 (brown), maigrün FAS 4 (pale green), gelb FAS 5 (yellow), hellgrau FAS 6 (light grey). (The FAS prefix was formed from abbreviation of the main words in the chart's title description.)

Those colours were used not for the general overall finish, but as part of the sequence of regional identification colours. However, no RAL equivalents were cited for them, even in the 1944 edition of Taschenbuch für Lackierbetreibe, reference being made only to the original document cited earlier. This appears unusual since, the latter, large book, cited RAL standards for every part of the Reichs industry, civil infrastructure and armed forces. It is well to reiterate here that the Luftwaffe had its own exclusive system of colour identification codes, mostly independent of the RAL standard. However, all other branches of the armed services and civil service organisations used the RAL standard exclusively, but the NSFK, a 'civil' organization, did not have its colours marked with their RAL equivalent. (The only other group so treated in the document was the Reichs Arbeits Dienst – German Workers Service; it had a list of ten colour descriptions without further cross reference to the RAL system.) From this it would appear that the NSFK's predecessor, the DLV, had used RAL colours.

As noted earlier, colour descriptions in use in the Luftwaffe prior to 1937 matched both the RAL and RLM colour identification system, the two diverging when RLM 65 hellblau had been introduced in 1936 (though technically the actual departure point was RLM 66, that being the last colour to match both systems). Retention of the full colour listing for the FAS, even though redundant, was not out of place with

other lists in the 1944 Taschenbuch für Lackierbetreibe document, e.g., RLM 61, 62 and 63 and their RAL equivalents were still recorded.

Established in 1925, the RAL system still functions today in its role as the German Federal Standard for colour identification, and its current extensive colour swatch Farbenfächer RAL-K5, Farbenregister RAL 840-HR contains a wide selection of colours, including several used by the Luftwaffe in the 1930s. As noted, it is probable, indeed logical, that colours prescribed for the DLV had been drawn from the RAL standard since that was the German national standard. The NSFK ivory colour FAS 1 elfenbein (the same name is used also for another RAL colour, which matches RLM 05, but that is a different shade of ivory) remains on the current colour swatch as RAL 1014. Similarly FAS 4 maigrün has also been retained and bears the designation RAL 6017. Christopher Wills published a more complete coverage of the range of colours, matched to American Fs 595a and British BS 381C colour standards, in the British Vintage Glider Club Newsletter (UK).[1] It recorded the following colour values.

    FAS 1 – 27855/No BS 381C equivalent (now identified as RAL 1014)
    FAS 2 – 25102/109 middle blue, two shades lighter
    FAS 3 – 20117/489 leaf brown
    FAS 4 – No Fs 595a equivalent/218 grass green, lighter and more
            yellow. (now identified as RAL 6017)
    FAS 5 – 23538/356 golden yellow
    FAS 6 – 26134/No BS 381C equivalent

These colours were matched to samples of the original colours used on sailplanes during the period under discussion. Other than for the RAL numbers identified above, the list provides the closest known equivalents. (see colour card Tafel 3, Volume One)

In addition to the NSFK, the Luftwaffe had its own sailplanes (by definition, high performance aircraft) and gliders, the aircraft of each organization distinguished by the style of registration carried. Colouring for these sailplanes followed the same style of a simple overall cream-coloured finish, adopted when the NSFK took over from the DLV. This was RLM 05, a colour, by reason of its number allocation, which was one of the original colours developed and adopted by the RLM around 1933. However, it did not appear on the 1936 Farbtontafel (see Volume One, Colour Charts), that colour atlas lacking also several colours that had been developed but not put into production, the sequence running 00, 01, 02, 04, 11 etc. In the case of 05 its omission had nothing to do with being rejected for production, but rather its contemporary use for non-military aircraft. To all outward appearances, gliding was still a civilian occupation, and as such beyond the military parameters of the 1936 Farbtontafel.

The creation of the NSFK, in 1937, and introduction into the Luftwaffe of glider flying as part of the initial phase of pilot training, eventually witnessed both operators using the common colouring of RLM 05. Despite the fact of its origins within the Luftwaffe range of colouring specifications, and its two-digit code, RLM 05 was never to appear on any of the three subsequent colour atlases of 1938, 1939 and 1941 for the reason explained above; an anomaly that has caused some confusion.

When war broke out, Luftwaffe sailplanes were subject to regulations issued by the RLM in terms of colouring, but no change occurred until 1944 when orders were issued to camouflage some classes of sailplanes.

Prior to that instruction it was rare to see such aircraft in a full military camouflage scheme. One such example was a Kranisch, photographed at Hornberg in 1941, which carried a full 71/02/65 scheme and military markings. The rear cockpit had been gutted to provide space to carry fuel or ammunition. Reputedly several Kranisch sailplanes were so modified in order to fly in supplies to the beleaguered troops on the Russian Front, but questions of weather and operational conditions makes the suggestion, and its fulfilment, open to conjecture.

Primary flying training in the Luftwaffe commenced with two classes of glider types: basic gliders (principally the Edmund Schneider-designed Grunau Baby); and high performance sailplanes (such as the two-seat DFS Kranisch, and the single-seat DFS Habicht) for more advanced training. Sailplanes were usually finished in clear-doped fabric with varnished wooden components, but exposure to sunlight (ultraviolet) gradually deepened the colour of the clear-doped fabric to a warmer shade of cream, while gliders generally were finished in 05.

ABOVE: Application of the sunrays marking was standardised for wing and horizontal tail surfaces as shown by this trio of Habicht gliders. (P. Selinger)

LEFT: The DFS Habicht provided advanced glider training. This example carries sunrays markings, in blue, of the type used by Gerhard Fiesler for his brilliant pre-war aerobatic displays. The marking allowed the viewer to determine the attitude of the aircraft during flight, a facility carried over to these primary trainers where it functioned as a safety feature in the air. (Peter Selinger)

RIGHT: Photographed on a bright winter's day, the rich blue of the sunrays markings stand out against the 05-base colouring of this Habicht being used for advanced training. The 'WL' code dates the photograph to the 1939/40 period, when the registrations for second-line military aircraft were revised. In the background is a Kranich 2 A, WL-XII-80, with another to its right marked '255' (possibly 'WL-XII-255'). Note the Kranich at the back had no sunrays on its wings, that marking being reserved for the higher performance single-seat Habicht. From the little that can be seen of the unit crest on the Habicht in the foreground, it appears to be similar in shape to that of FFS A/B 6. (Steve Coates)

In May 1943, a revised edition of L.Dv.521/2 (Behandlung-und Anwendungsvorschrift für Flugzeuglacke Teil 2: Segelflugzeuge) – (Handling and application instructions for aircraft lacquers. Book 2: Gliders.) was issued. It stated, in part, that sailplanes were to remain in clear lacquered finish, but without exception gliders were to be finished in 05-colouring.

Internal wooden parts were to be lacquered using 7171.99, replacing 7171.27 only after stocks of the latter were exhausted. Samples of wood from gliders of this period show the usual yellowish-green finish. Internal metal parts (Eloxieren or Dural) were to be undercoated with 7102.99. Cockpit areas on high performance gliders were to be lacquered in 7171.99, followed by 7172.99 and then a final single coat of 7174.02.

External finish for primary sailplanes was a priming coat of 7171.00 over all wood, with 7173.00 applied undiluted, by brush, to fabric parts. This was followed by a thinned, sprayed application of 7175.00. A note reminded the user that it was to be applied thinly, weight being more critical than on powered aircraft. For high performance gliders 7171.00 was first applied externally, with 7251.99 sealer-paste used to ensure a smooth finish at joints. The aircraft was then sanded back before a finish of 7172.99 was applied, followed by 7174.05. External metal fittings were in 7174.05, or if in the cockpit area, 7174.02. Hoheitszeichen and Kennzeichnen were to be applied with standard 7164-coloured 21, 22 and 23.

Repairs to fabric and lacquer on both classes of aircraft were to be given an intermediate coat of 7210.99 and allowed to stand for a few minutes, to soften the old paint edges, followed by the final colour coat. For metal repairs, minor damage was re-lacquered with 7102.99, while 7210.99 was used for major repair areas.

The decreasing air security over Germany in 1944 was reflected in Paragraph 6 of the Sammelmitteilung issued on 1 July 1944:

6.) *Camouflage for Sailplanes (not transport gliders).*

For the duration of the war, sailplanes and gliders are to receive camouflage paint, effective immediately. Following the last painting step according to L.Dv.521/2, all parts visible from above and the sides are to be lacquered with lacquer type 7174.81 and .82 until rescinded.

The camouflage colours on upper surfaces and fuselage sides are to be applied in similar manner to the mottle scheme for powered aircraft. Where drawings for mottle schemes have not already been distributed, these may be requested from the NSFK supply centre at Worms or Rhein airfield.

After section II D of L.Dv.521/1 on page 13, the following new paragraph is to be added.
[An instruction was then given to '*Cut out and paste in!*']

E. *Camouflage-painting*

Until further notice, all sailplanes and gliders are to be camouflaged.

After the coats of paint applied according to A., B., and C. have thoroughly dried (about 16 hrs. after the last coat), camouflaging will be accomplished with Flieglack 7174.81 and 7174.82, respectively, in accordance with the mottle scheme.

The paint will be applied only as thickly as is absolutely necessary for the camouflage effect.

The paints as delivered are ready for use. In cases of need, especially for spraying, they may be thinned with Lacquer Thinner 7211.00
Drying time: dry to touch in 1-2 hrs. Hardened through: overnight.

Until the issuance of these instructions, the overspraying of operational sailplanes has been, or is being carried out as an immediate measure. During this transitional period the overspraying of the aircraft with available Flieglack 7135 in shades 70 and 71 was authorized, as it is not possible to produce and deliver the above paint in the new shades at short notice.

It is brought to your attention that the overspray with the paints mentioned may result in the centre of gravity as well as weight changes.

The delivery of colour sample cards for the RLM shades 81 and 82 is for the present not possible. Thus testing of the lacquer for correct colour shade is omitted.

ABOVE: This Grunau Baby II B finish has the random application which complied with the final 1944 RLM order calling for gliders to be mottled in 81 and 82 on upper and side surfaces. Operated by the French in the immediate post-war period, it retained its late war camouflage scheme of 81 applied directly over the original regulation 05 base colouring. The finish was not in accordance with the directive for this class of aircraft, only a single camouflage colour having been applied. The Hakenkreuz has also been retained but is almost lost under the heavy strokes of 81. As with most primary gliders, no Balkenkreuz was added to the fuselage.

ABOVE AND ABOVE RIGHT:
Two photographs of one of many Grunau Baby IIs that passed into service with the Czechoslovak gliding schools in the immediate post-war period. This machine shows well the effectiveness of the heavy mottled camouflage of 81 and 82 that all but obliterated the original 05-finish. The close-up photograph illustrates how the 82 had been sprayed as a misting finish with heavier, soft-edged mottling with 81. Only the Hakenkreuz emblem had been deleted and a white '31' added. There is no evidence of a Stammkennzeichen marking having been applied to this airframe. The unidentified badge below the cockpit may have been original, but this is unconfirmed. (JaPo Publications)

ABOVE: The style of application could vary, as shown on this NSFK Grunau Baby marked with the registration D-13-650. The 81–coloured segments had been added as large 'spots' of colour over a base coat of 82, on the fin and tail plane surfaces. The 82-colouring however finished at a line approximately level with the horizontal tail surfaces. The fuselage was left uncamouflaged. The glider behind had what was possibly just the 81-colouring added over its base coat of 05-colouring. Note what looks like a thin line of cartoon-style teeth along the 81-coloured nose section. Such wide variation was the result of individual gliding units being left to organise the camouflage pattern for their gliders.

LEFT: This Kranisch II was used post-war by the Czechoslovak gliding fraternity. Apart from the addition of its new registration, OK-8012 marked in black, it retained its late war finish of 81/82 over the base colouring of 05 – plus some repair marks. (JaPo Publications)

ABOVE: Heavily camouflaged Stummel Habichts used by the Italian pilots sent to Germany in January 1945 for training to fly the Me 163 B. Nearest is LK-EB with an unidentified one slightly forward of it, and LA-HH to the left. The original 05-overall colouring had been camouflaged in accordance with Paragraph 6 of the Sammelmitteilung of 1 July 1944. All parts visible from above had been sprayed with 7174.81 and 7174.82. The middle aircraft had a much darker camouflage application, with 81 predominating. Note that only the Hakenkreuz marking was applied, in solid black, across both fin and rudder on the rear two aircraft. On the original photograph it could be seen that the middle aircraft had a Balkenkreuz marking of approximately half the size of those seen on the rear two aircraft.
(F. D'Amico and G. Valentini).

ABOVE: The official painting instruction called for gliders to be sprayed in a mottle scheme similar to powered aircraft. This close-up shows the mottle was formed by using first an overall 82-inish on upper and side surfaces with 81 applied in soft-edged strokes to break up the 82 into lozenges of a paler colour. (F. D'Amico and G. Valentini).

RIGHT: On this Habicht, the contrast of the 81 is more pronounced, indicating that the underpainting of 82 had been applied very thinly, leaving areas where the original 05-colouring showed through. The wing uppersurface camouflage of 81/82 ended at the front spar line, leaving only a thin application of 82 over the forward section. Note the dark anti-dazzle area of what appears to be 81-colouring in front of the cockpit.
(F. D'Amico and G. Valentini)

There are some significant implications to the instruction; as the least regarded of the second line aircraft, in effect, priority for supplying colour matching cards was very low. Relatively, it was inconsequential whether or not the colour was precisely matched. This is however the only known reference where both colour matching and difficulty in supplying colour cards is mentioned. These statements have been interpreted as representative of the entire process of introduction of the 81 and 82; but the relatively low status of gliders within a production system struggling to maintain first-line strength was more likely to have been the reason. This is supported by the accompanying comment about supplies of the lacquers; the new colours 81 and 82 were prioritised for front line aircraft production.

No written colour description was given for 81 and 82, though they may have been shown on the drawings referred to above, emphasising that the RLM numerical designation was considered sufficient identification. Implementation was erratic, reflecting the nature of the employment of these second-line aircraft and the rate of supply of the new paints. At some locations gliders remained in their old 05-colouring until war's end, while others received camouflage in one or both of the prescribed colours, (or in the old colours of 70 and 71, though no photographs so far located appear to show those two closely matching colours; so that stratagem may have been restricted to the initial period after the order was issued).

The style of application varied, some using large patches of 81 over a base coat of 82, or simply 81 sprayed in mottles and streaks over the existing pale finish, while others used a more subtle form of mottling with 81 and 82. Unlike front line aircraft, where soft mottling was used, in many cases it covered all the upper and side surfaces, no attempt being made to produce a two tone, segmented pattern as seen on other classes of aircraft. The reasons for the wide variation may have been predicated by the available facilities as much as the identity of the operator of the aircraft – NSFK or Luftwaffe. The NSFK used civilian facilities, based on relatively small airfields, while Luftwaffe-operated machines had the advantage of pre-war military base facilities, The eclectic and erratic applications bear out the contention that the work had had to be done at operational bases rather than by transfer to a Luftwaffe maintenance depot, something that would have been impractical given the non-powered type of aircraft in question. The use of a mobile work party from a Luftwaffe Maintenance Depot is also a reasonable possibility in the case of Luftwaffe-operated gliders and sailplanes.

Gliders were used as part of the conversion training programme for the Me 163 at Rangsdorf airfield near Berlin, the final stages being flown on the Habicht 14, 8 and 6 (the numbers indicated the wingspan in metres). The Habicht gliders were camouflaged with 82 used as the base colour, on the upper surfaces and sides, broken up with lines of 81. On some, the camouflage on the wings had been taken only to the line of the main spar; forward of that the original 05-colouring remained.

Flugzeugführerschulen (FFS A-Schule), training schools also provided basic powered flying instruction, using a range of aircraft, including the Ar 65, Ar 66, Ar 68, Ar 76, Go 145, He 72, Kl 25, Kl 35, Fw 44 and Bü 131. Initially, most were finished 63-overall, with a few random examples in silver, but by 1938 silver had begun to predominate, and aircraft produced after that time were delivered in 01-silver colouring. Because of the potential glare factor from the finish, anti-dazzle panels were introduced for the top decking of the fuselage. Usually they were added in the form of either black or dark blue, and extended from engine to fin in stylised form as a trim. Silver was a good choice of colour because of its reflective qualities, which helped make the aircraft more readily visible to other aircraft, something vital in the crowded air space of flying schools. In contrast, older 63-finish was counter-productive in terms of ready visibility. The weather proofing qualities of the silver (powdered aluminium) finish, especially on fabric surfaces, was also an advantage.

Aircraft of the FFS B-Schulen provided advanced flying on such types as the Ar 65, Bü 133 and Fw 56. (Often both types of school were combined into an FFS A/B-Schule.)

Seen initially in 63, aircraft colouring had changed to 01 in late 1938, However, as with the basic flying training school aircraft, older machines usually had been left in their original colour scheme until needing refurbishing, thus both the silver as well as 63-coloured aircraft were still in evidence well into the war period. At some locations, where possibility of attack from enemy aircraft was deemed to exist, the 1938 crisis had precipitated some rudimentary schemes, maintenance staff applying a form of camouflage to some machines, often simply by overpainting parts with one of the contemporary camouflage greens.

Fully camouflaged aircraft entered the system when obsolete front line aircraft were used for the final stage of advanced training. Official instructions stated that such aircraft were to retain their existing camouflage at time of delivery for training duties. At FFS C-Schulen, where final stages of multi-engine training occurred, Do 17s, Ju 86s and Ju 52s were present wearing either 61/62/63/65 or 70/71/65 colouring.

continued on page 392

ABOVE: An Albatross Al 101 basic trainer, of Fliegerschule Kitzingen, D-IMIV, in silver overall finish with the revised form of civil registration (introduced in 1934) applied in black. The school number 'K139' is marked on the fuselage side just below the cabane struts. The 'K' possibly identified the school and the number the aircraft on a flight (Staffel) basis. This aircraft had originally been registered to the DVS G.m.b.H in February 1934. (O. Hintze via J. Vasco)

ABOVE: An Ar 66 C in what was possibly overall 02-finish rather than 63 given its probable date of construction, the fin and rudder marking dating it as prior to June 1936. The school number 'K154' is marked in the usual place seen on aircraft at Kitzingen. (O. Hintze via J. Vasco)

LEFT: The Fw 44 C was a versatile trainer. This example, RB+DL, was still in its silver 01 finish but with correct Balkenkreuz and Hakenkreuz markings. However, the aircraft behind, almost obscured from view, shows just enough to see that it retained its Hakenkreuz in the pre-January 1939 position. (S. Wunder via F. Grabowski)

RIGHT: Registered D-ILAR, this is the Fw 56 V3, which first flew in 1934. It is seen here serving as an advanced trainer for fighter pilots. Finish is silver overall with red trim around the engine cowling including spinner) and forward fuselage. (O. Hintze via J. Vasco)

LEFT: Advanced fighter training was also carried out on the obsolescent Ar 65 E. These two, D-IPUU in the foreground and D-IPUO in the rear, retain the greenish-grey overall finish that was in force before the Nationalist Socialist take-over in 1933. (O. Hintze via J. Vasco)

LEFT: The Fw 56 was highly manoeuvrable and had excellent aerobatic qualities despite the seeming fragility of the parasol wing design. This example, SE+PF (or E) was finished overall on either 02 or 63, the types production spanning the changeover between these two very similar shades of grey-green. (S. Wunder via F. Grabowski)

RIGHT: Advanced training for reconnaissance crews was undertaken on the He 45 C. This machine, D-IKEL, was in the greenish-grey colouring in which the type entered service in 1934. Wheel centres were lacquered in what may have been a Staffel colour. (O. Hintze via J.Vasco)

LEFT: This He 45 C, D-IXXH, exhibits a typical flat finish. Note the pale grey colouring to the propeller blades with the Heinkel emblem in black and the dark, natural colour, clear lacquered centre section. The wheel centre appears to be in blue rather than red. The starboard side of the fin and rudder carried the tricolour of stripes, dating the photograph prior to June 1936. (O. Hintze via J. Vasco)

RIGHT: Also used for advanced reconnaissance training was the He 46 C. It entered service at a time when the RLM colour coding system was beginning to replace the individual paint company designations. Photographed at Kitzingen D-IKAO wears 02 overall and the school number of what appears to be 'K100'. (O. Hintze via J. Vasco)

LEFT: Fw 58 A-1 CR+KQ in 70/71/65 camouflage adopted for advanced fighter training. Positioning of the Hakenkreuz across the fin and rudder indicates that this aircraft was repainted in camouflage during the emergency period of late 1938. The aircraft's school number '823' was applied in yellow on the engine cowling. (I. Primmer)

RIGHT: This Fw 58 A-1 BA+HY, also finished in 70/71/65 camouflage, had the yellow fuselage band and wing tip lower surface markings denoting its role as an advanced flying training aircraft. Adoption of these yellow markings appears to have coincided with the deletion of the aircraft school numbering system. (I. Primmer)

LEFT AND BELOW: Views of two lines of Bü 181 advanced trainers left at Bøtø airfield in Denmark at the end of the war. In the top view the nearer aircraft is marked with two broad 04-yellow bands to signify its use as a blind flying training aircraft. It had 70/71/65 camouflage and a Stammkennzeichen of what appears to be SB(or P)+WF. Possibly what is a unit badge can be seen just forward of the wing leading edge. The other Bü 181s had their entire upper and lower surface camouflage oversprayed with a dark colour that appears to be a very thin coat of black, subduing the Balkenkreuz markings at the same time. Whether this was related to night flying training or something entirely different is unknown. The first Bü 181 in the second row appears to have been left in 02-overall and to have had its two broad bands of 04-colouring painted out with a very dark colour, possibly dark green or black. Only the middle two letters of its Stamm-kennzeichen can be seen, ?C+G?. The entire engine cowling had been painted in 04-colouring, with the colour being taken right back to the windshield on the upper section. Each aircraft had had its propeller and rudder removed. (Royal Danish Air Force)

ABOVE: Twin-engine blind flying training was done on the Si 204, this example being one form the same advanced training school based at Bøtø in Denmark. Camouflage was 70/71/65 with the aircraft's status as a instrument trainer identified by the two broad 04-yellow coloured bands around the fuselage. Even with the fuselage in deep shade, the two yellow bands stand out clearly. (Royal Danish Air Force via M. Jessen)

ABOVE: Compare the placement of the two broad bands of 04-yellow on this Si 204 with that shown in the photograph above. The two aircraft were serving at different schools, indicating that addition of the dual band marking was left to local interpretation.

OPPOSITE PAGE CENTRE: This collection of aircraft illustrates well the process of pre-war advanced stage fighter-pilot training. On the extreme right are a group of Fw 56s in plain 63-finish; the right hand line of the central group in the photograph contains three He 51s and six Ar 65 Es. The left column has ten Fw 56s and on the extreme left are six Ar 76s. The variety of markings and colour schemes also reflects the practice of using obsolete and obsolescent aircraft for the advanced training role. Some of the Ar 76s on the left, plus three of the He 51s on the right, wear camouflage of 70/71/65, types that would have been in front line use until recent times. The photograph was taken in 1939 when political tensions were running high and even obsolescent fighter aircraft might be needed in a crisis. Most of the Fw 44s had a red band marked around the rear of the fuselage, while the three He 51s had had a white band added; these were school 'Staffel' colour markings. The individual aircraft numbers were marked in a contrasting colour, white on the red, and black on the white. Note that the He 51s also had their 'Staffel' colour marked on the wing centre section; and also the variety of civil markings still visible beneath the school markings. The row of Fw 56s to the left have a mixture of the old civil D-series registrations and the interim military WL series introduced in 1939; the first two are marked D-IFQO and D-IFOO while the third is WL-IALO. All the aircraft in the row have a registration ending in the letter 'O', something of an oddity in itself. (Via D. Vincent)

RIGHT: A Do 17 E of a training school based in Prag-Ruzyne, BA+BF, retained its original 61/62/63/65 camouflage with the 04-markings applied around the front section of each engine, and has a yellow band around the rear of the fuselage immediately forward of the tail plane. Both rudders were also painted yellow. No evidence can be seen of yellow beneath the wing tip.

RIGHT: Do 23, S17+D66; the type entered service late in 1935, on the cusp of the changeover from 02-overall finish to one of 63 to which the newly introduced five-character black codes were added in June 1936. (O. Hintze via J. Vasco)

RIGHT: This example of an Ar 76 A, CA+FV, was serving with FFS A/B 5 when photographed, the unit's distinctive 'seahorse' emblem being marked just forward of the cockpit. A good design that lost out in competition with the Fw 56, it was still produced in very small numbers and delivered to the Luftwaffe training system in early 1936. That date points to the pale finish being 63 rather than 02. The turtle deck colour appears to be blue 24. The Balkenkreuz proportions show that this photograph was taken after January 1939. (J. Crow)

LEFT AND BELOW: Two views of He 51 B, PS+CQ, which had been camouflaged in 70/71/65. Incorrect proportions of the Hakenkreuz applied to the fin indicates that this aircraft was repainted in late 1938 when emergency measures were introduced and obsolete fighter aircraft were camouflaged for front line use. The aircraft's school number, '838' in yellow, was painted on both sides of the engine cowling above the exhaust stacks. (I. Primmer)

BELOW: Advanced training for bomber crews was done using standard front line aircraft, such as this Ju 88 of a training school in Denmark. Camouflage was standard for the type, 70/71/65, with the addition of 04-yellow beneath the engine cowlings and the marking of its school number, (White 70 in this instance) on the rudder. Camouflage netting had been draped over the rear section of the fuselage and around parts of the engines. The letter 'D' could be seen beneath the starboard wing.
(Royal Danish Air Force)

These captured Go 145 and an Ar 96 training aircraft exhibit the final range of camouflage for these types. Go 145 TD+BN in the middle, facing left, has 83 applied as a soft interlocking mottle over the 02-overall finish, the double 04-coloured band marking identifying it as a blind flying instruction aircraft. RP+NN in the far background has similar 04 markings, but the camouflage had been applied as a solid coat in what appears to be 83. A yellow '8' is marked on the rudder and the 'R' and the 'N' both have a thin yellow outline. The Go 145 in the foreground has a very rough application of 82/83 over the upper surfaces of the wings and the fuselage. The application appears to have been made very thinly and poorly applied as the upper surface of the top wing has much of its paint stripped away, indicating that the camouflage process had been applied at unit level without the benefit of proper facilities. No Balkenkreuz markings are visible on the latter surface. A short yellow bar is visible on the leading edge of each lower wing and possibly extended across the lower surface. The Ar 96 appears to be in standard 70/71/65 finish.

RIGHT: The Ar 96 B provided advanced pilot training. This example, from 3./JG 102 at Rodslet airfield (Aalborg West) in 1944, had standard 70/71/65-camouflage with 04-yellow markings beneath the wing tips and engine cowling lower section. The red band around the engine cowling was probably a Staffel marking within the school. The front section of the engine cowling had been replaced with a panel still painted in 02, as is the spinner and propeller hub; possibly the consequence of a nose over accident The school number on the side of the fuselage appears to be '331', marked in red, outlined thinly in white. (Royal Danish Air Force)

LEFT: Repainting obsolescent aircraft in current camouflage, while not mentioned in the 1941 edition of Der Flugzeugmahler, eventually was carried out when an aircraft was given a major overhaul. This Bf 109 D had its original 71/72/65 (or possibly 71/02/65) camouflage replaced with 74/75/76, dating the photograph to after spring 1941. The colour shift in the wartime photograph printing process has biased the red component of the original print. (M. Payne)

LEFT: This Fw 190 A, 'Blue 4' served with Jagdfliegerschule 4. Camouflage was standard for the type and period – 74/75/76. Note the hard division between upper and lower surface colouring along the fuselage side area. The spinner tip was also marked in blue 24. In the background a line of Ar 96 trainers can just be seen.

RIGHT: Advanced training conversion for single-seat fighter aircraft was eventually resolved by conversion of some machines to two-seat configuration. However, the numbers involved were relatively small, the war effort not allowing time or materials for a major production programme and all were conversions of existing single-seat airframes. This Fw 190 S-8, W.Nr. 388047, was a conversion of an A-8 series airframe and wore contemporary fighter camouflage of 74/75/76. Note the sharp division between upper and lower surface colouring and lack of mottling.

LEFT: The Bf 109 was also converted to two-seat configuration, in much larger numbers, using Bf 109 G airframes with some 500 being ordered. The main reason for this adaptation seems to have been the decline in the number of hours available for fighter training, requiring a more rapid transfer onto single-engine aircraft. Designated Bf 109 G-12, the type first entered service in early 1944. This machine was photographed at Augsburg at war's end. Its camouflage is enigmatic, but judging by the tonal difference between the 70-coloured propeller blades and the camouflage on the nose section, the colours were probably 74/75/76 with the sides heavily mottled in both colours plus probably 02. The quality of the 76 on the lower surfaces also points to this, it being a richer shade of colour than that seen on new production aircraft in 1944. A narrow yellow band - marking its training status - can be seen around the rear section of the fuselage. (J. Weidman via M. Olmsted)

RIGHT: Used for final operational conversion training, these Bf 109 G-6 aircraft had standard 74/75/76 camouflage with the addition of identifying numbers for the aircraft within the school, in this case in 04.

LEFT: The remains of a Bf 109 G used for advanced fighter training. Marked with its school number of '479' in black, thinly outlined in white, the general camouflage appears to be 81/82 with greenish-blue lower colouring, the brown being more easily detected on the port wing pattern behind the Balkenkreuz marking. The greenish tinge to the side surface colouring may have been from addition of 02, though there is no clear evidence of that colour having been added. The underside of the engine cowling was painted 04-yellow.

BELOW: Advanced single-seat training for the Me 262 was done using production aircraft that were not passed as fit for the stresses of air fighting, their special category being signified by the letter 'S' marked on the airframe, as seen here in white on both the fuselage and fin of W.Nr. 110956. 'White 17' was operated by III./EJG 2, which retained the marking style of a narrow yellow band in 04-colouring of its predecessor, Kommando Nowotny. The fabric sealing strip, used to cover the joint between the fuselage and empennage, had been replaced, the upper portion being painted over with a dark colour, probably undiluted 74-colouring, while the lower section had been painted with full strength 76-colouring. The overall camouflage was 74/75/76 with mottling in both upper surface colours on the side surfaces. The front section of the port engine (and probably also that of the starboard engine) was bare metal, the need for constant engine changes making it rather pointless to keep repainting that section, which housed the integral starter fuel tank for the engine.

ABOVE: Conversion training needs for jet aircraft produced the Me 262 B-1a. This captured example, W.Nr. 110639 'White 35', was finished in 81/82 with either green-blue or 76-coloured side and lower surfaces. The engine intakes, which housed the starter fuel tanks, are bare metal, replacement engines having been fitted as the aircraft was about to be ferried to the coast.

Eventually however, all passed through the major overhaul process, at which time their external paint finish was refurbished, contemporary colours replacing the older, obsolete colours stock of which which were no longer held by maintenance depots.

At Jagdgeschwaderschulen, (fighter training schools), the He 51 provided the final stage of training before pilots moved to contemporary fighter types. Following the international political crisis in late 1938 they had been camouflaged with 70/71/65, their rôle denoted by painting the wing upper surface centre section 21-white and adding a one metre wide 21-white band to the rear fuselage, ending immediately in line with the leading edge of the fin. The advanced two-seat fighter trainer, the Ar 96, also had filled that role. Pre-war they had been in overall 02, but following the outbreak of war many were camouflaged with 70/71/65. Obsolete fighter types, which provided final conversion training, retained their existing camouflage scheme at time of transfer; however, in due course the natural major overhaul and refurbishment cycle saw many wearing contemporary fighter camouflage. When the Bf 109 G-12 and Fw 190 A-8/U1 two-seat conversions entered service, colours were the contemporary 74/75/76, and those were retained by the trainer versions.

Advanced flying at schools training bomber crews also used obsolete types along with the ubiquitous Ju 52. Once more, the existing camouflage on aircraft at the time they were transferred to second line duties was retained, and initially this produced some examples of the pre-war 61/62/63/65 scheme amongst the 70/71/65-finished aircraft.

Not so consistent were the markings worn by some of these advanced training aircraft. It was normal for such aircraft to retain their Stammkennzeichen, usually in combination with a numerical sequence, the latter varying in colour to distinguish the Staffel within the training school. However, by late in the war that system had become a law unto itself at some establishments, with colour (Staffel) identification being expressed in some very unique forms as the following list illustrates. All these aircraft, found at Metz-Frescaty airfield in France, just south-west of the German border, belonged to Schuleschlachtgeschwader SG 103. They were recorded in Crashed Enemy Aircraft Report No. 266 , dated 21 February 1945.

Ju 87 D-3

CE+VF,	C+VF, blue,	E yellow (W.Nr. 31031)
CE+MD,	CE+M, black,	D red (W.Nr. 413721)
NG+HX,	NG+H, black,	G yellow
GO+AK,	GO+K, black,	A yellow
SH+BB,	H+BB, black,	S yellow (W.Nr 1188)

Ju 88

ST+PM,	ST+P, black,	M black outlined red (W.Nr. 3673)

Bf 110

DP+R.,	DP, black,	R black outlined yellow (W.Nr. 730070)

Me 210

IE+RC,	IE+C, blue,	R red outlined white (W.Nr. 848)
IE+UO,	IE+O, blue,	U red outlined black (W.Nr. 8165)

Ar 96 B

RL+KP,	RL+P, black,	K black outlined yellow (W.Nr. 425660)

Fw 190

F-5/R-1,	14 BV+LV	BV+LV, black,	14 white (W.Nr. ???653)
G-2,	21 NH+ZG	NH+ZG, black,	21 white (W.Nr. 01413)
F-3,	1 PM+II	PM+II, black,	1 yellow
F-8/R-1,	2 BU+LN	BU+LN, black,	2 yellow (W.Nr. 580646)
F-8,	15 DU+FK	DU+FK, black,	15 yellow (W.Nr. ???115)
F-8/R-1,	21 PL+DM	PL+DM, black,	21 yellow
F-8,	20 J + I	J+I, black,	20 yellow
F-8/R-1,	1 BV+LY	BV+LY, black,	1 red (W.Nr. 580657)
	4 CL+WI	CL+WI, black,	4 red
F,	PM+IF 4	PM+IF, black,	4 red (W.Nr. 670034)
G-2,	BH+CE 11	BH+CE, black,	11 red (W.Nr. 0815)
F-3/R-1,	GT+DI 17	GT+DI, black ,	17 red (W.Nr. 671129)
F-3,	23 BN+ZT	BN+ZD, black,	23 red W.Nr. 670641)
G-3,	VL+I 24	VL+I, black,	24 red (W.Nr. 160485)
F-8,	27 ST+IR	ST+IR, black,	27 red
F,	7 DO+SM	DO+SM, black,	7 white outlined red (W.Nr. ???411)
F-8,	16 D	D, white,	16 white outlined red (W.Nr. 931379)
A-4,	SK+OU 3	SK+OU, black,	3 yellow outlined red (W.Nr. 0799)
F-3/R-4,	21 BM+ZD	BM+Z, black,	21 yellow outlined red (W.Nr. 670455)
G-3,	25 SP+FF	SP+FF, black,	25 yellow outlined red (W.Nr. 160606)
	NA+YS	NA+S black,	Y, black outlined yellow (W.Nr. 5704)
	6 TO+GS	TO+GS, black,	6 violet

The variety of colours used was standard other than for the violet mentioned at the end of the list (possibly a blue or red which had been badly mixed or use of RLM 28). The Ju 87s, despite using the school number system earlier in the war, appear to have abandoned the practice by this time. Only the Fw 190s retained that system of identification at this school.

It will be noted also that in some instances, amongst the Fw 190s, the aircraft number within the training school was listed as positioned after the Stammkennzeichen. Of more interest is the manner in which the Stammkennzeichen markings had been used as a form of identification with a single letter painted in the training Staffel colour. Why the choice of a letter from various positions within the four is unclear; it may have been chosen on the basis of allocating an individual letter to each aircraft in the absence of the more usual additional numerical sequence. The choice of blue for the markings on the two Ju 87 D-3s and the two Me 210s may relate to Stab status with the addition of red and yellow identifying the Staffel under its control. The presence of the Bf 110 was probably for blind flying training, while the Ar 96 B would have served for advanced conversion training.

Whatever the actual nature of the various markings and choice of colouring, it gives a very good insight into the colourful variety of external markings carried by some training aircraft.

Liaison and light aircraft

Liaison aircraft were drawn from a mixture of aircraft types – Ar 69, Go 145, Kl 25, Bü 181, Bf 108, Fi 156, Ju W34, Fw 58, Si 104, plus some captured aircraft, generally of French origin, but to which some Italian aircraft were later added. The term liaison was a broad definition, covering transfer of individual personnel, mail, signals information, through to straight unit 'hack' machines. Colour schemes were as varied as the range of types. Pre-war, some had retained their original 02-overall finish, but many mimicked the schemes of the day, depending upon where they were stationed and by whom they were operated. While 70/71/65 was seen on many of the larger and more modern machines, aircraft operated by Jagdgeschwadern tended to be repainted in the contemporary fighter scheme, producing aircraft such as a Kl 25 in 74/75/76. The perennial Fi 156 sported a wide variety of schemes including 70/71/65, 78/79/80 and, very late in the war, 81/82/76. The Bf 108 also saw service on every operational front and wore every form of camouflage, from standard to hybrid, some fighter units having their's repainted to their own specification.

ABOVE: The elegant Siebel Fh 104 prototype, D-IQPG seen here, made its first flight in 1937 and with the second prototype the design proved very successful, winning the Italian Littorio Rally and excelling in the Europa-Rundflug of September 1938. The overall finish was a pale grey, with a lightning flash cheat line in black on the nose section. (Mello via S. Santos)

However, this general class of light aircraft had been seen widely during the 1920s and 1930s when the immediate post-First World War boom in flying swept across Europe. The restrictions of the Versailles Treaty had had its own effect in channelling aircraft manufacture in Germany toward light aircraft design work, and many companies owed their continuance to this new, expanding market. In Germany, where every effort was made to popularise flying, a wide range of light aircraft had emerged, not only from the old established manufacturers, but also via many small design and manufacturing teams. Designers, such as Willy Messerschmitt, became established in the aircraft design field through this period.

A quick listing of the types that were manufactured, and the names behind them, will illustrate just how extensive had been this success story. Messerschmitt, initially working for the Bayerische Flugzeugwerke, produced a number of designs, amongst them the M 23, M 27, M 29, M 31, M 35 and the M 37, later designated as the Bf 108 by the RLM (Messerschmitt having gained control of the bankrupt Bayersriche Flugzeugwerke in 1931). Arado produced the L I and L II series; Erla the M 5; Fieseler the Fi F 5, Fi 97 and the Fi 99; Klemm the L 20 and L 25 series, the L 26, L 31, L32, L33 and L 35 B; Junkers the A 50 and U 23 E, Gotha the Go 149; Heinkel the He 64, He 71 and He 72; Siebel the Si 202 series. Smaller companies and individuals are remembered for aircraft such as the Darmstadt D 18, Gerner G II R c, Schwalbe FR 2 and Mark R III b. In time, some of these aircraft, such as the He 72 and Bf 108, went on to serve the new Luftwaffe. The design types ranged from quite simple single-seat aircraft, with quite small engine capacity, through to two- and four-seat cabin monoplanes, while

changes of engine type and capacity extended the range even further. Initially, German aircraft constructors were often forced to resort to using imported (mainly British) engines, but that situation was slowly reversed as mainstream aircraft engine development and production once more resumed in Germany.

The immediate post war years witnessed a boom in light aircraft across most European countries and England, leading to the establishment of annual flying events designed, not simply for entertainment, but also to test developments in airframe and engine design. As a result, European flying seasons for team and individual racing with this class of aircraft supplied an annual focus for the flying fraternity, many of the aircraft produced and sold for leisure flying having found their way into the racing circuit via the multiple category entry system. Two of the major light aircraft races each year, within Europe, were the International Touring Competition (Challenge International), – known in Germany as the Europa-Rundflug – and the Deutschlandflug. The former was hosted each year by a different country, and was limited to aircraft less than 560 kg empty weight and was usually flown over a distance of between 7,000 km and 9,000 km. The Deutschlandflug, (which had started in the late 1920s as the Deutschen Rundfluge) was a national annual competition organised by the Aero Club of Germany, restricted to German pilots and aircraft, and flown around the borders of Germany. It too gradually developed in character as the years progressed, eventually drawing a wider and wider variety of competitors, including teams from the RLM and later individual Luftwaffe units after the new Luftwaffe came into being. The service pilots involved included some who were to become household names in the years that followed, either in the front line, or in the higher echelons of command. Both competitions used distinctive racing markings.

The International Touring Competition mounted each year by a host country, was another event with its roots in the 1920s. It usually drew a large field of competitors, from many countries, for instance, the 1930 event saw 97 aircraft entered, Initially, to identify competitors, it employed a logo in the form of a large black outline circle, divided horizontally by two parallel lines, one of which was placed at a point one quarter of the way up from the bottom, the other a similar position down from the top of the circle. In the top small section appeared, in black, the words identifying the title of that year's race, (e.g., Europa Rundflug, International Rundflug, Challenge International) placed one above the other; in the lower segment the year of the race was marked, also in black. Between the two segments was the racing number, which consisted of a combination of a letter and a number in black. For example in the 1930 race, three Junkers A 50s marked A8, A9 and E2,

ABOVE: The initial M 23 sports aircraft design by Willi Messerschmitt appeared in 1929 and proved to be extremely popular, about 70 being built in the ensuing years. It appeared in several variants, the M 23b version being seen here at Tempelhof airport during the 1936 Olympic celebrations in Berlin. Both aircraft were painted in gloss red and white but the areas of colour varied between the two aircraft. The colours matched the RAL-system, possibly RAL 3000 rot (or RAL 3001 Feuerrot) and RAL 9002 reinweiß. The machine to the right was registered D-ISI(?).

ABOVE: The Bf 108, in its military disguise, was also popular one with some of Germany's Allies. Resplendent in the tactical yellow markings of the mid-war period, this exported model was operated by the Bulgarian Air Force.

were all entered by the Junkers-Flugzeugwerk A.G.A Klemm L 26 v and an L 25 e, (respectively marked A2 and A3) were entered by the Leichtenflugzeugbau Klemm G.m.b.H., with another Klemm L 25, (marked B6) entered by the Düsseldorfer Aeroclub and two other Klemm 25s (B7 and B8) from the Luftdienst G.m.b.H in Berlin; each letter identified an individual team with the number identifying the entrant. Amongst the pilots of the 47 German entries that year were Rudolf Hess, later deputy Reichs Führer; Fritz Morzik, later General der Transportflieger, and Theo Osterkamp, a former First World War flier and later a Luftwaffe fighter commander.

For the earliest events, the natural colour of the aircraft's individual paint scheme was retained for the background to the circle and its markings, but by the time of the 1930 race, the marking was usually shown against a white circular background. Modification continued in the following years and the logo and date marking disappeared, allowing for a slight increase in the size of the letter/number combination. The black edge-colour to the circle was also changed to red, in a shade that appears to match the red banner section of the national tail marking (RAL 3001). In addition, the increasing number of entrants also led to addition of a single letter, to identify the individual aircraft/pilot, placed in a white square, with the same outline colour as the main racing number.

The Deutschlandflug was the premier air-racing event within Germany, and followed a circuitous route around the border cities and towns in the country. It was divided into two sections, a series of technical tests plus a handicap race around a two-day circuit within Germany; two weight categories of light aircraft were allowed, 460 kg and 322 kg empty weight. Thirty aircraft were entered for the 1931 competition (one from Junkers, two from Arado, the ultra-light BFW M 27, the only one in this class, while the rest were Klemm L-26s) and the technical tests were carried out at Berlin-Staaken airfield between 11 and 13 August. These tested dismounting and refitting (wing folding),

engine starting and time, take-off and landing run distances, lowest airspeed, fuel consumption, equipment and comfort. The actual race then started on 15 August, from the same airfield, ending the next day at Berlin-Tempelhof airfield after covering a circuit comprised of Berlin-Travemünde-Münster-Duisburg-Stuttgart-München-Wien-Breslau-Berlin-Tempelhof, some 2,120 km in all.

Initially, a simple square of variable size had been painted on each side of each aircraft, as well as beneath and above the wing tip area, in which a letter and number combination was marked. The outline to the square was quite wide and marked in black, and initially, as with the International Touring Competition system, the background pale colouring of the aircraft's paintwork was retained within the square. By 1931 white had been adopted as the background colour. Positioning of the marking was left to the discretion of the owner/entrant and varied from the engine cowling to just aft of the wing trailing edge, regardless of the configuration. However, in later competitions, where an aircraft had a dark colour scheme, (such as two BFW M 29a aircraft, D-2306 and D-2309, which wore the company's dark grey-blue overall colour with white civil registration), the respective racing numbers C3 and B4 were marked against a white square. The size of the square was standard, but the additional dark edging was not necessary. Sponsor's emblems, such as the familiar Shell Oil Company logo, also appeared on some aircraft.

Like the International Touring Competition event, the classification system expanded as the race's popularity drew more and more competitors. The original marking, in its black-edged square, was always painted on each side of the fuselage, plus occasionally both above and below the wing at the furthest outer point capable of containing the standard size square. This meant that it often overlapped the ailerons. The rule on the addition of wing markings appears to have been less stringent because photographs of competitors within the same racing year show a very erratic approach to this aspect; some with, some without, others with markings only on one wing, or on one surface of the wing.

By the 1934 race, this system had been replaced with what appears to be a dual marking consisting of a red-edged white circle containing a black alpha-numeric combination, which was required to be marked on each side of the engine cowling. This identified the class of the competitor, i.e., by aircraft numbers within the team and the team origin. An additional marking took the form of a white square containing a coloured letter to identify the individual aircraft within the group entry. For example, that year's race (at which aircraft wearing both the old numerical form of registration and those carrying the new alpha-type were present), He 72 B, D-EMES, wore 'G2' in its circular marking plus a 'V' in a square for its individual marking; this was one of six aircraft in a team entry. Teams often competed in both the Deutschlandflug as well as the International Touring Competition and other races, and some aircraft retained the 'number in a square' personal identification marking of the latter race, in combination with the markings of the Deutschlandflug. The Fliegergruppe Danzig entered a team of Fieseler F 5s, one of which, D-3093 marked 'G1' in red in a white circle, edged in the same colour, carried a red 'M' on a black-edged white square, plus a smaller black-edged square containing a black '23' over the cream-coloured background of

ABOVE: The halcyon days of sport flying in Germany are captured in this panorama of entrants for the 1934 Deutschlandflug, exclusively for German entrants, one of several premier flying events staged in Europe each year. In the foreground is an Fi F 5 R, D-3094, one of several entered; the 'G1' registration marking was in black, with red edging to the white circle. The cream overall-finish carries the additional individual marking of a 'V' in what appears to be red set in a white square, just forward of the registration on the fuselage, repeating the 'G1' marking colours. The white on black 'F' emblem on the nose is also present on the five Fw 44 D aircraft of the D2 team, standing in the background; the reason for this is unclear. D-2916 'R', D-2913 'V', D-2910 'K' are first in line, the individual letter of each marked in what appears to be blue or green; in line behind D-2913 are D-2915 'P' and D-2911 'M'. All five were from the Deutscher Luftfahrt Verband e.V.-Ortstgruppe based at Bremen. The bifurcated cheat line on each machine was possibly black or dark blue. Note the presence of Fw 44 D, D-EJOM 'P', immediately behind D-2910, confirming the date – this was the year in which the change was made from the numerical registrations to alpha registrations, both types appearing at the meeting. D-2915 and D-2916 were later re-registered, respectively, as D-EBMA and D-EQDY.

RIGHT: The pre-war light aircraft industry provided many types that were eventually to see military service. In the foreground of the line-up of 154 entrants for the 1935 Deutschlandflug are some of the five Fieseler F 5 R-equipped B2 team from Berlin-Staaken; D-EVEN 'P', D-EMIT 'L' and D-EFUX 'M'. Behind can be seen some of the He 72 aircraft of the B3 Reichsgruppe Lufthansa team; D-EFUK 'M' and D-EKUQ 'K'. The F 5s were finished in a pale cream colour while the He 72s wore the green-grey colouring that was currently being identified by the new RLM system as RLM 02. Every aircraft competing was marked with a red equilateral triangle enclosed in a yellow circle. (J. Radziwill)

LEFT: Four of the five cream-coloured Fi F 5 R aircraft of the Fliegersportsgruppe Langfuhr B1 team. Identifiable are D-ENYT 'K' and D-EZEF 'L'. The yellow circle with red triangle marking can be seen on the cowl of each of the aircraft. Placement varied between aircraft types and teams. (J. Radziwill)

BELOW LEFT AND BELOW: Seen at the same meeting as shown in the previous photograph, two views of D-IRYL 'K', one of seven Ar 66 c aircraft (some sub-designations were still being recorded in lower case at this time) of one of the three RLM teams competing. Colour was overall RLM 02 with dark blue (most likely RLM 24) turtle deck colouring and trim lines. The positioning of the team racing marking 'F1' and the individual letter 'K' on both sides can be seen. Racing numbers were marked in black on a white disc with red border, the red matching that of the national markings on the tail unit. Positioned above the dash of the civil registration is the yellow circle and red triangle marking. (J. Radziwill)

the aircraft. Another of the nine-aircraft team entry, D-3104, was marked 'G1' with a 'W' in a white square plus '27' in a smaller square. In each instance the latter number was part of the International Touring Competition racing markings, which appear to have been issued sequentially within each team, unlike the individual letter system as explained below.

Groups were divided by the number of aircraft entered and by the team's origin. The listing for the 1935 Deutschlandflug explains this system more clearly.

The RLM also entered a team of seven He 72s, which were allocated the team racing number 'F3'. Nearest the camera is 'S', with D-EXIF 'R' next, then D-EIYQ 'K' (the second letter is not a 'J' but the German manner of marking an 'I', a point which has caused some confusion in the past when interpreting German civil registrations of this period). The front of the fuselage, immediately behind the engine had a white band edged in black, covering the point where the black cheat line along the fuselage bifurcated into a 'Y' shape; black was also used on the wheel spats. Overall colouring of the aircraft was the contemporary RLM 02. (J. Radziwill)

Racing number	Origin	Aircraft Type
Groups of three aircraft.		
A1	Bremen	Focke-Wulf 44
A2	Braunschweig	Klemm L 25 d
A3	Nordhausen	Klemm L 25 d
A4	Weimar	Klemm L 25 d
A5	Osnabrück	Klemm L 25 d
B4	Königsberg	Klemm L 25 d
Groups of four aircraft		
A6	Nürnberg	Klemm L 25 d
B9	Hamburg	Klemm L 25 d
Groups of five aircraft		
B1	Langfuhr	Fieseler F 5 R
B2	Berlin-Staaken	Fieseler F 5 R
B3	Reichsgruppe Lufthansa	Heinkel He 72
B5	Essen	Adler-Gerner G II Re
B6	Danzig	Klemm L 25 d
B7	Dresden	Klemm L 25 d
B8	Breslau	Klemm L 25 d
C1	Hannover	Klemm L 25 d
C2	O.-S. Gleiwitz	Klemm L 25 d
C3	Mannheim	Klemm L 25 d
C4	Halberstadt	Klemm L 25 d
C5	München	Klemm L 25 d
C6	Münster	Klemm L 25 d
C7	Dortmund	Klemm L 25 e
C8	Essen	Klemm L 25 e
D1	Darmstadt	Klemm L 25 d
Groups of seven aircraft		
F1	RLM	Arado 66 c
F3	RLM	Heinkel He 72
F4	Karlsruhe	Klemm L 25 d

Racing number	Origin	Aircraft Type
Groups of nine aircraft		
G1	RLM	Klemm KL 32 A XIV
G2	Berlin Staaken	Klemm L 25 d
G3	Stuttgart	Klemm L 25 d

(*Note: with the exception of the Fieseler designation, the aircraft designation system in use at that time used a lower case letter following the aircraft type.*)

Some individual examples from the above list will clarify the system further. The RLM entry 'F1' D-IRYL (one of seven in the team), carried the individual identifying letter 'K' in the white square marking. The Langfur entry, 'B1' D-ENYT was also marked 'K', the number of individual entries exceeding 26 and thus requiring a repetition of individual letters. No confusion though could follow from this because the entry was also marked with its alphanumeric code. Entry D-ETET was marked 'G1' plus 'V'; the 'B1' entry D-EZEF was marked 'L'. As an example taken across an entire team, four of the five Fieseler F 5 Rs of the Berlin-Staaken 'B2'-marked team were, D-EQOP with the individual letter 'K', D-EMIT with 'L', D-EFUX with 'M', and D-EVEN with 'P'. This illustrates that issuing of individual racing letters was not necessarily sequential, the remaining aircraft could have been either 'N' or 'O' – and again that was not necessarily so because of the dual combination of markings carried by each aircraft. On the 'G1' team of nine aircraft, three were marked 'M', 'R' and 'V', clearly spanning a much greater range than nine letters of the alphabet. That particular race involved 30 groups (154 aircraft), comprising 105 Klemm L 25s, 10 Fieseler F 5 Rs, 10 Heinkel He 72s, nine Klemm Kl 32s, eight Focke-Wulf Fw 44s, seven Arado Ar 66 cs and five Adler G II Rcs. This gives some idea of how flexible the marking system needed to be.

By the 1937 Deutschlandflug, the system of markings had again changed with the circular marking allowing the letter/number combination to be placed 'one above the other as on the Stuttgarter Taxis' entry, which had the letter 'P' marked above the '16'. Another entry in the same race had both racing number (B1) and individual letter (B), combined in the circle, marked approximately two thirds of the height of the racing number. The 1938 meeting employed a further revision, the main team letter/number combination appearing as before, but with the individual entry within each team being identified by a lower case letter immediately below the main marking, all marked in black within the usual red-edged white circle. As an example, the all-silver He 72 D-EMSE, flown by Oblt. Matuschek and Lt. Neubert from the Kampfgruppe Wels team, had a lower case 'b' beneath its 'F6' designation marking.

As noted earlier, the Deutschlandflug had attracted ever-increasing numbers of competitors with each passing year, many from the RLM and Luftwaffe. By 1938 the listing was exclusively comprised of government and military teams, including several from the RLM, e.g., RLM-LB (C2), RLM C-Amt (two teams, registered C1 and G9), RLM Rangsdorf (4), RLM Genst. 1. Abt. III (G1); RLM Genst. 2 Abt. (G8); RLM Aufklarungsgruppe Lehrgeschwader Jüterbog (G4); RLM - Lkrsch. Gatow (G2); RLM - Lkrsch. Dresden-Klotzsche (G6); RLM - Lkrsch. Fürstenfeldbruck (G5); RLM - L.Nachr.Sch.Köthen/Anh (K1); RLM - Flugber, Staaken (K2); RLM - Höh. Kdr. D. Lehrtr (G3).

The Luftwaffe units, both secondary and front-line, fielded several others, e.g., Aufklarungsgruppe Würzburg, Aufkl. Gr. 13, 23 and Stuka gruppe 163 Brieg (K5), Aufkl. Gr. Stargard (K8), Aufkl. Gr. Neuhasusen/Ostpreussen (L9), J Gr. Jesau/Ostpreussen (L8), JG Jever, Oldenburg (F4), JG Richthofen Jüterbog-Damm (K9), Kampfgruppe Fritzlar, z.Z. Diepholz (F5),

ABOVE: Another season... another set of team marking allocations. This was possibly the 1936 event as the system of marking changed in 1937. Some of the He 72 Bs of the D1 team are seen here, the nearest, D-EBOR, marked with the individual letter 'R'. Overall colour was silver with what was either black or dark blue trim.

Kampfgruppe Wels (F6), Kdo. Fliegerschule u Fl. Ers.Abt Dresden (K6), Kdo. Fl. Sch. Dresden (K7), Fliegerführerschule Frankfurt am Oder (L1), Flfsch. C. Ludwigslust L2), Flfsch. Neubiberg (L6), KG Gotha (K3), KG Merseburg (K4), KG Ansbach (L7), KG Hindenburg, Neubrandenburg (L3).

The NSFK were represented by three teams, the F7-registered team representing Stand. 22, Frankfurt am Oder, Gruppe 4, piloted by instructors from the organization, the G1 team representing Gruppe 8, and the Gruppe 17 team C3. Teams C1 to C4 flew Bü 131s.

Teams F1 to F8 used He 72s and the remainder Fw 44s. This listing represents only about half the entries of that year.

Note the reluctance to identify the front line units in a more precise manner – probably due to intelligence restrictions for what was a public document in this year of political turmoil and military brinkmanship. The identity of some were obvious (in hindsight), the F4, 'J.G. Jever' team listing Maj. Schumacher and Lt. Steinhoff in the six man team.

Aircraft of mixed fabric and wood design of this period were seen in several finishes, depending on ownership, but a simple gloss, pale ivory to cream colouring was common, black or a deep blue being added as both decoration and for anti-dazzle purposes on the nose section. The Kl 36 cabin monoplane, which had emerged in 1934, designed and produced

for the Europa-Rundflug race, followed the same general colouring. The Bf 108, although produced to a military contract, had been built to compete in the 4th Challenge de Tourisme Internationale of 1934 and, as noted above, subsequently became a popular private owner light aircraft. It too appeared in cream with black trim and civil registration, as well as alternatively in the company's dark grey-blue with white registration.

It is difficult to identify the precise shade of colours used during this period, but most were drawn from the RAL range of standard colours. The very popular ivory finish was RAL 1014 elfenbein, while the Messerschmitt company colour was RAL 5008 graublau. (This colour was also used on the Bf 109 V14, registered D-ISLU, which crashed during the Dübendorf flying meeting in 1937, and also on the Me 209 V1, D-INJR, which established the world air speed record 755.138 km/h on 26 April 1939.) These colours were all gloss finish. The palest of the cream finishes appears to have been RAL 9001 cremeweiß (cream white). Red and blue were among the colours used for cheat lines and trim around engines and, where fitted, spats. Registrations were marked in RAL 9005 tiefschwarz (jet black) on pale colours and RAL 9010 reinweiß (pure white) on dark colours.

After the outbreak of the Second World War many of the remaining light aircraft still in civil ownership were impressed for military service and those remaining were seen less and less as fuel restrictions took force. It was the end of a very colourful period in German flying history.

1 Martin Simons research.

APPENDIX

German Paint Technology 1930-1945

A Synopsis by Jürgen H. Kiroff – Farben-Kiroff-Technik

(See booklet in inside back cover wallet)

APPENDIX

External Stores

A wide variety of external stores were seen beneath Luftwaffe aircraft ranging from bombs to weapons packs, external fuel tanks, etc. The range of German bombs varied from 1 kg to 2,000 kg, plus sea mines adapted for use over land. Bombs were designated SC for Sprengbombe Cylindrisch (thin-walled bomb, high explosive for general purpose use); SD for Sprengbombe Dickwändig (thick-walled bomb; high explosive armour piercing or semi-armour piercing); PC for Panzerbombe Cylindrisch (extra thick walled, high explosive armour-piercing bomb). These prefixes were followed by the bomb weight, e.g., SD 250, SC 1800, etc.

Colouring used to denote the type, SD or SC, usually took the form of a stripe running vertically between the bottom and top point of the tail cone, marked between each fin segment. Stripe width was approximately 40 mm on smaller bombs and 65 mm on larger bombs. Colour designations were yellow (SC), red (SD) and blue (PC). Bombs also carried stencilled notations in black or red to denote type etc. Colour identification was sometimes not marked on 50 kg and 250 kg bombs these having distinguishing physical features. The SC bombs had a smooth parallel body surface while the SD bombs had their tapered body fitted with a cylindrical collar from about the last third of the body length back to the fins. This produced a thin weld line around the body. The SD 250 was also some 25 cm shorter than the 1.80 m long SC 250 giving the weapon the appearance of a more rotund shape.

Document Az 74b Nr 4724/39 geh. Genst.6. Ab. (IVC) of 20 December 1939 list the following examples of the stripe colouring used to identify each class of bomb:

Splitter und Minenwirkung [leicht] (e.g., SC 50) – kepelflächen
      der Steuerschwänze im rot
nur Minenwirkung (e.g., SC 50) – gelb
Durchschlagwirkung (e.g., SD 500) – blau
nur Splitterwirkung (e.g., SB 50) – vollkommen Grün Anstrich

Body colouring varied with the type of bomb, there being a range within each of the smaller size category. The SC 50 appeared in buff as well as dark green. The SC 250 appeared in field grey for the weapons fitted with the Stabo device (a long rod attached to the nose) or dark green. The SC 500 appeared in a buff colour, SC 1000, SC 1200 and SC 1800 bombs were finished sky overall. (Colour descriptions used here are from British documents and are not definitive colour terms. 'Sky' in English parlance was a blue-green or a blue, probably the latter in this instance.) The SC 2000 type was black overall while the SC 2500 were finished in 65 overall with a yellow stripe on the body. The PC-range of bombs usually were painted 65 overall regardless of size. The colour terms listed for the types appear to be a mixture of RLM and RAL standard colours listed under table 840 R for both Wermacht and Luftwaffe. In German documents NC 2505 bombs were described as feldgrau colouring with a white ring around the nose section and the central part of the body with the type description NC 2505 added in white lettering. Use of feldgrau as the paint description points to RAL 6006 feldgrau (subtitled dunkelgrüngrau) being the colour described (see colour card 3 in Volume One of this work).

ABOVE: An SC 1000 (code named Hermann) finished in 65-overall with its prominent suspension band and yellow-coloured stripe on the tail cone. The armorer gives some scale to this weapon. (E. Sommer)

ABOVE: Carried externally below a He 111H, 1H+DN of II./KG 26, this SD 1000 shows how well the red identifying stripe stood out against the overall sky-colouring. (H. Nowarra)

Stencilled markings were added to the body of each class of bomb in 80 mm high lettering, e.g.,

Güteklasse I	SC 50JA	250JA	250L	500L2		
II	SC 50JB	250JB	50JC	250JC		
III	SC 50K	250K	500K	50B	250B	500B

Early examples of the SC 2500 had no identifying description on the body, but later examples had 'C2500' in 40 mm high lettering marked in two places.

Smaller bombs carried externally by such types as the Bf 109, Bf 110, and Ju 87 were usually left in production colouring; any alteration amounted to a hasty splash of 65-colouring on part of the body of the bomb, so that it would not adversely compromise the aircraft carrying it. In this class were the SC and SD 250, SC and SD 500. When fighter-bomber camouflage changed to 74/75/76 there is some evidence that occasionally ground staff painted 76-colouring over the bombs carried by such types as the Fw 190 and Bf 109, but the 'sky' colour appears to have been adequate in most instances. During winter operations on the Eastern Front bombs of these sizes were sometimes given a coat of temporary 21 white to blend with the aircraft, but this was at unit discretion.

ABOVE: An SB 1000 mounted on an Fw 190 G-3, showing how its lower fin had been renoved for ground clearance. Colouring is sky on the body, with the tail cone and fins in buff.

Night attacks by fighter-bombers against British civil targets in 1942 and 1943 usually saw the externally carried bombs coated in temporary black. The same colouration was used for night attacks by standard bombers where larger weapons were externally carried.

In addition to bombs, the Luftwaffe also employed two types of sea mines adapted for land use; the 500 kg Luftmine A (LMA) and the 1,000 kg Luftmine B (LMB). These had a metal tail fairing housing a parachute that was usually torn away as the parachute deployed. Overall colouring was a dark green, as these devices were normally dropped in the sea where dark colouration was advantageous. A third such weapon was the 1,000 kg Bombenmine (BM). Unlike the LMA and LMB this weapon was fitted with a conventional tail cone made of bakelised paper painted 'sky blue' according to official reports, although some photographs show this part in a much darker colour.

Larger types of incendiary bombs ranged in size from the 50 kg Sprengbrandbombe, a phosphorus filled weapon, to the 250 and 500 kg

oil filled Flammbombe.Overall they resembled the SC/SD range of weapons. Overall colouring was similar, but red stencilling replaced the black of the HE weapons.

Disposable weapon containers were also employed in a number of sizes. These 'Abwurf Behalter' were marked AB in black followed by a number, which denoted the equivalent physical size, not weight, of a PC/PD range of bomb. On weapons marked ABB the last B denoted Brandbomben (Fire bombs). The range of weapon containers was large and colours included dark green, red, light grey, silver, slate grey and buff. Non-expendable weapons containers came in three sizes and three distinct colours. The BSB 320 was black, the BSB 700 sky blue and the BSB 1000 buff. Occupying the same space as 500 kg or 1,000 kg bombs they were carried externally.

Externally mounted bomb racks were usually painted in the prevailing under surface colour of 65 or 76, depending on which type of aircraft were employed. Notations on the racks were applied in black and red lettering. Externally mounted weapons packs were treated in the same manner.

Non-jettisonable external fuel tanks, where they protruded beyond the wing, (as on the Bf 110), were finished in the prevailing upper surface colouring with the remainder in either the standard lower surface camouflage colour or natural metal. The large external fuel tank, code named 'Dackelbauch', fitted externally to the under fuselage surface on Bf 110 Ds was painted in 65. On night fighter Bf 110s employing the tactical marking of a black-coloured starboard wing lower surface, the external fuel tank under that wing was usually also painted permanent black, their stencilled instructions appearing over the top of this colour. Jettisonable tanks mounted completely below the aircraft were usually given a coat of the appropriate under surface colouring, i.e., 65 or 76. Late in the war occasionally some examples were seen in natural metal finish, possibly as a result of austerity measures.

Torpedoes were usually left in bare metal on the main body of the weapon, with the warhead section painted in a dark colour, possibly one of the RAL system colours as the weapons were manufactured by the munitions industry. Training torpedoes were sometimes marked with longitudinal red stripes or left in a buff colour.

Weapons such as the Henschel Hs 293 A and PC 1400X, carried externally, were finished 65 overall as they were usually employed in daylight hours. Some night operations were carried out with the Hs 293 A by II./KG 100 in late 1943 and it is possible that the weapons were given a coat of temporary black.

ABOVE: An Fw 190 F-8 finished in 74/75/76 camouflage fitted with a BV 246 glider bomb, photographed during trials with this weapon. Upper surfaces of the BV 246 were 70, with 65 lower surfaces.

ABOVE: Ju 87 D-4, W.Nr. 142891, fitted with anti-personnel bomb canisters, each of which housed 48 fragmentation bombs. Photographed at Prag-Letnany airfield in 1945, the aircraft was finished in standard 70/71/65 with 65-coloured under surfaces, the bomb containers being in the latter colouring. Note that this aircraft had not had the final revised range of yellow tactical markings applied to it.

The collapsible freight container, code named 'Dobbas', usually employed one of the upper surface greens, and tonal value suggests 71, and 65 lower surface camouflage. Spraying equipment was also carried by a variety of aircraft, the large tanks beneath each wing being left in 02 or painted with one of the upper surface greens.

The Luftwaffe also used air-dropped containers to re-supply troops on the ground. These were usually painted in RAL 6006 feldgrau.

RIGHT: A stock of SC 50 bombs, awaiting use by the He 111s of K/88 in Spain in 1937. The dark colouring is green (an RAL colour) with the bomb type marked in black stencilling. The smooth parallel-sided body identifies the SC type. (H. Obert)

ABOVE: This PC 250 bomb being loaded under a Ju 87 B of St.G. 77 during the Polish campaign in 1939 has a buff coloured body with white nose cap and a dark blue band around its middle. Note the ground equipment colouring - RAL not RLM colours. In this instance probably dunkelgrün or olivgrün plus erdgelb.

RIGHT: France 1940: an SC 250 in overall grey-green. The yellow identifying stripe can just be seen between the fins. Black stencil marks identified sub-types amongst the general class of bomb. (J. Vasco)

ABOVE: The yellow 65 mm-wide colour stripe between the fins on the SC 500 bomb is easily seen against the grey-green colouring. (J. Vasco)

ABOVE: A pair of practice SC 50s under the wing of an Hs 123. Colouring is buff with white nose cap, and a yellow double oblong edged in black. (R. Lutz)

LEFT: Loading an SC 500 beneath a Bf 110 of Erp.Gr.210 in 1940. The weapon is coloured grey-green with a white nose cap. Lack of a weld joint near the fin end identifies it as an SC type (J. Vasco)

RIGHT: A mixture of SC and SD bombs. In the front row are dark green-coloured SC 500s identified by their 65 mm-wide yellow stripe. In the middle row are SD 500s, three in sky colouring and two in dark green colouring, the red stripe showing more clearly on the paler coloured bombs.

ABOVE: An SD 500 Type 1 bomb, distinguishable by its annular tail ring, finished in sky-colouring, lies beside two others coloured grey-green overall. An SC 500 in sky finish is immediately behind them, its yellow identifying stripe visible between the fins. More of the latter type, in grey-green colouring can be seen on the other side of the Fw 190 A-8. The distorted circular flange on the bomb in the left foreground shows the rough handling to which these weapons could be subjected.

ABOVE: An externally fitted paired ETC 500 bomb rack (from a Ju 88 A) painted in standard 65-colouring, with lettering in black and red. The letters 'ETC' stood for Elektrische Trägervorrichtung für Cylinderbomben. The camera equipment and bombsights on the tables behind are painted in 02.

LEFT: An Fw 190 F (or G) trop of SG 4 fitted with an ER-4 adaptor bomb rack to house four SC 50 bombs. The adaptor was painted 66 on its upper surface, and 76 on its lower surface. Found abandoned at Bizerta, the aircraft was camouflaged in 74/75/76.

ABOVE AND LEFT: Two views of the paired ETC 250 external bomb rack fitted beneath a captured Bf 110. The colouring matches the undersides of this aircraft, which had retained its European camouflage finish. The yellow-coloured tips to the propeller blades were added by the RAF.

RIGHT: An unusual modification to a Ju 52/3m. External bomb racks had been fitted just forward and aft of the wheel bracing struts. The racks appear to be finished in 02. The crude metal doors for a small internal load appear to have been fashioned at unit-level, as well as the unidentified V-shaped metal shroud, which passed well to rear of the fuselage. (D. Vincent)

LEFT: A 300 litre Type D external fuel tank fitted to a Ju 87 R-2. Colour is 65 to match the aircraft's under surfaces; the under surfaces of the wing tips are in 04-colouring. (H. Nowarra)

BELOW: A Fi 156 C-3, B1+BB of Transportstaffel I.Fliegerkorps, serving on the Eastern Front in 1941. It is fitted with a fixed external fuel tank finished overall in 65-colouring.

ABOVE AND RIGHT: Two views of a Do 23 G, SA+FJ, fitted with a ring for exploding electrically detonated sea mines, photographed at Stendal in the second half of 1941. Overall colouring is 63 with the ring and the large ventral pannier, housing the electric motor, in the same colour. The positioning of the Hakenkreuz marking determines that the aircraft had not been repainted in 02. Note the apparent colour difference between the two shots, one taken in strong sunlight, the other on an overcast day after a rain shower.
(H. Jonas via D. Vincent)

ABOVE: A Ju 88 A, 1H+GN, of 5./KG 26 carrying an aerial torpedo. The body of the weapon was left in bare metal, but the warhead section was in a dark colour. As a weapon the colour used may have been from the RAL range rather than an RLM standard, both sources of colour being used at times for a wide range of weapons, largely dependent upon the individual supplier. As an expendable device precise colour control was not relevant.

LEFT: A Ju 88 A-17 fitted with a pair of LT F5b torpedoes. The weapons were usually left in natural metal, but the weapon racks were finished in 65. The half black-half white nose section of this Ju 88 indicates that it was used for weapons trials, the colouring facilitating camera telemetry tracking.

ABOVE: The 'Dobbas' freight pannier was used for transporting ammunition and light weapons. Seen here below a Ju 87 B, the pannier was made of plywood and finished in 70 on its upper surface and 65 underneath.

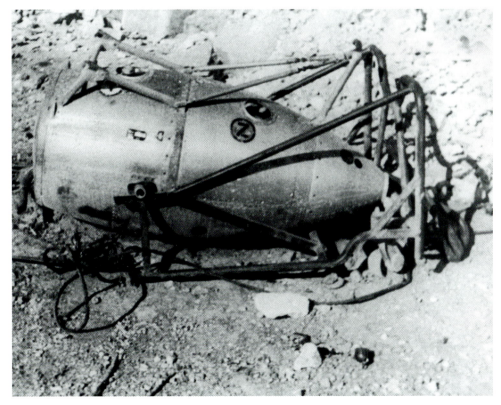

ABOVE: Fw 58 Cs of EKdo 40 (formerly Fliegerforstchutzverband - Aerial Forest Protection Unit) finished in 70/71/65. The aircraft in the foreground, XB+HM, shows the 65-coloured spray equipment fitted below the wing centre section. The aircraft are marked with an 04-coloured half-metre band around the fuselage as they were last employed on the Eastern Front, spraying potential disease sources such as malarial swamps. The equipment also was used at one point in the Middle Danube area for laying smoke over potato crops to prevent frost damage.

LEFT: The externally mounted RATO pack, used by the Ar 234 for rocket-assisted take-offs, is seen here on its transportation frame, which was in a dark colour (possibly 70 or 71), with the top securing rods that attached to the wing in 02. The rocket pack was left in bare metal other than for the black, stencilled. Circular markings of 'Z' on a pink background, 'T' on a white background, 'E' on a green background and 'L' on a blue background – each situated by the relevant filler point for the chemicals used by the rocket. The manufacturer's data plate can be seen on the forward section, near the joint band. The parachute pack, fitted to the front face, was usually in natural fabric colouring.

Maintenance and Safety Markings

ircraft structures of all classes had a wide variety of small markings applied to them. The average airframe wore a significant number of such markings, both externally and internally, many of which were readily visible only when close to the structure concerned. Such markings broadly fall into two main categories - maintenance markings and safety markings, with the latter also including identification of the structural materials (as detailed later in this text).

General maintenance markings provided all necessary warnings needed to ensure that specific parts of the airframe, and its requirements, were clearly identified. As such, maintenance itself can be divided into two distinct categories; (a) airframe and control systems, (b) engine, fuel, oil, oxygen and electrical services.

Under caregory (a), among the most common basic markings found on all airframes was the numbering of the individual fuselage frame positions, indicated by simple black numbers starting from the primary frame of the front section. Deutsche Normen DIN Luftfahrt 1929-1939 (German Standards DIN relating to aircraft 1929-1939) was a collected revision of the original Luftfahrt-Normen Ausgabe Dezember 1929 (Aircraft Standards, Issue December 1929), which covered all aspects of the airframe – fabric, tyres and wheel rims, bracing wires, instruments and colour coding for piping – but by 1939 only the numerical marking of frame positions of DIN L46 was retained for more modern aircraft structures. The original order had required not only numbering of the main frames of the fuselage, but also each individual wing rib and part-rib commencing at the fuselage and including the suffix 'L' (Linke for left) and 'R' (Recht for right) plus 'a' for part ribs, e.g., 5aL (part rib 5 left wing). There were even more elaborate aspects to this original system, but as stated, only individual fuselage frame marking survived.

In the case of twin-engine aircraft marking commenced at the first frame of the fuselage, but on single engine aircraft it usually began at the firewall, or the first full frame at the rear section of the cockpit. Another marking common to all types was the two-letter combination WE (Waagerecht Einstellung – 'horizontal position') marked at intervals along the fuselage structure, to indicate the horizontal datum rigging line. These were painted in black, but occasionally had a red spot of paint applied to an accompanying dome-headed rivet that served as an exact datum point. A similar style of datum point sometimes was provided for the aircraft painter to enable accurate positioning of markings. Official instructions specifically forbade over painting of either type of marking point.

Lifting and jacking points were marked with plain language instructions, as were tie-down points, internal stowage of equipment such as crew access ladders, and entrance hatches. Foot and hand-holds were outlined on their opening sides with a solid line of colour, either red or black. Indication of where and where not to step was marked either in wine red, black or white. The wine red colour, RLM 28, was more usually found on bomber aircraft wing structures, providing a better contrast to the dark greens of the camouflage, though towards the end of the war that colour appeared on some single-engine fighter aircraft as camouflage colouring moved to the darker colours of brown and green.

Markings for walkway boundaries and quick release fasteners on panels were restated in the 1944 edition of Der Flugzeugmahler:

"Wing walkway boundaries must be delineated with a broken red line 10 mm in width (length of strokes 20 mm; spacing 20 mm). In the stencil formed broad middle script lettering (block letters DIN 1451) 25 mm high as follows

"Nur hier betreten!" Delicate parts as well as trim tabs are stencilled "Nicht anfassen!"

Quick release fasteners will have a red line painted across them generally in the direction of flight. The red line should overlap the fasteners for a distance of 1 cm right and left."

(Despite specifying red, by the late war period white was sometimes used, and the appropriate stencils were not always available, hand-painted lettering being used on some aircraft.)

Flying control surfaces, particularly trim tabs, were marked with a warning in red, black or white. Gust lock positions were precisely indicated with

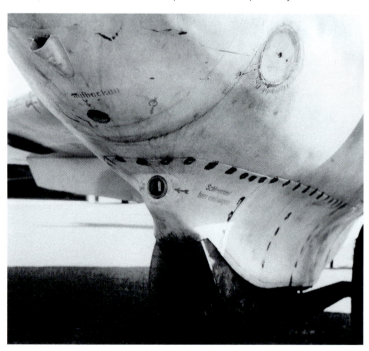

ABOVE: Under the nose section of Me 163 B, W.Nr. 191907, the jacking point is labelled **aufbocken** in black with a red arrow pointing to the hole outlined in red. At the front of the skid housing is the towing attachment point, identified on the port side by a red arrow and the marking in black of:

Schleppseil
hier einhangen

ABOVE: Me 163s carried the following legend beneath the wing root:
Hier aufbocken
Nur mit leeren Behaltern
(Jack here only with empty fuel tanks). (RAAF)

dotted lines, usually in red or black. Wing leading edges on fighter aircraft and training aircraft sometimes were marked with a red line along their extent with a warning, also in red, 'Nicht hier schieben' ('Do not push'). Where the wing flap position could be viewed by the pilot, a series of red or white lines were sometimes painted on the curve of the port flap as a visual indicator of the angle of setting. Undercarriage visual position indicators, in the form of a simple vertical rod, painted red, were fitted to Fw 190s and later models, and protruded from the wing uppersurface when the undercarriage was lowered.

The basic airframe maintenance markings common to all classes of Luftwaffe aircraft were;

Hier unterbocken	(trestle here)
Hier aufbocken	(jack here)
Hier anheben	(lift here)
Hier eingreifen	(grip here)
Einstiegklappe	(boarding step)
Hier nicht schieben	(do not push)
Nicht betreten	(do not step)
Nur hier betreten	(step here only)
Nicht anfassen	(do not touch)
WE	(horizontal datum levelling point)

Application of these, and other markings, was done usually with the aid of a set of stencils developed by individual aircraft companies for each specific type of aircraft produced. These were included in an aircraft's painting schedule as a set of lists, each marking having its company stencil number alongside the reference number followed by the DIN standard code for the size of the characters and numerals. Company abbreviations were quite easily identifiable, e.g., DoN for Dornier, HsN for Henschel, etc.

The maintenance category also had a set of basic markings that referred to weights and loadings and these were promulgated in the Luftwerkhersvorschrift (Air Traffic Regulation) of 29 August 1936. However, that was only an upgrading document as there is photographic evidence of the fuselage weights and loadings table in use in 1935, e.g., on the He 112 V2 and Hs 123 V2.

The 1935 form of table required the following data:

Leergewicht	(gross weight)
Gesamtlast	(load capacity)
Fluggewicht	(flying weight)
Höchstzul Pers.	(maximum persons)
Letzte Prüf.	(date of last major service)
Nachste Prüf.	(date of next major service)
Eigent}	(specific)
Halter}	(owner)

The 1936 issue of the air traffic regulation was slightly truncated, setting down only the following requirements:

An identification plate giving name and address of manufacturer, aircraft type, construction number, year of manufacture of each part is to be firmly affixed to fuselage, wings and other parts of aircraft.

On the left rear fuselage, in black characters of at least 25 mm height and 4 mm width on light background, the following information is to be stencilled:
a) name and address of owner.
b) tare weight, payload and maximum take-off weight in kg.
c) maximum number of persons, including crew.
d) date of last annual inspection and due date of next inspection.

Airships carry this information in a prominent place on the gondola. In the cargo hold, a diagram showing the stowing of cargo to be affixed.

On engines, a metal plate with the following details has to be affixed in a prominent place
a) name and address of manufacturer
b) type, series, construction number and year
c) maximum power and maximum permissible RPM."

Details of the weights and loading table however did vary slightly, with the class of airframe being added and the weights divided up into different lines as set out here.

BELOW: Fw 56s of Fliegergruppe Damm lined up. The weights and loading table can be seen on the first two aircraft, marked just ahead of the rudder sternpost. The nearer one reads:

LEERGEWICHT:	**670kg**
GESAMTLAST:	**315kg**
FLUGGEWICHT:	**985kg**
HÖCHSTZÜHL PERS. ZAHL 1	
LETZTE PRUF:	**28.8.35**
NACHSTE PRÜF:	**28.8.36**
EINGENT} FLIEGERGRUPPE	
HALTER } DAMM	

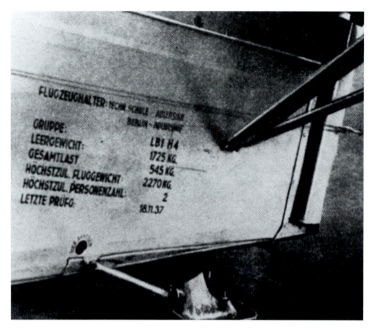

ABOVE: The weights and loading table, marked below the port horizontal stabilizer on the port side of the fuselage of a He 46 from the Technical School at Adlershof in Berlin.

Flugzeughalter	(aircraft owner)
Gruppe	(class of airframe)
Leergewicht	(gross weight)
Gesamtlast	(load capacity)
Höchstzul. Fluggewicht	(maximum flying weight)
Höchstzul. Personenzahl	(maximum number of crew)
Letzte Prüfg.	(date of last major service)

While the weights and loading table continued in use on second line and civil aircraft, for security reasons the outbreak of hostilities witnessed deletion of this information on front line aircraft. Transition was not immediate and some examples continued to be seen during the first months of the war.

In late 1940 the airframe manufacturing plate had its plain language information replaced by a series of coded details (shown as either a two

ABOVE: The weights and loading data, stencilled in white on the red oxide-primed fabric of the inside of the door of a DFS 230 glider. The data listed the empty weight (845 kg), load (1255 kg), all up weight (2100 kg) and maximum number of personnel (10). The marking was placed on the inside of the door where it could be seen when loading the aircraft, the door being locked in the open position. Note that each line had been constructed using stencils for each letter, producing a slightly ragged alignment and spacing. The other side of the fabric was in 70 or 71-colouring; the passing of time having made it difficult to establish the exact shade of green.

or three letter, lower case, combination) that attempted to deny the enemy any intelligence details on production sources, etc. These plates were aluminium and details were individually stamped into each one.

A second table of information, relating to paint finish, also was marked on the rear section of the port side of the fuselage of some aircraft. This was intended to facilitate the maintenance of the overall external finish of the airframe, but this form of marking gradually disappeared, the requisite data instead being recorded only in the individual aircraft's maintenance logbook. Even so, examples were to be seen on some front line aircraft right through to 1940.

The second category (of maintenance), (b) engine, fuel, oil, oxygen and electrical services, retained the most common series of maintenance markings as originally codified into DIN L5, the first edition being issued in April 1927 and upgraded periodically in the following years. These were colours used to identify various systems by means of colour combinations and specific sequences, later with set dimensions as the accompanying colour diagrams on pages 424/425 show. The colours used were all from the RAL colour range and comprised just red (fire extinguisher), green (water), blue (air), yellow (fuel), brown (oil) and black (exhaust gas). This initial standard did not specify anything other than colour, which was added to the various pipe runs and connectors as a single solid colour. While external identification colours were marked using the colours from the RLM 21 to 28 range that mimicked their equivalent, but not quite identical RAL colours, internal systems were pre-painted with RAL colours by the supplying sub-contractor. The RAL colours were RAL 3000 (red), RAL 6010 (green), RAL 5009 (blue), RAL 1012 (yellow), RAL 8003 (brown), RAL 9005 (black), RAL 9002 (white).

As aircraft systems became more complex, revisions refined the process, adding both combinations of colours (and introducing white into the system) as well as marking dimensions. Modern engines for example required more than just water for their coolant systems, glycol being added, Thus while green was retained as the primary identification colour for water, green/white/green identified a combination of both. Compressed air also served a number of systems, requiring a combination of blue with the appropriate service colour, e.g., the compressed air pressure equalizing system for oil was identified with a blue/black/blue band around the pipe.

Internally the DIN L5 standard was used on all engine services. Colouring of the service component itself was covered in DIN L43. Cockpit instrumentation used to monitor specific services was marked with the same colour code on the instrument rim. Electrical cabling was also colour coded along its length, the appropriate colour combination being woven into the sheathing. Where instruments or electrical services terminated on the instrument panels, an alpha-numeric combination was usually marked to identify each system for maintenance purposes.

Commonly seen servicing markings were:

Glykol/Wasser 50/50	(glycol/water 50/50)
Ölpeilstab	(oil dipstick cover)
Preßluft	(compressed air)
Sauerstoff	(oxygen)
Federbeindruck … atü	(strut pressure)
Reifendruck … atü	(tyre pressure)

Fuel filler points were marked with a white-edged yellow (04) triangle containing the appropriate octane rating number in black. Later in the war a simple stencil was sometimes used, which left the octane rating marked in the underlying camouflage colour. Late in the war, some symbols used to identify items, like the fuel primer filler point on Bf 190s and the MW 50 sign, varied slightly between parent and licensed manufacturers (a distinguishing point sometimes useful for identifying an aircraft's manufacturing source).

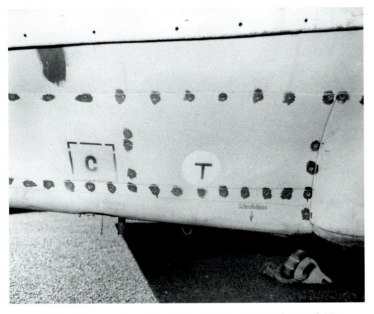

ABOVE: On the lower section of the starboard side of the airframe of this Me 163 B are the identification markings for the two types of fuel. A black 'C' stencilled on an 04 yellow square edged in black with a black 'T' stencilled on a white disc further forward. The quick release point for the skid is marked **Schnellablass** in 23 red, with a red arrow pointing down. (RAAF)

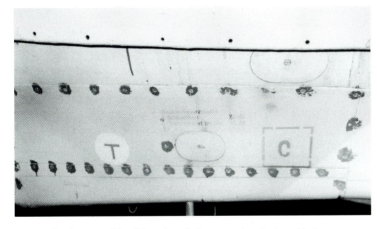

ABOVE: On the port side of the aircraft the same two fuel markings appear plus three lines of stencilling, giving compressed air pressure details, marked above the access hatch.

Drück für Federzylinder	
1) Schleppstart	**2.8 atü**
2) Treibwerkstart	**3.0 atü**
3)	**3.2 atü**
Pressure table for spring cylinder	
1) Towed start	2.8 atmospheres
2) Powered start	3.0 atmospheres
3)	3.2 atmospheres

(RAAF)

Engines were sent for part or full overhauls after a specific set of hours of use. To signify their overhaul status, equilateral triangles, 15 mm per side, were used. After each part overhaul, the engine block had to be marked with a yellow (04) triangle. This was applied on the port side for in-line engines and on the gearbox or front housing on radial engines. The engine number was painted, either in red, white or yellow 40 mm high numerals, immediately above the triangle marking. The number of yellow triangles painted alongside each other indicated the number of part overhauls carried out; once a full overhaul had been carried out, the yellow triangle markings were painted out and replaced by a single red triangle of the same dimensions. Adding a yellow triangle alongside of the red triangle signified further part overhauls. A further complete overhaul repeated the painting out process of the yellow triangles and another red triangle was added. By this means the current number of full and part overhauls could be seen.

That system however was modified in 1942, following complaint that some overhauls had proved less than satisfactory, and that there were no means of identifying where and when the work had taken place. The RLM issued an instruction on 28 May 1942 that resulted in the process of marking being revised. Henceforth, triangles were to be displayed one below the other, and each was to be marked with a code identifying the factory that had carried out the overhaul, plus the date of the work. Those markings were to appear in 3 cm high white lettering. A British intelligence report recorded that the type of marking used for identification was similar to the existing OKL two and three letter code system, but four letters were used. Why that variation to the existing, extensive code system was introduced is unknown. [1]

Internally, markings were either hand-painted or applied by means of decals or stencils. Lettering styles in the cockpit area were usually fairly basic, as ground staff rather than tradesmen painters added identification codes to many instruments and specific controls. In addition to the standard range of markings ground staff, often on a one-off basis, added a plethora of minor markings. For maintenance purposes individual instrument locations were marked with an alpha-numeric code that identified the service to which they were attached. These were usually hand-painted in white or, occasionally, yellow. As the war progressed decals were sometimes utilised. The system was standardised right across the service and used the following groupings:

- **A** – electrical current supply and storage (e.g., batteries)
- **B** – circuit breakers for main electrical system
- **C** – lighting (internal and external)
- **D** – heating (e.g., for pitot tube)
- **E** – electrically operated ancillary services (e.g., undercarriage and flaps, airscrew pitch change)
- **FT** (usually recorded only as **F**) – radio equipment
- **K** – circuit breakers for electrically operated trim controls
- **L** – blind-flying instruments
- **M** – engine instruments (e.g., temperature gauge for oil)
- **P** – weapons (e.g., gun sight, cannons)
- **R** – release circuits of disposable weapon loads (e.g., rockets, bombs)
- **S** – fusing circuits for disposable weapons

Notations referring to cockpit fittings were also applied by hand, stencil or decal, colouring usually being white but with red used for emergency services. Individual instruments had their outer rim painted in a colour that either related to their function, or denoted limitations that were not to be exceed by the particular system.

Externally, the range of markings was extensive and each aircraft type, and often sub-model of the same type, exhibited variations and additions. Lettering style also varied considerably; standard stencilled DIN block lettering was sometimes replaced with hand-painted block lettering, or even script form lettering (including pseudo-Gothic script). Often a mixture of styles, and colours, would appear on a single aircraft – inconsistencies such as a mixture of stencils, some using upper case while others were in lower case also occurred.

As a result it is necessary to examine aircraft on an individual basis to determine both style and colouring used despite some clearly defined standards set in the pre-war period. The full range would fill a small book in itself. To give the reader an appreciation of the extent to which such markings were employed, the internal and external markings standards for the Do 17 E, Do 217 E-1, E-2, E-3, E-4, Do 217 J, Do 217 M-1 and

Do 217 N-1 series are presented here in full. Many markings were common to all, but each type exhibited its own variations. The general instructions notes sometimes specified colours; those for the Do 217 M-1 for instance listed that all emergency markings were to be in 'Ton 23 (rot)' (tone red), while the remaining internal markings were all to be in 'RLM 77 (grau)'. Each marking was also accompanied by a Dornier stencil reference, e.g., 22 DoN 1302; the style of letters and numbers of each was, in turn, dictated by the appropriate DIN 1451 standard. The diagrams showing placement of each stencil also included dimensions for setting up the position of the Balkenkreuz and Hakenkreuz and also the Stammkennzeichen.

With the shift to all-metal construction in 1936, a wide range of metals became common to German aircraft production. This short extract from a document entitled, Technische Lehrmittel (Technical training methods), published pre-war, provides a brief oversight to some of the range of such materials. [2]

"The main construction material for the skinning of the fuselage and the wings is Duraluminium, also for sheet metal up to 1 mm thickness [used as] plated material which is Duraluminium covered on both sides with a thin layer of Dural. This layer protects the inside material from corrosion, which is comparable to the rusting of iron.

Normal commercially used names of this protected material are Duralplat, Bondur etc. For single parts, e.g. wing- and tail plane, flaps, Pantal is used, which can be welded as good as aluminium, but has a higher stability. Pressed-, wrought- and turned-parts are made from highly refined chromium-nickel-steel, also in small quantities chromium-molybdenum-steel is used. All steel-parts are protected against weathering by applying cadmium [plating] and paint. The different materials and surface protection materials are described in more detail in the 'Adviser' published by the Junkers-Works which can be ordered from the Dunnhaupt-Publisher at Dessau."

Key to external stencilling on Do 17 E as per aircraft handbook.

Anlage 18
Blatt 12

Bemerkungen:

1) Die Klappen sämtlicher Verschlußdeckel zum Öffnen sind rot zu bemalen

2) Die Verschlußstellung von Drehverschlüssen, z. B. an der Motorhaube, ist durch einen roten Strich zu tennzeichnen

3) Der Hals und der Sechstant sämtlicher Schmiernippel sind rot zu bemalen

4) Sämtliche Ausbauteile, wie Stromsammler, abnehmbare Deckel usw. sind mit Werknummer und Baumuster-Bezeichnung zu beschriften

5) Die Schraubenköpfe der Rüstmarken (MLE) oben auf den Spanten (4, 8, 13, 17, und 27) werden rot bemalt

Nr.	Aufschrift	Zeichnung
1	Hier unterboden	1 DoN 1656
2	Für Lagerjoch 25	2 DoN 1656
3	Druck im Federbein, Reifendruck usw.	3 DoN 1656
4	Preßluft	4 DoN 1656
5	Ottan, Grünring usw.	5 DoN 1656
6	Nicht drücken	6 DoN 1656
7	Kraftstoff Peilstab	7 DoN 1656
8	Schmierstoff Peilstab usw. (Nur 17 E)	8 DoN 1656
9	Glytol	9 DoN 1656
10	Schmierstoff Ablaß (Nur 17 E)	10 DoN 1656
11	Kraftstoff Ablaß	11 DoN 1656
12	Hier unterboden	12 DoN 1656
13	Verankerung	13 DoN 1656
14	Motor heizen	14 DoN 1656
15	Heizen	15 DoN 1656
16	Außenbordanschluß (Bodenstromquelle)	16 DoN 1656
17	Sauerstoff	17 DoN 1656
18	Leergewicht, Gesamtlast usw.	18 DoN 1656
19	Nicht betreten	19 DoN 1656
20	WE · —100	20 DoN 1656
21	Hier unterboden	21 DoN 1656
22	Fahrwerk („Ace" auffüllen)	22 DoN 1656
23	Nur „Ace"-Bremsöl einfüllen	23 DoN 1656
24	Feuerlöschmittel einfüllen	24 DoN 1656
25	Skala für Höhenflossenverstellung	25 DoN 1656
26	WE (siehe Anlage 11 Bl. 4)	26 DoN 1656
27	Schmierstoff Peilstab usw. (Nur 17 F)	27 DoN 1656
28	Schmierstoff Ablaß (Nur 17 F)	28 DoN 1656
29	Motor heizen	29 DoN 1656
30	Kraftstoff Peilstab (Nur 17 F)	7 DoN 1656
35	Rotes Kreuz	13 DoN 1637
36	Balkenkreuz	DoN 1670
40	4 5 6 usw. (Spanten)	40 DoN 1656
41	Leuchtpistole	41 DoN 1656
42	Leuchtpatronen	42 DoN 1656
43	Fahrwerk Notauslaß usw.	43 DoN 1656
44	Bei Notausstieg usw.	44 DoN 1656
45	oben	45 DoN 1656
46	Nur für Leuchtbomben	46 DoN 1656
47	Nicht betreten	47 DoN 1656
48	Nur für Leuchtbomben	48 DoN 1656
49	L R	49 DoN 1656
65	Rotes Kreuz	13 DoN 1637

Innen- und Außenbeschriftung

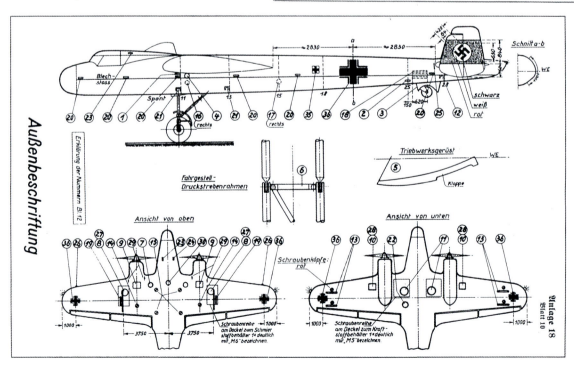

Außenbeschriftung

Anlage 18
Blatt 10

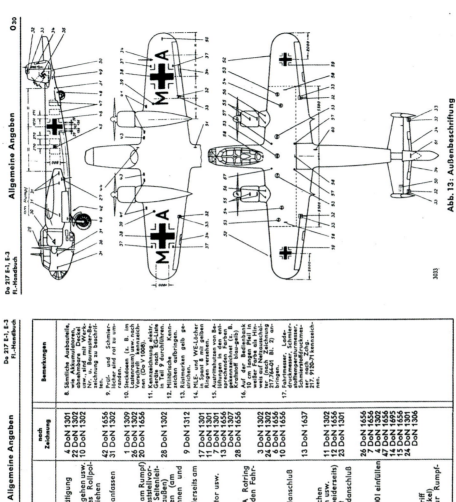

O 30

Do 217 E-1, E-3
Fl.-Handbuch

Allgemeine Angaben

Abb. 13: Außenbeschriftung

Key to internal and external stencilling on Do 217 E-1, E-3 as per aircraft handbook.

O 29

Do 217 E-1, E-3
Fl.-Handbuch

Allgemeine Angaben

Lfd. Nr.	Aufschrift	nach Zeichnung	Bemerkungen
22	Bombenklappenbetätigung	4 DoN 1301	8. Sämtliche Ausbauteile, wie Akkumulatoren, abnehmbare Deckel usw., sind mit Werk-Nr. u. Baumuster-Bezeichnung zu beschriften.
23	Handgriff	22 DoN 1302	
24	Vorsicht nachhintengehen usw.	10 DoN 1302	
25	Vor Betätigung des Rollpolsters Okular einziehen		
26	Leuchtpatronen	42 DoN 1656	9. Prüf- und Schmierlöcher sind rot zu umranden.
27	Antennenstab nicht anfassen	31 DoN 1302	
28	Nicht betreten	1 DoN 1309	10. Steckdosen (z. B. im Lastenraum) usw. nach Vorschrift kennzeichnen. (Do V 1008).
29	87	20 DoN 1302	
30	WE-100 (beiderseits am Rumpf)	20 DoN 1656	
31	Kennzeichen für Feststellvorrichtungen (am Seitenleitwerk innen und außen)		11. Kennzeichnung elektr. Geräte nach EG-Liste in Teil 9 durchführen.
32		28 DoN 1302	12. Militärische Kennzeichen aufbringen.
33	Feststellvorrichtung (am Seitenleitwerk innen und außen)	9 DoN 1312	13. Rüstmarken gelb gestrichen.
34	Nicht anfassen (beiderseits am Trimmruder)	17 DoN 1301	14. MLE- und WE-Löcher in Spant 8 mit gelben Ringen versehen.
35	Hoheitszeichen	11 DoN 1301	15. Austrittshutzen von Belüftungen in den entsprechenden Farben gekennzeichnet (z. B. Kraftstoff blau-gelb)
36	Zurück um den Motor usw.	7 DoN 1301	
37	Balkenkreuz	13 DoN 1656	
38		1 DoN 1307	
39	Schmierstoffablaß	28 DoN 1656	16. Auf der Bedienbank 10 cm langen Pfeil in weißer Farbe als Hinweis auf Netzauschalter (nach Zeichnung 217.7264-01 Bl. 2) anbringen.
40	Oktan 87 INTAVA Rotring usw. (außen an den Fahrgestellklappen)	3 DoN 1302	
41	Schrauben 6 x 28	24 DoN 1302	
42	Nicht drücken	6 DoN 1656	
43	Hier unterbocken	10 DoN 1656	17. Fahrtmesser, Ladedruckmesser, Schmierstofftemperaturmesser, Schmierstoffdruckmesser nach Zeichnung 217. 9120-71 kennzeichnen.
44	Elektr. Außenbordanschluß (rechts)		
45	Rotes Kreuz	13 DoN 1637	
46	Balkenkreuz		
47	Raum für Kennzeichen	11 DoN 1302	
48	Druck im Federbein usw.	12 DoN 1656	
49	Hier unterbocken (beiderseits)	23 DoN 1301	
50	Isolierlack gespritzt		
51	Sauerstoffaußenbordanschluß (rechts)		
52	WE	26 DoN 1656	
53	Kraftstoff-Peilstab	7 DoN 1656	
54	INTAVA Rotring 2001 einfüllen	4 DoN 1302	
55	Nicht betreten	47 DoN 1656	
56	Motor heißen	14 DoN 1695	
57	Heißen	15 DoN 1656	
58	Nur hier betreten	24 DoN 1301	
59	Balkenkreuz	DoN 1306	
60	Roter Hand-Drehgriff (Schlauchbootdeckel)		
61	Nicht betreten (nur Rumpfendkappe)		

3033

O 28

Do 217 E-1, E-3
Fl.-Handbuch

Allgemeine Angaben

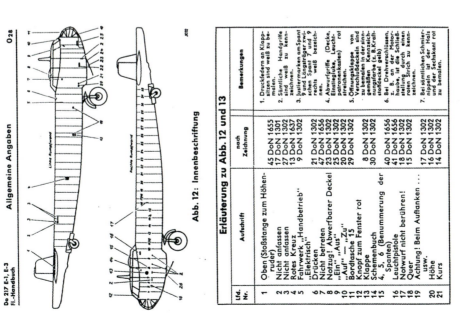

Abb. 12: Innenbeschriftung

Lfd. Nr.	Aufschrift	nach Zeichnung	Bemerkungen
1	Oben (Stoßstange zum Höhenruder)	45 DoN 1655	1. Druckfedern an Klappsitzen sind weiß zu bemalen.
2	Nicht anfassen	17 DoN 1301	
3	Nicht anfassen	27 DoN 1302	2. Sämtliche Handgriffe sind weiß zu kennzeichnen.
4	Rotes Kreuz	13 DoN 1637	
5	Fahrwerk „Handbetrieb" „Elektrisch"	9 DoN 1302	3. Jusiermarken am Spant 9 und Längsträger zwischen Spant 7 und 9 rechts weiß bezeichnen.
6	Drücken	21 DoN 1302	
7	Nicht betreten	47 DoN 1656	
8	Notzug! Abwerfbarer Deckel	23 DoN 1302	4. Abwurfklappe (Decke, Einstiegluke, Leuchtpatronenkasten) rot streichen.
9	„Ein" „Aus"	25 DoN 1302	
10	„Auf" „Zu"	20 DoN 1302	
11	Bordflasche 15	29 DoN 1302	5. Öffnungsklappe von Verschlußdeckeln sind zu bemalen. Kennzeichnungen gemäß Kennzeichnungsfarbe (s. a. Kraftstoffdeckel gelb)
12	Knopf zum Fenster rot		
13	Klappe	8 DoN 1302	
14	Schemenbuch	30 DoN 1302	
15	4, 5, 6 (Benummerung der Spanten)		6. Bei Drehverschlüssen, z. B. an der Motorhaube, ist die Schließstellung durch einen roten Strich zu kennzeichnen.
16	Leuchtpistole	40 DoN 1656	
17	Notwurf nicht berühren!	41 DoN 1656	
18	Nur hier betreten	15 DoN 1302	
19	Quer		7. Bei sämtlichen Schmiernippeln ist der Hals und der Sechskant rot zu bemalen.
19	Achtung! Beim Aufflanken ... usw.		
20	Höhe	17 DoN 1302	
21	Kurs	14 DoN 1302	

Erläuterung zu Abb. 12 und 13

415

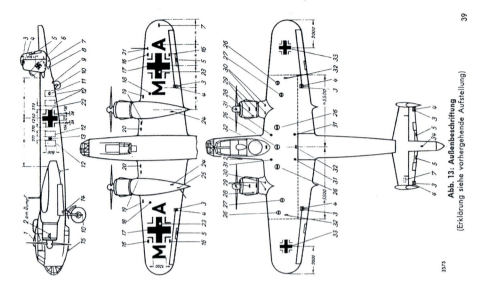

39

Abb. 13: Außenbeschriftung
(Erklärung siehe vorhergehende Aufstellung)

3575

Key to internal and external stencilling on Do 217 E-3 and E-4 as per aircraft handbook.

c) Außenbeschriftung (folg. Aufstellung und Abbildung)
Vgl. auch „d" Bemerkungen".

Nr. auf Abb.13	I	II	Mi	re	Aufschrift	Ort	Nach Zeichnung
1				1	Nicht betreten	Astralon-Haube über E-Peilrahmen	1 DoN 1309
2	1				Oktan 87	Rumpfvorderteil	26 DoN 1302
3	1			1	Feststellvorrichtung	Seitenleitwerk oben	9 DoN 1312
4	1			1	Kennzeichnung für Feststellvorrichtung	Seitenleitwerk oben	28 DoN 1302
5	1				Nicht anfassen	Seitenhilfsruder	17 DoN 1301
6	1				Hoheitszeichen	Seitenflosse	11 DoN 1301
7				1	isolierlack gespritzt		23 DoN 1301
8	1				Hier unterbocken	Spant 34 unten	12 DoN 1656
9	1			1	Druck im Federbein	bei Spant 34 unten	10 DoN 1312
10	1				Reifenrutschmarken	Sporn- u. Laufräder	10 DoN 1312
11	1				Hier anheben	Spant 29	13 DoN 1312
12	1				Raum für Kenn-zeichen	siehe Bemaßung in Abb. 13	—
13	1				Rotes Kreuz	Zwisch.Spant 23 u.24	13 DoN 1637
14	1				Oktan 87, Intava Rotring usw.	Fahrgestellklappen außen	3 DoN 1312
15				1	Zurück, um den Motor usw.	Einstiegluke innen und außen	7 DoN 1301
16	2				Verankerung	Außenfläche Außenfl.	13 DoN 1656
17	1				Balkenkreuz	Unterseite Außenfl.	DoN 1307
18	2				Schmierstoff-Ablaß	Unterseite Außenfl.	28 DoN 1656
19	2				Schraubenlänge 6 x 28	Unterseite Außen-fläche	24 DoN 1302
20	1				Hier unterbocken	Querriegel I — Vor-derholm	10 DoN 1656
21	1				Nicht anfassen	bei Staurohrmast	17 DoN 1301
22	1				Balkenkreuz	siehe Bemaßung in Abb. 13	—
23	1				Abreißen bei An-bau	Außenfläche Unter-seite	12 DoN 1312
24							
25	2	1			Antennenmast nicht anfassen	Rechte Motorgondel	31 DoN 1302
26	2	1			Kraftstoffpeilstab	Hauptbehälterköpfe (Kraftstoff)	7 DoN 1656
27	1				Intava Rotring nur 200 l einfüllen	Über Schmierstoff-behälter	4 DoN 1302
28	1				P₁, P₂	Auf Kraftstoff-För-derpumpe und Zu-führungsschläuchen	1 DoN 1312
29	2				Nicht betreten	Auf Motorgondel-oberseite	47 DoN 1656
30	2				Motor heißen	Auf innerer Strö-mungsverkleidung (Oberseite)	14 DoN 1695
31	2				Heißen	Querriegel I	15 DoN 1656
32	2				Nur hier betreten	Flächenoberseite	24 DoN 1301
33	1	1			Balkenkreuz	Außenfläche Obers.	DoN 1306
34				1	Nicht betreten	Rumpfendkappe	1 DoN 1309

38

b) Innenbeschriftung (folg. Aufstellung mit Abbildung)
Vergleiche auch „d" Bemerkungen".

Nr. auf Abb.12	I	II	Mi	re	Aufschrift	Ort	Nach Zeichnung
1	1				Nicht anfassen	bei Spant 28	27 DoN 1302
2	1				Drücken	Spant 12	21 DoN 1302
3	1				Notzug für abwerf-bare Glaskuppel	B-Stand	8 DoN 1312
4	1				Handgriff	bei Spant 11/12	
5	1			1	Fahrwerkhandkurbel	am Spant 10	5 DoN 1312
6				1	Reserve-Munition	am Spant 9½	6 DoN 1312
7	1				Elt. Wartungsunter-lagen	bei Spant 10	
8	1				Leuchtpistole	oben bei Spant 9	41 DoN 1656
9		1			MG-Bordtasche	bei Spant 9	29 DoN 1302
10	1				Klappe	bei Spant 4 (Bedien-bank)	8 DoN 1302
11	1				MG-Bordtasche	im Rumpfbug	29 DoN 1302
12	1				„Auf — Zu"	im Rumpfbug	20 DoN 1302
13	1				Vorsicht nach hinten gehen ... usw.	auf Einstiegluke	10 DoN 1302
14	1				Handgriff	an der Einstiegluke	22 DoN 1302
15	1				Objektivbelüftung, Auf, Zu	am Spant 10	4 DoN 1312
16	1				Quer	am Spant 12	15 DoN 1302
17	1				Höhe	am Spant 12	16 DoN 1302
18	1				Kurs	am Spant 12	14 DoN 1302
19				2	Achtung! Beim Auf-tanken ... usw.	am Spant 14 und 16	17 DoN 1302
20	1				Notzug! Abwerf-barer Deckel	Führerraumdecke	23 DoN 1302
21				1	Notwurf nicht be-rühren	bei Spant 17	18 DoN 1302
22	4				Nicht anfassen	Rumpfvorderteil	17 DoN 1301
23	1				Leuchtpistole	bei Spant 6	41 DoN 1656
24				1	4, 5, 6, 7 ...	Spantbenummerung	40 DcN 1656

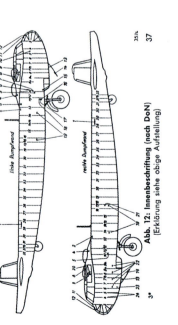

357a

Abb. 12: Innenbeschriftung (nach DoN)
(Erklärung siehe obige Aufstellung)

3*

37

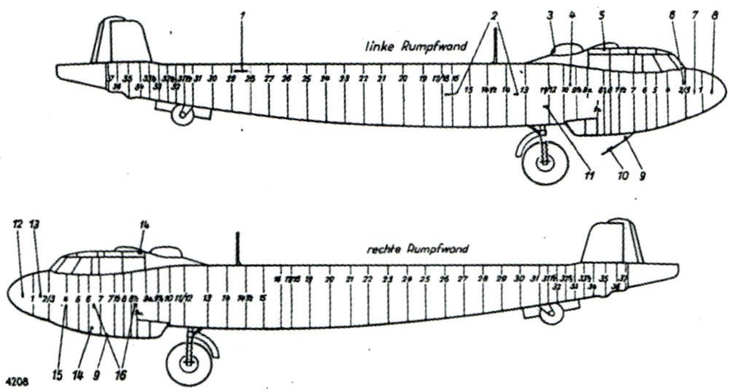

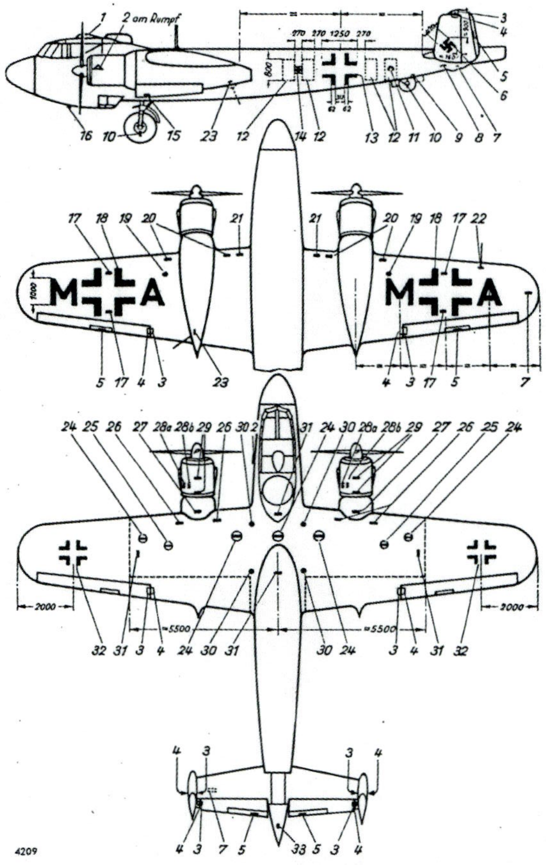

Abb. 13: Außenbeschriftung
(Erklärung siehe vorhergehende Aufstellung)

c. Außenbeschriftung (folg. Aufstellung und Abbildung)

Vgl. auch „d) Bemerkungen", wo sich auch Angaben über Anstrichmittel finden.

Nr. auf Abb.13	li	Mi	re	Aufschrift	Ort	Nach Zeichnung
1	1	—		Nicht betreten	Astralon-Haube über E-Peilrahmen	1 DoN 1309
2		1		Oktan 87	Rumpfvorderteil	26 DoN 1302
3		1		Festtellvorrichtung	Seitenleitwerk oben	9 DoN 1312
4		1		Kennzeichnung für Festtellvorrichtung	Seitenleitwerk oben	28 DoN 1302
5		1		Nicht anfassen	Seitenhilfsruder	17 DoN 1301
6		1		Hoheitszeichen	Seitenflosse	11 DoN 1301
7		1		Isolierlack gespritzt		23 DoN 1301
8		1		Hier unterbocken	Spant 34 unten	12 DoN 1656
9		1		Druck im Federbein	bei Spant 34 unten	12 DoN 1312
10		1		Reifenrutschmarken	Sporn- und Laufräder	10 DoN 1312
11		1		Hier anheben	Spant 29	13 DoN 1312
12		1		Raum für Kennzeichen	siehe Bemaßung in Abb. 13	—
13		1		Balkenkreuz	Unterseite Außenfläche	—
14		1		Rotes Kreuz	Zwischen Spant 23 und 24	13 DoN 1637

Nr. auf Abb.13	li	Mi	re	Aufschrift	Ort	Nach Zeichnung
15		1		Oktan 87, Intava Rotring usw.	Fahrgestellklappen außen	3 DoN 1312
16	—	1		Zurück, um den Motor usw.	Einstiegluke innen und außen	7 DoN 1301
17		2		Verankerung	Außenfläche Unterseite	13 DoN 1656
18		1		Balkenkreuz	Unterseite Außenfläche	DoN 1307
19		1		Schmierstoff-Ablaß		28 DoN 1656
20		2		Schraubenlänge 6 × 28	Unterseite Außenfläche	24 DoN 1302
21		1		Hier unterbocken	Querriegel I — Vorderholm	1 DoN 1314
22		1		Nicht anfassen	bei Staurohrmast	17 DoN 1301
23		2		Antennenmast nicht anfassen	Rechte Motorgondel	31 DoN 1302
24		2		Kraftstoffpeilstab	Hauptbehälter-köpfe (Kraftstoff)	7 DoN 1656
25		1		Intava Rotring nur 200 l einfüllen	Über Schmierstoffbehälter	4 DoN 1302
26		2		Motor heißen	Auf innerer Strömungsverkleidung (Oberseite)	14 DoN 1695
27		1		Drücken	Unterseite Motorgondel	21 DoN 1302
28a	1			P_2	Auf Kraftstofförderpumpe u. Zuführungsschläuchen	1 DoN 1312
28b	—			P_1		
29		2		Nicht betreten	Auf Motorgondeloberseite	47 DoN 1656
30		2		Heißen	Querriegel I	15 DoN 1656
31	2	1		Nur hier betreten	Flächenoberseite	24 DoN 1301
32		1		Balkenkreuz	Außenfläche Oberseite	DoN 1306
33	—	1		Nicht betreten	Rumpfendkappe	1 DoN 1309

Abb. 12: Innenbeschriftung (nach DoN)
(Erklärung siehe obige Aufstellung)

Nr. auf Abb.12	li	Mi	re	Aufschrift	Ort	Nach Zeichnung
1	1		1	„Nicht anfassen"	Spant 28—29 oben	27 DoN 1302
2		2		„Achtung! Beim Auftanken" usw.	Vorn an den Zusatzbehältern	17 DoN 1302
3		1		„Notzug für abwerfbare Glaskuppel"	Oben am B-Stand	8 DoN 1312
4		1		„Reserve-Munitionskasten"	Rechts, unterhalb der Hauptschalttafel	6 DoN 1312
5		1		„Notzug! Abwerfbarer Deckel"	Führerraumdecke	23 DoN 1302
6		1		„Klappe"	Links an der Bordwand	8 DoN 1302
7		1		„Links hinten"	Zwischen Spant 1 und 2 links	5 DoN 1314
8		1		„Links vorn"	Vor Spant 1 links	4 DoN 1314
9		1		„Handgriff"	Innen auf der Einstiegluke	22 DoN 1302
10		1		„Vorsicht! Nach hinten gehen" usw.	Innen auf der Einstiegluke	10 DoN 1302
11		1		„Kurs"	Bei Spant 11 links	14 DoN 1302
12		1		„Rechts vorn"	Vor Spant 1 rechts	22 DoN 1314
13		1		„Rechts hinten"	Zwischen Spant 1 und 2 rechts	3 DoN 1314
14		1		„Leuchtpistole"	—	14 DoN 1656
15		42		Spantbenummerung („1" „2" usw.)	Oben am Spant 9	40 DoN 1656
16			2	„Nicht anfassen"	Bei Spant 6 und 8 rechts	17 DoN 1301

*) Für andere Einsätze können selbstverständlich andere Sichtschutzanstriche nach Vorschrift aufgebracht werden. Zum Beispiel nach Zeichnung 8—217 N Bl. 10.

Key to internal and external stencilling on Do 17 J as per aircraft handbook.

b. Innenbeschriftung (folgende Aufstellung mit Abbildung 13)
Vgl. auch „d. Bemerkungen", wo sich Angaben über Anstrichmittel finden.

Nr. auf Abb. 13	li	mi	re	Aufschrift	Ort	Nach Zeichnung
1	1	1		„Nicht anfassen"	auf Stoßstangen bei Spant 28 bis 29 oben	28 DoN 1302
2		2		„Achtung! Beim Auftanken" usw.	Vorn an den Zusatzbehältern	17 DoN 1302
3	1		1	„Leuchtpistole"	Oben am B-Stand	8 DoN 1312
4	1			„Notzug für abwerfbare Glaskuppel"	Am Schloßträger rechts und links	23 DoN 1302
5		2		Transportwanne für Bordsack	Fuhrerraumdecke	
6	1			„Notzug! Abwerfbarer Deckel"	Links an der Bordwand	8 DoN 1302
7	1			„Klappe"	Zwischen Spant 1 u. 2 links	5 DoN 1314
8	1			„Links hinten"	Vor Spant 1 links	4 DoN 1314
9	1			„Links vorn"	Innen auf der Einstiegluke	22 DoN 1302
10	1			„Handgriff"	Innen auf der Einstiegluke	10 DoN 1302
11	1			„Vorsicht! Nach hinten gehen" usw.		
12	1			„Kurs"		14 DoN 1656
13		1		„Rechts vorn"	Vor Spant 1 rechts	2 DoN 1314
14		2		„Rechts hinten"	Zwischen Spant 1 u. 2 rechts	3 DoN 1314
	2			„Leuchtpistole"	Oben am Spant 9 u. 2 unten am Spant 6	41 DoN 1656
15			42	Spantenbenummerung („1", „2" usw.)		40 DoN 1656
16	2			„Nicht anfassen"	Bei Spant 6 u. 8 rechts	17 DoN 1301
17	1			„Kurbel für Bombenklappe"	zw. Spant 8 u. 9 links	
18	2			„Links"	auf Gurkasten links	
19		1		„Rechts unten"	auf Gurkasten rechts	
20	1			„Rechts mitte"	auf Gurkasten rechts	
21		1		„Rechts oben"	auf Gurkasten rechts	
22	1			„Für Funkgerät"	auf Handkurbel en Spant 9 ½	
23		1		„Achtung! Bei Beschuß usw."	am Drehkranz	
24		1		„Achtung! Bei gezurrter Waffe usw."	am Drehkranz	2 DoN 1313
25			1	„LRO"	zw. Spant 3 u. 4	3 DoN 1313
26			1	„LRu"	zw. Spant 3 u. 4	

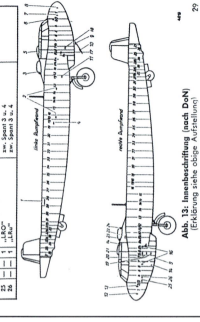

Abb. 13: Innenbeschriftung (nach DoN)
(Erklärung siehe obige Aufstellung)

linke Rumpfwand

rechte Rumpfwand

Key to internal stencilling on Do 217 N as per aircraft handbook.

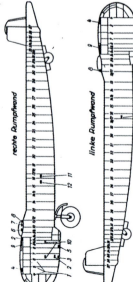

Abb. 14: Außenbeschriftung
(Erklärung siehe vorhergehende Aufstellung)

Key to internal and external stencilling on Do 217 M as per aircraft handbook.

---

b. **Innenbeschriftung.**

Anstrichmittel: Für Not, Gefahr, Schmierung: Kennzeichnungsfarbe Ton 23 (rot).
Für alles übrige: Kennzeichnungsfarbe 2401/77 (grau).

Lfd. Nr.	li	Ort mi	re	Aufschrift	Nach Zeichnung
1		1	1	„4", „5", „6" usw. (Benummerung der Spanten)	40 DoN 1656
2		1		„Leuchtpistole"	41 DoN 1656
3		1		„Handgriff"	22 DoN 1302
4		1		„Notzug"	1 DoN 1313
5		1		„Vorsicht! Nach hinten gehen" usw.	10 DoN 1302
6		1		„Achtung! Beim Schließen" usw.	2 DoN 1313
7		1		„Notzug für abwerfbare Glaskuppel"	8 DoN 1312
8		1		„Notzug! Abwerfbarer Deckel"	3 DoN 1313
9		1		„Achtung! Bei gezurrter Waffe" usw.	23 DoN 1302
10		1		„Nicht anfassen"	17 DoN 1301
11		1		„Sämtliche Schrauben" usw.	4 DoN 1313
12		1		„Vor Abnahme" usw.	5 DoN 1313

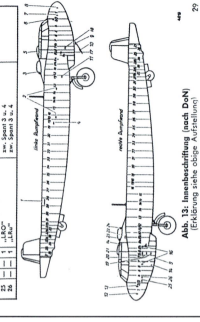

Abb. 13: Innenbeschriftung (nach DoN)
(Erklärung siehe obige Aufstellung)

rechte Rumpfwand

linke Rumpfwand

c. **Außenbeschriftung** (Abb. 14)

Anstrichmittel: Siehe unter „b. Innenbeschriftung".

Lfd. Nr.	li	Ort mi	re	Aufschrift	Nach Zeichnung
1		1		„Nicht betreten"	1 DoN 1309
2		1		„87"	26 DoN 1302
3		1		„Feststellvorrichtung"	18 DoN 1301
4		1		Kennzeichen für Feststellvorrichtungen	28 DoN 1301
5		1		„Nicht anfassen"	17 DoN 1301
6		1		Hoheitzeichen	11 DoN 1301
7	Versch. Stellen			„Hier unterbocken"	12 DoN 1656
8	Versch. Stellen			„Druck im Federbein"	2 DoN 1312
9		1		Reifenrutschmarkierung	10 DoN 1312
10		1		„Hier anheben"	13 DoN 1312
11		1		Raum für Kennzeichen	
12		1		Siehe „d" Bemerkungen	13 DoN 1637
13		1		Rotes Kreuz	3 DoN 1312
14		1		„Oktan 87 INTAVA-Rotring usw."	7 DoN 1301
15		1		„Zurück um in den Motor"	13 DoN 1307
16		1		„Verankerung"	13 DoN 1307
17		1		Balkenkreuz	28 DoN 1302
18	Versch. Stellen			„Schmierstoffablaß"	24 DoN 1302
19	Versch. Stellen			„Schraubenlänge 6 x 28"	1 DoN 1312
20		1		„Hier unterbocken"	1 DoN 1302
21		1		„Feststellvorrichtung"	7 DoN 1656
22		1		„Antennenstab nicht anfassen"	3 DoN 1302
23		1		„INTAVA-Rotring nur 200 l einfüllen"	14 DoN 1695
24		1		„Motor heißen"	21 DoN 1302
25		1		„Nicht betreten"	13 DoN 1302
26		1		„Drücken"	47 DoN 1656
27		1		„Achtung! Höhenruder 217.358 nur . . ."	13 DoN 1656
28		1		„Achtung! Bei Verschieben" usw.	32 DoN 1302
29		4		„Heißen"	28 DoN 1656
30				„Nur hier betreten" usw.	32 DoN 1656
31		1		Balkenkreuz	3 DoN 1302
32	Versch. Stellen			„Kühlstoff ablassen"	15 DoN 1656
33		1		„Heißen"	15 DoN 1656
34		1		„Kühlstoff auffüllen"	15 DoN 1304

Identification of each metal type was done by means of numerical codes, marked usually on the inside surfaces of all classes of aircraft; this identified the type and grade of metal. A system of four numbers followed by a period (full stop), and then a single number (i.e., 0000.0) was marked on each piece of metal, usually in black, but sometimes in white or red. While this was normally on the inside surface, late in the war the RLM issued an instruction stating that cutting metal parts just to ensure conformity with this aspect of the regulation was not necessary (saving time in labour and materials). In addition, even though the marking (applied with paint) could bleed through the surface of the very thin lacquers by then in use, it was not cause for complaint from the end user. However, E-Stelle Travemünde was to be informed of those sub-manufacturers whose paints bled through the final finish, so that they could be advised to use a different (more stable) form of paint for marking. While the numerical code marking often appeared on its own, it was not uncommon for the manufacturer's identity to be marked as well, sometimes with the company initials, or sometimes with the company logo. The intention was clear, but some materials with unstable markings had continued to slip through and the bleed marks were seen in some instances.

Divided into three major groups, the class of metal was identified by the first digit in the four-digit group – **1** for Stahl (steel), **2** for Schwermetall (heavy metal), **3** for Leichtmetall (light metal). Each major group was broken into sub-groups that identified specific types of metal within the parent group, numbering running from 0 to 9, though not all numbers were used in each sub-group. Group 1 had eight sub-divisions, Group 2 six and Group 3 five. Numbering commenced from 0 (not 1). Each sub-group was further divided into numbered categories depending on specific characteristics, the system continuing in this manner to provide the full four-digit identification. While some terms appear to be simple repeats of previous ones, the degree of alloy composition or treatment varied, requiring the numerical distinction.

1- Steel
0 - carbon steel, unalloyed.
1 - carbon steel, ratio to aged steel.
2 - basic alloyed steel.
4 - compound alloyed steel.
5 - compound alloyed steel.
6 - compound alloyed steel.
8 - cast steel.
9 - cast steel.

2 - Heavy metal
0 - without copper alloying.
1 - brass (hard and pressure formed).
2 - special pressing.
3 - aluminium, lead bronze.
4 - special bronze.
5 - white metal.

3 - Light metal
0 - pure aluminium.
1 - aluminium - copper -magnesium Duraluminium.
2 - aluminium - silveralloy silumin.
3 - aluminium - magnesium Hydronalium.
5 - magnesium - alloy Elektron.

The fifth digit, the last number after the period mark, indicated the status of the semi-finished material for delivery. The numbers 0 to 9 flagged pre-treatment of the semi-finished material and provided information as to whether the material was treated, hardened or heat-treated, or cold worked. Since the physical properties essentially were changed by thermal treatment of the material, great importance was to be attached to the correct specification of the code marking.

From the following table it is evident that again, as the quality of the material rose so did the status number value.

1 - Steel
0 - without additional treatment.
1 - annealed.
2 - annealed.
3 - annealed.
4 - hardened in addition to tempered.
5 - hardened in addition to tempered.
6 - hardened in addition to tempered.
7 - cold hardened.
8 - cold hardened.
9 - after specific treatment.

2 - Heavy Metal
0 - without additional treatment.
1 - annealed.
2 - ————
3 - ————
4 - externally hardened.
5 - externally hardened and cold hardened.
6 - externally hardened and cold hardened.
7 - cold hardened.
8 - cold hardened.
9 - after specific treatment.

3 - Light metal
0 - without additional treatment.
1 - annealed.
2 - annealed and treated.
3 - ————
4 - externally hardened.
5 - externally hardened and treated.
6 - externally hardened and cold hardened.
7 - cold hardened.
8 - cold hardened.
9 – after specific treatment.

Luftwaffe aircraft carried a host of such materials markings, often marked only a few centimetres apart, sometimes almost touching in a continuous stream, indicating that a roller, etched with the relevant marking had been used, rather than individual stamps. The markings were sometimes interspersed with company logo markings, but in most instances, just lines of numerical code groups appeared.

1 M. Pegg research.
2 P. Cohausz research.

ABOVE: The crew access ladder on the Bf 110 G was stored in the fuselage and could be extended by pressing a button and pulling the ladder down. The marking is in 22 black on the 76-coloured background. It reads **Einsteigleiter Knopf drücken** (Boarding Ladder. Press Button) and has a black arrow pointing down. Note also the fuselage frame numbers marked in black. (Steve Haggard)

BELOW LEFT AND BELOW: Port and starboard detail of the wing root radiator flap marking on Bf 109 G W.Nr. 613824. In each case **Klappen Ausschlag auf = 220mm begrenzt** (flap deflection out = 220mm limit) has been hand painted in 22 white, and by the same person. Note the mistake on the port flap (left), the 'auf' in the wording having been added afterwards. Official colour code standard for such markings were becoming increasingly difficult to comply with in the last months of the war within the aircraft rebuilding factories, as shown here.

LEFT: A section of an Me 210 fuselage showing the oxygen filler point (on left) with its blue and white markings and the hand hold just below the rear canopy marked **Hier eingrieffen** in black. The dark square forward of the gun barbette is black with white lettering which reads

> **Vor dem Start -**
> **auf O-Stellung der Höhen**
> **flossen achten Hydr.-**
> **Schalter für Sturzflug**
> **"Ein,, betätigen**

(Before take-off check horizontal stabilizer is in O-position, hydraulic selector for dive brakes set "on").

The gun barbette is marked with six rows of lettering, the centre two being larger, in 23 red.

> **Vor Aufsetzen der Verkleidung**
> **Zündstromschalter "Ein,,!**
>
> **Zum Nachfüllen der Preßluft**
> **Verkleidung abnehmen**
>
> **Bei Abnehmen der Verkleidung**
> **Zündstromschalter "Aus,,!**

(Before replacing fairing electrical switch "On"! To refill compressed air remove fairing. Upon removing fairing electrical switch "Off"! (MBB Archiv via R. Lutz)

RIGHT: Detail of the oxygen filler point marking on Me 163 B W.Nr. 191907. It can be seen that an oval shaped stencil has been used first for the 24 blue background with a second stencil for the two 21 white horizontal lines and the word **Sauerstoff**. Note that the marking **Oel u. Fettfrei halten** (oil and fat free) has been painted in white by hand, resulting in **Fett** and **Frei** running into each other because of lack of space. (RAAF)

RIGHT: The oil filler marking on the engine cowling of this Ar 68 F-1 was identified by a brown triangle, outlined in white. Each of the fasteners on the cowling panels had a thin red line marked across them, parallel to the line of flight, to identify the locked position. The black oblong marking on the inside of the wheel spat carried instructions for removal of the wheel. The small panel on the outside of the spat provided access to the tyre filling point and is marked **federbeindruck 2 atü** (air pressure 2 atmospheres). (H. Obert)

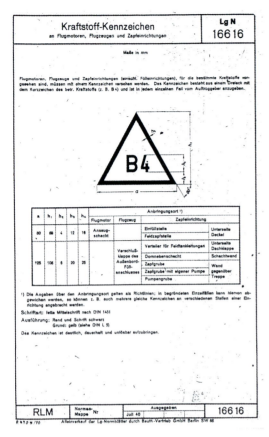

ABOVE: The July 1940 RLM diagram Lg N 16616 Kraftstoff-Kennzeichen setting out marking dimensions and colours for fuel points; B4 grade is shown here, but dimensions and colours were identical for other grades of fuel. Note the cross-references to DIN L 5 and DIN 1451 diagrams, which are included in this Appendix.

ABOVE: Typical of the fuel marking triangles used on all Luftwaffe piston-powered aircraft is this 87 octane fuel marking on a Bf 109 F. The triangle was a standard shape with 04-yellow centre and white edging. Usually the fuel identification was marked in black, but sometimes, when the entire marking was applied by stencil, the background camouflage colouring was used for the marking. (F. Grabowski)

LEFT: Fuel and oil markings can be seen on this Ju 87 D or G. Directly beneath the cockpit is a fuel marking triangle with 'E 87' marked in it. The same proportions and colouring were used as in the previous photographic example. The triangle just below the open access panel in front of the windscreen was for the oil, and carried the identification details in three lines of yellow (ASM, Rotring, ATAV 100) on a brown background edged in yellow.

BELOW: This Ju 87 D shows several standard markings. Just visible is **NICHT HIER BETRETEN** in 22 black on the inboard flap section, but it is almost lost against the dark green background. Note the non-slip wing walk is edged with a solid 23 red border instead of the more usual 20 mm long oblongs of colour. On the fuselage is the filler point for the oxygen bottles - marked in 24 blue with two 21 white lines across the panel. To the left of it is the electrical socket marked with '**24V**' in white to the right, and with its electrical circuit code '**A4**' marked in white to the left. On the armour plate below the front cockpit a white-edged 04 yellow triangle, bearing a black '**E**' over an '**87**', marks the fuel tank filler point and grade of fuel to be used. The radio mast has a red section marked with white lettering, **VORSICHT. Nicht Anfassen.** (CAUTION. Do not touch). (MBB Archiv via R. Lutz)

ABOVE: The oil cooler carries the white inscription
**Filtereinsatz nach zwei Starts
ausbauen u. reiningen Filter in
Oel tauchen, abtropfen lassen
u. wieder einbauen.**
(Remove and clean filter insert after two take-offs, dip filter in oil, let it drain and replace again).
(MBB Archiv via R. Lutz)

BELOW: Ground staff of JG 53, checking over the engine of a Bf 109 E, reveal some of the internal piping runs. The red oblong-shaped marking on the spinner indicated the correct joint alignment position for the back-plate of the spinner.

BELOW: The lower elements of radar aerials were usually marked with alternating stripes of 21 white and 23 red to prevent damage from equipment or personnel while on the ground. (S. Haggard)

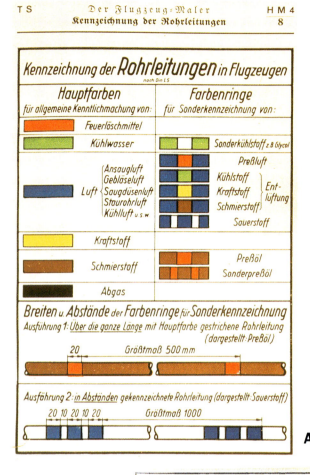

DOCUMENT A: The official markings chart for internal piping runs and external points established by the DIN L5 of March 1935.

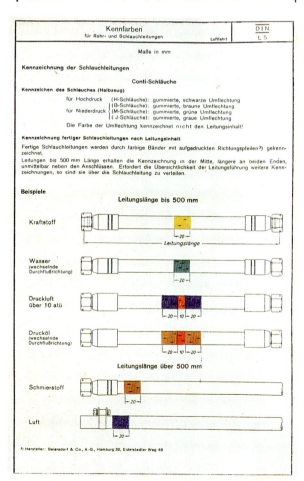

DOCUMENT B: The first chart as shown above was revised and replaced by the four-page issue (Document B), reflecting the changes to technology. Note that colours were now specified by their RAL code.
(JaPo)

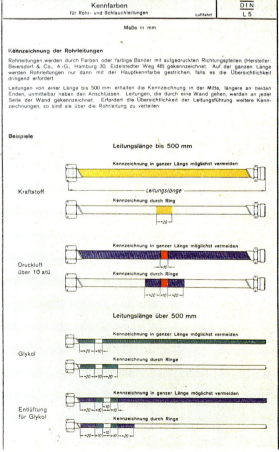

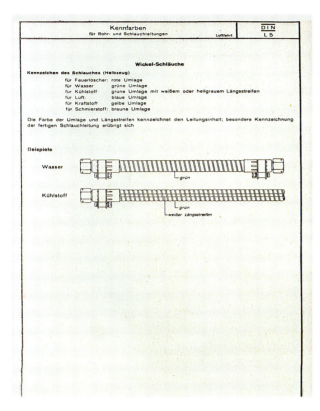

B

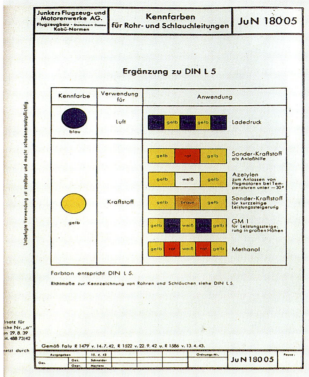

C

C

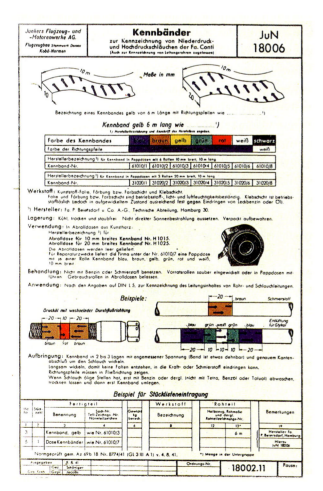

C

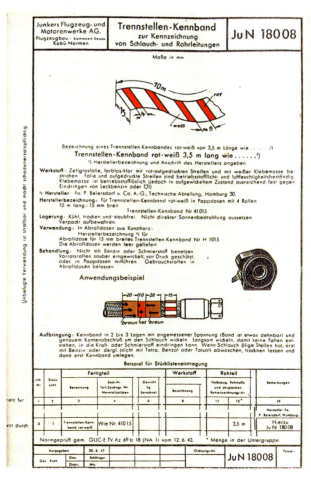

DOCUMENT C: Individual companies also issued their own internal documentation based on the L5 standard. These three samples of Junkers company documents start with a repeat of the basic L5 chart; the JuN 18005 15 April 1943 revision of the 29 August 1939 issue, which included markings for the new engine boosting mixtures (note the mistake in the use of yellow instead of white for the middle band of the Methanol marking); the JuN 18006 colour marking code for low and high pressure flexible hose markings; and finally the JuN 18008 chart of 20 June 1942 spacing markings for colour coding of flexible and metal pipes. (JaPo)

LEFT: Lettering was regulated under the German Standards DIN 1451. The Junkers Flugzeug- und Motorenwerke AG chart JuN 10102 of 18 August 1937 set out the style and measurements to be used when applying lettering. (JaPo)

RIGHT: Page two of the document, HgN 10151, revised and issued in November 1940, illustrating how to set out the lettering and numbers on a standard grid to guide the construction of company stencils. (JaPo)

BELOW LEFT AND RIGHT: Two pages from the October 1943 edition of DIN 1451 showing the changes to lettering that had occurred since the first edition, including a graphed layout. (JaPo)

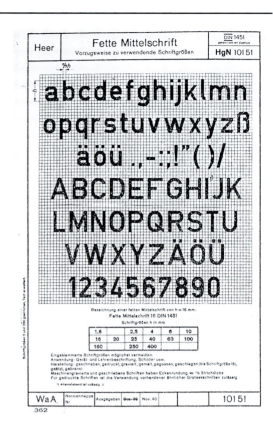

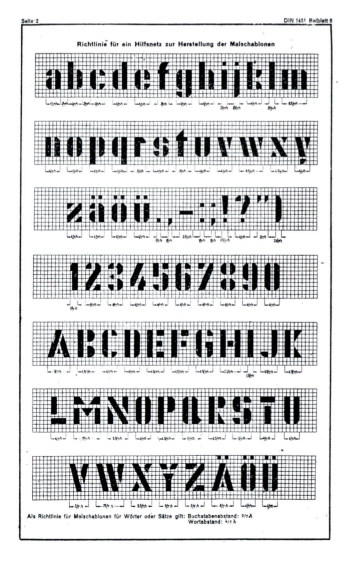

BELOW: The interior of the rear section of Me 262 W.Nr. 500200, 'Black X', held by the Australian War Memorial. The bare metal sheeting has barely any markings, just a blurred application bottom left, giving the usual 3116.5 information, with a manufacturers' logo. On the right-hand side the metal surface has been used to mark information by hand, 3010.455, possibly relating to equipment data. The D/F compass aerial motor, mounted under the top section was painted in the same dark green colour that was used for some cockpit interiors late in the war. The motor unit has its identifying number, 'AAG16', hand painted in white. The zinc chromate coated structure in the foreground was the mount for the master compass. The yellow-coloured wiring looms on the right were marked at regular intervals with small colour coded sections, part of the vertically mounted radio equipment board and its fittings can be seen on the right. The wiring on the left of the photograph connected to the adjustable tail incidence electric motor.

ABOVE: Looking aft from the battery tray installation, the duraluminium skin of the repaired section of the fuselage carries the grade of metal marking 'OKD 3116.5' marking in 22 black. The OKD marking identified the supplier of the metal sheet – (this was not the three-letter security code used on equipment and airframes, but rather the company logo identification). The last frame visible carries the production marking 109 100 1707. The radio equipment fitting at the top right has its circuit identity, F102, hand painted in 23 red on its dark green paintwork. This is the same dark green that began to replace regulation 66 in some very late war production aircraft as noted for the Me 163 B.

ABOVE: This sheet of 3116.5 Cu 30 (copper magnesium Duraluminium) had the additional data appended to the code. Produced by VDM, better known for its airscrew manufacturing skills, the company included its logo on the sheets. What is particularly interesting is that they must have been supplied already lap joined and riveted for the metal grade marking to have been applied across both sheets, which was done by a rubber roller in this instance. VDM possibly made prepared sheets of pre-fabricated metal for use by the aircraft industry – Messerschmitt in this instance. (M. Ullmann)

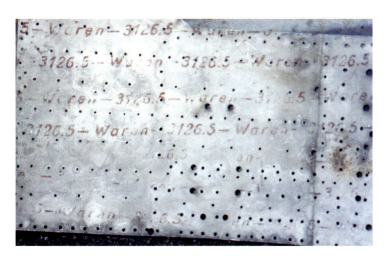

LEFT: This metal sheeting was found on part of the spar wing web structure in a Fw 190. It has the metal coded applied in red, again by means of a roller, but in a less formal form of lettering and numbering. The grade code here is 3126.5, indicating a different chemical structure for the sheet metal, which was used for internal purposes. (M. Laing)

APPENDIX

Werknummern

By J. Richard Smith

Comprehensive information on the method of German aircraft serial number (Werknummer) allocation is difficult to discover, but from thorough examination of manufacturer's records and Luftwaffe loss reports, it has been possible to draw the conclusions as described in this appendix.

The original system

By the time the National Socialists came to power in 1933, each aircraft manufacturer was using the logical scheme of having a consecutive number for each aircraft produced by the company, no matter what the type. This was the first 60 aeroplanes built by the Focke-Wulf company at Bremen illustrates this:

Aircraft type	W.Nr.	Registration	Name and owner
Focke-Wulf A VII	1	D-264	Focke-Wulf, Bremen
Focke-Wulf A 16	2	D-437	Fliegerhorst Nordmark, Altona
Focke-Wulf A 16 c	3	D-469	DLH
Focke-Wulf A 16 c	4	D-647	*Hansa*, DLH
Focke-Wulf A 16 c	5	D-548	*Baden*, DLH
	6		
Focke-Wulf A 16 b	7	D-814	DLH
Focke-Wulf A 16 b	8	D-659	*Borkum*, DLH
Focke-Wulf A 16	9	D-731	Norddeutsche LV AG, Bremen
Focke-Wulf A 16 a	10	D-671	LVG Niedersachsen, Hannover
Focke-Wulf A 16 d	11	D-747	LVG Niedersachsen, Hannover
Focke-Wulf A 16 d	12	D-804	LVG Niedersachsen, Hannover
Focke-Wulf A 16 a	13	D-776	
Focke-Wulf A 16 d	14	D-763	LVG Halle AG, Halle
Focke-Wulf S I	15	D-790	Luftfahrt GmbH, Halberstadt
	16		
	17		
Focke-Wulf A 16 c	18	D-566	DVS
Focke-Wulf A 16 d	19	D-162	LVG Wilhelmshaven-Rüstringen
Focke-Wulf A 16 c	20	D-914	DVS
	21		
Focke-Wulf S I a	22	D-853	DVL, Adlershof
	23		
Focke-Wulf A 16 d	24	D-894	LVG Niedersachsen, Hannover
Focke-Wulf A 16 d	25	D-916	LVG Niedersachsen, Hannover
Focke-Wulf A 16 d	26	D-959	LVG Niedersachsen, Hannover
Focke-Wulf S I a	27	D-966	DVS
Focke-Wulf GL 18	28	D-967	*Helgoland*, DLH
Focke-Wulf S I b	29	D-1056	DVS
	30		
	31		
Focke-Wulf A 17	32	D-1149	Norddeutsche LV AG, Bremen
Focke-Wulf A 16 d	33	D-1129	*Dortmund*, LV AG, Westfalen
Focke-Wulf A 20	34	D-1159	Deutsche Verkehrsflug, Nürnberg

Aircraft type	W.Nr.	Registration	Name and owner
Focke-Wulf FW 19 a	35	D-1960	DVL, Adlershof
Focke-Wulf S 2	36	D-1293	DVL, Adlershof
	37		
Focke-Wulf A 17 a	38	D-1345	DVL, Adlershof
Focke-Wulf GL 22	39	D-1375	DVS
Focke-Wulf GL 22	40	D-1418	DVS
Focke-Wulf GL 22	41	D-1462	DVS
Focke-Wulf A 17 a	42	D-1342	*Emden*, DLH
Focke-Wulf A 17 a	43	D-1358	*Aurich*, DLH
Focke-Wulf A 17 a	44	D-1367	*Leer*, DLH
Focke-Wulf A 17 a	45	D-1380	*Oldenburg*, DLH
Focke-Wulf A 17 a	46	D-1388	DLH
Focke-Wulf A 17 a	47	D-1403	*Lüneburg*, DLH
Focke-Wulf A 17 a	48	D-1416	*Osnabrück*, DLH
Focke-Wulf A 17 a	49	D-1430	*Hannover*, DLH
Focke-Wulf A 17 a	50	D-1444	*Münster*, DLH
Focke-Wulf A 17 a	51	D-1481	*Bielefeld*, DLH
Focke-Wulf A 20 a	52	D-1482	Focke-Wulf, Bremen
Focke-Wulf A 20 a	53	D-1439	LVG Wilhelmshaven-Rüstringen
Focke-Wulf A 21	54	D-1737	DVL, Adlershof
Focke-Wulf W 4	55	D-1730	DVL, Adlershof
	56		
Focke-Wulf A 26	57	D-1752	DVL, Adlershof
Focke-Wulf A 29	58	D-1867	*Westfalen*, DLH
	59		
Focke-Wulf A 28	60	D-1664	Norddeutsche LV AG, Bremen

This format was retained until the late 1930s when a new system seems to have been adopted by all manufacturers. In this, each main aircraft *type* had its own serial number series. It was therefore possible, and indeed likely, for two different aircraft types manufactured by the same company to have identical Werknummern. To endorse this point, it is worth examining a batch of Bf 109 and Bf 110 fighters lost or damaged during the Battle of Britain period, together with the Luftwaffe unit to which they were delivered:

Messerschmitt Bf 109

3177 17 Sep 40 Bf 109 E-1 9./JG 53
3182 12 Sep 40 Bf 109 E-1 2./JG 52
3185 29 Sep 40 Bf 109 E-4 4./JG 54
3187 20 Aug 41 Bf 109 E-7 1.(E)/JG 3
3192 30 Sep 40 Bf 109 E-1 6./JG 52

3209 5 Apr 42 Bf 109 E-7 I./JG 5
3217 27 Sep 40 Bf 109 E-1 9./JG 3

Messerschmitt Bf 110

3185 7 Sep 40 Bf 110 D-0 II./ZG 2

3193 2 Sep 40 Bf 110 D-0 I./ZG 2
3197 2 Sep 40 Bf 110 D-0 II./ZG 2
3207 9 Sep 40 Bf 110 C-? III./ZG 76

Messerschmitt Bf 109

3225	6 Sep 40	Bf 109 E-1	3./JG 27
3228	3 Aug 41	Bf 109 E-7	1./JG 54
3237	1 Sep 40	Bf 109 E-4	III./JG 53
3250	30 Oct 40	Bf 109 E-1	1./JG 77
3251	15 Oct 40	Bf 109 E-1	5./JG 3
3266	15 Sep 40	Bf 109 E-4	7./JG 51
3269	6 Sep 41	Bf 109 E-7	1./JG 54
3273	29 Oct 40	Bf 109 E-1	Erg./JG 2
3279	14 Oct 40	Bf 109 E-1	I./JG 2
3284	28 Aug 40	Bf 109 E-1	2./JG 27
3309	12 Oct 40	Bf 109 E-1	II./JG 77

Messerschmitt Bf 110

3225	3 Sep 40	Bf 110 C-2	I./ZG 2
3226	2 Sep 40	Bf 110 C-2	7./ZG 26
3229	4 Sep 40	Bf 110 C-?	II./ZG 76
3231	11 Sep 40	Bf 110 C-4	9./ZG 26
3235	30 Aug 40	Bf 110 C-2	III./ZG 76
3246	7 Sep 40	Bf 110 C-4	I./ZG 2
3251	24 Sep 40	Bf 110 C-4	III./ZG 76
3254	4 Sep 40	Bf 110 C-4	I./ZG 76
3257	30 Aug 40	Bf 110 C-?	4./ZG 76
3263	25 Sep 40	Bf 110 C-4	III./ZG 26
3269	2 Sep 40	Bf 110 D-0	II./ZG 2
3280	31 Aug 40	Bf 110 ?	Stab/ZG 26
3283	7 Oct 40	Bf 110 C-4	III./ZG 26
3285	11 Sep 40	Bf 110 C-?	II./ZG 76
3287	4 Sep 40	Bf 110 C-?	II./ZG 76
3290	27 Sep 40	Bf 110 C-4	8./ZG 26
3294	3 Sep 40	Bf 110 C-4	3./ZG 26
3297	27 Sep 40	Bf 110 C-4	9./ZG 26
3298	9 Sep 40	Bf 110 ?-?	15./LG 1
3299	26 Aug 40	Bf 110 C-4	9./ZG 26
3302	16 Oct 40	Bf 110 ?-?	I./NJG 3
3303	4 Sep 40	Bf 110 ?-?	14.(Z)/LG 1
3304	27 Sep 40	Bf 110 D-0	13.(Z)/LG 1
3308	7 Oct 40	Bf 110 D-1	9./NJG 1
3309	2 Sep 40	Bf 110 D-1	2./ZG 26
3310	3 Sep 40	Bf 110 D-0	6./ZG 26

It may also have been noticed from the above that the sub-types of each aircraft appear to have been allocated somewhat randomly vis a vis Werknummer blocks, at least with the Messerschmitt company. Logically, one would expect the Bf 109 E-1 series to have been produced before the E-4 series, and for production of the F-series to have been completed before the first Gs appeared, but the random shuffling of Werknummer blocks between sub-types (for security reasons) produced these apparent 'anomalies'. Some extracts culled by the author from contemporary Luftwaffe loss reports will serve to illustrate this point:

Bf 109 Werknummer 5450 to 5700 series

5460	22 June 41	Bf 109 F-2	4./JG 52
5462	10 August 42	Bf 109 F-2	10./JG 51
5463	8 July 41	Bf 109 F-2	?./JG 3
5495	21 March 42	Bf 109 F-2	1./JG 54
5496	13 August 42	Bf 109 F-2	12./JG 51
5515	4 November 41	Bf 109 F-2	II./JG 2
5519	27 June 41	Bf 109 F-2	4./JG 3
5531	11 February 42	Bf 109 F-2	7./JG 51
5541	12 August 41	Bf 109 F-2	4./JG 52
5543	31 July 41	Bf 109 F-2	6./JG 54
5547	13 November 41	Bf 109 F-2	2./JG 51
5549	24 July 41	Bf 109 F-2	6./JG 51
5558	25 June 41	Bf 109 F-2	6./JG 51
5562	29 October 40	Bf 109 E-4	4.(S)/LG 2
5563	12 October 40	Bf 109 E-4	2.(J)/LG 2
5564	4 September 40	Bf 109 E-7	II.(S)/LG 2
5566	7 October 40	Bf 109 E-4	4.(S)/LG 2
5567	6 September 40	Bf 109 E-7	II.(S)/LG 2
5569	15 October 40	Bf 109 E-4	II.(S)/LG 2
5572	3 September 40	Bf 109 E-7	I.(J)/LG 2
5573	4 September 40	Bf 109 E-7	II.(S)/LG 2
5574	18 September 40	Bf 109 E-7	1./JG 27
5576	29 September 40	Bf 109 E-4B	II.(S)/LG 2
5581	22 October 40	Bf 109 E-4	7./JG 27
5582	27 September 40	Bf 109 E-4	3./JG 51
5583	26 August 40	Bf 109 E-4	2./JG 2
5587	24 August 40	Bf 109 E-4	6./JG 51
5592	27 September 40	Bf 109 E-7	2.(J)/LG 2
5593	29 October 40	Bf 109 E-4	4.(S)/LG 2
5598	20 October 40	Bf 109 E-1	3.(J)/LG 2
5600	31 August 40	Bf 109 E-7	I.(J)/LG 2
5637	5 June 41	Bf 109 F-1	12./JG 51
5647	11 August 41	Bf 109 F-1	3./JG 3
5650	30 August 40	Bf 109 E-?	I./JG 26
5660	10 May 42	Bf 109 F-1	8./JG 51
5667	11 August 41	Bf 109 F-2	9./JG 51
5678	22 June 41	Bf 109 F-2	3./JG 51
5684	5 December 41	Bf 109 F-2	1./JG 54

In addition, all Bf 109 Werknummern in the series from 10300 onwards were of the G-1, G-2, G-3 and G-4 variant, but all those in the 12000 and 13000 series up to 13400 were F-2s and F-4s. No Werknummern in the 11000 series were allocated to the Bf 109.

Although for the historian, Messerschmitt used this somewhat erratic and most confusing system, other manufacturers adopted a more logical arrangement. Take for example the Werknummer system devised by Focke-Wulf for the Fw 190. It comprised a ten or eleven digit code, such as 190.0125.386. In this the first three digits, '190' identified the aircraft type. The next two digits, '01' indicated the main sub-type, in this case the Fw 190 A. The sixth digit, '2' indicated the sub-series, in this case the Fw 190 A-2. The seventh digit, '5' indicated the manufacturer, in this case Arado. The final three digits indicated the individual aircraft. Thus in the example above, 190.0125.386 indicated an Arado-built Fw 190 A-2, serial number 386. (When production numbered in excess of 100 the eleventh digit appeared).

The batches known to have been allocated to the Fw 190 were as follows:

Fw 190 A-1

Focke-Wulf	0110.001-102

Fw 190 A-2 & A-3

Focke-Wulf	0120.201-558
Ago	0122.053-290
Arado	0125.201-532
Fieseler	0137.001-019

Fw 190 A-4

Focke-Wulf	0140.561-810
Ago	0142.291-497
Arado	0145.533-817
Fieseler	0147.020-203

Fw 190 B-1

Focke-Wulf	0210.811 (one aircraft only)

Fw 190 A-5

Focke-Wulf	0150.812-1793
Ago	0152.501-719
Arado	0155.823-999
unknown	0156.006-020
Fieseler	0157.202-395

To take another example, the Dornier company seemed to use a similar system to Messerschmitt, as can be seen from the following overview of Do 217 production:

W.Nr.

1001 to 1100	Do 217 E-1
1101 to 1200	Do 217 E-2, E-4, J-1 and J-2
1201 to 1240	Do 217 E-2
1241 to 1245	Do 217 M-0
1246 to 1300	Do 217 E-2
1301 to 1400	Do 217 J-1 and J-2
1401 to 1500	Do 217 N-1
1501 to 1600	Do 217 N-2
2801 to 2900	Do 217 M-1
2901 to 3000	Do 217 M-11
3001 to 3100	Do 217 K-3 and M-11
4201 to 4300	Do 217 E-4 and E-5
4301 to 4400	Do 217 E-4
4401 to 4410	Do 217 K-0
4411 to 4500	Do 217 K-1
4501 to 4600	Do 217 E-4, E-5, K-2 and K-3
4701 to 4800	Do 217 K-3
5301 to 5400	Do 217 E-4
5401 to 5500	Do 217 E-4 and E-5
5501 to 5600	Do 217 E-4
5601 to 5700	Do 217 E-5
6401 to 6500	Do 217 M-11
24301 to 24400	Do 217 E-4
52401 to 52500	Do 217 E-4
56101 to 56200	Do 217 M-1

The six-figure system

Sometime during the spring of 1943, the various systems of Werknummern adopted by the different aircraft manufacturers was replaced by a new common principal. Each aircraft type was allocated a six-figure serial number batch, the first two digits of which indicated both the sub-type and the manufacturer. For example, all Bf 109 K-4s had six figure serial numbers beginning with 33 and were built by Messerschmitt and all He 177 A-5s had numbers beginning with 55, those built by Heinkel at Oranienburg being numbered 550001 to 550201 and those by Arado at Warnemünde 550202 to 550333.

An example of how these Werknummer batches were allocated can be seen in the production schedule proposed for the Focke-Wulf Ta 152 given below. Although these batch numbers were allocated to all the manufacturers shown below, few were actually used before the end of the war:

110000 series	Focke-Wulf, Sorau	Ta 152 H-0 and H-1
150000 series	Focke-Wulf, Cottbus	Ta 152 H-0 and H-1
200000 series	Focke-Wulf, Bremen	Ta 152 H-1
360000 series	Siebel, Halle	Ta 152 C-1 and C-3
380000 series	Ago, Oschersleben	Ta 152 C-0 and C-1
440000 series	Siebel, Halle	Ta 152 C-1 and C-3
480000 series	Fieseler, Kassel	Ta 152 C-1 and C-2
510000 series	Erla, Leipzig	Ta 152 B-5, H-1 and H-2
580000 series	Gothaer Waggonfabrik, Gotha	Ta 152 B-5, C and H
600000 series	Mimetall, Erfurt	Ta 152 C, E and H
640000 series	Erla, Leipzig	Ta 152 B-5, H-1 and H-2
710000 series	Norddeutsche Dornier, Wismar	Ta 152 C-1, C-2 and C-4
720000 series	Gothaer Waggonfabrik, Gotha	Ta 152 B-5, C and H
790000 series	Arbeitsgesellschaft Roland	Ta 152 C-1, C-2 and C-4
830000 series	ATG, Leipzig	Ta 152 C-1 and C-3
870000 series	Mimetall, Erfurt	Ta 152 C, E and H
920000 series	ATG, Leipzig	Ta 152 C-1 and C-3
950000 series	Mimetall, Erfurt	Ta 152 C, E and H

The reader will notice that the earlier numbers were allocated to the parent manufacturer (in this case Focke-Wulf) first, with the various licence builders following. It should also be noted that the batches themselves were allocated in groups of ten, twenty, thirty, etc., with large gaps in-between. To illustrate this point, take the Werknummer batches allocated to the Arado Ar 234:

130001 to 130010	Ar 234 V1 to V10
130021 to 130030	Ar 234 V11 to V20
130061 to 130067	Ar 234 V21 to V27
140101 to 140120	Ar 234 S-0 to S-20
140141 to 140180	Ar 234 B-2
140301 to 140360	Ar 234 B-2
140450 to 140500	Ar 234 B-2
140571 to 140608	Ar 234 B-2
250001 to 250020	Ar 234 C-3

Most examples of German aircraft Werknummern quoted above have been pieced together by the author from various documentary sources; only one document so far having been discovered that lists the Werknummern allocated to an aircraft type. This was for Messerschmitt AG production of the Me 262, and is included, in abbreviated form, below. It should be noted that Augsburg, Leipheim, Schwäbisch Hall and "Kuno"[1] were all final assembly plants for Messerschmitt AG. The publicly-owned Messerschmitt GmbH at Regensburg used final assembly plants at Obertraubling, Neuburg am Donau and Erding and the Me 262s produced there were allocated Werknummern in the 500000 series.

262 000 0001 to 0005	Me 262 V1 to V5

Messerschmitt, Augsburg

130006 to 130010	Me 262 S1 to S5	Messerschmitt, Augsburg
130011 to 130027	Me 262 S6 to S15 and A	Messerschmitt, Leipheim
130163 to 130165	Me 262 A	Messerschmitt, Leipheim
130166 to 130185	Me 262 A	

Messerschmitt, Schwäbisch Hall

130186 to 130190	Me 262 A	Messerschmitt, Leipheim
170001 to 170015	Me 262 A	Messerschmitt, Leipheim
170016 to 170017	Me 262 A	Messerschmitt, Schwäbisch Hall
170036 to 170053	Me 262 A	Messerschmitt, Schwäbisch Hall
170054 to 170073	Me 262 A	Messerschmitt, Leipheim
170074 to 170093	Me 262 A	Messerschmitt, Schwäbisch Hall
170093 to 170118	Me 262 A	Messerschmitt, Leipheim
170119 to 170124	Me 262 A	Messerschmitt, Schwäbisch Hall
170269 to 170287	Me 262 A	Messerschmitt, Schwäbisch Hall
170288 to 170312	Me 262 A	Messerschmitt, Leipheim
110305 to 110307	Me 262 B-1a/U1	Blohm und Voss, Wenzendorf [2]
110361 to 110385	Me 262 A	Messerschmitt, Schwäbisch Hall
110386 to 110410	Me 262 A	Messerschmitt, Leipheim
110411 to 110430	Me 262 A	Messerschmitt, Schwäbisch Hall
110466 to 110470	Me 262 A	Messerschmitt, Schwäbisch Hall
110471 to 110495	Me 262 A	Messerschmitt, Leipheim
110496 to 110520	Me 262 A	Messerschmitt, Schwäbisch Hall
110521 to 110545	Me 262 A	Messerschmitt, Leipheim
110546 to 110570	Me 262 A	Messerschmitt, Schwäbisch Hall
110571 to 110595	Me 262 A	Messerschmitt, Leipheim
110596 to 110620	Me 262 A	Messerschmitt, Schwäbisch Hall
110621 to 110645	Me 262 A	Messerschmitt, Leipheim
110646 to 110649	Me 262 A	Messerschmitt, Schwäbisch Hall
110718	Me 262 A	Messerschmitt, Schwäbisch Hall

110719 to 110743	Me 262 A	Messerschmitt, Leipheim
110744 to 110768	Me 262 A	Messerschmitt, 'Kuno'
110769 to 110845	Me 262 A	Messerschmitt, Leipheim
110911 to 110960	Me 262 A	Messerschmitt, Schwäbisch Hall
110961 to 111011	Me 262 A	Messerschmitt, Leipheim
111538 to 111636	Me 262 A	Messerschmitt, Leipheim
110637 to 110736	Me 262 A	Messerschmitt, Schwäbisch Hall
111737 to 111811	Me 262 A	Messerschmitt, 'Kuno'
111812 to 110886	Me 262 A	Messerschmitt, Schwäbisch Hall
110887 to 112000	Me 262 A	Messerschmitt, Leipheim
112311 to 112414	Me 262 A	Messerschmitt, Leipheim
113046 to 113???	Me 262 A	Messerschmitt, Leipheim
113??? to 113394	Me 262 A	Messerschmitt, Leipheim
113395 to 113694	Me 262 A	Messerschmitt, Schwäbisch Hall
113695 to 113728	Me 262 A	Messerschmitt, Leipheim
113395 to 113694	Me 262 A	Messerschmitt, Schwäbisch Hall

A widely held belief is that production batches from a factory were delivered to a specific Luftwaffe unit. For example W.Nr.1235 to 1270 might have been delivered to II./JG 26 and 453462 to 453489 to III./KG 77. However, detailed examination of German records gives little support to this belief. It is possible that aircraft were delivered to a holding unit in batches, but by the time they reached an operational unit, these batches had been widely scattered. It is just possible that batches of aircraft were delivered to a specific unit at a late stage in the war when Germany's borders were rapidly shrinking and some units were based closed to a factory, but if this did happen, it was rare.

Method of application

With few exceptions, German Werknummern were painted in black on the tail fin of the aircraft, usually just above the tail plane.

To the frustration of historians, dark green camouflage often meant that these numbers are virtually invisible because of the lack of contrast. During the early part of the Second World War, the serial number was often prefixed with the abbreviation 'W.Nr.', but this practice ceased around late 1940. The method of application of Fw 190 serials described in this appendix varied. Sometimes just the last three figures of the sequence appeared, eg: '235', sometimes five, eg: '20 235' (indicating a Focke-Wulf built A-2). In the latter case, the first two figures were painted in smaller characters than the remaining three.

Towards the end of the war, it became common practice with six-figure serial numbers to paint the last three figures almost twice the size of the preceding three. Also, it was more common for the serial to be painted on the top of the fin, above the Hakenkreuz, rather than beneath. In the Sammelmitteilung issued on 1 July 1944, under an order instructing manufacturers, for security reasons, to cease marking Stammkennzeichen on aircraft, it was stated that:

> "Only the number [Werknummer] itself, is to be painted on both vertical tail surfaces. Shade 22 or 21, Flieglacke 7160 or 7164 or 7165. The height of the numbers is 25 cm, or if necessary – e.g., when infringing on the Hakenkreuz – smaller."

This order was loosely interpreted by some production centres. Many late production Bf 109s had their Werknummer stencilled along the bottom edge of the rudder, while others had the number marked just above the horizontal tail plane/elevator line, usually with just the first digit on the fin. Some Ju 88 Gs were recorded with both the full Werknummer at the top of the fin as well as an abbreviated form low on the fin; variations were prolific by war's end.

ABOVE: During construction and flight testing of Bf 109s, it was common practice at most centres to mark the last three digits of the Werknummer in a prominent place, as shown here, '138' having been applied by hand painting in a dark colour. It would be painted over once the aircraft had reached acceptance standard.

ABOVE: Sometimes a more prominent form was used during the flight-testing stage, as on this Bf 109 E, CD+ED, which had the entire Werknummer (7667) marked on the engine cowling, port side. The paint used was removable with benzine.

---

1 "Kuno" was a construction complex situated in the Horgau Forest with a production area of 4,700 m2 (5,621 sq yds). The complex used the nearby autobahn for flight testing and delivery.

2 These serial numbers do not appear in the document quoted, but are known to have been allocated to three night fighter conversions produced by the Blohm und Voss company.

BELOW: The RLM order included in the 1 July 1944 Sammelmitteilung banning the further marking of Stammkennzeichen on production aircraft caused some confusion with its reference to using only the Werknummer "...painted on both vertical tail surfaces." This produced the form of marking seen on this Fw 190, with its Werknummer '681330' marked part on the fin and part on the rudder, (note the elaborate numeral style used also on the very earliest production Fw 190s). Rudders were liable to damage and to be changed at unit-level, requiring marking of three of the digits each time – and under battle conditions such niceties were not always carried out. Late production Bf 109 Gs and Ks also adopted this 'split' application, but usually marked only one digit on the fin. In the last months of the war, some Bf 109 manufacturers took to placing the entire Werknummer low down on the rudder. (J. Crow)

ABOVE: The usual form of Werknummer marking on Fw 190s was at the tip of the fin, in black, as shown here by '430674'. Note that the style of the '3' and '4' conformed to the standard as shown in the accompanying diagram in Appendix G. Early production aircraft often used a more abbreviated form with just the last three digits, or with the last three digits in larger size than the first three.

LEFT: Junkers 52s often were marked with their Werknummer on the panel just forward of the leading edge of the wing, as shown here. In this instance the numbers, '6119', had been painted by hand in black, though usually they were applied by stencil, often in white. The aircraft was from II./KG.z.b.V 1, the dual shield emblem of that Gruppe being marked on the engine cowling.
(A. Fleuret via M. Jessen)

Werknummern

BELOW: The very large fin of the He 111 made the numerals look even smaller, the manufacturer choosing to place the Werknummer markings low, near the base of the fin as shown on this example, the fin recovered by personnel of No.145 Sqn, RAF, from a He 111 of Stab./KG 27, W.Nr.2648, shot down by F/Lt Adrian Boyd on 18 July 1940. (E. Marsden)

ABOVE: Junkers was one of the few manufacturers to mark the Werknummer on both sides of the fin, most using only the port side location. Late production Ju 88s also tended to have the Werknummer marked in various locations, sometimes high on the fin, sometimes low, as shown here by '130378'. In some instances, they chose to mark the Werknummer twice on the same side of the fin, one high, often abbreviated to the last three or four digits, and in full low down. The aircraft in the photograph is also unusual in having its Hakenkreuz positioned much lower than normal. The large, hand-painted yellow '395' was the quick identification marking applied to aircraft at some advanced flying training units. (J. Crow)

LEFT: Werknummer were marked in small digits on some types. Size was regulated by the DIN standards proportions, which, technically at least, allowed for wide scope of overall size as shown in the diagrams in Appendix G, but some manufacturers still chose a smaller size ratio as shown by '750597' marked on the fin of this derelict Ju 88. The style matches that shown in the JuN 10102 document.

433

APPENDIX

Balkenkreuz and Hakenkreuz

Hakenkreuz markings

After coming to power in 1933 the National Socialist Party had incorporated its political party emblem as part of the German National emblem and it retained its international status for both civilian and military organizations, until May 1945. The old Imperial German flag had been replaced by the Reichs-und Nationalflagge, which incorporated the National Socialist Party Hakenkreuz (swastika) emblem in black on a white circle, surmounted on a red background. As such it was not unique to the National Socialist Party, only having been adopted by the fledgling NSDAP (National Socialist Democratic Workers Party) in 1920.

Initially, replacement of the old Imperial flag with that of the symbol of the National Socialist Party was done without addressing necessary international legalities. This was redressed by a unanimous resolution of the Seventh Reichsparteitag Congress on 15 September 1935, the NSP flag being legally incorporated as part of the German national emblem, a fact promulgated into force with effect from that same day. The existing black, white and red (black uppermost) horizontal tricolour (in the old colours of Prussia), the merchant ensign displayed on the port side of the fin and rudder of all German aircraft, was replaced by what was now the legal Reichs-und Nationalflagge.

ABOVE: The Reichs und Nationalflagge, introduced on 6 July 1933, is seen here marked on the starboard side of the fin and rudder of a Habicht glider, identifying the date as post-15 September 1935. After that date, this marking replaced the horizontal tricolour of black, white and red on the starboard side of the empennage of all aircraft. (P. Selinger)

On 3 July 1933 instructions were issued to adopt the dual set of markings across the vertical tail surfaces in order to identify them as German. In a very small number of instances these markings were confined to the rudder area; generally however they were applied as per the official instruction. Both markings were to be coincident and to occupy the same area on both sides of the vertical tail surfaces. Colouring of each component of the two designs was carried around the curve of the rudder leading edge to the vertical mid-point line. This ensured that visual integrity of each marking was retained when the rudder was moved from side to side.

An Air Traffic Ordinance (Luftverkehrsvorschrift) promulgated on 29 August 1936, in the Reich Government Gazette No. 78, incorporated the new

standards (Encl No. 1 to Paras 4, 12 and 75 of LuftVO, Reichsgesetzblatt Nr. 78 - 29/8/36) and laid down applications and dimensions for the marking. This publication was, itself, an amended version of air traffic regulations that had been published on 21 August 1936. The section dealing with the Reichs-und Nationalflagge read:

> "2. Aircraft and towed aircraft carry the Reichs-und Nationalflagge in colour on both sides of the vertical fin above the horizontal stabiliser. Minimum size is half the height of the fin above the horizontal stabiliser. Length and height of the two flag bands should be in a 3:5 ratio.
>
> The flag is to be applied as follows:
> A black Hakenkreuz, angled at 45 degrees, in a white disk on a red band, all possessing a common centre. The arm of the Hakenkreuz nearest to the leading edge of the fin is open at the top. Diameter of the white disk is three-quarters of the width of the red band. Length of the centre arms of the Hakenkreuz is half the width of the red band. Thickness of the arms of the Hakenkreuz and their distance from each other [is] in one-tenth of the width of the red band.
>
> Airships carry the Reichs-und Nationalflagge on both sides of the vertical stabilisers. Size of the flag is determined by the Air Minister on a case by case basis.
>
> Sailplanes carry the Reichs-und Nationalflagge as prescribed for powered aircraft.
>
> Free balloons carry the Hakenkreuz marking.
>
> Aircraft on which standard markings cannot be applied due to peculiarities of their construction or for other reasons will receive markings authorised by the Air Minister."

The Reichsdienstflagge (Reich Service Flag) had come into use the year before, Dr Frick, Minister of the Interior, having issued regulations governing its use on 31 October 1935, supported by an order of the Führer issued on 7 December 1935. It had replaced the existing Service Flag and comprised a red rectangular field, in the proportions 3:5, with a white disk on its central axis. The disk was to have a narrow black border on its inner rim, edged with a narrow white outer border. An upright black Hakenkreuz was placed centrally on the white disk and outlined thinly in white and black. The bent sections of the marking extended to the circumference of the black outline circle; the lower section of the marking being open towards the hoist. Both obverse and reverse designs mirrored each other.

Regulations stated that this flag was to be used by all public administration authorities. It was to be flown on administration buildings when so ordered; service vessels on inland waters, as well as the high seas, in place of the former Service Flag; on service cars in place of the original Service Flag.

ABOVE: While of indifferent quality, this photograph illustrates the unusual interpretation put on the introduction of the new military markings by an unidentified unit at Döberitz, as mentioned in the text.

In the Luftwaffe the Reichsdienstflagge was marked on second line aircraft bearing civil registrations used for VIP transport and air ambulance duties, that status lasting until 1940. To distinguish it further, a German eagle emblem was added in the top corner nearest the direction of flight. The regulation concerning central placement of the white circle and emblem was not always adhered to however; at least one example has been noted, D-TABX, an all white Ju 52/3m air ambulance showing the disk off-set on the rudder.

Use of the Reichsdienstflagge on white-painted ambulance aircraft came to an abrupt end in mid-1940. During the opening phases of the air war against Britain He 59 seaplanes, carrying this tail marking and bearing civil registration, were constantly engaged in the rescue of downed aircrew. That had raised some controversy about their neutrality as they were often seen near convoys following air actions – an explanation of which would have been logical enough had not war and propaganda issues intervened. On 14 July 1940 the British Government instructed RAF Fighter Command to order its pilots to shoot down enemy ambulance aircraft. This decision was later ratified in Air Ministry Order No. 1254 of 29 July which, while still guaranteeing continuing immunity under the International Red Cross Convention, would do so with exception of:

> "…aircraft flying over areas in which operations are in progress on land and at sea, or approaching British or Allied territory, or territory in British occupation, or British and Allied ships.
>
> Ambulance aircraft which do not comply with the above requirements will do so at their own risk and peril."

This information was notified to the German Government and soon after ambulance aircraft reverted to camouflage and use of the Reichs und Nationalflagge. On other classes of aircraft use of the Reichsdienstflagge continued until the end of the Second World War.

Balkenkreuz markings

Around October 1935, military markings had been reintroduced for the first time since 1918. A black and white cross marking was adopted, which resembled the style, but not the exact proportions, of the final form of this military marking used in 1918 and sometimes referred to as a Greek cross. It was applied in six positions; at the wing tips on the top surface of upper wings and bottom surface of lower wings and on either side of the fuselage. The markings were applied with the fore and aft centre line of each parallel to the centre line of the fuselage. In the instance of the fuselage marking, the

horizontal alignment was parallel to the theoretical ground line when the aircraft was in flight. The initial form was a black cross with only a narrow white border. In previous publications it has been speculated that this form of the Balkenkreuz marking was in error as it lacked the narrow black edge to the white border, and was seen only on a few aircraft. However, further research has shown this to be incorrect.

When first introduced, initially it mimicked the 1918-style marking in so far as it carried plain white edging along the sides of the black arms. In 1918, in most instances, contemporary camouflage had provided a dark background against which the white edging was clearly visible, a narrow black border not being required. Even in that period black edging had not been used even when marked against a pale background, e.g., on Albatros Dr II or Junkers J 11 aircraft. It was in that general form that the marking had been reintroduced. However, even though the proportions were promulgated, initially some odd interpretations resulted. At Döberitz, the He 45 Cs of an unidentified training unit were photographed with the correctly proportioned black section of the cross but marked on a solid white square large enough to just contain the cross, a style reminiscent of the First World War. At Galgenberg, a He 45 C of 3.(F)/125, 50+A13, was photographed wearing a 1918-style Greek cross with its narrower, elongated proportions and without black outline.

ABOVE: An He 46 C of Aufkl. Gr. (H)/125 photographed after October 1935, by which time both military codes and Balkenkreuz markings had been introduced for front line aircraft. This is the original form of Balkenkreuz marking with only a white edging to the black cross. (D. Vincent)

Not until mid-1936 do reliably dated photographs appear that show addition of a narrow black border to the white outline. Prior to this there are photographs from as early as March of that year showing Balkenkreuz markings without black edging, in combination with the five-figure military codes, on He 51s. That form of code structure for fighters was rescinded from 1 September 1936, and subsequent photographs of aircraft wearing the new style of fighter markings, show the addition of the black edging.

Directive LA Nr. 1290/36 geh. LA II/Fl. In. 3., issued on 2 July 1936, had specifically addressed fighter aircraft, of which only two types were in service, the He 51 and Ar 68. It set out the physical dimensions for placement of both unit and national markings. Balkenkreuz markings were positioned on the fuselage such that the vertical centre line of the marking was equidistant between wing trailing edge and horizontal tail plane leading edge. It had been able to set down precise measurements because of only two types of fighter in service. The Balkenkreuz markings on the top surface of the upper wing and bottom surface of the lower wing were set with their centre line on the half chord point of the main section of the wing. In both instances the markings were placed with their longitudinal centre line 900 mm from the wing tip. All Balkenkreuz markings illustrated in the accompanying diagrams were marked with a narrow black edge. This revised form of the Balkenkreuz marking

Luftwaffe Camouflage and Markings 1933-1945

ABOVE: Ar 78s of 3./JG 134 photographed during the fly-past over Wartburg on Reichsparteitag (Reichs Party Day) of 1937. Despite the date, the Balkenkreuze still lack the thin black edging, demonstrating how visual effectiveness of the marking was reduced without that extra outlining. The sheen of the overall lacquer finish is more easily seen on the darker paintwork of the upper fuselage. The Hakenkreuz marking is in the form of the Reichs- und Nationalflagge. (O. Hintze via J. Vasco)

appears then to have been introduced either with, or about the time of this directive for fighter aircraft. The reason for the black edging simply was to increase visual identification range of the marking against the 63-coloured background; the standard Luftwaffe overall colour scheme adopted that year. However, examples of unmodified Balkenkreuz markings remained right through until 1937, probably as a result of waiting for aircraft to reach their major overhaul and refurbishment date.

With the introduction of the new Bf 109 B monoplane into service in early 1937, the fighter aircraft markings directive was superseded by a new one, Fl. In. 3. Nr. 730/37 II. Existing dimensions and positioning of the fuselage Balkenkreuz marking did not allow sufficient room for both aircraft identifying number and Staffel marking. The position of the Balkenkreuz was set at 1500 mm aft of the wing trailing edge (excluding the root fairing), which placed the marking overlapping Frame 4. That position was retained until the 24 October

ABOVE: This Bf 109 B-2 demonstrates the effectiveness of adding the narrow black outline to the white border of the Balkenkreuz on the 65-coloured wing under surfaces. With the change to 70/71 for upper surfaces, the narrow black edging was sometimes omitted, the background of dark greens providing the high contrast needed to make the white edges effective. This seems to have been an aberration not intended by the official RLM markings directive. (Real Photographs)

1939 instruction when the marking was moved slightly further aft and situated with its vertical centre line superimposed on Frame 5.

A further directive, Az. 19 d 10 Genst. 2. Abt. (III B), reflecting the growing international tensions, was promulgated on 15 December 1938, effective from 1 January 1939 at which date all production military aircraft had to have the red banner and white circle marking deleted from the painting specification. The instruction was also promulgated in the Luftwaffen=Verordnungsblatt – Luftwaffe Instructions Gazette – of 30 January 1939 to ensure that order was not unnoticed by any unit of the Luftwaffe. The Hakenkreuz marking was henceforth to be marked only on the fin. Exception was permitted only where design of the vertical tail surfaces provided insufficient fin area; in such instances the marking was applied in full proportions to the rudder. Existing aircraft held by units were to have the red and white portions of the marking painted out leaving only the Hakenkreuz marking in its original central position.

The marking was to retain its existing dimensions, plus a narrow white border equivalent to 1/6th the width of the black stroke. The narrow white border was to be achieved by masking out a portion of the existing white area and spraying out the remaining sections of the marking. On aircraft using the old three-tone scheme 61-colouring was to be used, on aircraft using the new two-tone scheme 70-colouring was to be used. After spraying out the old marking, the white edge to the Hakenkreuz was to have a narrow black line added. By this time military aircraft were finished in dark camouflage colours against which the Hakenkreuz marking could only be seen if it retained a white border, a factor that seems to have influenced some units to disregard the instruction to add the superfluous thin black outline.

On 24 October 1939, the Balkenkreuz marking was again revised. The white angles were increased proportionately to 1/8th the overall width of the entire marking with the black outer edge increased proportionately to 1/32nd of the overall width to better define the increased white areas. This enlarged form of the Balkenkreuz marking was to be applied only to the lower surface of the bottom wing and to the fuselage side surface, the original, revised 1936-proportioned marking being retained for the wing upper surface.

In addition to the changes to proportions, positioning of the markings on the wing upper and lower surface also had been revised. On single-engine aircraft the marking on the lower surface of the bottom wing was centred on a point determined by the intersection of lines dividing the wing in half both longitudinally and chord-wise at a point half way between wing root and wing tip. The marking was to be aligned parallel with the centre line of the fuselage. On the lower surface of twin-engine aircraft this process was applied at a point half way between the centre line of the engine and the wing tip. The wing upper surface marking had its longitudinal centre line set at 2000 mm maximum inboard from the wing tip, maximum overall size for single-engine aircraft being set at 1000 mm.

In practice these locations varied from aircraft type to aircraft type and close examination shows that in each case the marking has one point or edge touching or aligned against a specific prominent feature of the structure. The changes had resulted in both upper and lower markings being almost diametrically opposite on the Bf 109, a result of the physical dimensions of the wing and the order to place the upper surface marking 2000 mm from the tip. The position was modified slightly for ease of painting, enabling the stencil to be placed with its lower outermost corner at the junction of the flap and aileron. Such minor variations were apparently acceptable as they simplified setting up the markings with a consequent saving in man-hours.

That general revision had addressed problems of rapid identification that had arisen during the recently completed Polish campaign, many Luftwaffe losses reputedly having been caused by German ground fire; which accords with the consequent official increase in size of markings visible only from a ground perspective. The resultant spate of ambiguities that resulted when the revised markings were applied, points strongly to the fact that no diagrams had been reissued with the written instruction. Incorrect marking of the wing upper surface Balkenkreuz would appear on most front line types, the proportions used being those stipulated for the wing lower surface.

436

LEFT: This photograph of an He 111 (possibly a J-1 judging by the bulge to the canvass cover) taken during the winter of 1939/40 shows the huge size of the Balkenkreuz markings applied to the lower surfaces of the wings. These were in the correct ratio of proportions for the revised markings but like so many aircraft of this period, grossly over normal size. (Peter Petrick)

BELOW: This may be the same aircraft. It has the same size and proportionately immense wing Balkenkreuz as on the previous He 111. It is possible to determine that some elements of the code were marked on each wing tip. As this was possibly an obsolescent He 111 J, these may have been part of the old five character code that had been superseded by then on front line aircraft, but which lingered on some second line machines. (Peter Petrick)

The confusion occurred at both front line and industry level; for example the Fw 190 V-1 used the under wing/fuselage size in all six positions. The original Überführungskennzeichen FO+LY (where FO identified Focke-Wulf) had been replaced with the Stammkennzeichen RM+CA from the new series introduced in October 1939, confirming the date of those particular incorrect wing upper surface Balkenkreuz markings. Another manufacturer to make the same error was Heinkel, which also marked its He 113s (He 100 Ds) in the same incorrect manner in all six positions.

The disorder was even greater in some cases where not only were ratio of proportions incorrect, but in many cases also the overall dimensions, resulting in extremely large markings. Amongst some bomber and maritime units that very large form of incorrect marking occasionally was seen with retention of the original marking on wing upper surfaces. Dual markings were also noted in a combination of correctly proportioned and positioned wing upper surface markings. Clearly it was a time of great confusion, again reinforcing the notion that diagrams were not issued.

The speed with which those new revisions had been applied may be judged from the He 111P of KG 26 shot down on the Lammermuir Hills in Scotland on 28 October 1939, just four days after the revisions were introduced. It displayed a combination of the original and revised correctly proportioned and positioned, but grossly oversize, wing upper surface markings. The Balkenkreuz marking on the fuselage was also incorrect, the old form having been retained. Central location of the Hakenkreuz marking on the fin and rudder of this aircraft identified that its markings had been repainted at unit level and all known examples of such excessively incorrect revisions were to be found on aircraft that had been repainted at unit level. A common misinterpretation seems to have been the size of the wing upper surface marking, which was often marked across the full chord of the wing fixed surfaces (excluding flaps). As on the KG 26 machine, the fuselage Balkenkreuz marking was often left in original form, a mistake that persisted well into 1940. The 1941 edition of L.Dv.521/1 did contain the requisite diagrams, but probably that aspect had already been corrected with an interim issue of an instruction, the excessively large Balkenkreuz markings generally having disappeared by early 1940.

Officially the revised proportions would remain unaltered for the remainder of the war and appear to have been adhered to at production centres until around mid-1943. Field modifications to markings however would produce

Luftwaffe Camouflage and Markings 1933-1945

RIGHT: As detailed in the text, the He 111, IH+JA of the Stab of KG 26 shot down on 28 October 1939, just four days after the official change to Balkenkreuz markings illustrates the confusion that followed. The retention of the original wing markings as well as the grossly oversize new markings, and the incorrect proportions of the fuselage marking speak volumes for the uncertainty of the period. Note that the Hakenkreuz marking was still centrally placed, showing that this was a pre-January 1939 production aircraft.

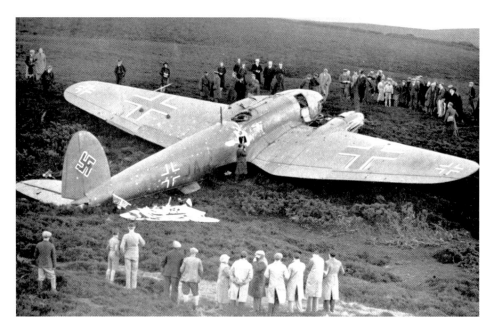

LEFT: In this view of a He 111, the oversize wing Balkenkreuz can just be seen. Close examination shows that when the white area was sprayed, the over spray drifted sufficiently to leave a slight fuzzing of white around the finished cross. Markings of this size could not be accommodated easily by the usual stencil system the Luftwaffe and aircraft industry employed for such markings. Most probably the larger areas were marked in chalk, after the fashion of application of the general camouflage segments, then had the area sprayed in. The thin black outer edges would have been painted over any such spray drift of white paint.

RIGHT: The sudden increase in dimensions and change of proportions to the Balkenkreuz markings following the Polish campaign was obviously not well documented in terms of instruction. The range of aircraft seen wearing those massive markings was fairly wide. Here a Do 18 D-2, K6+KL W.Nr.0874, exhibits yet another anomaly, which also occurred on some bomber aircraft during this period of confusion. Not only were the oversize markings applied to the new inboard location, but the old markings also were retained. Note in this instance, that while the ratio of proportions was correct for the white angles, only those elements had been applied and not the black infill (something that would not occur officially until much later in the war).

LEFT: This Do 17 P of 3./(F) 11 was photographed at Kassel during January 1940. While the Balkenkreuz markings on the lower wing surfaces are both of incorrect proportions and grossly oversize, the fuselage marking is correct for the revised proportions. The two aircraft in the background have the same combination of incorrect wing but correct fuselage markings. The confusion was slowly abated.

variation, almost inevitably a reflection of battle conditions. In 1940 when the air fighting was at its peak some fighter units modified the fuselage Balkenkreuz marking in order to less compromise the camouflage. That resulted in Balkenkreuz markings of pre-October 1939 proportions, achieved either by increasing the thickness of the black outline into the white edging and thus reducing the latter; or by painting over the black outline and part of the white edging to produce a narrower surround. Several examples have been noted amongst JG 2 aircraft and this practice may have been specific to this unit. Well-known photographs taken in October 1940 of the Bf 109 Es of Major Wick of JG 2 provide examples of both these modifications.

Another anomaly seen on Bf 109 Es of the 1940 period was retention of the original overall size of Balkenkreuz marking, based on a square of 660 mm, but in the revised proportions. When the 24 October 1939, revisions had been introduced the fuselage size had been increased to 880 mm, and wing upper and lower surface size to 990 mm. While production aircraft were so marked, those repainted at unit-level ended up with a mixture of sizes. These are easily detected in photographs of Bf 109 Es of this period, the smaller size being quite evident.

While the process of applying the Balkenkreuz and Hakenkreuz markings were done with a series of metal templates, size still did vary slightly at different manufacturing centres. Templates were manufactured to a set of DIN standards, but it would appear that production centres and field staff may have had to construct their own at times. The Australian War Memorial's Bf 109 G has some interesting variations that are reflected in the differing origins of its three major components, i.e., fuselage from one factory and each wing from a separate source. The fuselage marking is based on an 895 mm sized square; wing lower surface markings are 955 mm (port) and 942 mm (starboard); upper surface markings are 1000 mm (port) and 986 mm (starboard). The discrepancy between the two wings underlines the variation between sources. The original Hakenkreuz marking was 300 mm square, but this had been replaced with one 295 mm square. In both cases the plain white outline was slightly oversize at 10 mm. According to the specification for this marking a 10 mm surround accorded with a square of 315 mm.

A distinct, but localised, variation to the Balkenkreuz marking had emerged at unit-level in two different theatres of operation and for two diametrically opposed reasons. The first appeared on Fw 200s of KG 40 engaged on anti-shipping sorties. The black centre portion of the Balkenkreuz had been expanded to the full overall size of the revised marking, to which had then been added a white outline and black edging in the original 1936 proportions. The purpose was to reduce the visual impact of the revised marking with its distinctive broad white outline edges – a less than useful feature for aircraft engaged on long-range solo operations where cloud and weather conditions were sought to mask approach to shipping.

The second, and identical form of marking, had turned up on some of the Bf 110s of LG 1 serving in the North African campaign. A third variation had also appeared in the same theatre of operations, in slightly different form, on various Bf 109s of 6./JG 27 and 7./SKG 210; in the latter instances the black centre portion of the marking had been enlarged to the overall size of the original marking; to that had been added the regulation size (original) white edges, but without the narrow black outline. Those modifications were all noted on aircraft wearing 79-camouflage colouring on the fuselage surfaces. The reason in that instance was to make the marking far more visible. The same aberration had also appeared on the wing upper surface marking of some JG 27 Bf 109 Fs.

Deletion of the narrow black edging to the fuselage Balkenkreuz had begun appearing at factory -level on some Bf 109 production aircraft, commencing with the F-2 model and continuing intermittently until appearance of the G-2 model in mid-1942, after which time the plain white edge predominated. Two versions of the wing upper surface Balkenkreuz marking also appeared on the G-6 model, even at the same production centre and at the same time. In some instances only the white angles of the cross were marked. That appears to occur from around late 1943, but both forms of the Balkenkreuz continued to be seen well into 1944.

Such anomalies were not restricted to fighter aircraft. Do 217s engaged on anti-shipping operations in particular appeared with a range of incorrect Balkenkreuz markings. The most common fault was adoption of the revised fuselage and wing under surface-style marking for the wing upper surfaces. Conversely some of KG 40's Do 217s exhibited a 1936-style fuselage marking, incorporating a white surround slightly wider than specified, which produced a marking style similar to the last form seen in 1918.

The Hakenkreuz marking had been less affected by these changes. With removal of the red banner and white disc background on 1 January 1939, at production centres the marking had been moved onto the fin, its original centre point position and alignment coordinates then being applied to just the fin dimensions. Despite the revisions to camouflage at production centres in December 1939, when 65-colouring had been taken right up the fuselage sides to include the vertical tail surfaces, initially the white outline had been retained without any narrow black edging. The latter refinement made random appearances throughout 1940 and onwards, becoming a factory standard in either mid-1941 (some Bf 109 F machines were without it) or a little later. That revision had then remained in force on production aircraft until 1942 when several changes had been introduced.

As with the earlier revisions to Balkenkreuz markings, oversized examples of the Hakenkreuz had also occurred, though far fewer than its companion marking. From the meagre photographic record those appear to have occurred primarily at training establishments, e.g., several Kl 35 Bs and a Praga E 39

LEFT: The revision to markings promulgated after the end of the Polish campaign called for an increase in overall size, as well as a change to the ratio of proportions. This Bf 109 E of 3./JG 2, photographed during the subsequent winter, shows the inaccurate interpretation of those instructions. The fuselage Balkenkreuz marking had the revised ratio of proportions but retained its original overall dimensions. The wing marking, which should have retained the old proportions but been moved inboard and slightly increased in overall size, had instead been applied greatly oversize and using the ratio of proportions applicable to the fuselage and underwing marking.

RIGHT: Retention of the pre-October 1939 Balkenkreuz proportions continued well into 1940, despite an official directive that stipulated increase in overall size to 880 mm and a revision of the ratio of proportions. Uffz. Fröba damaged this Bf 109 E-3, W.Nr. 820 of 4./JG 77, when he landed in Sweden in error on 24 October 1940. His unit was based in Norway and he had made a navigational error. The aircraft provides some interesting insights into the delays in correcting major factors relating to markings. Despite the date, the fuselage Balkenkreuz marking was still retained its oversize dimensions, which probably accounts for why it was marked too far forward by half a frame, and lacked also the prescribed increased proportions to the white and black edging. These differences underline the confusion that accompanied the change of markings order. (Air Historic Research Bo. Widfeldt)

LEFT: The lower surface of the port wing of Fröba's aircraft shows that while the original pre-October 1939 proportions had been retained, the overall size had been grossly exaggerated. The fact that this aircraft still retained these anomalous markings may relate to it being an older E-3 model, one possibly kept as a reserve aircraft. (Air Historic Research Bo Widfeldt)

of A/B 23 at Kaufbeuren. The other noted examples were seen on captured aircraft flown for evaluation purposes, e.g., Spitfire, P-38, and P-47, which wore special identification markings of an all yellow 04-tail section with a solid, oversize black Hakenkreuz marking. The larger size was no doubt adopted as an additional identification aid. The other source of that form of incorrect marking occurred on Italian aircraft pressed into Luftwaffe service at the time of the split of Italian forces into pro- and anti-German forces.

A directive issued in 1942, TAGL IP 10 g, Nr. 37/42, had first addressed simplification of the Balkenkreuz and Hakenkreuz markings, calling for deletion of the black outline and centre on wing upper surfaces and the deletion of the black outline to the Hakenkreuz marking. As noted above, that order had been complied with only intermittently. Precise date of issue is unknown, but judging by photographic evidence it was in the second half of the year.

The 1944 edition of Der Flugzeugmaler restated those marking styles for Balkenkreuz and Hakenkreuz. In doing so it attempted once again to eliminate the fairly widespread non-conformist state of these markings.

> *"The Balkenkreuze of the wing undersurfaces remains unchanged.*
>
> *Simplified outline insignia is to be utilised on dark camouflage colours (70/71 for land planes, 72/73 for sea planes, 74/75 for fighter aircraft). In these instances the following is eliminated:*
>
> *The black outline of the Balkenkreuze*
>
> *The black inner part of the insignia (i.e., both Balkenkreuze and Hakenkreuze); if the fuselage Balkenkreuz lies partly on a light camouflage background (65 or 76), the dark upper surface colour (70 to 75) is to be brought down between the white angles, as far as this lies on the colour.*
>
> *The black surround to the Hakenkreuz on the fin, independent of the background colour.*
> *(See TAGL, section IP 10 g, Nr. 37/42)."*

In the 15 August Sammelmitteilung reference was again made to that instruction as follows;

> *"Insignia*
> *It is apparent that, despite repeated instructions for simplification, economy measures, etc., Balkenkreuze and Hakenkreuze are still being applied in the original manner.*
>
> *Only the outlines of the Balkenkreuze and either the black portion or the white surrounds of the Hakenkreuze are to be painted as follows;*
>
> *On light colours 76 and 21 only the black outlines of the Balkenkreuz and the black Hakenkreuz,*
>
> *On dark colours 72, 73, 75, 81, 82 and 83 only the white outline Balkenkreuze and the white outline Hakenkreuze.*
>
> *These instructions also apply to the use of removable or decal markings, although remaining stocks are naturally to be used up. Future orders, however, will conform to the present directive. For night camouflage (22 black), colour 77 grey instead of 21 will be used for the outline insignia."*

These were the last known instructions issued on the subject. Despite their appeal, the occurrence of incorrect styles of markings continued to the end of the war, aided in part by the inevitable inclusion of approval to use up existing stocks.

Nationality markings of convenience

Luftwaffe units had, of course, seen front line service during the years of the Spanish Civil War, where they had adopted the nationality markings of their allies, the Nationalist Forces of General Franco.

In keeping with the Nationalist Air Force units, a plain black disk had been marked in the standard six positions of wing upper and lower surfaces and fuselage side surfaces. The rudder was marked with a black cross on a white background, the latter usually covering the entire rudder surface. For types that had a complex wing structure, such as He 59s, a black disc marking was used on the fuselage, fore and aft of the wings, to ensure rapid air-to-air recognition. By the time that the first Bf 109 Bs arrived in March 1937, a white cross had been added to wing upper and lower surfaces markings, and wing tips marked in white on all aircraft types.

ABOVE: Retention of the pre-October 1939 proportions, combined with the prescribed increase in overall size to 880 mm, continued to be seen well into 1940. This Bf 109 E-4, W.Nr. 1506 of 7./JG 53, was lost on 6 September 1940. The modified camouflage has been taken down to the pre-December 1939 low division line between side and lower surfaces. The original Type 4 pattern, in 71/02, had been almost eliminated beneath a background spray, possibly 02, which had then been heavily mottled with a darker colour.

ABOVE: The rudder of Helmut Wick's, the Staffelkapitän of 3./JG 2, Bf 109E-4, 'Yellow 2' was adorned with 22 victory bars at the beginning of September 1940. The fuselage Balkenkreuz displays the unit modification to reduce its visibility. The white borders had been painted with black to reduce them to the pre-October 1939 proportion. Whether this was done with official RLM sanction, or on the initiative of the unit command staff is unknown, but the evidence points to the latter being the most likely source of the change. Note the dense application of the modified camouflage, a mixture of stippling and narrow short lines making a lace-like effect.

ABOVE: Wearing Balkenkreuz markings of both correct proportion and size Bf 110 C-5, 5F+CM W.Nr. 2177 of 4.(F)/14, was forced down on 21 July 1940. Previously, this aircraft sometimes has been incorrectly identified as W.Nr. 2187, which was completely destroyed on 26 September 1940. Note that though the Hakenkreuz does not have a narrow black border, the darker background colouring produces the illusion of one. Camouflage is 71/02, with heavy mottling in both colours.

LEFT: Bombers exhibited their share of non-standard applications of the Balkenkreuz during the early months of 1940, but this Ju 88 A-1 of I/KG 51 is finished in accordance with the prevailing regulations. The black portions of the unit code, 9K+EL, are barely discernible against the dark greens of the camouflage, but the Balkenkreuz and Hakenkreuz markings, and the aircraft letter 'E', stand out boldly as the regulations intended. (H. Obert)

LEFT: KG 40 was still employing this oversized marking during the winter of 1942/43 as shown by this photograph of F8+HK, a Fw 200 C of 2. Staffel. On the original print it was possible to discern how the inner portion of the white angles had been painted black to increase the size of the black cross.

RIGHT: Disproportionate Balkenkreuz markings also appeared in North Africa, but for a quite different purpose. There they were meant to rapidly identify nationality as the air war became more intense. Shot down on 14 August 1942, Lt. Mix's Bf 109 F-4 trop of 6./JG 27 had the oversize Balkenkreuz markings applied to both fuselage and wing upper surfaces. Against the sand-coloured background they stood out starkly – as intended.
(AWM via D. Vincent)

RIGHT: Another Bf 109 F trop of JG 27 burns after crash-landing in the desert. It too displays the oversized Balkenkreuz on the fuselage, illustrating that the markings on Mix's aircraft were not an exception.

LEFT: Oversize Balkenkreuz markings also were used by other units; here Uffz. Hans Sennholz's Bf 109 F trop of 7./ZG 1 S9+DR, W.Nr. 4964, lies in the desert after being shot down by flak on 31 August 1942 near El Alamein. Propeller damage shows that it had stopped rotating at the time of impact. Again the oversize fuselage Balkenkreuz marking is present, but the upper surface of both wings display standard markings. Note however the discrepancy in the camouflage; the fuselage and horizontal tail surfaces are in 78 and 79 finish while the wings have Type 4 pattern camouflage in 71/02 to which white tactical markings had been added. Either it was lost before re-painting could be completed or, more likely, it had had replacement wings

RIGHT: A Bf 109 F-4 trop of 7./JG 53 found by 92 Squadron, RAAF personnel at Daba displays another variation to the fuselage Balkenkreuz. Careful measurement shows that the proportions are about halfway between standard and the oversize marking seen on other Bf 109s in this theatre of operations. The Stammkenzeichen markings had been painted out with 79 before applying the unit markings. The slight difference in colour between the original and newer 79-coloured paintwork can be seen as angular areas that look, at first, like some form of segment pattern to the camouflage.
(J. L. Waddy)

ABOVE: Not all Luftwaffe aircraft in North Africa adopted oversize markings. This dump at Daba shows two Bf 109 Es, a Bf 110 (W. Nr. 2354) and a Ju 87, all of which wear correctly proportioned fuselage Balkenkreuze.The pair of Bf 109 F wings in the foreground illustrate the regulation positioning and standard proportioned wing lower surface Balkenkreuz.

BELOW: Bf 110s did, however, utilize this oversize form of marking as seen on LI+O? of I (ZG)/LG 1, camouflaged in tropical colouring, being inspected by American service personnel, possibly at Wright Patterson AFB. It wears the abnormal size Balkenkreuz marking on its fuselage. Deformation of the bottom edge of the fin indicates that the aircraft had made a belly landing. (D. Vincent)

ABOVE: Other differences to markings noted on Bf 109s serving in North Africa was a slightly oversize Hakenkreuz as shown here on the fin of W.Nr.7200. Note also the vertical alignment was slightly different, the top rear edge being aligned with the slope of the fin balance area, probably done for expediency. The regulation black edging to the white surround was also absent, a common occurrence.

ABOVE: Painting of the Hakenkreuz and Balkenkreuz was normally done using a series of stencils. Application varied between production centres, sometimes after camouflaging, sometimes before. This Bf 109 G had its second stencil application during marking of the Balkenkreuz to paint in the black centre. Using a metal stencil the 76-coloured side area had been left blank in the shape of the outside dimensions. of the marking during camouflage painting. Note the segment of 74/75-camouflage above the top of the stencil area, which confirms that the camouflage scheme already had been applied in full. A third stencil was then used to apply the white outline, while a final stencil produced the thin black outline. Each stencil had its individual identifying DIN reference number.

Balkenkreuz and Hakenkreuz

LEFT: Unlike their larger counterparts, DFS 230 gliders rarely wore a Hakenkreuz on their vertical tail surfaces. This machine also displays the reduced, but correctly proportioned, fuselage Balkenkreuz more commonly seen on this type of glider.

BELOW: The mid-war style of markings is seen on this Bf 109 G. The Balkenkreuz markings are outline form, but of different proportions, on fuselage and wing upper surface. The Hakenkreuz is also correct for the period other than for the lack of a thin black outline.

BELOW: At some production centres Balkenkreuz and Hakenreuz were sometimes added before application of the primer coat; at others, after the primer had been applied. In most instances, regardless of the order, the markings were masked out before the final camouflage colours were added. At the facility where this Bf 109 was being built, the practice was to spray a large area of white directly over the treated bare metal finish, then to mark in the Balkenkreuz. As shown here, camouflage was then applied, the area around the marking being added last of all. (See also photograph on page 400)

RIGHT: The revised form of outline wing Balkenkreuz marking is shown here, being applied with a stencil set to the regulation DIN dimensions set by the RLM (though small variations occurred as noted in the text). The dark background is the dark segment of the camouflage, not a black centre marking.

LEFT: No regulation has been found calling for simplified outline-type Balkenkreuz markings on wing lower surfaces, but during the last months of the war many fighters exhibited the style of marking seen on this Fw 190 G-8. The yellow band around the nose of the aircraft was applied as part of the last change to tactical markings as detailed in Chapter 11. (S. Haggard)

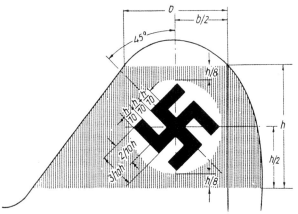

ABOVE: Proportions for the original form of the Hakenkreuz marking. No dimensions were specified because of the variety of aircraft in use made that impractical.

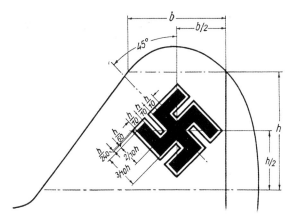

ABOVE: The revised form introduced on 1 January 1939 after deletion of the background red banner and white disc. Proportions remained unaltered.

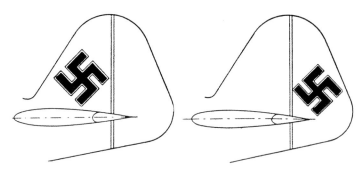

ABOVE: Aircraft with restricted space on the fin were allowed to mark the Hakenkreuz across the rudder (e.g., Fieseler Fi 156).

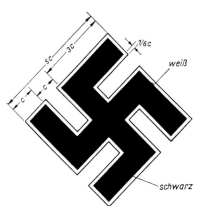

Abmessungen

Größe 5c	315	(400)	500	(630)	800	
c	63	80	100	126	160	
3c	189	240	300	378	480	
1/6c	10	13	17	21	27	

Auf Sichtschutzanstrich Farbton 70÷75 fällt schwarzes Innenteil des Hakenkreuzes fort.

ABOVE: The proportions and dimensions for marking of the Hakenkreuz.

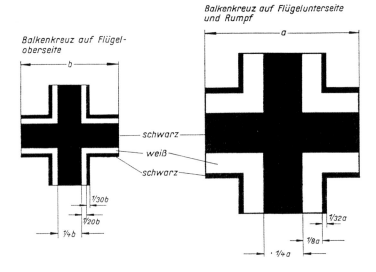

ABOVE: The standard proportions for both forms of Balkenkreuz carried after size revision in 1939. These proportions (but not style of presentation) remained in force until 1945.

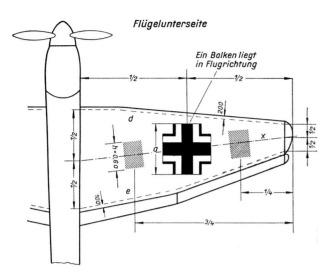

ABOVE: Positioning of the wing under surface Balkenkreuz marking for single-engine aircraft. Note positioning for Stammkennzeichnung or unit codes also shown.

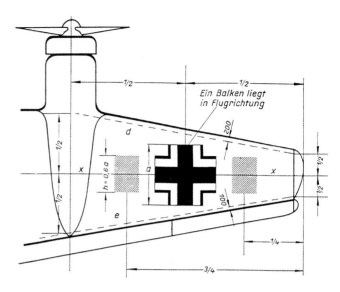

ABOVE: Positioning of the wing under surface Balkenkreuz marking for twin-engine aircraft.

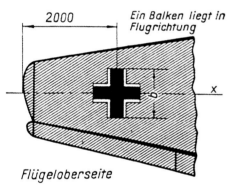

Flügeloberseite

Der Mittelpunkt des Balkenkreuzes auf Flügeloberseite liegt auf der festgelegten Mittellinie X 2000mm vom Flügelende entfernt.

ABOVE: Positioning of the wing upper surface Balkenkreuz marking.

RIGHT: Individual aircraft types were provided with specific markings diagrams – that for the Ju 88 A—1 and A-5 being shown here. Note that the extension of the wing for the A-5 variant was not accompanied by a repositioning of the upper surface Balkenkreuz marking. The lower wing surface markings were moved slightly outboard as they relied on being positioned at the mid-point between engine and wing tip.

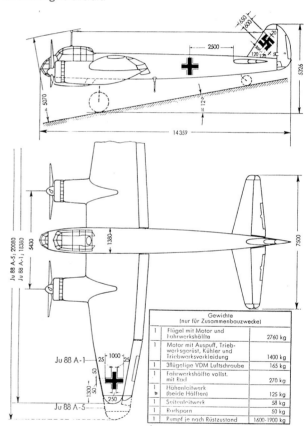

Abb. 2 Übersicht, Hauptmaße und Gewichte der Ju 88 A-1, A-5

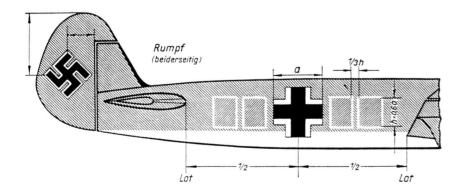

LEFT: Positioning and proportions for marking of Balkenkreuz and Hakenkreuz on fuselage and vertical tail surfaces. Note the purely representational positioning of the Hakenkreuz marking shown on the rudder of the stylised Ju 88 drawing to illustrate the permissible alternative position for this marking on some types (but not the Ju 88). Positions for the Stammkennzeichnung or unit codes are also shown.

Addendum and Corrigenda to Volume One

Page 8 — (left hand column), in the 'Acknowledgements': Sergio Luis dos Santos' name was incorrectly spelled (as Louis). Helmut Stubert was also incorrectly named as Hans Stubert. My apologies to both.

Page 191 — Caption to middle photograph: the location is Kassel-Rothwestern.

Page 194 — Captions to top and middle photographs: the location is Kassel-Rothwestern.

Colour cards and chips: on colour card *Tafel 3) nicht in den RLM-Karten veröffentlichte Farbtöne* ['Card 3' not in the RLM cards of published colours], the colour samples shown on the bottom line, items 19 to 24 inclusive, were not adequately identified in the text.

Chip 19 — 'gelbchromatiert' was a yellow chromate plating finish for metal surfaces.

Chip 20 — 'kadmiert' was a cadmium plating finish for metal surfaces.

Chip 21 — 'Ikarol 201 (grün)' was Warnecke & Böhm 'Ikarol light metal primer green 201'.

Chip 22 — 'FLIEGLACK 7142 (rotbraun)' was a metal primer, Warnecke & Böhm 'Ikarol propeller lacquer red 135'.

Chip 23 — 'FLIEGLACK 7130 (rotbraun)' was a fabric primer, Atlas Ago A.G. 'Celesta nitro aviation primer red 1603 C'.

Chip 24 — 'FLIEGLACK 7132 (grau)' was Atlas Ago A.G. 'Celesta wood primer filler grey 2070'.

Errata

Page 103 — caption to bottom photograph: the correct identification should be Fw 190 F-8, W.Nr. 584592, 'Yellow 14'.

Page 104 — photograph caption; the location was Neubiberg, not Oberpfaffenhofen.

Page 116 — photograph caption: the aircraft was a Bf 109 G-10, W.Nr. 612769, 'Yellow 12' not a Bf 109 K-4, 'Red 12'. The engine cowlings were not from the Bf 109, but from the Me 262 on the left of the photograph, and were finished in 02 with filler along the rivet lines.

Page 116 — (left hand column): the paint formula listed under the heading D.K.H. Metallack 10100.76 should read D.K.H. Metallack 10.100.76. In the text, in the paragraph above I made the comment that this was an unusual identifying number. A second document has since emerged to show that the '10100' was missing a decimal point between the '10' and the '100'. The nature of this full designation was part of the D.K.H. company system, with just the colour defined by its RLM two-digit designation '76'.

Page 146 — caption to bottom photograph: S9+PH on the extreme left of the photograph is a Bf 110 C-6, one of the 1. Staffel aircraft armed with a 30 mm cannon in a belly pack.

Page 148 — all three photographs: this was a Bf 110 E, not a Bf 110 D as stated.

Page 166 — caption to bottom photograph: the location was St Dizier, not a production centre, so the likelihood is that this aircraft had been delivered to a unit in the area.

Page 167 — caption to top photograph: this is Fw 190 G-3, W.Nr. 160022. The location is reported to be Montecorvino, in Italy, not a production centre in Germany.

The colour card titled *farbtontafel*: the colour chip on line three, marked '28 weinrot', was a production error, the actual paint chip used being colour FLIEGLACK 7142, the fabric primer colour shown also on *Tafel 3) nicht in den RLM- Karten veröffentlichte Farbtöne.* The correct 28 weinrot colour is included in the facsimile 1938 colour card titled *farbtontafel zur Behandlungs= und Anwendungsvorschrift für flugzeuglacke (Ausgabe 1938)*.

APPENDIX

German Paint Technology 1930-1945

A Synopsis by Jürgen H. Kiroff – Farben-Kiroff-Technik

A Brief Insight into German Paint Technology 1930-1945

INTRODUCTION

Historians and enthusiasts continue endlessly discussing the colours of historical aircraft, yet nobody has bothered to ask the experts in this field, i.e., manufacturers of the original colours. Perhaps the topic was not important enough to promote such an idea?

It is a simple fact that a building of historical value is restored according to the original blueprint, materials and colours used to construct it. The restoration of an historic aircraft, on the other hand, seems to rely more often than not on the instruction sheet of a model aircraft kit, and paint colours prepared by model paint manufacturers.

We are delighted then that Ken Merrick has given us the opportunity to support him with our professionally based knowledge, and also to contribute a little to the history of chemistry as it relates to colour. It is to his credit that he is first one to deal exclusively with the colour schemes of the former German Luftwaffe on a more detailed technical basis. However, a cautionary word to fellow chemists: the target audience of this book is not you, but rather the circle of historians, restoration experts, air enthusiasts and model builders.

DEFINITION OF THE CONCEPT OF COLOUR

Colour is a sensory impression transmitted by the eye to the brain. A colour is signified by its name or tone, how pure or thinned out it is, and its value or lightness. Our physical perception of colour originates as an external stimulant, just as all physical objects influence the light waves that reach our eyes; however, colour is a paradox, only becoming visible to the eye when an object is illuminated by a light source that is, in reality, invisible to our eye. Depending on the combination and the energy (wave length) of the reflected light, we perceive a variety of visual colours. Yet we do not live in a world of varied coloured objects, but rather in a world of surfaces that reflect light in various ways that then appear to have colour.

Colour impressions can be produced in two ways whereby light can be mixed and modulated, in a plus or minus range termed additive and subtractive. The additive mixture process, for instance, is applied in colour television tubes, where the basic colours are red, green and blue-violet (RGB signal) for the endless range of colours and tones that we see. The mixing of colour pigments, however, deals with a subtractive approach that works back from the three primary colours – yellow, blue and red, none of which can be mixed from any other colour combination. It is by subtracting (taking away) colour from any of those three primaries that moves our colour perception through the full range of the colour spectrum that we see.

Focus on the subject of this book requires that we deal with scientific paint standards that applied – and still do – in Germany in the 1930s and 1940s. The very basis of those German Standards parameters that specify the basic concept of all colour substances is one entitled 'Pigmentation DIN 55943'.

The paramount problem in any technical discourse –and the very nature of this subject requires that we do deal with the technical aspects – is to define the concept of variation (alteration and change); a definition that rests on the factors of physical and chemical change (both chemical and optical) to the properties of a substance that has had to withstand storage and use over any reasonable period of time. Such variables inevitably occur because of natural influences, such as exposure to temperature change and sunlight etc.; or are induced artificially through application of high temperatures or exposure to UV light.

TECHNICAL CHARACTERISTICS OF AGEING OR CHANGE

Plastics and elastomeres or latex based paint can undergo chemical changes due to the impact of such variable influences as light, heat, oxygen, humidity and radiation, any of which can produce specific changes such as a reduction or rearrangement of macro-molecules (large molecules). With the ageing of latex based paints there are incidents of molecular linkage problems (the physical bonding between atoms) as well as molecular linkage breakage (the bonding between the atoms of different chemicals in the substance) that reduces the capacity for thinning with benzene, hardening of the paint and a lack of viscosity.

Exterior paints are exposed to extreme variations in temperature that, depending on geographical location, such as the artic to the tropics , can vary from –50 to +70 degrees Centigrade. These types of paints belong, like plastics, glass etc., to the class of amorphous materials made from macro-molecules whose binding materials do not have a fixed melting point, such as metals. Instead, they have a wide softening, or melting threshold that can be as broad as 10 to 30 degrees Centigrade . This temperature band is sometimes called the 'glass-melting threshold' (based on the terminology of glass melting from rigid, to brittle, to soft). In this range, macro-molecules begin to expand, reducing their bonding rigidity, as the temperature is increased. Morphologically, the paint film goes from a rigid, frozen state to a soft, viscous, elastic state. First the outer layer of macro-molecules move (known as the 'Brown movement'), then this movement is transferred to the main molecules of the paint layer.

Simply expressed, through heat-induced movement, molecules expand and collide with each other as they attempt to make more room for themselves – and thus the paint film expands. This larger space is referred to as a 'free volume'. This process is reversible when a cooling process sets in; the molecules shrink again, regaining their rigidity as the volume decreases, and the paint film shrinks. This process is known as the 'freezing process'.

During the 'glass-melting threshold' many properties of the macro-molecular materials change, such as the elasticity module as a measurement tool for hardness and elasticity, the expansion coefficient, the specific heat capacity, the electrical constant and the density of the specific volume.

This is a simple overview of the processes of change. For those interested, the following provides a more detailed analysis of the processes involved – and provides reasons for changes that occurred to German camouflage lacquers.

Normally, the type of paint film we are concerned with here consists of straight, branched out, or integrated strings of molecules. Readers may recall the common school textbook illustration of molecules, shown as masses of atoms clustered together in an endless range of patters. Below the temperature gradient norm (Tg- norm) the paint film is frozen in a fixed state, and the molecules barely move. With increasing temperature (i.e., an increase in energy) the outer strings of the molecules begin to vibrate until all molecules of the paint film are affected, in keeping with their interrelated nature. As the depth of penetration of movement into the paint layer increases, the E-module (the elasticity factor, for the technically minded expressed as =ca. 10 squared N/mm squared) is increased. During the first phase the paint film becomes softer and more ductile, assuming the characteristics of a viscous and elastic substance. At the end of this process the paint film is either rubbery or viscous-elastic, depending on the degree of linkage density of the molecules.

In this state, especially where a high degree of linkage density occurs, the paint layer can display rubber-like elasticity and hence suffer no permanent deformation when the process is reversed. This elasticity phenomenon, commonly known as the 'change to glass' threshold, works the same way in reverse when the warm paint film cools down. The technical literature refers to it as the 'change to glass' temperature, or the temperature at which the paint film turns glassy – a precise point in an otherwise broad area of transition.

Evidence of the weathering process is especially evident in dry oxidation prone areas producing strong linkage of macro-molecules, and resulting in a hardening of the top (external) layer. This is connected to a clear increase in the 'change to glass' temperature. An increase in the Tg value is the same as an increased shift upwards of the 'change to glass' temperature.

INTERNAL STRESS AS A CAUSE FOR CRACKING PAINT

During the last two decades, paint experts have become acquainted with a phenomenon known as 'Internal Stress'. The work of English and Scandinavian researchers had been preceded by the work of D. Y. Perera, from the Belgian Research Institute 'Cori', contributing important studies to the characteristics of paint. But what does the term really mean?

Internal Stress with paint film arises when layers behave in different mechanical ways (different Tg- values) as for instance in the 'state of glass' as opposed to that of rubber elasticity.

According to Perera and other authors (i.e., Funke) there are two causes of IS (internal stress) formation that can be measured on flexible substrata; firstly, contraction of the top paint film layer due to different rates of evaporation of thinners and softeners used, and because of increased linkage of molecules (rigidity) through ageing and weathering, causing cracks to form on solid. Secondly, expansion or swelling of the paint film because of water absorption in high humidity locales, producing additional wrinkling of the solid surface.

However, The IS however can revert because of increase movement of molecules. In the first instance, because of an increase of temperature above the Tg-value; in the second, because of the normal drying out values of the RF (approximately 50 degrees). These two physical factors for change of paint structure are not the only ones to be considered in relationship to variation in the appearance of 'standard' lacquers.

CONSTANCY OF PIGMENTS

A major factor with any interpretation of colours relates to the consistency of pigments, the component in any paint that produces the colour we actually perceive with the naked eye.

Eyewitnesses and primary sources can provide valuable information – but only if one is careful to consider the following parameters.

Wrecked aircraft parts

The environment in which the part was found, as well as the composition of the paints used on it, determine the optical changes that

have inevitably taken place, e.g., all matt paints contained talcum so that the surface was more scratch resistant, because the Tg value was increased by its inclusion. However, weathering caused 'chalking' , producing a floury coating (that can be wiped off) on the surface that made the colour appear whitish-grey.

Even when professional museum archaeological standards are applied to the storage of such objects, at best the changes can only be slowed down. Even parts that have been completely shielded from light do not show their absolutely true original colour tone today.

Colour charts

In the paint industry, colour charts have a deterioration time of 12 months. The colour charts that we are concerned with here are 600 months old.

All such RLM reference charts were produced on paper painted white with a non-RLM cellulose-nitrate paint, a method still used today. As a result, from these surviving charts no conclusions can be made about the actual degree of lustre.

The cardboard carrier, the paper structure of the actual colour chart, inevitably acquires a brownish-yellow tint, and has a microscopic loose fibrous surface. The optical changes then stem from the age and the composition of the cardboard, a result of a chemical change that also influences subtle but discernible changes in the colour chips they contain.

Further, each colour chip does not show an homogenous colour over its complete area, having minute areas that are lighter and darker than the original base colour.

The authority for colour standards within Germany since the 1920s is the Reichsausschuss für Lieferbedingungen (RAL), which has in its possession two original RLM charts. However, the institute would never certify any colour, even after comparison their charts, as a 100 per cent accurate RLM colour (statement of Herr Helmut Wigger, RAL, Feb. 2003).

Colour data from the earliest dated colour charts surviving today, 1936 are based on comparisons carried out by the RAL (using those original RLM charts) in the nineteen-seventies. That constitutes a time span of 300 months, much too late to serve as a 100 per cent reliable reference. If we say "…that it is not the right colour tone anymore" we may mean a slight change, but change could also be a shift from white into red, blue into white and green into red.

The value of the best colour photographs

Colour photographs also are a source to be treated with great circumspection, and can be used only for the broadest interpretations of what a particular colour tone actually was.

A primary problem is that different types, and manufacturing processes of film can portray the same colours in different ways. The sensitivity of electromagnetic radiation of silver halides used in photography ranges from g-radiation to the short wave part of the visible spectrum. By using spectral sensibilies (sensitivity enhancers) with organic colours, sensitivity can be expanded into the infrared realm. Halides are in most cases imbedded in the form of granules in the thin layers of a gelatinous mass that not only serves as a binder, but also plays a major rôle in the photographic process because of its sensiometric (light sensitive) properties.

One generally speaks) about photographic emulsion, but actually what takes place is actually a dispersion of silver halide granules (granule size 1mm^3) in a chemical carrier base (Xerogelen). Most often silver bromide (AgBr) is used with a little silver iodide added, while silver chloride (AgCl) is used in only a few low sensitivity photo papers. Since the light sensitivity of silver bromide occurs in the ultraviolet and blue ranges of light one has to make the other layers sensitive for photography. That happens through addition of certain colours, especially Cyanin, Mercocyanin, and Polymethin to the emulsion. By using certain sensitising agents one can reach sensitivities even with infrared radiation up to a wavelength of 1.3mm. Layers that are sensitive to the whole spectrum, other than red, are referred to as orthochromatic or orthopanchromatic and panchromatic; however, in layers sensitive to the total spectral range, red appears lighter and green darker.

The circumstances under which an object was photographed also play a major rôle. Since those circumstances often are not known, a definitive conclusion is hard reach when dealing with colour tones. Natural filters, such as dust clouds etc., also play a rôle, as do polarizing filters such as water, desert, grassland and forest.

Mistakes can also be made during developing and can lead to different results.

The colour chemistry of photography is different in a fundamental way from the real surface (objective reality) colour of the object photographed. Lastly, the photo itself is subject to ageing. Most significant of all, even a photograph taken under optimal conditions cannot stand up to direct comparison with the real surface of the object (objective reality).

Conclusions

This exposition shows how impractical it has been, up to now, to search for accurate original colours and to make copies from such sources. But one may then ask; is this futile effort even necessary in order to search for the authentic colours?

THE SEARCH FOR THE SOLUTION

Before and during WW II, major technical breakthroughs were accomplished, not just by the producers of aircraft in Germany, but in particular by the chemical industry, primarily represented by I.G. Farben (An industry of world rank that was deliberately dismantled by the allies after WWII.) Many people still do not look at paints for what they really are: a complex, chemical, highly developed technical product. Instead, they unwittingly tend to trivialize it as, "Oh, it needs only a little paint".

To achieve a high quality standard for paint it is obvious that strict procedures and quality control have to be followed. The most important aspect of this is the documentation of the production steps. The industry refers to this as the formulation procedure.

One can understand then, that as suppliers of materials for military production, the demand for quality was very high. This then was the origin of the high technology standard that applied, especially when raw materials, financial capital etc., were tight. The loose phrase "They used what they received" has to be carefully scrutinized. Its validity becomes even more doubtful when one reads of the penalties that were incurred if one did not follow the particular colour formulations, even in 1945.

The question now is, How can one duplicate old surface paints today? The simple answer is that precise application of the following points will lead to success:

Analytical and Physical Chemistry

Old paint surfaces cannot show us the original, true colour tone, or properties, but they do give us a good idea of the chemical composition. The latter is still largely present in the paint film. Changes will have occurred, because of the chemical and physical interaction with the environment, contact chemistry and the substrata, and thus the distribution of the original chemical content is not the same any more. Molecular movement, caused by chemical, electrical and gravimetric imbalances and accelerated by temperature and radiation interactions, influence the changes. However, by using classical analytical chemistry, spectra analysis and microscopy we can determine the composition of the paint film at hand. The more we know about the environmental conditions (i.e., chemical make-up of the ground where the object was found such as clay, lime dirt, salt water, depth, oxygen content,

temperature, sun exposure and period in the ground or water) the 'easier' will be a determination.

The history of Chemistry

At the beginning of every search, we establish the limitation of possibilities; and to reach this point we have to ask ourselves what was technically possible during the historical period in question.

In turn, it is impossible to avoid the need to research the technical development of paint up to this specific point and only be content with the period in which we are interested. For the layperson it seems exaggerated to go back to the Roman period; and such a bizarre requirement would only be warranted if that degree of knowledge contributed to the particular period we are interested in.

Contemporary documents in Chemistry

Michael Ullman (who also has written on this subject of Luftwaffe colours) also explored a path that led to a solution of our problem. Because the German war industry planned and documented everything to the last detail, he asked whether this should also have been true with paint. If so, there must be documents that would make the duplication of the exact colour tones possible. Since 1928, within Germany all industrial issues and standards have been the concern of the Reichsausschuss für Lieferbedingungen (Reichscommittee for delivery terms and conditions i.e. standards), which still exists today as the RAL. It was only obvious to look to that institute for solutions and clarification.

The intriguing idea of Michael Ullmann was to find the old RLM colours under a different nomenclature in the RAL colour listings. Unfortunately, this was found to apply only to the following colours: RLM 00, 01, 02, 04, 21, 22, 24, 25, 26, 27, 28, 61, 62, 63, 66.

The solution however was not only to be found with the RAL but also in the archives of the German paint industry, and the reports of the Allied interrogators who wanted such formulae for their own industries.

Individually those documents comprised:

Surface Paint Lists;
L.Dv. 521 and added regulations (table 3)
Instructions and orders of the RLM, the High Command of the Wehrmacht, the High Command of the Luftwaffe, the Testing Facilities (table 4)

Correspondence from and within the Industry (table 4)

It sounds incredible, but historians have not looked at these key documents.

Colour formulae

Most available formulae are not encoded in a single standard. As is still customary today, the chemical compounds involved are not designated as such appearing instead as company brand names. Many of these brands are still protected but it was possible to track down most of these formulations through the technical literature of the time, as well as the current owners of the brand.

This line of resolution was then pursued through a technically exacting, time consuming process that began first in a laboratory setting, using small quantities; then, in the case of the binders, in 100 kg quantities, and for the pigments, in 5 kg quantities. In order to duplicate exactly the technology of the time, the following original plant equipment was employed: a Spangenberg Dissolver, type ESM1 (built in 1939) to dissolve pigments; and to abrade the mixture, a Spangenberg drum roller. This ensured that all the original factors were re-established in their entirety.

Luftwaffe Camouflage and Markings 1933-1945

With the help of pigmentation charts, reference pigmentation paints could be made. Those where then mixed with white and black reference paint, in clearly defined proportions, and tested to determine the tonal range.

All such samples were then spectrally measured. With the help of these values we can now use original documents to come up with formulations based on the original pigments. The spectral values provided by the RAL could now be adjusted to the original colour tones. Thus a combination of original technology, ingredients and the spectral measurements of the RAL have been employed to reverse engineer the original paints.

Which formula components are responsible for surface characteristics?

L.Dv 521, published in 1938, described three basic binding materials:

(1) For fireproof paints for aircraft – Polyvinyl chloride (vinoflex), which used antimony white and acted as a flame retardant in combination with chlorine.

(2) For opaque finishes or body varnishes in the remaining colour ranges – cellulose nitrate, in high to middle viscosity, combined with synthetic resin varnishes (type 4 per cent to a maximum of 24 per cent for 400pas. One used about 30 per cent for opaque finishes, but in mixtures today only up to 24 per cent is used). It was very difficult to add pigmentation to Lacquer 7109, and as a result it contained only about 10 per cent pigment. This was especially true with colours containing white or yellow. The low pigmentation did not produce good opaque covering qualities.

(3) In lacquers 7121.22, and in light metal primers 7101.02 – Phenolakyd resin was used, manufactured in that form worldwide by Warnecke & Boehme, and sold as a light metal primer. A higher pigmentation content of 20 per cent was possible with 7122, a significant increase over what was possible with 7109.

In addition, solvents, emollients and colourless fillers, like talcum powder, chalk, shale powder and tinters added there own l characteristics to surface qualities.

Pigments

Pigments are simply finely ground powders. They are insoluble in the binding material and give paint its property to cover the base material with a specific colour. The following were used.

Titanium oxide (Anatas)	Hansa blue (Phtalocyanine,
Zinc white	unstable.)
Lemon yellow	Burned soot (smoke)
Gold ochre	Iron oxide red
Ultramarine blue	Iron oxide yellow
Cobalt blue	

Colour solutions

Colour solutions are soluble colouring materials of a very intense colouring strength, but lacking in covering (opaque) ability – basically they are inks. In order to achieve covering ability (colour lacquers) enamels have to be produced first. They form as a result of the deposit of the colour solution on a covering pigment layer. Such pigment layers consist of barium sulfate, calcium carbonate, zinc oxide, iron oxide, etc.

By following this exacting, scientific approach to reproduce the original colours, based on the L.Dv. documented references and the

history of chemistry as noted above, we can certify as conclusive all of the formulations.

FORMULATIONS OF INDIVIDUAL PAINTS AND PAINT TONES

Covering (opaque) paints.

RLM 7109 was a cellulose nitrate/ ketone resin combination paint with the following properties. Pigmentation was difficult to add; it could not be sprayed on; it did not withstand the elements well; it did not adhere to light metals well; it tended to flake when used in combination with primer 7101.02 because of a higher change to glass threshold. However, it could be matted, with retention of all properties, as a semi-gloss finish.

RLM 7114 and 7115 were paints of the non-flammable range, based on vinyl chloride combined with antimony white. They were salt water resistant and relatively thick (heavy) paints. They were not very compatible with other binders and hence it was difficult to paint over them. Antimony white acts as a pigment and hence has an effect on colour tone. These paints were also difficult to matt with talcum powder. The result is that not all RLM colours can be exactly reformulated today. It could be matted and made durable to the maximum only if mixed to semi-gloss standard.

RLM 7121 and 7122, with the 20 per cent pigmentation, had decidedly higher opacity than that of 7109, which ensured that the colour beneath no longer mattered. Because of the good adhesion, even on light metals, primers were not necessary. Phenol alkyd resin was the new binder whose qualities were known from its use in the primers 7101 and 7102. This new paint showed excellent durability and had the added advantage that phenol alkyd resin was manufactured from non-strategic materials. Fatty acids were boiled with plant oils and acids and made for a good air-drying paint, but it was not as durable as heat (kiln) dried Durophene. It could be matted to maximum durability as a full matt finish.

The light colour tones

Light colour tones are involved in all paints where the pigmentation of white and yellow dominates. With these colours especially, there have been many unanswered questions. The camouflage colours for the underside of aircraft, such as RLM 65, RLM 76 and RLM 78, RLM 79, as well as the light grey overall aircraft colour of the pre-war years, used such pigmentation.

RLM 7107.63, 7108.63, lacquer Groups 01 and 02 raise the first persistent question. Colour tone 63 (RAL 7004, 840R) was used in conjunction with colour range 01 and 02, always sprayed over a silver (and later a grey intermediate paint 7106). Earlier, for instance, painting of the He 51, used the Avionorm- Nitro paint silver Nr.1708, over sprayed with Avionorm Nr. 7007 grey. Because of the low pigmentation qualities of the Nr 1708 lacquer, the resulting colour impression moved closer to the RLM 02 range; or alternatively if the intermediate paint used was grey combined with RLM 63, retained its own colour tone. The subsequent replacement with 7109.02 had not been done for reasons of time or material considerations, but rather as an improvement in colour uniformity. Aircraft from that time period show a decidedly 'RLM 02' colour tone. (RAL 7004, 840R was deleted after 1942 from the 840R register.) This course of action, to achieve uniformity and balance, might throw some light on the inconsistencies of the underside camouflage colours of the Luftwaffe.

RLM 7109.65, lacquer Group 04. Although higher in pigmentation density than the Nitro paints then in use, RLM 7109.65 contained only

10 per cent pigmentation, which was still not very dense in terms of opacity. The poor covering quality of the white pigments, such as zinc white, titanium oxide, and antimony white in the formulation added to this inadequacy. As noted above, with RLM 7121 and 7122 the pigmentation was considerably higher at 20 per cent. That led to the situation that the colour tone represented in the charts could only be matched after the introduction of individual, single colours. This has also lead to the conclusion on the part of some historians that there was more than one shade of RLM 65, something that has never been proven.

This has to be looked at more closely. Before the introduction of the revised painting standards listed in L.Dv. 521/1 of 1938, painting of aircraft had always been done with three different coats. This three-layered build up consisted of a primer coat, an intermediate coat, and a finishing or topcoat. The intermediate coat served to cover the various primer coat colours (red, green, grey) to give a neutral finish for the topcoat. However, topcoats were very low-pigmented Cellulose paints (only 5 per cent) and the intermediate coats were mostly aluminium in colour. Introduction of the Lacquer Group 04 paints in 1938 dispensed with the requirement for an intermediate coat because the colours listed within that group contained twice as much pigmentation as previous topcoat colours – but the pigmentation was still not sufficient to fully obliterate the effects of primer coat colouring. The poor covering quality of 7109.65, because of the unstable quality of its whites – and also because it was applied over different primer colours – created an overall impression of a colour tone that differed from the one included on the L.Dv 521/1 reference chart. The topcoat colour shown on the official chart colour chip appears uniform only because it was applied to a consistent base colour of white paper.

The primer coat for steel and canvas was reddish brown, for light metal it was olive grey, for hydraulic lines it was RLM 02. The result was that whatever primer 7109.65 was sprayed on, different colour tones resulted. Furthermore the touch-up colour 7121.65 was used, and that led to further colour discrepancies. Using iron oxide red for the transition from canvas covered parts (red base) to light metal parts (olive green base) also could vary the appearance of RLM 65. This state of affairs that was not permitted to continue and Lacquer group 04 was withdrawn.

A further factor was that the base lacquer did not weather very well in comparison with more modern paints that had become available. And there were other reasons for its replacement. We can read the following remarks, even in later OS lists (painting schedules) based on earlier camouflage drawings, e.g.,"....avoid mist spraying, paint must be as 7122". (RLM 7122 had been introduced in 1938, as part of Lacquer group 04, but had not been included in the March issue of L.DV.521/1.) When the historically minded aircraft painter and restorer Jürgen Kretschmann painted the Bf 109 E of the Technical Museum in Berlin with the paints from Lacquer Group 04, he found that the paint was well suited for solid spraying, but not for mist spraying. The misted areas showed a lack of adhesion and when it was sprayed over a previous coat of paint, there were differences in sheen. That meant that only sharp edged separation lines were possible for transitions from one colour tone to another. This clarifies the regular stipulation in OS lists for 100 mm zigzag lines to blend the perimeters of two different camouflage colours with each other. With the introduction of mottled camouflage on the side surfaces of aircraft this shortcoming became even more troubling. The first tentative blotches and lines, seen in 1940 on Bf 109 Es, had been done by hand application or sprayed use of 7122.

RLM 7121.65 and 7122.65. Only with the introduction of these paints was it possible to make the appearance of RLM 65 more uniform and to make it more of a match with the official colour charts. A new colour tone did not have to be added to RLM register to replace the existing 65 colour tone. However, the Anatas white added to these formulations did show incompatibility with oils. This created a situation analogous with the problem encountered with talcum powders, and eventually began to cause chalking and lighter appearance. Because of the disuse of primers, the topcoat had to have the corrosion resistant qualities of the old primer, and zinc chromate was added to accomplish this. While the yellow content of the zinc chromate did not have a particularly strong covering (opaque) quality, and could easily be toned down, as it aged it gradually became chalky and the colour tone turned greenish.

RLM 76 behaved in a similar fashion to RLM 65. Because of gradual change from cobalt blue to Hansa blue (unstable phatlocyanine blue) the green tone became even more pronounced. The unstable phatlocyanine blue, with age, turned into stable phatlocyanine green.

The Primers

The task of primers was seldom employed for optical appearance, and therefore considered in the L.Dv. documents as not 'colour tone relevant', a primer disappearing under a multitude of succeeding paint layers. It served instead as an adhesion agent, providing various protective functions. Metals naturally become 'active' under atmospheric exposure, and hence are protected from corrosion by primers, while biological materials like wood or canvas are protected from micro-organisms. With stretched canvas, the necessary shrinkage of the paint film is accomplished. The colour tone RLM 02 had a special place among primers because its colour tone was compatible with the colours that were used to cover it.

RLM 7109.02 and 7122.02. RLM 02 contained in its pigment formulation aluminium powder and zinc chromate, and was used from the beginning of the war for landing gear paint; as such it was almost certain that this paint had been developed originally for corrosion protection. Even today we still use 'landing gear primer' that contains aluminium powder for corrosion protection against hydraulic fluid. The positioning of colour designation '02' between 00 and 19 shows that originally it was a primer colour. With silver intermediate paints, RLM 63 appeared optically like RLM 02, and was introduced as a topcoat colour. Aluminium colour does not, as one might believe, act upon the eye as a metallic colour but rather as grey or green grey as with RAL 7004, 840 R.

NOTES